Hands-on Nuxt.js Web Development

Build universal and static-generated Vue.js applications using Nuxt.js

Lau Tiam Kok

Packt>

BIRMINGHAM - MUMBAI

Hands-on Nuxt.js Web Development

Copyright © 2020 Packt Publishing

All rights reserved. No part of this book may be reproduced, stored in a retrieval system, or transmitted in any form or by any means, without the prior written permission of the publisher, except in the case of brief quotations embedded in critical articles or reviews.

Every effort has been made in the preparation of this book to ensure the accuracy of the information presented. However, the information contained in this book is sold without warranty, either express or implied. Neither the author, nor Packt Publishing or its dealers and distributors, will be held liable for any damages caused or alleged to have been caused directly or indirectly by this book.

Packt Publishing has endeavored to provide trademark information about all of the companies and products mentioned in this book by the appropriate use of capitals. However, Packt Publishing cannot guarantee the accuracy of this information.

Commissioning Editor: Pavan Ramchandani
Acquisition Editor: Karan Gupta
Content Development Editor: Keagan Carneiro
Senior Editor: Sofi Rogers
Technical Editor: Shubham Sharma
Copy Editor: Safis Editing
Project Coordinator: Kinjal Bari
Proofreader: Safis Editing
Indexer: Tejal Daruwale Soni
Production Designer: Alishon Mendonca

First published: August 2020

Production reference: 1130820

Published by Packt Publishing Ltd.
Livery Place
35 Livery Street
Birmingham
B3 2PB, UK.

ISBN 978-1-78995-269-8

www.packt.com

To my mother, who gave me this humble life to wonder about the universe and the Heaven that she looks down from.

Packt>

Packt.com

Subscribe to our online digital library for full access to over 7,000 books and videos, as well as industry leading tools to help you plan your personal development and advance your career. For more information, please visit our website.

Why subscribe?

- Spend less time learning and more time coding with practical eBooks and Videos from over 4,000 industry professionals

- Improve your learning with Skill Plans built especially for you

- Get a free eBook or video every month

- Fully searchable for easy access to vital information

- Copy and paste, print, and bookmark content

Did you know that Packt offers eBook versions of every book published, with PDF and ePub files available? You can upgrade to the eBook version at www.packt.com and as a print book customer, you are entitled to a discount on the eBook copy. Get in touch with us at customercare@packtpub.com for more details.

At www.packt.com, you can also read a collection of free technical articles, sign up for a range of free newsletters, and receive exclusive discounts and offers on Packt books and eBooks.

Contributors

About the author

Lau Tiam Kok, aka **Lau Thiam Kok**, is a cross-disciplinary full stack web developer/designer and analyst. He was born in Penang, Malaysia. His studies include a Bachelor of Applied Arts degree at University Malaysia Sarawak (1996 - 1999), and an MSc in Digital Futures at the Institute of Digital Art and Technology, University of Plymouth, UK (2002 - 2003).

Lau has freelanced for more than 10 years for various individuals, institutions, and companies. He works with designers or independently, from designing layouts to coding the frontend and server-side programs to produce responsive websites. He also works collaboratively on air-quality monitoring projects for Citizen Sense (based in the United Kingdom), which uses R, openair, Shiny, MongoDB, RethinkDB, Express.js, Koa.js, Socket.IO and Nuxt.js for data analysis web apps and IoT data platforms.

> *I would like to thank Packt for giving me this opportunity to write this book, to share my knowledge, to reach a wider audience. I want to thank the editorial team for giving me the support, patience, and encouragement throughout the journey of writing this book. I want to thank the graphics team involved in the production of this book. Also, I want to thank the technical reviewers and external editors for improving this book tremendously, the authors of various sources that are used in this book. Last but not least, I want to thank my family and friends for supporting and loving me. Without any of these people in this journey of writing, this book would be impossible.*

About the reviewer

Timi Omoyeni is an experienced frontend engineer who crafts responsive user interfaces that are cross-browser compatible. He uses Vue.js and Nuxt.js to build web applications and also writes technical articles on those technologies for Smashing Magazine and Log Rocket Blog.

Packt is searching for authors like you

If you're interested in becoming an author for Packt, please visit `authors.packtpub.com` and apply today. We have worked with thousands of developers and tech professionals, just like you, to help them share their insight with the global tech community. You can make a general application, apply for a specific hot topic that we are recruiting an author for, or submit your own idea.

Table of Contents

Preface   1

Section 1: Section 1: Your First Nuxt App

Chapter 1: Introducing Nuxt   11
  From Vue to Nuxt   11
  Why use Nuxt?   13
    Writing single-file components   13
    Writing ES2015+   14
    Writing CSS with a preprocessor   15
    Extending Nuxt with modules and plugins   16
    Adding transitions between routes   17
    Managing the <head> element   18
    Bundling and splitting code with webpack   18
  Types of applications   20
    Traditional server-side rendered app   20
    Traditional single-page app (SPA)   22
    Universal server-side rendered app (SSR)   23
    Static-generated app   25
  Nuxt as a universal SSR app   26
  Nuxt as a static site generator   28
  Nuxt as a single-page app   28
  Summary   29

Chapter 2: Getting Started with Nuxt   31
  Technical requirements   31
  Installing Nuxt   32
    Using create-nuxt-app   32
    Starting from scratch   34
  Understanding the directory structure   35
    The assets directory   36
    The static directory   36
    The pages directory   37
    The layouts directory   37
    The components directory   37
    The plugins directory   38
    The store directory   38
    The middleware directory   39
    The package.json file   39
    The nuxt.config.js file   40

Table of Contents

The aliases	40
Understanding custom configuration	**41**
The mode option	42
The target option	42
The head option	42
The css option	43
The plugins option	44
The components option	44
The buildModules option	45
The modules option	45
The build option	46
The dev option	46
The rootDir option	47
The srcDir option	48
The server option	49
The env option	49
The router option	50
The dir option	51
The loading option	53
The pageTransition and layoutTransition options	53
The generate option	54
Understanding asset serving	**55**
webpack assets versus static assets	57
Summary	**58**
Chapter 3: Adding UI Frameworks	**59**
Adding Foundation and Motion UI	**60**
Creating grid layouts and website navigations with Foundation	62
Using JavaScript utilities and plugins from Foundation	64
Creating CSS animations and transitions with Motion UI	68
Adding icons with Foundation Icon Fonts 3	71
Adding Less (Leaner Style Sheets)	**72**
Adding jQuery UI	**75**
Adding AOS	**78**
Adding Swiper	**81**
Summary	**84**
Section 2: Section 2: View, Routing, Components, Plugins, and Modules	
Chapter 4: Adding Views, Routes, and Transitions	**89**
Creating custom routes	**90**
Introducing Vue Router	90
Installing Vue Router	91
Creating routes with Vue Router	91

[ii]

Creating basic routes	93
Creating dynamic routes	94
Creating nested routes	96
Creating dynamic nested routes	101
Validating route params	104
Handling unknown routes with _.vue files	105
Creating custom views	**107**
Understanding the Nuxt view	107
Customizing the app template	108
Creating a custom HTML head	109
Introducing Vue Meta	109
Installing Vue Meta	110
Creating metadata with Vue Meta in Vue apps	111
Customizing the default meta tags in Nuxt apps	113
Creating custom meta tags for Nuxt pages	113
Creating custom layouts	114
Modifying the default layout	114
Creating new custom layouts	115
Creating custom error pages	116
Creating custom pages	117
Understanding pages	118
The asyncData method	118
The fetch method	120
The head method	121
The layout property	121
The loading property	121
The transition property	126
The scrollToTop property	126
The validate method	126
The middleware property	127
Creating custom transitions	**127**
Understanding Vue transitions	128
Making transitions with the pageTransition property	130
Making transitions with the layoutTransition property	133
Making transitions with CSS animations	135
Making transitions with JavaScript hooks	137
Understanding transition modes	142
Summary	**143**
Chapter 5: Adding Vue Components	**145**
Understanding Vue components	**146**
What is a component?	147
Passing data to child components with props	148
Listening to child component events	151
Emitting a value with an event	152
Creating custom input components with v-model	153
Customizing the model in custom input components	154

Table of Contents

Understanding the key attribute in v-for loops	156
Controlling reusable elements with key attributes	161
Creating single-file Vue components	**162**
Compiling single-file components with webpack	164
Passing data and listening to events in single-file components	166
Adding Vue components in Nuxt	169
Refactoring navigation and social links	170
Refactoring the copyright component	172
Registering global and local components	**174**
Registering global components in Vue	174
Registering local components in Vue/Nuxt	175
Registering global components in Nuxt	178
Writing basic and global mixins	**180**
Creating basic mixins/non-global mixins	181
Creating global mixins	183
Defining component names and using naming conventions	**184**
Multi-word component names	185
Component data	185
Prop definitions	186
Component files	187
Single-file component filename casing	188
Self-closing components	188
Summary	**189**
Chapter 6: Writing Plugins and Modules	**191**
Writing Vue plugins	**192**
Writing a custom plugin in Vue	193
Importing Vue plugins into Nuxt	196
Importing external Vue plugins without SSR support	197
Writing global functions in Nuxt	**198**
Injecting functions into the Vue instance	199
Injecting functions into the Nuxt context	200
Injecting functions into both the Vue instance and the Nuxt context	201
Injecting client-only or server-only plugins	204
Writing Nuxt modules	**207**
Writing a basic module	208
Writing async Nuxt modules	**213**
Using async/await	213
Returning a Promise	214
Writing Nuxt module snippets	**215**
Using top-level options	215
Using the addPlugin helper	217
Using Lodash templates	219
Adding a CSS library	221
Registering custom webpack loaders	223

Registering custom webpack plugins	226
Creating tasks on specific hooks	227
Summary	**230**
Chapter 7: Adding Vue Forms	**231**
Understanding v-model	**231**
Using v-model in text and textarea elements	232
Using v-model in checkbox and radio elements	233
Using v-model in select elements	235
Validating forms with basic data bindings	**236**
Validating text elements	237
Validating textarea elements	238
Validating checkbox elements	239
Validating radio elements	240
Validating select elements	241
Making dynamic value bindings	**243**
Replacing Boolean – checkbox elements	244
Replacing strings with dynamic properties – radio elements	245
Replacing strings with objects – select options elements	245
Using modifiers	**246**
Adding .lazy	247
Adding .number	247
Adding .trim	247
Validating forms with VeeValidate	**248**
Applying custom validation to a Nuxt application	**251**
Summary	**256**

Section 3: Section 3: Server-Side Development and Data Management

Chapter 8: Adding a Server-Side Framework	**259**
Introducing Backpack	**259**
Installing and configuring Backpack	260
Creating a simple app using Backpack	261
Introducing Koa	**262**
Installing and configuring Koa	262
What is ctx?	263
Understanding how Koa cascading works	264
Installing dependencies for Koa apps	265
Integrating Koa with Nuxt	**268**
Adding routes and other essential middleware	270
Understanding async data	**274**
Returning a promise	274
Using async/await	275
Merging the data	275

Table of Contents

Accessing context in asyncData   276
- Accessing the req/res objects   277
- Accessing the dynamic route data   277
- Listening to the query changes   278
- Handling errors   278

Fetching async data with Axios   280
- Installing and configuring Axios   280
- Fetching data with Axios and asyncData   281
- Listening on the query change   283

Summary   284

Chapter 9: Adding a Server-Side Database   287
Introducing MongoDB   287
- Installing MongoDB   288
- Installing on Ubuntu 20.04   288
- Starting MongoDB   289

Writing basic MongoDB queries   291
- Creating a database   291
- Creating a new collection   292

Writing MongoDB CRUD operations   293
Injecting data with MongoDB CRUD   294
- Inserting documents   294
- Querying documents   295
- Updating documents   298
- Deleting documents   300

Integrating MongoDB with Koa   301
- Installing the MongoDB driver   301
- Creating a simple app with the MongoDB driver   302
- Configuring the MongoDB driver   304
- Understanding ObjectId and the ObjectId method   305
- Injecting one document   306
- Fetching all documents   309
- Updating one document   310
- Deleting one document   312

Integrating with Nuxt Pages   313
- Creating an add page for adding new users   313
- Creating an update page for updating existing users   314
- Creating a delete page for deleting existing users   315

Summary   317

Chapter 10: Adding a Vuex Store   319
Understanding the Vuex architecture   319
- What is Vuex?   320
- State management pattern   320

Getting started with Vuex   322

[vi]

Table of Contents

Installing Vuex	322
Creating a simple store	323
Understanding Vuex core concepts	**323**
The state	324
Accessing the state	324
The mapState helper	325
Getters	327
The mapGetters helper	329
Mutations	330
The mapMutations helper	331
Actions	332
The mapActions helper	334
Modules	335
Understanding the local state and root state	336
Understanding namespacing	337
Structuring Vuex store modules	**341**
Creating a simple store module structure	341
Creating an advanced store module structure	343
Handling forms in a Vuex store	**345**
Using v-bind and v-on directives	346
Using a two-way computed property	347
Using a Vuex store in Nuxt	**348**
Using module mode	348
Using module files	352
Using the fetch method	354
Using the nuxtServerInit action	356
Summary	**360**

Section 4: Section 4: Middleware and Security

Chapter 11: Writing Route Middlewares and Server Middlewares	**363**
Writing middlewares with Vue Router	**364**
What is middleware?	364
Installing Vue Router	365
Using navigation guards	366
Creating global guards	366
Creating per-route guards	368
Creating in-component guards	369
Understanding the navigation guard arguments: to, from, and next	373
Introducing Vue CLI	**376**
Installing Vue CLI	376
Understanding Vue CLI's project structure	377
Writing middlewares and a Vuex store with Vue CLI	379
Writing route middlewares in Nuxt	**384**
Writing global middlewares	385
Writing per-route middlewares	388

[vii]

Table of Contents

Writing Nuxt server middlewares — 392
- Using Express as Nuxt's server middleware — 393
- Using Koa as Nuxt's server middleware — 397
- Creating custom server middleware — 400

Summary — 401

Chapter 12: Creating User Logins and API Authentication — 403

Understanding session-based authentication — 404
- What are sessions and cookies? — 404
- The session authentication flow — 405

Understanding token-based authentication — 406
- What are JSON Web Tokens? — 406
- The token authentication flow — 407
- Using Node.js modules for JWT — 408

Creating backend authentication — 409
- Using MySQL as the server database — 410
- Structuring cross-domain app directories — 411
- Creating API public/private routes and their modules — 413
- Using the bcryptjs module for Node.js — 422
- Using the mysql module for Node.js — 424
- Refactoring login code on the server side — 427
- Verifying the incoming token on the server side — 429

Creating frontend authentication — 431
- Using cookies on the (Nuxt) client side — 432
- Using cookies on the (Nuxt) server side — 434

Signing in with Google OAuth — 436
- Adding Google OAuth to the backend authentication — 436
- Creating frontend authentication for Google OAuth — 441

Summary — 444

Section 5: Section 5: Testing and Deployment

Chapter 13: Writing End-to-End Tests — 447
End-to-end testing versus unit testing — 447
End-to-end testing tools — 448
- jsdom — 448
- AVA — 452

Writing tests with jsdomn and AVA for Nuxt apps — 454
Introducing Nightwatch — 458
Writing tests with Nightwatch for Nuxt apps — 462
Summary — 464

Chapter 14: Using Linters, Formatters, and Deployment Commands — 465
Introducing linters – Prettier, ESLint, and StandardJS — 466
- Prettier — 466
  - Configuring Prettier — 468

ESLint	469
Configuring ESLint	471
StandardJS	473
Integrating ESLint and Prettier	**474**
Using ESLint and Prettier for Vue and Nuxt apps	**477**
Configuring Vue rules	478
Running ESLint and Prettier separately in Nuxt apps	484
Deploying Nuxt apps	**485**
Deploying a Nuxt universal server-side rendered app	486
Deploying a Nuxt static-generated (pre-rendered) app	488
Hosting the Nuxt universal SSR app on virtual private servers	490
Hosting the Nuxt universal SSR app on shared hosting servers	491
Hosting the Nuxt static generated app on static site hosting servers	493
Summary	**494**

Section 6: Section 6: The Further Fields

Chapter 15: Creating an SPA with Nuxt	**497**
Understanding classic SPAs and Nuxt SPAs	**497**
Installing a Nuxt SPA	**500**
Developing a Nuxt SPA	**501**
Creating the client-side nuxtServerInit action	502
Creating multiple custom Axios instances with plugins	504
Installing the custom Axios plugin in the Nuxt config file	505
Importing the custom Axios plugin manually	506
Deploying a Nuxt SPA	**508**
Deploying to GitHub Pages	511
Summary	**514**
Chapter 16: Creating a Framework-Agnostic PHP API for Nuxt	**515**
Introducing PHP	**516**
Installing or upgrading PHP	516
Configuring PHP 7.4	518
Running PHP apps with a built-in PHP web server	519
Understanding HTTP messages and PSRs	**520**
Why PSRs?	526
PSR-12 – Extended Coding Style guide	528
PSR-4 – Autoloader	531
PSR-7 – HTTP Message Interfaces	536
PSR-15 – HTTP Server Request Handlers (request handlers)	541
PSR-15 – HTTP Server Request Handlers (middleware)	542
PSR-7/PSR-15 router	544
Writing CRUD operations with PHP database frameworks	**548**
Creating MySQL tables	548
Using Medoo as a database framework	549
Inserting records	552

Querying records	553
Updating records	554
Deleting records	554
Structuring cross-domain app directories	555
Creating the API's public routes and their modules	559
Integrating with Nuxt	**562**
Creating CRUD pages	564
Summary	**565**
Chapter 17: Creating a Real-Time App with Nuxt	**567**
Introducing RethinkDB	**567**
Installing RethinkDB Server	568
Introducing ReQL	569
Integrating RethinkDB with Koa	**574**
Restructuring API directories	574
Adding and using the RethinkDB JavaScript client	577
Enforcing schema in RethinkDB	584
Introducing changefeeds in RethinkDB	586
Introducing Socket.IO	**587**
Adding and using Socket.IO server and client	588
Integrating Socket.IO server and RethinkDB changefeeds	592
Integrating Socket.IO with Nuxt	**594**
Summary	**600**
Chapter 18: Creating a Nuxt App with a CMS and GraphQL	**603**
Creating headless REST APIs in WordPress	**604**
Installing WordPress and creating our first pages	605
Creating custom post types in WordPress	607
Extending the WordPress REST API	610
Integrating with Nuxt and streaming images from WordPress	615
Introducing Keystone	**621**
Installing and securing PostgreSQL (Ubuntu)	621
Installing and securing MongoDB (Ubuntu)	624
Installing and creating Keystone apps	626
Creating lists and fields	630
Introducing GraphQL	**637**
Understanding the GraphQL schema and resolvers	639
Understanding GraphQL default resolvers	645
Creating a GraphQL API with Apollo Server	647
Using the Keystone GraphQL API	651
Integrating Keystone, GraphQL, and Nuxt	**653**
Summary	**660**
Other Books You May Enjoy	**663**
Index	**667**

Preface

Nuxt.js (we will call it Nuxt in this book) is a progressive web framework built on top of Vue.js (we will call it Vue in this book) for **server-side rendering** (**SSR**). With Nuxt and Vue, building universal and static-generated applications is easier than ever before. This book will help you get up and running with the fundamentals of Nuxt and how to integrate it with the latest version of Vue, enabling you to build an entire project, including authentication, testing, and deployment, with Nuxt and Vue.js. You will explore Nuxt's directory structure and get your Nuxt project created by using Nuxt's pages, views, routing, and Vue components, and by writing plugins, modules, a Vuex store, and middlewares. Furthermore, you will learn how to create Node.js and PHP APIs or data platforms from scratch by using Koa.js (we will call it Koa in this book), **PHP Standards Recommendations** (**PSRs**), MongoDB, and MySQL, as well as using WordPress as a headless CMS and REST API. You'll also use Keystone.js as a GraphQL API to complement Nuxt. You will learn how to create a real-time Nuxt application and API with Socket.IO and RethinkDB, and finally generate static sites with Nuxt and streaming resources (images and videos) from a remote API, whether a REST API or a GraphQL API.

Who this book is for

The book is for any JavaScript or full-stack developer who wants to build server-side-rendered Vue.js apps. A basic understanding of the Vue.js framework will assist in understanding the key concepts covered in the book.

What this book covers

Chapter 1, *Introducing Nuxt*, is where you will learn about the main features of Nuxt. You will learn about the types of web applications there are today and which categories Nuxt is in line with. Then, you will find out what you can use Nuxt for in the coming chapters.

Chapter 2, *Getting Started with Nuxt*, is where you will install Nuxt, using a scaffolding tool, or doing so from scratch, to create your first basic Nuxt application. You will learn about the default directory structure in your Nuxt project, configuring Nuxt to suit your project and understanding asset serving.

Chapter 3, *Adding UI Frameworks*, is where you will add custom UI frameworks, such as Zurb Foundation, Motion UI, Less CSS, and many more, to make your UI development in Nuxt easier and more fun.

Preface

Chapter 4, *Adding Views, Routes, and Transitions*, is where you will create navigation routes, custom pages, layouts, and templates in your Nuxt application. You will learn how to add transitions and animations, create custom error pages, customize global meta tags, and add specific tags to individual pages.

Chapter 5, *Adding Vue Components*, is where you will add Vue components to your Nuxt application. You will learn how to create global and local components and reuse them, writing basic and global mixins and defining component names that comply with the naming convention.

Chapter 6, *Writing Plugins and Modules*, is where you will create and add plugins, modules, and module snippets in your Nuxt application. You will learn how to create Vue plugins and install them in your Nuxt project, writing global functions, and registering them.

Chapter 7, *Adding Vue Forms*, is where you will create forms with `v-model` and `v-bind`, validating form elements and making dynamic value bindings by using modifiers. You will also learn to use a Vue plugin, VeeValidate, to make your frontend validation easier.

Chapter 8, *Adding a Server-Side Framework*, is where you will use Koa as the server-side framework to create an API to complement your Nuxt application. You will learn how to install Koa and its essential Node.js packages to create a fully working API and integrate it with your Nuxt application. Also, you will learn about using async data in Nuxt to fetch data from the Koa API, accessing Nuxt context via async data, listening to query changes, handling errors, and using Axios as the HTTP client for requesting data from the API.

Chapter 9, *Adding a Server-Side Database*, is where you will use MongoDB to manage the database for your Nuxt application. You will learn how to install MongoDB, writing basic MongoDB queries, adding some dummy data into your MongoDB database, integrating MongoDB with your API from the previous chapter with Koa, and then fetching the data from your Nuxt application.

Chapter 10, *Adding a Vuex Store*, is where you will use Vuex to manage and centralize the store data for your Nuxt application. You will learn about the Vuex architecture, mutating store data with the store's mutation and action methods, structuring your store program modularly when it gets bigger, and handling forms in the Vuex store.

Chapter 11, *Writing Route Middlewares and Server Middlewares*, is where you will create route middlewares and server middlewares in your Nuxt application. You will learn how to create middlewares using Vue Router, creating Vue applications using Vue CLI and using Express.js (we will call it Express in this book), Koa, and Connect.js (we will call it Connect in this book) as server middlewares.

Chapter 12, *Creating User Logins and API Authentication*, is where you will add authentication to the restricted page in your Nuxt application using session, cookies, **JSON Web Tokens (JWTs)**, Google OAuth, and the route middlewares that you learned about in the previous chapter. You will learn how to create backend authentication with JWTs, using cookies on the client side and server side in your Nuxt application (frontend authentication), and adding Google OAuth to the backend and frontend authentication.

Chapter 13, *Writing End-to-End Tests*, is where you will create end-to-end tests with AVA, jsdom, and Nightwatch.js. You will learn how to install these tools, setting up the testing environment, and writing tests for the pages in your Nuxt application from the previous chapter.

Chapter 14, *Using Linters, Formatters, and Deployment Commands*, is where you will use ESLint, Prettier, and StandardJS to keep your code clean, readable, and formatted. You will learn how to install and configure these tools to suit your needs and integrate different linters in your Nuxt application. Finally, you will learn how to deploy your Nuxt application with Nuxt commands and learn about what hosting service to publish your application.

Chapter 15, *Creating an SPA with Nuxt*, is where you will learn how to develop a **single-page application (SPA)** in Nuxt, understanding the differences between the SPA in Nuxt and the classic SPA and generating a static SPA to deploy to a static hosting server, GitHub Pages.

Chapter 16, *Creating a Framework-Agnostic PHP API for Nuxt*, is where you will use PHP to create an API to complement your Nuxt application. You will learn how to install the Apache server and PHP engine, understand HTTP messages and PHP standards, install MySQL as your database system, write CRUD operations for MySQL, create a framework-agnostic PHP API by complying with the PHP standards, and then integrate your API with your Nuxt application.

Chapter 17, *Creating a Real-Time App with Nuxt*, is where you will develop a real-time Nuxt application with RethinkDB, Socket.IO, and Koa. You will learn how to install RethinkDB, be introduced to ReQL, integrate RethinkDB with your Koa API, add Socket.IO to the API and your Nuxt application, and finally turn your Nuxt application into a real-time web application with RethinkDB changefeeds.

Preface

Chapter 18, *Creating a Nuxt App with a CMS and GraphQL,* is where you will use a (headless) CMS and GraphQL to complement your Nuxt application. You will learn how to turn WordPress into a headless CMS, creating custom post types in WordPress and extending the WordPress REST API. You will learn how to use GraphQL in your Nuxt application, understand GraphQL schema and resolvers, create a GraphQL API with Appolo Server, and use the Keystone.js GraphQL API. Also, you will learn how to install and secure PostgreSQL and MongoDB, generating static sites with Nuxt and streaming resources (images and videos) from the remote API, whether it is a REST API or a GraphQL API.

To get the most out of this book

You will need a version of Nuxt.js throughout the book – the latest version, if possible. All code examples have been tested using Nuxt 2.14.x on Ubuntu 20.10. Here is a list of other essential software, frameworks, and technologies for this book:

Software/hardware covered in the book	OS requirements
Koa.js v2.13.0	Any platform
Axios v0.19.2	Any platform
Keystone.js v11.2.0	Any platform
Socket.IO v2.3.0	Any platform
MongoDB v4.2.6	Any platform
MySQL v10.3.22-MariaDB	Any platform
RethinkDB v2.4.0	Linux, macOS
PHP v7.4.5	Any platform
Foundation v6.6.3	Any platform
Swiper.js v6.0.0	Any platform
Node.js v12.18.2 LTS (at least v8.9.0)	Any platform
NPM v6.14.7	Any platform

If you are using the digital version of this book, we advise you to type the code yourself or access the code via the GitHub repository (link available in the next section). Doing so will help you avoid any potential errors related to the copying and pasting of code.

Download the example code files

You can download the example code files for this book from your account at www.packt.com. If you purchased this book elsewhere, you can visit www.packtpub.com/support and register to have the files emailed directly to you.

You can download the code files by following these steps:

1. Log in or register at www.packt.com.
2. Select the **Support** tab.
3. Click on **Code Downloads**.
4. Enter the name of the book in the **Search** box and follow the onscreen instructions.

Once the file is downloaded, please make sure that you unzip or extract the folder using the latest version of:

- WinRAR/7-Zip for Windows
- Zipeg/iZip/UnRarX for Mac
- 7-Zip/PeaZip for Linux

The code bundle for the book is also hosted on GitHub at https://github.com/PacktPublishing/Hands-on-Nuxt.js-Web-Development. In case there's an update to the code, it will be updated on the existing GitHub repository.

We also have other code bundles from our rich catalog of books and videos available at https://github.com/PacktPublishing/. Check them out!

Conventions used

There are a number of text conventions used throughout this book.

CodeInText: Indicates code words in text, database table names, folder names, filenames, file extensions, pathnames, dummy URLs, user input, and Twitter handles. Here is an example: "Then, you can just create the transition style in a .css file."

Preface

A block of code is set as follows:

```
// pages/about.vue
<script>
export default {
  transition: {
    name: 'fade'
```

When we wish to draw your attention to a particular part of a code block, the relevant lines or items are set in bold:

```
[default]
exten => s,1,Dial(Zap/1|30)
exten => s,2,Voicemail(u100)
exten => s,102,Voicemail(b100)
exten => i,1,Voicemail(s0)
```

Any command-line input or output is written as follows:

```
$ npm i less --save-dev
$ npm i less-loader --save-dev
```

Bold: Indicates a new term, an important word, or words that you see onscreen. For example, words in menus or dialog boxes appear in the text like this. Here is an example: "Select **Manually select features** to pick **Router** from the options that you are prompted to select, to choose the features you need."

> Warnings or important notes appear like this.

> Tips and tricks appear like this.

Get in touch

Feedback from our readers is always welcome.

General feedback: If you have questions about any aspect of this book, mention the book title in the subject of your message and email us at customercare@packtpub.com.

Errata: Although we have taken every care to ensure the accuracy of our content, mistakes do happen. If you have found a mistake in this book, we would be grateful if you would report this to us. Please visit www.packtpub.com/support/errata, selecting your book, clicking on the Errata Submission Form link, and entering the details.

Piracy: If you come across any illegal copies of our works in any form on the Internet, we would be grateful if you would provide us with the location address or website name. Please contact us at copyright@packt.com with a link to the material.

If you are interested in becoming an author: If there is a topic that you have expertise in and you are interested in either writing or contributing to a book, please visit authors.packtpub.com.

Reviews

Please leave a review. Once you have read and used this book, why not leave a review on the site that you purchased it from? Potential readers can then see and use your unbiased opinion to make purchase decisions, we at Packt can understand what you think about our products, and our authors can see your feedback on their book. Thank you!

For more information about Packt, please visit packt.com.

Section 1: Your First Nuxt App

In this section, we will provide a short introduction to Nuxt, its features, its folder structures, and more. Then, we'll start building our first Nuxt app by following some simple steps and integrating Nuxt routing, configuration, Vue components, and more.

This section comprises the following chapters:

- `Chapter 1`, *Introducing Nuxt*
- `Chapter 2`, *Getting Started with Nuxt*
- `Chapter 3`, *Adding UI Frameworks*

1
Introducing Nuxt

Welcome to your journey of *Hands-on Nuxt.js Web Development*. In this chapter, we will peer inside Nuxt to see what constitutes this framework. We will walk you through Nuxt's features and you will get to know the pros and cons of the different types of applications that Nuxt falls in line with. Last but not least, you will discover the great potential of using Nuxt as a universal SSR app, a static site generator, and a single-page app.

In this chapter, we will cover the following topics:

- From Vue to Nuxt
- Why Use Nuxt?
- Types of applications
- Nuxt as a universal SSR app
- Nuxt as a static site generator
- Nuxt as a single-page app

Let's get started!

From Vue to Nuxt

Nuxt is a higher-level Node.js web development framework for creating Vue apps that can be developed and deployed in two different modes: universal (SSR) or **single-page application** (**SPA**). Furthermore, you can deploy SSR and SPA in Nuxt as static-generated apps. Even though you can choose the SPA mode, the full power of Nuxt lies in its universal mode or **server-side rendering** (**SSR**) for building universal apps. A universal app is used to describe JavaScript code that can execute both on the client and the server-side. But if you wish to develop a classic (or standard/traditional) SPA, which executes on the client-side only, you may want to consider using vanilla Vue.

Introducing Nuxt

> Note that an SPA mode Nuxt app is slightly different from a classic SPA. You will find out more about it later in this book and briefly in this chapter.

Nuxt is created on top of Vue, supercharged with some extra features such as asynchronous data, middleware, layouts, modules, and plugins that execute your app on the server-side first, and then on the client-side. This means the app generally renders quicker than the traditional server-side (or multiple-page) apps.

Nuxt is pre-installed with the following packages so that you don't have to install them, which you would do in a standard Vue app:

- Vue (https://vuejs.org/)
- Vue Router (https://router.vuejs.org/)
- Vuex (https://vuex.vuejs.org/)
- Vue Server Renderer (https://ssr.vuejs.org/)
- Vue Meta (https://vue-meta.nuxtjs.org/)

On top of that, Nuxt uses webpack and Babel to compile and bundle your code with the following webpack loaders:

- Vue Loader (https://vue-loader.vuejs.org/)
- Babel Loader (https://webpack.js.org/loaders/babel-loader/)

In a nutshell, webpack is a module bundler that bundles all the scripts, styles, assets, and images in your JavaScript app, while Babel is a JavaScript compiler that compiles or transpiles the next-generation JavaScript (ES2015+) to browser-compatible JavaScript (ES5) so that you can run your code on current browsers.

> For more information about webpack and Babel, please visit https://webpack.js.org/ and https://babeljs.io/, respectively.

webpack uses what they call loaders to preprocess your files when you import them via the JavaScript `import` statement or `require` method. You can write your loaders but you don't have to do so when compiling your code in Vue files since they have been created for you by the Babel community and Vue team. We'll discover the great features that come with Nuxt and those contributed by these loaders in the next section.

Why use Nuxt?

Frameworks such as Nuxt exist because of the shortcomings of the traditional SPA and the server-side rendering of **multi-page applications** (**MPAs**). We can regard Nuxt as a hybrid of server-side rendering MPA and traditional SPA. Hence, it is dubbed "universal" or "isomorphic". So, being able to do server-side rendering is the defining feature of Nuxt. In this section, we will walk you through other prominent features of Nuxt that will make your app development easy and fun. The first feature we'll look at allows you to write single-file Vue components by using a .vue extension in your files.

Writing single-file components

There are a few methods we can use to create a Vue component. A global Vue component is created by using Vue.component, as follows:

```
Vue.component('todo-item', {...})
```

On the other hand, a local Vue component can be created using a plain JavaScript object, as follows:

```
const TodoItem = {...}
```

These two methods are manageable and maintainable if you're using Vue for a small project, but it becomes difficult to manage for a big project when you have tons of components with different templates, styles, and JavaScript methods all at once.

Hence, single-file components come to the rescue, in which we only use one .vue file for each Vue component. If you need more than one component in your app, then just separate them into multiple .vue files. In each of them, you can write the template, script, and style that relate to that particular component only, as follows:

```
// pages/index.vue
<template>
  <p>{{ message }}</p>
</template>

<script>
export default {
  data () {
    return { message: 'Hello World' }
  }
}
</script>
```

Introducing Nuxt

```
<style scoped>
p {
  font-size: 2em;
  text-align: center;
}
</style>
```

Here, you can see how we have an HTML template that prints the message from the JavaScript script and the CSS style that describes the presentation of the template, all in one single .vue file. This makes your code more structured, readable, and organizable. Sweet, isn't it? This is only made possible by vue-loader and webpack. In Nuxt, we only write components in .vue files, regardless of whether they are components in the /components/, /pages/, or /layouts/ directory. We will explore this in more detail in Chapter 2, *Getting Started with Nuxt*. Now, we'll look at the Nuxt feature that allows you to write ES6 JavaScript out of the box.

Writing ES2015+

Nuxt compiles your ES6+ code out of the box without you having to worry about configuring and installing Babel in webpack. This means you can write ES6+ code straight away and your code will be compiled into JavaScript that can be run on older browsers. For example, you will see the following destructuring assignment syntax often when using an asyncData method:

```
// pages/about.vue
<script>
export default {
  async asyncData ({ params, error }) {
    //...
  }
}
</script>
```

The destructuring assignment syntax is used in the preceding code to unpack the properties from the Nuxt context into distinct variables that we can use for the logic inside the asyncData method.

> For more information about the Nuxt context and ECMAScript 2015 features, please visit https://nuxtjs.org/api/context and https://babeljs.io/docs/en/learn/, respectively.

Writing ES6 in Nuxt is only made possible by `babel-loader` and webpack. There's more than just the destructuring assignment syntax that you can write in Nuxt, including the `async` function, the `await` operator, the `arrow` function, the `import` statement, and many more. What about the CSS preprocessor? If you write CSS styles with a popular CSS preprocessor such as Sass, Less, or Stylus, but if you are a Sass person and not a Less person, nor a Stylus person, can Nuxt support any of them? The short answer is yes. We'll find out the long answer to this question in the next section.

Writing CSS with a preprocessor

In Nuxt, you can choose your favorite CSS preprocessor to write the styles for your app, whether it is Sass, Less, or Stylus. They are already pre-configured for you in Nuxt. You can check out their configurations at https://github.com/nuxt/nuxt.js/blob/dev/packages/webpack/src/config/base.js. So, you just need to install the preprocessor and its webpack loader in your Nuxt project. For example, if you want to use Less as your CSS preprocessor, just install the following dependencies in your Nuxt project:

```
$ npm i less --save-dev
$ npm i less-loader --save-dev
```

Then, you can start writing your Less code by setting the `lang` attribute to "less" in the `<style>` block, as follows:

```
// pages/index.vue
<template>
  <p>Hello World</p>
</template>

<style scoped lang="less">
@align: center;
p {
  text-align: @align;
}
</style>
```

From this example, you can see that writing modern CSS styles is as easy as writing modern JavaScript in Nuxt. All you are required to do is install your favorite CSS preprocessor and its webpack loader. We will use Less in this book in the upcoming chapters, but for now, let's find out what other features Nuxt offers.

Introducing Nuxt

For more information about these preprocessors and their webpack loaders, please visit the following links:

- `http://lesscss.org/` for Less
- `https://webpack.js.org/loaders/less-loader/` for less-loader
- `https://sass-lang.com/` for Sass
- `https://webpack.js.org/loaders/sass-loader/` for sass-loader
- `http://stylus-lang.com/` for Stylus
- `https://github.com/shama/stylus-loader` for stylus-loader

> Even though PostCSS is not a preprocessor, if you want to use it in a Nuxt project, please visit the guide provided at `https://nuxtjs.org/faq/postcss-plugins`.

Extending Nuxt with modules and plugins

Nuxt was created on top of a modular architecture. This means you can extend it with endless modules and plugins for your app or Nuxt community. This also means you can choose tons of modules and plugins from the Nuxt and Vue communities so that you don't have to reinvent them for your app. The links to these are as follows:

- Awesome Nuxt.js at `https://github.com/nuxt-community/awesome-nuxt#official` for Nuxt modules
- Awesome Vue.js at `https://github.com/vuejs/awesome-vue#components--libraries` for Vue components, libraries, and plugins

Modules and plugins are simply JavaScript functions. Don't worry about the distinction between them for now; we will get to this in `Chapter 6`, *Writing Plugins and Modules*.

Adding transitions between routes

Unlike traditional Vue apps, in Nuxt, you don't have to use the wrapper `<transition>` element to handle JavaScript animations, CSS animations, and CSS transitions on your elements or components. For example, if you want to apply a `fade` transition to the specific page when navigating to it, you can just add the transition name (for example, `fade`) to the `transition` property of that page:

```
// pages/about.vue
<script>
export default {
  transition: {
    name: 'fade'
  }
}
</script>
```

Then, you can just create the transition style in a `.css` file:

```
// assets/transitions.css
.fade-enter,
.fade-leave-to {
  opacity: 0;
}

.fade-leave,
.fade-enter-to {
  opacity: 1;
}

.fade-enter-active,
.fade-leave-active {
  transition: opacity 3s;
}
```

The "fade" transition will apply to the `about` page automatically when navigating to the `/about` route. Cool, isn't it? Don't worry if the code or the class names look a bit overwhelming to you at this point; we will look at this transition feature and explore it in more detail in Chapter 4, *Adding Views, Routes, and Transitions*.

Introducing Nuxt

Managing the <head> element

Also, unlike traditional Vue apps, you can manage the `<head>` block of your app out of the box without installing the additional Vue package that handles it – `vue-meta`. You just add the data you need for `<title>`, `<meta>`, and `<link>` via the `head` property to any page. For example, you can manage the global `<head>` element via the Nuxt config file of your app:

```
// nuxt.config.js
export default {
  head: {
    title: 'My Nuxt App',
    meta: [
      { charset: 'utf-8' },
      { name: 'viewport', content: 'width=device-width, initial-scale=1' },
      { hid: 'description', name: 'description', content: 'My Nuxt app is
        about...' }
    ],
    link: [
      { rel: 'icon', type: 'image/x-icon', href: '/favicon.ico' }
    ]
  }
}
```

Nuxt will convert this data into the HTML tags for you. Again, we will learn about this feature and explore it in more detail in `Chapter 4`, *Adding Views, Routes, and Transitions*.

Bundling and splitting code with webpack

Nuxt uses webpack to bundle, minify, and split your code into chunks that can speed up the load time of your app. For example, in a simple Nuxt app with two pages, index/home and about, you will get similar chunks for the client-side:

```
Hash: 0e9b10c17829e996ef30
Version: webpack 4.43.0
Time: 4913ms
Built at: 06/07/2020 21:02:26
                         Asset       Size  Chunks
Chunk Names
../server/client.manifest.json   7.77 KiB          [emitted]
                      LICENSES  389 bytes          [emitted]
                 app.3d81a84.js   51.2 KiB       0  [emitted] [immutable]
app
        commons/app.9498a8c.js    155 KiB       1  [emitted] [immutable]
commons/app
```

```
commons/pages/index.8dfce35.js         13.3 KiB       2  [emitted] [immutable]
commons/pages/index
         pages/about.c6ca234.js        357 bytes      3  [emitted] [immutable]
pages/about
         pages/index.f83939d.js        1.21 KiB       4  [emitted] [immutable]
pages/index
              runtime.3d677ca.js       2.38 KiB       5  [emitted] [immutable]
runtime
 + 2 hidden assets
Entrypoint app = runtime.3d677ca.js commons/app.9498a8c.js app.3d81a84.js
```

The chunks that you would get for the server-side will look as follows:

```
Hash: 8af8db87175486cd8e06
Version: webpack 4.43.0
Time: 525ms
Built at: 06/07/2020 21:02:27
              Asset        Size  Chunks              Chunk Names
      pages/about.js    1.23 KiB       1  [emitted]  pages/about
      pages/index.js    6.06 KiB       2  [emitted]  pages/index
           server.js    80.9 KiB       0  [emitted]  app
server.manifest.json   291 bytes          [emitted]
 + 3 hidden assets
Entrypoint app = server.js server.js.map
```

These chunks and the build information are generated when you use Nuxt `npm run build` command to build your app for deployment. We will look at this in more detail in Chapter 14, *Using Linters, Formatters, and Deployment Commands*.

This aside, there are other great features and plugins from webpack that are used by Nuxt, such as static files and asset serving (asset management), hot module replacement, CSS extraction (`extract-css-chunks-webpack-plugin`), a progress bar while you're building and watching (webpackbar), and so on. For more information, please visit the following links:

- `https://webpack.js.org/guides/code-splitting/` for code splitting
- `https://webpack.js.org/concepts/manifest/` for the manifest
- `https://webpack.js.org/guides/asset-management/` for asset management

Introducing Nuxt

- `https://webpack.js.org/concepts/hot-module-replacement/` for hot module replacement
- `https://webpack.js.org/plugins/mini-css-extract-plugin/` for CSS extraction
- `https://github.com/nuxt/webpackbar` for `webpackbar` (a plugin developed by Nuxt core team)

These great features from webpack, Babel, and Nuxt itself will make your modern project development fun and easy. Now, let's take a look at the various application types to see why you should or shouldn't use Nuxt when you're building your next web app.

Types of applications

The web applications of today are very different from the ones from decades ago. We had fewer options and solutions in those days. Today, they are blooming. Whether we call them "applications" or "apps", they are the same. We will call them "apps" in this book. So, we can categorize our current web apps as follows:

- Traditional server-side rendered app
- Traditional SPA
- Universal SSR app
- Static-generated app

Let's go through each of them and understand the pros and cons. We will first look at the oldest type of app – the traditional server-side rendered app.

Traditional server-side rendered app

Server-side rendering is the most common approach for delivering the data and HTML to the client side on the browser on your screen. It was the only way to do things when the web industry just started. In traditional server-rendered apps or dynamic websites, every request requires a new page re-rendered from the server to the browser. This means you will reload all the scripts, styles, and template(s) once more with every request you send to the server. The idea of reloading and re-rendering does not sound compelling and elegant at all. Even though some of the reloading and re-rendering burdens can be lifted by using AJAX these days, this adds more complexity to the app.

Let's go through the advantages and disadvantages of these types of apps.

Advantages:

- **Better SEO performance:** Because the client (browser) gets the finished page with all the data and HTML tags, especially the meta tags that belong to the page, search engines can crawl the page and index it.
- **Faster initial load time:** Because the pages and content are rendered on the server side by a server-side scripting language such as PHP before sending it to the client browser, we get the rendered page fast on the client side. Also, there is no need to compile the web pages and content in JavaScript files like we do in traditional SPAs, so the app is loaded quicker on the browser.

Disadvantages:

- **Poorer user experience:** Because every page has to be re-rendered and this process takes time on the server, the user has to wait until everything is reloaded on the browser and that may affect the user experience. Most of the time, we want the new data only when provided with the new request; we don't need the HTML base to be regenerated, for example, the navigation bar and the footer, but still, we get these base elements re-rendered, regardless. We can make use of AJAX to render just a particular component, but this makes development more difficult and complex.
- **Tight coupling of the backend and frontend logic:** The view and data are usually handled together within the same app. For example, in a typical PHP framework app such as Laravel, you may render the view (https://laravel.com/docs/7.x/views) with a template engine such as Laravel Pug (https://github.com/BKWLD/laravel-pug) in a route. Or, if you are using Express for a traditional server-side rendered app, you may use a template engine such as Pug (https://pugjs.org/api/getting-started.html) or vuexpress (https://github.com/vuexpress/vuexpress) for rending the view (https://expressjs.com/en/guide/using-template-engines.html). In these two frameworks for a typical, traditional server-side rendered app, the view is coupled with the backend logic, even though we can extract the view layer with a template engine. The backend developer has to know what view (for example, `home.pug`) to use for each specific route or controller. On the other hand, the frontend developer has to work on the view within the same framework as the backend developer. This adds more complexity to the project.

Traditional single-page app (SPA)

As opposed to server-side rendered apps, SPAs are client-side rendered (CSR) apps that render content in the browser using JavaScript without requiring new pages to be reloaded during use. So, instead of getting the content rendered to the HTML document, you get barebones HTML from the server, and the content will be loaded using JavaScript in the browser, as follows:

```
<!DOCTYPE html>
<html>
<head>
  <meta charset="utf-8">
  <title>Vue App</title>
</head>
<body>
  <div id="app"></div>
  <script src="https://unpkg.com/vue/dist/vue.js" type="text/javascript"></script>
  <script src="/path/to/app.js"type="text/javascript"></script>
</body>
</html>
```

This is a very simple Vue app in which you have a container, `<div>`, with `app` as its ID only and nothing else inside it, followed by two `<script>` elements. The first `<script>` element will load the Vue.js library, while the second one will load the Vue instance that renders the content of your app, as follows:

```
// path/to/app.js
const app = new Vue({
  data: {
    greeting:'Hello World!'
  },
  template: '<p>{{ greeting }}</p>'
}).$mount('#app')
```

Let's go through the advantages and disadvantages of this type of app.

Advantages:

- **Better user experience:** SPA is fast when rendering content after the initial load. Most resources, such as CSS styles, JavaScript code, and HTML templates, are only loaded once throughout the lifespan of the app. Only data is sent back and forth afterward; the base HTML and layout stay unchanged, thus offering a smooth and better user experience.

- **Easier development and deployment:** SPA development is comparatively easier to get started without the need for a server and a server-side scripting language. You can simply kick off the development from your local machine with `file://URI`. It is easier to deploy as well because it consists of HTML, JavaScript, and CSS files; you can just drop them to the remote server and go live right away.

Disadvantages:

- **Poor performance on the search engine:** SPAs are bare-bone single HTML pages, mostly with no headings and paragraph tags for search engine crawlers to crawl. The SPA content is loaded via JavaScript that the crawlers mostly cannot execute, so SPAs usually perform poorly in SEO.
- **Slow initial load time:** Most resources such as CSS styles, JavaScript code, and HTML templates are only loaded once throughout the lifespan of the app, so we need to load tons of these resource files all at once at the beginning. By doing this, the app usually slows down regarding its initial loading time, especially in a large SPA.

Universal server-side rendered app (SSR)

As we learned in the previous section, there are advantages and disadvantages to both traditional server-side rendered apps and SPAs. There are benefits in writing SPAs, but there are things that you lose: the ability for web crawlers to traverse your app and slower performance while the app is initially loaded. This is the opposite of writing traditional server-side rendered apps, also there are things you do not have, such as better user experience and the fun of client-side development in SPAs. Ideally, client-side and server-side rendering can be balanced for user experience and performance. Here is where universal server-side rendering (SSR) comes to bridge the gap.

JavaScript has become an isomorphic language since the release of Node.js in 2009. By isomorphic, we mean that codes can run both on the client side and the server side. Isomorphic (universal) JavaScript can be defined as a hybrid of client-side and server-side applications. It is a new approach for web apps to compensate for the shortcomings of both traditional SSR apps and traditional SPAs. This is the category that Nuxt falls into.

In universal SSR, your app will first pre-load on the server side, pre-render the pages, and send the rendered HTML to the browser before switching to the client-side operation for the rest of its lifespan. Building universal SSR apps from scratch can be tedious as it requires lots of configuration before the actual development process begins. This is what Nuxt aims to achieve by presetting all the configuration needed for you to create SSR Vue apps easily.

Even though universal SSR apps are a great solution in our modern web development, there are still advantages and disadvantages to these types of apps. Let's go through them.

Advantages:

- **Faster initial load time:** In universal SSR, JavaScript and CSS are split into chunks, assets are optimized, and pages are rendered on the server-side before being served to the client browser. All of these options help make the initial loading time faster.
- **Better SEO support:** Since all pages are rendered on the server side with the appropriate meta content, headings, and paragraphs before being served on the client side, the search engine crawlers can traverse the page to increase the SEO performance of your app.
- **Better user experience:** Universal SSR apps work like traditional SPAs after the initial load in that the transition between pages and routes is seamless. Only data is transmitted back and forth without re-rendering the HTML content holders. All these features have helped to provide a better user experience overall.

Disadvantages:

- **Node.js server required:** Running JavaScript on the server side requires a Node.js server, so the server must be set up before you can use Nuxt and write your app.
- **Complex development:** Running JavaScript code in universal SSR apps can be confusing because some JavaScript plugins and libraries are meant to run on the client side only, such as Bootstrap and Zurb Foundation for styling and DOM manipulation.

Static-generated app

Static-generated apps are pre-generated with the help of a static site generator and stored as static HTML pages on the hosting server. Nuxt comes with a `nuxt generate` command that generates **static pages** out of the box for you from the universal SSR or SPA app that you've developed in Nuxt. It pre-renders HTML pages for each of your routes into a generated `/dist/` folder during the build step, as follows:

```
-| dist/
----| index.html
----| favicon.ico
----| about/
------| index.html
----| contact/
------| index.html
----| _nuxt/
------| 2d3427ee2a5aa9ed16c9.js
------| ...
```

You can deploy these static files to a static hosting server without the need for Node.js or any server-side support. So, when the app is initially loaded on the browser – no matter what route you are requesting – you will always get the full content (if it's been exported from the universal SSR app) immediately, and the app will perform like a traditional SPA afterward.

Let's go through the advantages and disadvantages of these types of apps.

Advantages:

- **Fast initial load time:** Since each route is pre-generated as a static HTML page that has its own content, it is fast to load on the browser.
- **Good for SEO:** Static-generated web apps allow your JavaScript app to be crawled perfectly by search engines, just like traditional server-side rendered apps.
- **Easier deployment:** Because static-generated web apps are just static files, this makes them easy to deploy to static hosting servers such as GitHub Pages.

Introducing Nuxt

Disadvantages:

- **No server-side support:** Because static-generated web apps are just static HTML pages and run on the client side only, this means there's no runtime support for Nuxt's `nuxtServerInit` action method and Node.js HTTP request and response objects, which are only available on the server side. All data will be pre-rendered during the build step.
- **No real-time rendering:** Static-generated web apps are suitable for apps that only serve **static pages** that are pre-rendered at **build time**. If you are developing a complex app that requires real-time rendering from the server, then you should probably use universal SSR instead to utilize the full power of Nuxt.

From these categories, you have probably figured out that Nuxt falls in line with universal SSR apps and static-generated apps. Apart from this, it also falls in line with single-page apps, but not the same as traditional SPAs, which you will find out more about in `Chapter 15`, *Creating an SPA with Nuxt*.

Now, let's take a better look at Nuxt regarding the types of applications that you will be creating in this book. We'll start with Nuxt as a universal SSR app.

Nuxt as a universal SSR app

Many years ago, we had server-side scripting languages such as ASP, Java, server-side JavaScript, PHP, and Python to create traditional server-side apps with template engines to render the view of our apps. This resulted in the tight coupling disadvantage that we went through in the previous section.

So, with the rise of universal SSR frameworks such as Nuxt, Next (https://nextjs.org/), and Angular Universal (https://angular.io/guide/universal), we can utilize their full power to decouple the view from the server-side scripting app for good by replacing the template engine, such as Pug (https://pugjs.org/), Handlebars (https://handlebarsjs.com/), Twig (https://twig.symfony.com/), and many more that we have been deeply replying on. If we consider Nuxt a **frontend server-side** app and Express (or others) a **backend server-side** app, we can see how they complement each other perfectly. For example, we can use Express to create a backend server-side app for serving data in JSON format on an API route (for example, /) at `localhost:4000`:

```
{
  "message": "Hello World"
}
```

[26]

Chapter 1

Then, on the frontend server side, we can use Nuxt as a universal SSR app running on `localhost:3000` to consume the aforementioned data by sending an HTTP request from a page in our Nuxt app, as follows:

```
// pages/index.vue
async asyncData ({ $http }) {
  const { message } = await $http.$get('http://127.0.0.1:4000')
  return { message }
}
```

Now, we have Nuxt as both a server and a client that handles our app's view and templates, while Express just handles our server-side logic. We no longer need a template engine to present our content. So, for once, perhaps we don't need to learn so many template engines and we don't need to worry about the battle between them because we now have the universal one – Nuxt.

We will show you how to create cross-domain apps with Nuxt and Koa (another Node.js server-side framework similar to Express) in `Chapter 12`, *Creating User Logins and API Authentication*.

> Note that in the preceding code, we used the Nuxt HTTP module to make the HTTP request. However, we will mostly use vanilla Axios or the Nuxt Axios module throughout this book for HTTP requests. For more information about the Nuxt HTTP module, please visit `https://http.nuxtjs.org/`.
>
> You also can use the Nuxt Content module to act as headless CMS so that you can serve your app content from Markdown, JSON, YAML, XML, and CSV files that can be stored "locally" in your Nuxt project. However, in this book, we will be using and creating external APIs to serve our content in order to avoid the tightly coupled issue that we found in the traditional server-side apps in the first place. For more information about the Nuxt Content module, please visit `https://content.nuxtjs.org/`.

Nuxt as a static site generator

Even though server-side rendering is the main feature of Nuxt, it is also a static site generator that pre-renders your Nuxt app in a static site, as shown in the example provided for the static-generated app category. It is perhaps the best of both worlds between a traditional single-page application and a server-side-rendered app. While benefiting from the static HTML content for a better SEO, you no longer need the runtime support from Node.js and Nuxt. However, your app will still behave like an SPA.

What's more is that during static generation, Nuxt has a crawler that crawls the links in your app to generate dynamic routes and save their data from the remote API as `payload.js` files in a `/static/` folder inside the `/dist/` folder. These payloads are then used to serve the data that was originally requested from the API. This means you are not calling the API anymore. This can secure your API from the public, and possibly from attackers.

You'll learn how to generate static sites from Nuxt with a remote API in Chapter 14, *Using Linters, Formatters, and Deployment Commands*, and in the final chapter of this book, Chapter 18, *Creating a Nuxt App with CMS and GraphQL*.

Nuxt as a single-page app

Nuxt is well-suited for developing single-page apps if you have any reason that prevents you from using Nuxt as a server-side rendering app. As we mentioned at the beginning of this chapter, Nuxt comes with two modes for developing your app: `universal` and `spa`. This means you just have to specify `spa` in the `mode` property in your project configuration, which we'll explore in more detail in the next chapter.

So, you might be thinking that if we can use Nuxt for developing a SPA, then why bother with Vue anymore? In fact, the SPA you can develop from Nuxt is slightly different from the SPA from Vue. The SPA you build from Vue is a traditional SPA, while the SPA from Nuxt is a "static" SPA (let's refer to it as Nuxt SPA) – your app pages are pre-rendered at build time. This means deploying a Nuxt SPA is technically the same as statically generating a Nuxt universal SSR app – both require the same Nuxt command: `nuxt generate`.

This can be confusing and you may want to ask what is the difference between the static-generated SSR app and the static-generated SPA? The difference is very obvious – the static-generated SPA has no page content compared to the static-generated SSR app. The static-generated SPA is pre-rendered with your app pages and "empty" HTML, just like the traditional SPA – devoid of page content. This is confusing, but rest assured, we will figure all this out in the upcoming chapters of this book. In particular, you learn about the trade-offs of developing SPAs in Nuxt and how to overcome them.

You'll learn how to develop a Nuxt SPA and generate a static Nuxt SPA with a remote API in `Chapter 15`, *Creating an SPA with Nuxt*.

Summary

Well done! You have made it through the first chapter of your journey into Nuxt. In this chapter, you learned what makes up the Nuxt framework; that is, Vue (the origin of Nuxt), webpack, and Babel. You learned about the various features Nuxt provides, such as the ability for you to write Vue single-file components (`.vue` files), ES2015+ JavaScript (ES6), CSS with a preprocessor (Sass, Less, Stylus). You are also able to extend your app with modules and plugins, to add transitions between the routes of your app, to manage the `<head>` element and the meta content of each route or page in your app. Apart from this you also covered tons of great features that are imported from webpack and Babel, such as bundling, minifying, and splitting code. You also learned that you can access tons of plugins and modules from the Nuxt community for your Nuxt projects.

Apart from these great features, you learned about the pros and cons of each type of available application: traditional server-side rendered apps, traditional single-page apps (SPAs), universal server-side rendered apps (SSRs), and static-generated apps. You also learned that Nuxt apps actually fall in line with the categories of universal SSR apps and static-generated apps. And then, you learned that Nuxt also falls in line with single-page apps, but not the same as traditional SPAs. Lastly, you looked into using Nuxt for universal SSR apps, static-generated apps, and single-page apps, all of which you'll learn more about throughout this book.

In the next chapter, you will learn how to install Nuxt and create a simple Nuxt app and understand the default directory structure that comes with the Nuxt scaffolding tool. You will also learn how to customize your Nuxt app and understand the assets that are served in Nuxt. So, stay tuned!

Getting Started with Nuxt

This chapter will guide you through the process of installing a Nuxt project from scratch or with the Nuxt scaffolding tool. Installing Nuxt is the first thing you should do when developing Nuxt apps. We'll use the Nuxt scaffolding tool for all of our example apps throughout this book as it generates essential project folders and files (which we will explore in this chapter) for us automatically; but of course, you can do it from scratch for small app development. We will go through the directory structure and the use and purpose of each directory. If you are installing your Nuxt project from scratch, you'll still need to know the directory structure and the official directories that Nuxt will read automatically from your project. You'll also learn how to configure Nuxt to suit the needs of your app specifically, even though Nuxt is already configured to cover most practical cases by default. So, we will guide you through the nuts and bolts of the configuration. Also, we will cover asset serving in Nuxt apps, particularly for serving images.

The topics we will cover in this chapter are as follows:

- Installing Nuxt
- Understanding the directory structure
- Understanding custom configuration
- Understanding asset serving

Technical requirements

You should be familiar with the following terms:

- JavaScript ES6
- Server-side and client-side development basics
- Application program interface (API)

The supported operating systems are as follows:

- Windows 10 or above with PowerShell
- macOS with a terminal (Bash or Oh My Zsh)
- Linux systems (such as Ubuntu) with a terminal

The suggested cross platform softwares are as follows:

- Node.js: `https://nodejs.org/`
- Node Package Manager (npm): `https://www.npmjs.com/`

Installing Nuxt

There are two ways to get started with Nuxt easily. The easiest way is by using the Nuxt scaffolding tool, `create-nuxt-app`, which installs all the Nuxt dependencies and default directories automatically for you. The other way is to start from scratch by using a `package.json` file only. Let's discover how you can do this.

Using create-nuxt-app

`create-nuxt-app` is a scaffolding tool created by the Nuxt team that you can use to install your project quickly. What you need to do is use `npx` to run `create-nuxt-app` on your favorite terminal:

```
$ npx create-nuxt-app <project-name>
```

npx is shipped by default since npm 5.2.0, but you can make sure you have it installed by checking its version on your terminal, as follows:

```
$ npx --version
6.14.5
```

During the process of installing the Nuxt project, you will be asked some questions to integrate with Nuxt, as follows:

- Choose a programming language:

    ```
    JavaScript
    TypeScript
    ```

- Choose a package manager:

    ```
    Yarn
    Npm
    ```

- Choose a UI framework:

    ```
    None
    Ant Design Vue
    Bootstrap Vue
    ...
    ```

- Choose a testing framework:

    ```
    None
    Jest
    AVA
    WebdriverIO
    ```

Let's create your first Nuxt app, called `first-nuxt`, using npx. So, choose a local directory on your machine, open a terminal on that directory, and run `npx create-nuxt-app first-nuxt`. When you come across the questions like the previously mentioned ones in the installation process, choose `JavaScript` for the programming language, Npm for the package manager, and `None` for the UI framework and the testing framework. Then, skip the rest of the questions (just don't pick any options) so that we can add them at a later stage when we need to. You should have a list of questions similar to the following, with the same options we have suggested, on your terminal:

```
$ npx create-nuxt-app first-nuxt
create-nuxt-app v3.1.0
:: Generating Nuxt.js project in /path/to/your/project/first-nuxt
? Project name: first-nuxt
? Programming language: JavaScript
? Package manager: Npm
? UI framework: None
? Nuxt.js modules: (Press <space> to select, <a> to toggle all, <i> to
invert selection)
? Linting tools: (Press <space> to select, <a> to toggle all, <i> to invert
selection)
? Testing framework: None
? Rendering mode: Universal (SSR / SSG)
? Deployment target: Server (Node.js hosting)
? Development tools: (Press <space> to select, <a> to toggle all, <i> to
invert selection)
```

Getting Started with Nuxt

You should choose `Universal (SSR / SSG)` for the question about the rendering mode. We will cover the option for single-page applications (SPAs) in Chapter 15, *Creating an SPA with Nuxt*. We will use SSR for all of our example apps throughout this book, except the examples in Chapter 15, *Creating an SPA with Nuxt*. We will also use `npm` as our package manager in this book as well, so make sure you pick this option. Once the installation is completed, we can get it started with:

```
$ cd first-nuxt
$ npm run dev
```

The app is now running on `localhost:3000`. You should see a default index page generated by Nuxt on your screen when you run that address in your favorite browser. It is easy peasy to install a Nuxt project using the scaffolding tool, isn't it? But sometimes you may not need a full stack installation like this; you may just need a "barebones" installation. If so, let's find out how you can install Nuxt from scratch in the next section.

> You can find the source files for this simple app in `/nuxt-packt/chapter-2/scaffolding/` in our GitHub repository.

Starting from scratch

If you don't want to use the Nuxt scaffolding tool, you can use a `package.json` file and `npm` to install a Nuxt app for you. Let's find out how with the following steps:

1. Create a `package.json` file in your root project:

    ```
    {
      "name": "nuxt-app",
      "scripts": {
        "dev": "nuxt"
      }
    }
    ```

2. Install Nuxt in the project via npm:

    ```
    $ npm i nuxt
    ```

3. Create a `/pages/` directory in your root project, and then create an `index.vue` page in it:

    ```
    // pages/index.vue
    <template>
    ```

```
    <h1>Hello world!</h1>
</template>
```

4. Launch the project with npm:

   ```
   $ npm run dev
   ```

The app is now running on `localhost:3000`. You should see the index page you created with the `Hello world!` message on your screen when you run that address in your favorite browser.

However, whether you are going for the "barebones" or full stack option, you should understand the default directories that Nuxt requires for running your app. So, let's find out what these directories are in the next section.

> You can find this simple app in `/nuxt-packt/chapter-2/scratch/` in our GitHub repository.

Understanding the directory structure

If you have installed a Nuxt project successfully using the `create-nuxt-app` scaffolding tool, you should get the following default directories and files in your project folder:

```
-| your-app-name/
---| assets/
---| components/
---| layouts/
---| middleware/
---| node_modules/
---| pages/
---| plugins/
---| static/
---| store/
---| nuxt.config.js
---| package.json
---| README.md
```

Let's go through each of them and understand what they are intended for in the following sections.

The assets directory

The `/assets/` directory is used to contain the assets of your project, such as images, fonts, and Less, Stylus, or Sass files, that will be compiled by webpack. For example, you may have a Less file, as follows:

```
// assets/styles.less
@width: 10px;
@height: @width + 10px;

header {
  width: @width;
  height: @height;
}
```

webpack will compile the preceding code into the following CSS for your app:

```
header {
  width: 10px;
  height: 20px;
}
```

We will discuss the benefits of serving images in this directory later in this chapter, and we will use this directory often in this book when generating static pages.

The static directory

The `/static/` directory is used to contain files that you don't want to be compiled by webpack or cannot be compiled, such as favicon files. If you don't want to serve your assets, such as images, fonts, and styles, in the `/assets/` directory, you can keep them in the `/static/` directory instead. All files in this directory are mapped to the server root directly, so they are accessible under the root URL directly. For example, `/static/1.jpg` is mapped as `/1.jpg`, so you can access it as follows:

```
http://localhost:3000/1.jpg
```

We will discuss the difference in serving images between the `/assets/` and `/static/` directories later in this chapter. Note that you get a `favicon.ico` file by default in this directory when you use the Nuxt scaffolding tool, but you can create your favicon file to replace it.

The pages directory

The `/pages/` directory is used to contain the views and the routes of the app. Nuxt will read and convert all the `.vue` files inside this directory and generate the app router automatically for you. For example, take the following:

```
/pages/about.vue
/pages/contact.vue
```

Nuxt will take the preceding filenames without the `.vue` extension and create the following routes for your app:

```
localhost:3000/about
localhost:3000/contact
```

If you install Nuxt via `create-nuxt-app`, you will get an `index.vue` file created automatically for you, and you can see this page at `localhost:3000`.

We will look at this directory in more detail in `Chapter 4`, *Adding Views, Routes, and Transitions*.

The layouts directory

The `/layouts/` directory is used to contain the layouts of your app. You get a layout called `default.vue` by default when you use the Nuxt scaffolding tool. You can modify this default layout or add new ones to this directory.

We will look at this directory in more detail in `Chapter 4`, *Adding Views, Routes, and Transitions*.

The components directory

The `/components/` directory is used to contain Vue components. You get a component called `Logo.vue` by default when you use the Nuxt scaffolding tool. The obvious and important difference between the `.vue` files in this directory and those in the `/pages/` directory is that you cannot use the `asyncData` method for the components in this directory; however, you can use the `fetch` method to set in them if you need to. You should keep small and reusable components in this directory.

We will look at this directory in more detail in `Chapter 5`, *Adding Vue Components*.

The plugins directory

The `/plugins/` directory is used to contain JavaScript functions, such as global functions that you want to run before the root Vue instance is instantiated. For example, you may want to create a new `axios` instance that sends API requests specifically to https://jsonplaceholder.typicode.com only, and you may want to make this instance available globally without importing `axios` and creating a fresh instance each time. You can create a plugin that injects and plugs into the Nuxt context, as follows:

```js
// plugins/axios-typicode.js
import axios from 'axios'

const instance = axios.create({
  baseURL: 'https://jsonplaceholder.typicode.com'
})

export default (ctx, inject) => {
  ctx.$axiosTypicode = instance
  inject('axiosTypicode', instance)
}
```

Then, you can use this `axios` instance on any page by calling `$axiosTypicode`, as follows:

```js
// pages/users/index.vue
export default {
  async asyncData ({ $axiosTypicode, error }) {
    let { data } = await $axiosTypicode.get('/users')
  }
}
```

We will look at this directory in more detail in Chapter 6, *Writing Plugins and Modules*.

> Note that `axios` is an HTTP client that we will use often throughout this book. You will need to install it in your project directory before importing it in the preceding plugin file. For more information about this Node.js package, please visit https://github.com/axios/axios.

The store directory

The `/store/` directory is used to contain the Vuex store files. You don't need to install Vuex in Nuxt because it already comes with Nuxt. It is disabled by default and you just have to add an `index.js` file to this directory to enable it. For example, if you want to have a property called `auth` that can be accessed from anywhere throughout your app.

You will have that property stored in the `state` variable in the `index.js` file, as follows:

```
// store/index.js:
export const state = () => ({
  auth: null
})
```

We will look at this directory in more detail in Chapter 10, *Adding a Vuex Store*.

The middleware directory

The `/middleware/` directory is used to contain middleware files that are JavaScript functions that run before rendering a page or a group of pages. For example, you may want to have a secret page that only can be accessed when the user is authenticated. You can use the Vuex store to store the authenticated data and create a middleware to throw a 403 error if the `auth` property is empty in the `state` store:

```
// middleware/auth.js
export default function ({ store, error }) {
  if (!store.state.auth) {
    error({
      message: 'You are not connected',
      statusCode: 403
    })
  }
}
```

We will look at this directory in more detail in Chapter 11, *Writing Route Middlewares and Server Middlewares*.

The package.json file

The `package.json` file is used to contain the dependencies and scripts of the Nuxt app. For example, you get the following default scripts and dependencies in this file if you are using the Nuxt scaffolding tool:

```
// package.json
{
  "scripts": {
    "dev": "nuxt",
    "build": "nuxt build",
    "start": "nuxt start",
    "generate": "nuxt generate"
```

Getting Started with Nuxt

```
  },
  "dependencies": {
    "nuxt": "^2.14.0"
  }
}
```

We will work on this file a lot in Chapter 8, *Adding a Server-Side Framework*, and in Chapter 14, *Using Linters, Formatters, and Deployment Commands*.

The nuxt.config.js file

The `nuxt.config.js` file is used to contain the custom configuration that applied to your app specifically. For example, you get these custom meta tags, title, and link by default for your HTML `<head>` block when you use the Nuxt scaffolding tool:

```
export default {
  head: {
    title: process.env.npm_package_name || '',
    meta: [
      { charset: 'utf-8' },
      { name: 'viewport', content: 'width=device-width, initial-scale=1' },
      { hid: 'description', name: 'description', content:
        process.env.npm_package_description || '' }
    ],
    link: [
      { rel: 'icon', type: 'image/x-icon', href: '/favicon.ico' }
    ]
  }
}
```

We can modify the preceding custom head block. You will learn how to do so in Chapter 4, *Adding Views, Routes, and Transitions*. Besides `head`, there are other key properties for making the custom configuration, which we will cover in the upcoming section.

The aliases

In Nuxt, the ~ or @ aliases are used to associate with the `srcDir` property, and the ~~ or @@ aliases are used to associate with the `rootDir` property. For example, if you want to link an image to the `/assets/` directory, you can use the ~ alias, as follows:

```
<template>
  <img src="~/assets/sample-1.jpg"/>
</template>
```

On the other hand, if you want to link the image to the /static/ directory, you can use the ~ alias, as follows:

```
<template>
  <img src="~/static/sample-1.jpg"/>
</template>
```

Note that you also can link your assets in the /static/ directory without these aliases:

```
<template>
  <img src="/sample-1.jpg"/>
</template>
```

The value of srcDir is the same as the value of rootDir, by default, which is process.cwd(). We will cover these two options in the next section and you will learn how to change their default values. So, let's explore how you can fiddle with custom configuration in your project.

Understanding custom configuration

You can configure your Nuxt app to suit your project by adding a nuxt.config.js file (we will call it a **Nuxt config file** in this book) in the project's root directory. You get this file by default if you use the Nuxt scaffolding tool. You should get the following options (or properties) when you open this file:

```
// nuxt.config.js
export default {
  mode: 'universal',
  target: 'server',
  head: { ... },
  css: [],
  plugins: [],
  components: true,
  buildModules: [],
  modules: [],
  build: {}
}
```

Most of them are empty, except mode, target, head, and components. You can customize Nuxt to suit your project specifically through these options. Let's go through each of them, and then the other options, to see what you can use them for.

The mode option

The `mode` option is used to define the "nature" of your app – whether it is universal or an SPA. Its default value is *universal*. If you are developing an SPA using Nuxt, then change this value to `spa`. We will focus on the universal mode in the upcoming chapters of this book, except `Chapter 15`, *Creating an SPA with Nuxt*.

The target option

The `target` option is used to set the deployment target of your app – whether it is deployed as a server-side rendering app or a static-generated app. Its default value is `server` for server-side rendering deployment. Our deployment target for most of the example apps in this book is server-side rendering. We will target static-generated deployments as well in a few chapters, especially the final chapter – `Chapter 18`, *Creating a Nuxt App with CMS and GraphQL*.

The head option

The `head` option is used to define all default meta tags in the `<head>` block of our app. You get the following custom `head` configuration in the Nuxt config file if you use the Nuxt scaffolding tool:

```
// nuxt.config.js
export default {
  head: {
    title: process.env.npm_package_name || '',
    meta: [
      { charset: 'utf-8' },
      { name: 'viewport', content: 'width=device-width, initial-scale=1' },
      { hid: 'description', name: 'description', content:
        process.env.npm_package_description || '' }
    ],
    link: [
      { rel: 'icon', type: 'image/x-icon', href: '/favicon.ico' }
    ]
  }
}
```

You can modify the preceding configuration or add more custom configuration – for example, add some JavaScript and CSS libraries that are required for your project:

```js
// nuxt.config.js
export default {
  head: {
    titleTemplate: '%s - Nuxt App',
    meta: [
      //...
    ],
    script: [
      { src: 'https://cdnjs.cloudflare.com/.../jquery.min.js' },
      { src: 'https://cdn.jsdelivr.net/.../foundation.min.js' },
    ],
    link: [
      { rel: 'stylesheet', href:
      'https://cdn.jsdelivr.net/.../foundation.min.css' },
    ]
  }
}
```

We will cover this option in more detail in Chapter 3, *Adding UI Frameworks*, and in Chapter 4, *Adding Views, Routes, and Transitions*. Note that jQuery is a core dependency of Foundation (Zurb), which we will explore in Chapter 3, *Adding UI Frameworks*. So, it is currently required that you install jQuery in your project to use Foundation. This may become optional in future releases.

The css option

The css option is used to add global CSS files. These can be .css, .less, or .scss files. They also can be the modules and libraries loaded from the Node.js /node_modules/ directory in your project directly. For example, take the following:

```js
// nuxt.config.js
export default {
  css: [
    'jquery-ui-bundle/jquery-ui.min.css',
    '@/assets/less/styles.less',
    '@/assets/scss/styles.scss'
  ]
}
```

Getting Started with Nuxt

In the preceding configuration, we load the CSS file from the jQuery UI module that is installed in the `/node_modules/` directory, as well as the Less and Sass files that are stored in the `/assets/` directory. Note that if you are writing styles using `.less` and `.scss` files, you need to install the Less and Sass modules with their webpack loaders, as follows:

```
$ npm i less less-loader --save-dev
$ npm i node-sass --save-dev
$ npm i sass-loader --save-dev
```

We will use this option more in Chapter 3, *Adding UI Frameworks*, and in Chapter 4, *Adding Views, Routes, and Transitions*.

The plugins option

The `plugins` option is used to add JavaScript plugins that run before the root Vue instance. For example, take the following:

```
// nuxt.config.js
export default {
  plugins: ['~/plugins/vue-notifications']
}
```

We often use this option with the `/plugins/` directory, which we covered in the previous section. We will work on this option a lot in Chapter 6, *Writing Plugins and Modules*.

The components option

The `components` option is used to set whether the components in the `/components/` directory should be auto-imported. This option is very useful if you have tons of components to be imported into a layout or a page. You don't have to import them manually if you set this option to `true`. Its default value is `false`. We set this option to `true` for all apps in this book.

> For more information and (advanced) usage of this option, please visit https://github.com/nuxt/components.

[44]

The buildModules option

The `buildModules` option is used to register built-only modules – modules that are required only for development and build time in your app. In this book, note that we will only leverage some modules from the Nuxt community and create the custom ones that are needed during the Node.js runtime in Chapter 6, *Writing Plugins and Modules*. But for more information about the `buildModules` option and the built-only modules for build-time only, please visit https://nuxtjs.org/guide/modules#build-only-modules.

The modules option

The `modules` option is used to add Nuxt modules to your project. For example, take the following:

```
// nuxt.config.js
export default {
  modules: [
    '@nuxtjs/axios',
    '~/modules/example.js'
  ]
}
```

We also can create inline modules directly with this option:

```
// nuxt.config.js
export default {
  modules: [
    function () {
      //...
    }
  ]
}
```

Nuxt modules are essentially JavaScript functions, just like plugins. We will discuss the difference between them in Chapter 6, *Writing Plugins and Modules*. Just like the `plugins` option, which is used often with the `/plugins/` directory, the `modules` option is often used with the `/modules/` directory. We will work on this option often in Chapter 6, *Writing Plugins and Modules*.

The build option

The `build` option is used to customize the webpack configuration for building your Nuxt app the way you prefer. For example, you may want to install jQuery globally in your project so that you don't have to use `import` whenever you need it. You can automatically load jQuery by using webpack's `ProvidePlugin` function, as follows:

```
// nuxt.config.js
import webpack from 'webpack'

export default {
  build: {
    plugins: [
      new webpack.ProvidePlugin({
        $: "jquery"
      })
    ]
  }
}
```

We will use this `build` option again in `Chapter 4`, *Adding Views, Routes, and Transitions*, in `Chapter 6`, *Writing Plugins and Modules*, and in `Chapter 14`, *Using Linters, Formatters, and Deployment Commands*.

> For more details and examples of things that you can do with this option for your Nuxt app, visit https://nuxtjs.org/api/configuration-build. For more information about webpack's `ProvidePlugin` function, visit https://webpack.js.org/plugins/provide-plugin/. If you are new to webpack, we encourage you to visit and learn about it from https://webpack.js.org/guides/.

The following sections outline some of the additional options that you can use to customize your Nuxt app further and more specifically. Let's explore some of them that can be useful in your projects. Some of them are used often in this book. So, let's get to them!

The dev option

The `dev` option is used to define the `development` or `production` mode of your app. It is not added to the Nuxt config file, but you can add it manually when you need to. It only takes a Boolean type and its default is set to `true`. It is always forced to be `true` with the `nuxt` command and always forced to be `false` with the `nuxt build`, `nuxt start`, and `nuxt generate` commands.

Hence, technically you *can't* customize it, but you can use this option in a Nuxt module, as follows:

```
// modules/sample.js
export default function (moduleOptions) {
  console.log(this.options.dev)
}
```

You will get either `true` or `false`, depending on which Nuxt command you use. We will cover this module in Chapter 6, *Writing Plugins and Modules*. Alternatively, you can use this option when you are importing Nuxt as a package in a server-side framework, as follows:

```
// server/index.js
import { Nuxt, Builder } from 'nuxt'
import config from './nuxt.config.js'

const nuxt = new Nuxt(config)

if (nuxt.options.dev) {
  new Builder(nuxt).build()
}
```

The `new Builder(nuxt).build()` line will be run when the `dev` option is `true`. We will get to the server-side framework in Chapter 8, *Adding a Server-Side Framework*.

> You can find an example app for this option in `/chapter-2/configuration/dev/` in our GitHub repository.

The rootDir option

The `rootDir` option is used to define the workspace of your Nuxt app. For example, say you have your project in the following location:

```
/var/www/html/my-project/
```

Then, the default value of the `rootDir` option for your project is `/var/www/html/my-project/`. However, you can change it by using the Nuxt command in your `package.json` file, as follows:

```
// my-project/package.json
{
  "scripts": {
```

Getting Started with Nuxt

```
    "dev": "nuxt ./app/"
  }
}
```

Now, the workspace of your Nuxt app is in `/var/www/html/my-project/app/` and your app structure has become the following:

```
-| my-project/
---| node_modules/
---| app/
------| nuxt.config.js
------| pages/
------| components/
------| ...
---| package.json
```

Note that now, the Nuxt config file must be put inside the `/app/` directory. We will cover the Nuxt commands in Chapter 14, *Using Linters, Formatters, and Deployment Commands*.

> You can find an example app for this option in `/chapter-2/configuration/rooDir/` in our GitHub repository.

The srcDir option

The `srcDir` option is used to define the source directory of your Nuxt app. The default value of `srcDir` is the value of `rootDir`. You can change it as follows:

```
// nuxt.config.js
export default {
  srcDir: 'src/'
}
```

Now, your app structure has become the following:

```
-| my-project/
---| node_modules/
---| src/
------| pages/
------| components/
------| ...
---| nuxt.config.js
---| package.json
```

Note that the Nuxt config file is outside the `/src/` directory.

> You can find an example app for this option in `/chapter-2/configuration/srcDir/` in our GitHub repository.

The server option

The `server` option is used to configure the server connection variables of our Nuxt app. It has the following default server connection details:

```
export default {
  server: {
    port: 3000,
    host: 'localhost',
    socket: undefined,
    https: false,
    timing: false
  }
}
```

You can change them as follows:

```
export default {
  server: {
    port: 8080,
    host: '0.0.0.0'
  }
}
```

Now, your app is running at `0.0.0.0:8080`.

> You can find an example app for this option in `/chapter-2/configuration/server/` in our GitHub repository.

The env option

The `env` option is used to set environment variables for the client side and the server side of your Nuxt app. The default for this option is an empty object, `{}`. This option is useful when you use `axios` in your project.

Take the following example:

```
// nuxt.config.js
export default {
  env: {
    baseUrl: process.env.BASE_URL || 'http://localhost:3000'
  }
}
```

Then, you can the `env` property in the `axios` plugin, as follows:

```
// plugins/axios.js
import axios from 'axios'

export default axios.create({
  baseURL: process.env.baseUrl
})
```

Now, the `baseURL` option is set to `localhost:3000`, or whatever `BASE_URL` is if it is defined. We can set `BASE_URL` in `package.json`, as follows:

```
// package.json
"scripts": {
  "start": "cross-env BASE_URL=https://your-domain-name.com nuxt start"
}
```

You will need to install `cross-env` for the preceding example to work on Windows:

```
$ npm i cross-env --save-dev
```

We will get to plugins in Chapter 6, *Writing Plugins and Modules*. We will use this `env` option often in this book when creating cross-domain apps.

> You can find an example app for this option in `/chapter-2/configuration/env/` in our GitHub repository.

The router option

The `router` option is used to overwrite the default Nuxt configuration on the Vue router. The default Vue router configuration is as follows:

```
{
  mode: 'history',
  base: '/',
```

[50]

```
  routes: [],
  routeNameSplitter: '-',
  middleware: [],
  linkActiveClass: 'nuxt-link-active',
  linkExactActiveClass: 'nuxt-link-exact-active',
  linkPrefetchedClass: false,
  extendRoutes: null,
  scrollBehavior: null,
  parseQuery: false,
  stringifyQuery: false,
  fallback: false,
  prefetchLinks: true
}
```

You can change this configuration, as follows:

```
// nuxt.config.js
export default {
  router: {
    base: '/app/'
  }
}
```

Now, your app is running at `localhost:3000/app/`.

> For more information about this property and the rest of its configuration, visit https://nuxtjs.org/api/configuration-router.
>
> You can find an example app for this option in `/chapter-2/configuration/router/` in our GitHub repository.

The dir option

The `dir` option is used to define custom directories in our Nuxt app. The default directories are as follows:

```
{
  assets: 'assets',
  layouts: 'layouts',
  middleware: 'middleware',
  pages: 'pages',
  static: 'static',
  store: 'store'
}
```

You can change them as follows:

```js
// nuxt.config.js
export default {
  dir: {
    assets: 'nuxt-assets',
    layouts: 'nuxt-layouts',
    middleware: 'nuxt-middleware',
    pages: 'nuxt-pages',
    static: 'nuxt-static',
    store: 'nuxt-store'
  }
}
```

Now, you can use the preceding custom directories as follows:

```
-| app/
---| nuxt-assets/
---| components/
---| nuxt-layouts/
---| nuxt-middleware/
---| node_modules/
---| nuxt-pages/
---| plugins/
---| modules/
---| nuxt-static/
---| nuxt-store/
---| nuxt.config.js
---| package.json
---| README.md
```

> You can find an example app for this option in /chapter-2/configuration/dir/ in our GitHub repository.

The loading option

The `loading` option is used to customize the default loading component in your Nuxt app. If you don't want to use this default loading component, you can set it to `false`, as follows:

```
// nuxt.config.js
export default {
  loading: false
}
```

We will cover this option in more detail in `Chapter 4`, *Adding Views, Routes, and Transitions*.

The pageTransition and layoutTransition options

The `pageTransition` and `layoutTransition` options are used to customize the default properties of the page and layout transitions in your Nuxt app. The default properties for the page transition are set as follows:

```
{
  name: 'page',
  mode: 'out-in',
  appear: false,
  appearClass: 'appear',
  appearActiveClass: 'appear-active',
  appearToClass: 'appear-to'
}
```

The default properties for the **layout** transition are set as follows:

```
{
  name: 'layout',
  mode: 'out-in'
}
```

You can change them as follows:

```
// nuxt.config.js
export default {
  pageTransition: {
    name: 'fade'
  },
  layoutTransition: {
    name: 'fade-layout'
  }
}
```

[53]

We will cover these options in more detail in Chapter 4, *Adding Views, Routes, and Transitions*.

The generate option

The `generate` option is used to tell Nuxt how to generate dynamic routes for a static web app. Dynamic routes are routes that are created by using an underscore in Nuxt. We will cover this type of route in Chapter 4, *Adding Views, Routes, and Transitions*. We use the `generate` option with dynamic routes that *cannot be detected automatically by the Nuxt crawler* if we want to export our Nuxt app as a static web app or as an SPA, instead of using Nuxt as a universal app (SSR). For example, you may have the following dynamic routes (pagination) in your app, if the scrawler fails to detect them:

```
/posts/pages/1
/posts/pages/2
/posts/pages/3
```

Then, you can use this `generate` option to generate and transform the content of each of these routes into an HTML file for you, as follows:

```
// nuxt.config.js
export default {
  generate: {
    routes: [
      '/posts/pages/1',
      '/posts/pages/2',
      '/posts/pages/3'
    ]
  }
}
```

We will show you how to use this option to generate routes, if they cannot be detected by the crawler in Chapter 15, *Creating a Nuxt SPA*, and in Chapter 18, *Creating a Nuxt App with CMS and GraphQL*.

> For more information and more advanced usage of this `generate` option, please visit https://nuxtjs.org/api/configuration-generate.

We will cover and discover other configuration options in the upcoming chapters as we go along. However, these are the basic custom configuration options you should know about at this point. Now, let's explore asset serving with webpack further in the next topic.

Understanding asset serving

Nuxt uses the `vue-loader`, `file-loader`, and `url-loader` webpack loaders to serve the assets in your app. Firstly, Nuxt will use `vue-loader` to process the `<template>` and `<style>` blocks with `css-loader` and `vue-template-compiler` to compile elements such as `<img src="...">`, `background-image: URL(...)`, and CSS `@import` in these blocks into module dependencies. Take the following example:

```
// pages/index.vue
<template>
  <img src="~/assets/sample-1.jpg">
</template>

<style>
.container {
  background-image: url("~assets/sample-2.jpg");
}
</style>
```

The image element and the assets in the preceding `<template>` and `<style>` block will be compiled and translated into the following code and module dependencies:

```
createElement('img', { attrs: { src: require('~/assets/sample-1.jpg') }})
require('~/assets/sample-2.jpg')
```

> Note that from Nuxt 2.0, the `~/` alias will not be correctly resolved in your styles, so use `~assets` or the `@/` alias instead.

After the preceding compilation and translation, Nuxt then will use `file-loader` to resolve the `import/require` module dependencies into a URL and emit (copy and paste) the assets into the output directory – or, use `url-loader` to transform the assets into Base64 URIs if the asset is under 1 KB. However, if the asset is larger than the 1 KB threshold, it will fall back to `file-loader`. That means any files below 1 KB will be inlined as a Base64 data URL by `url-loader`, as follows:

```
<img src="data:image/png;base64,iVBO...">
```

Getting Started with Nuxt

This can give you more control over the number of HTTP requests from your app to the server. Inlined assets cost you fewer HTTP requests, while any file beyond 1 KB will be copied and pasted into the out destination and named with a version hash for better caching. For example, the images in the preceding `<template>` and `<style>` blocks are emitted as follows (via `npm run build`):

```
img/04983cb.jpg 67.3 KiB [emitted]
img/cc6fc31.jpg 85.8 KiB [emitted]
```

You will see the image on the front side of your browser, as follows:

```
<div class="links">
  <img src="/_nuxt/img/04983cb.jpg">
</div>
```

The following is the default configuration for these two webpack loaders (`url-loader` and `file-loader`):

```
[
  {
    test: /\.(png|jpe?g|gif|svg|webp)$/i,
    use: [{
      loader: 'url-loader',
      options: Object.assign(
        this.loaders.imgUrl,
        { name: this.getFileName('img') }
      )
    }]
  },
  {
    test: /\.(woff2?|eot|ttf|otf)(\?.)?$/i,
    use: [{
      loader: 'url-loader',
      options: Object.assign(
        this.loaders.fontUrl,
        { name: this.getFileName('font') }
      )
    }]
  },
  {
    test: /\.(webm|mp4|ogv)$/i,
    use: [{
      loader: 'file-loader',
      options: Object.assign(
        this.loaders.file,
        { name: this.getFileName('video') }
      )
```

```
    }]
  }
]
```

You can customize this default configuration as we did in the previous topic using the `build` option for webpack configuration.

> For more information about `file-loader` and `url-loader`, please visit https://webpack.js.org/loaders/file-loader/ and https://webpack.js.org/loaders/url-loader/.
>
> For more information about `vue-loader` and `vue-template-compiler`, please visit https://vue-loader.vuejs.org/ and https://www.npmjs.com/package/vue-template-compiler.

If you are new to webpack, please visit https://webpack.js.org/concepts/. Also, visit https://webpack.js.org/guides/asset-management/ for its asset management guide. In a nutshell, webpack is a static module bundler for JavaScript apps. The main purpose of it is to bundle JavaScript files, but it also can be used to transform assets such as HTML, CSS, images, and fonts. If you don't want to serve your assets in the way that webpack does for you, you can also use the `/static/` directory for static assets, just as we mentioned before in the previous section, *Understanding Directory Structure*. However, there are benefits to serving assets using webpack. Let's find out what they are in the next section.

webpack assets versus static assets

One of the benefits of using webpack for asset serving is that it optimizes them for production, whether they are images, fonts, or preprocessed styles such as Less, Sass, or Stylus. webpack can transform Less, Sass, and Stylus into generic CSS, while a static folder is just a place where you can put all of your static assets that will *never* be touched by webpack. In Nuxt, if you don't want to use the webpack assets from the `/assets/` directory for your project, you can use the `/static/` directory instead.

For example, we can use the static image from the `/static/` directory, as follows:

```
// pages/index.vue
<template>
  <img src="/sample-1.jpg"/>
</template>
```

Getting Started with Nuxt

Another good example is the favicon file in the Nuxt config file:

```
// nuxt.config.js
export default {
  head: {
    link: [
      { rel: 'icon', type: 'image/x-icon', href: '/favicon.ico' }
    ]
  }
}
```

Note that if you use the ~ alias to link your assets in the /static/ directory, webpack *will* process these assets, just like those in the /assets/ directory, as follows:

```
// pages/index.vue
<template>
  <img src="~/static/sample-1.jpg"/>
</template>
```

We will work on the /assets/ directory a lot for asset serving in Chapter 3, *Adding UI Frameworks*, and in Chapter 4, *Adding Views, Routes, and Transitions*, as well as in Chapter 5, *Adding Vue Components*, to serve assets dynamically. Right now, let's summarize what you have learned in this chapter.

> You can find an example app for serving assets and files from these two directories in /chapter-2/assets/ in our GitHub repository.

Summary

In this chapter, you learned how to install Nuxt with create-nuxt-app, and how to install it from scratch, and about the default directories installed by the Nuxt scaffolding tool. You also learned how to use the nuxt.config.js file to customize your app. Lastly, you learned to understand how assets work in Nuxt and the difference between using webpack and the /static/ folder for assets serving.

In the upcoming chapter, you will learn how to install custom UI frameworks, libraries, and tools, such as Zurb Foundation, Motion UI, jQuery UI, and Less CSS for your app. You will write some basic code to style your index page and add some animations to it. You will also start using some of the directories we have just covered in this chapter, such as the /assets/, /plugins/, and /pages/ directories, to develop your Nuxt app.

3
Adding UI Frameworks

In this chapter, we will guide you through the process of installing a selection of frontend UI frameworks in your Nuxt project that will style your app templates. The frameworks we have selected in this book are Foundation for designing your layouts, Motion UI for creating animations, Less as the style sheet language, jQuery UI for adding animations to your DOM, AOS for animating your contents on scrolling, and Swiper for creating carousel images. These frameworks can speed up frontend development in your Nuxt project, making it fun and easy.

The topics we will be covering in this chapter are as follows:

- Adding Foundation and Motion UI
- Adding Less (Leaner Style Sheets)
- Adding jQuery UI
- Adding AOS
- Adding Swiper

Adding Foundation and Motion UI

Foundation is a frontend framework for creating responsive sites. It is shipped with HTML and CSS templates for grid layouts, typography, buttons, tables, navigation, forms, and much more, as well as optional JavaScript plugins. It works with any device, mobile or desktop, and is an alternative to Bootstrap (https://getbootstrap.com/), another popular frontend framework. We focus on Foundation in this book. So, just as in the previous chapter, we have a list of suggested UI frameworks that you can choose from for your app when using the `create-nuxt-app` scaffolding to install the skeleton of your Nuxt project. We should choose None so that we can add Foundation as the UI framework:

```
? Choose UI framework (Use arrow keys)
> None
  Ant Design Vue
  Bootstrap Vue
  ...
```

Once you have answered the questions in the installation process, navigate to your project directory, and then you can install and integrate Foundation into your Nuxt app. The easiest way is to use **content delivery networks** (**CDNs**), but is not encouraged. The simplest reason is that the CDN link won't work if you are developing offline. Also, you will lose control of the source files because they are handled by large web companies, such as Google, Microsoft, and Amazon. However, if you want to use a CDN in your Nuxt project for a quick start, simply add the CDN source to the `head` option in the Nuxt config file as follows:

```js
// nuxt.config.js
export default {
  head: {
    script: [
      { src: 'https://cdn.jsdelivr.net/.../foundation.min.js' },
    ],
    link: [
      { rel: 'stylesheet', href:
      'https://cdn.jsdelivr.net/.../foundation.min.css' },
    ],
  },
}
```

> You can find the latest CDN links from the official Foundation site at https://get.foundation/sites/docs/installation.html#cdn-links.

That's easy, isn't it? But it is not ideal if you want to host the source files locally. Let's find out the proper way of integrating with Nuxt in the following steps:

1. Install Foundation and its dependencies (jQuery and what-input) via npm on your terminal:

    ```
    $ npm i foundation-sites
    $ npm i jquery
    $ npm i what-input
    ```

2. Add the Foundation CSS source from the `/node_modules/` folder to the `css` option in the Nuxt config file as follows:

    ```
    // nuxt.config.js
    export default {
      css: [
        'foundation-sites/dist/css/foundation.min.css'
      ],
    }
    ```

3. Create a `foundation.client.js` file in the `/plugins/` directory with this code:

    ```
    // plugins/client-only/foundation.client.js
    import 'foundation-sites'
    ```

    This plugin will make sure that Foundation runs on the client side only. We will cover plugins in more detail in Chapter 6, *Writing Plugins and Modules*.

4. Register the preceding Foundation plugin in the `plugins` option in the Nuxt config file as follows:

    ```
    // nuxt.config.js
    export default {
      plugins: [
        '~/plugins/client-only/foundation.client.js',
      ],
    }
    ```

5. Then you can use the JavaScript plugins from Foundation in any page where you need them, for example:

    ```
    // layouts/form.vue
    <script>
    import $ from 'jquery'

    export default {
    ```

[61]

Adding UI Frameworks

```
    mounted () {
      $(document).foundation()
    }
  }
</script>
```

That's it. You have installed and integrated it successfully in your Nuxt project. Now, let's explore how you can create a grid-structure layout and website navigation with Foundation to accelerate frontend web development in the next section.

Creating grid layouts and website navigations with Foundation

The very first thing we should look at is the grid system from Foundation, which is called XY Grid. In web development, a grid system is a system that structures our HTML elements into a grid-based layout. Foundation comes with CSS classes that we can use to structure our HTML elements easily and effortlessly, for example:

```
<div class="grid-x">
  <div class="cell medium-6">left</div>
  <div class="cell medium-6">right</div>
</div>
```

This will responsively structure our elements into two columns on large screens (for example, iPad, Windows Surface), but a single column on small screens (for example, iPhone). Let's create a responsive layout in the default `index.vue` page and website navigation in the `default.vue` layout generated by the `create-nuxt-app` scaffolding tool in the following steps:

1. Delete the `Logo.vue` component in the `/components/` directory.
2. Remove the `<style>` and `<script>` blocks in the `index.vue` page in the `/pages/` directory, but replace the `<template>` block with the following elements and grid classes:

```
// pages/index.vue
<template>
  <div class="grid-x">
    <div class="medium-6 cell">
      <img src="~/assets/images/sample-01.jpg">
    </div>
    <div class="medium-6 cell">
      <img src="~/assets/images/sample-02.jpg">
    </div>
```

```
    </div>
</template>
```

In this template, the images are structured side by side when the page is loaded on a large screen. But they will responsively stack upon each other when the page is resized to, or loaded on, a small screen.

3. Remove the `<style>` and `<script>` blocks in the `default.vue` layout in the `/layouts/` directory, but replace the `<template>` block with the following navigation:

```
// layouts/default.vue
<template>
  <div>
    <ul class="menu align-center">
      <li><nuxt-link to="/">Home</nuxt-link></li>
      <li><nuxt-link to="/form">Form</nuxt-link></li>
      <li><nuxt-link to="/motion-ui">Motion UI</nuxt-link></li>
    </ul>
    <nuxt />
  </div>
</template>
```

In this new layout, we have just created a basic website horizontal menu with a `<ul>` element filled with three `<li>` elements and `<nuxt-link>` components by adding a `.menu` class to the `<ul>` element. We also have aligned the menu items to center by just adding `.align-center` right after the `.menu` class.

That's it. You now have a responsive layout with navigation that works beautifully on any device. You can see how quickly you can get it done without writing any CSS styles yourself. It's sweet, isn't it? But what about JavaScript? Foundation comes with some JavaScript utilities and plugins that we can make use of too. Let's find out in the next section.

> For more information about the XY grid and navigation in Foundation, please visit https://get.foundation/sites/docs/xy-grid.html.
> and https://get.foundation/sites/docs/menu.html.

Adding UI Frameworks

Using JavaScript utilities and plugins from Foundation

Foundation comes with many useful JavaScript utilities, such as MediaQuery. This MediaQuery utility can be used to get the screen size breakpoints (small, medium, large, extra large) for creating responsive layouts in your app. Let's find out how you can make use of it in the following steps:

1. Create a `utils.js` file for keeping your custom global utilities in the `/plugins/` directory and add the following code:

   ```
   // plugins/utils.js
   import Vue from 'vue'
   Vue.prototype.$getCurrentScreenSize = () => {
     window.addEventListener('resize', () => {
       console.log('Current screen size: ' +
         Foundation.MediaQuery.current)
     })
   }
   ```

   In this code, we have created a global plugin (which is a JavaScript function) that will get the current screen size from the `current` property in the MediaQuery utility and log the output whenever the browser's screen size is changed. A resize event listener is added to the window object by using the JavaScript `EventTarget` method, `addEventListener`. This plugin is then injected into the Vue instance by naming it `$getCurrentScreenSize`.

2. Call this `$getCurrentScreenSize` function in the default layout as follows:

   ```
   // layouts/default.vue
   <script>
   export default {
     mounted () {
       this.$getCurrentScreenSize()
     }
   }
   </script>
   ```

   So, if you open the console tab on your Chrome browser, you should see the log of the current screen size when you are resizing your screen, such as `Current screen size: medium`.

[64]

> For more information about Foundation MediaQuery and other utilities, please visit `https://get.foundation/sites/docs/javascript-utilities.html#mediaquery` and `https://get.foundation/sites/docs/javascript-utilities.html`.
>
> For more information about the JavaScript EventTarget and addEventListener, please visit `https://developer.mozilla.org/en-US/docs/Web/API/EventTarget` and `https://developer.mozilla.org/en-US/docs/Web/API/EventTarget/addEventListener`.

Apart from the JavaScript utilities, there are many JavaScript plugins that come with Foundation, such as Dropdown Menu for creating dropdown navigation, Abide for form validation, and Tooltip for displaying extended information on an element in your HTML page. These plugins can be activated by simply adding their class names to your elements. Furthermore, you can modify and interact with them by writing JavaScript just like we have shown you in this section. Let's take a look at the Abide plugin in the following steps:

1. Create a `form.vue` page in the `/pages/` directory with the following HTML elements to create a form containing two blocks of `.grid-container` elements:

```
// pages/form.vue
<template>
  <form data-abide novalidate>
    <div class="grid-container">
      <div class="grid-x">
        <div class="cell small-12">
          <div data-abide-error class="alert callout"
            style="display: none;">
            <p><i class="fi-alert"></i> There are errors in your
              form.</p>
          </div>
        </div>
      </div>
    </div>
    <div class="grid-container">
      <div class="grid-x">
        //...
      </div>
    </div>
  </form>
</template>
```

Adding UI Frameworks

In this form, the first grid container contains the general error message while the second container will contain the form input fields. We activated the Abide plugin just by adding `data-abide` to the form element. We also added a `novalidate` attribute to the form element to prevent the native validation from the browser so that we can pass the job to the Abide plugin.

2. Create a `<div>` block with the `.cell` and `.small-12` classes containing an email `<input>` element and two default error messages in `<span>` elements as follows:

```
// pages/form.vue
<div class="cell small-12">
  <label>Email (Required)
    <input type="text" placeholder="hello@example.com" required
      pattern="email">
    <span class="form-error" data-form-error-on="required">
      Sorry, this field is required.
    </span>
    <span class="form-error" data-form-error-on="pattern">
      Sorry, invalid Email
    </span>
  </label>
</div>
```

In this cell block, there are three custom attributes that come from Foundation: the `pattern` attribute is used to validate the email string, the `data-form-error-on` attribute is used to display the input error responding to the `required` and `pattern` attributes, and the `placeholder` attribute is used to display an input hint in the input field. Note that the `required` attribute is an HTML5 default attribute.

3. Create two `<div>` blocks containing two `<input>` elements for collecting passwords in which the second password is used to match the first password by adding a `data-equalto` attribute from Foundation to the second password `<input>` element as follows:

```
// pages/form.vue
<div class="cell small-12">
  <label>Password Required
    <input type="password" placeholder="chewieR2D2" required >
    <span class="form-error">
      Sorry, this field is required.
    </span>
  </label>
</div>
<div class="cell small-12">
```

```
      <label>Re-enter Password
        <input type="password" placeholder="chewieR2D2" required
          pattern="alpha_numeric"
          data-equalto="password">
        <span class="form-error">
          Sorry, passwords are supposed to match!
        </span>
      </label>
    </div>
```

4. Create the last `<div>` block containing a submit button and reset button as follows:

```
// pages/form.vue
<div class="cell small-12">
  <button class="button" type="submit" value="Submit">Submit</button>
  <button class="button" type="reset" value="Reset">Reset</button>
</div>
```

5. Initiate the Foundation JavaScript plugin in the `<script>` block when the Vue component is mounted:

```
// pages/form.vue
<script>
import $ from 'jquery'

export default {
  mounted () {
    $(document).foundation()
  }
}
</script>
```

That's it. Without writing any JavaScript, you have created a beautiful frontend form validation by just adding HTML elements with classes and attributes. That is extremely useful!

> For more information about the Abide plugin in Foundation, please visit https://get.foundation/sites/docs/abide.html.

Besides JavaScript utilities and plugins, there are a few useful libraries from Zurb Foundation that we can benefit from: Motion UI for creating Sass/CSS animations, Panini for creating pages and layouts with reusable partials, and Style Sherpa for creating style guides for your code base. We will explore how we can use Motion UI to create CSS animations and transitions in the next section. Let's find out!

Creating CSS animations and transitions with Motion UI

Motion UI is a handy Sass library from Zurb Foundation for creating CSS transitions and animations quickly. You can download the Starter Kit from the Motion UI site and fiddle around with it, but that lacks the control of your own because it comes with many built-in defaults and effects that you have to stick with. So, if you want to have more control and take full advantage of Motion UI, you must know how to customize and compile the Sass code yourself. Let's find out how you can write your Sass animations in the following steps:

1. Install Motion UI and its dependencies (Sass and Sass loader) via npm on your terminal:

   ```
   $ npm i motion-ui --save-dev
   $ npm i node-sass --save-dev
   $ npm i sass-loader --save-dev
   ```

2. Create a `main.scss` file in a `/css/` folder in the `/assets/` directory and import Motion UI as follows:

   ```
   // assets/scss/main.scss
   @import 'motion-ui/src/motion-ui';
   @include motion-ui-transitions;
   @include motion-ui-animations;
   ```

3. Followed by the custom CSS animation as follows:

   ```
   // assets/scss/main.scss
   .welcome {
     @include mui-animation(fade);
     animation-duration: 2s;
   }
   ```

4. Register the custom Motion UI CSS resource in the `css` option in the Nuxt config file:

   ```
   // nuxt.config.js
   export default {
     css: [
       'assets/scss/main.scss'
     ]
   }
   ```

5. Apply the animation to any element by using its class name, for example:

   ```
   // pages/index.vue
   <img class="welcome" src="~/assets/images/sample-01.jpg">
   ```

   Then you should see that the preceding image is taking 2 seconds to fade in gradually whenever the page is loaded.

Motion UI also provides two public functions that we can interact with to trigger its built-in animations and transitions: `animationIn` and `animateOut`. Let's find out how you can use them in the following steps:

1. Create a `motion-ui.client.js` file in the `/plugins/` directory with this code:

   ```
   // plugins/client-only/motion-ui.client.js
   import Vue from 'vue'
   import MotionUi from 'motion-ui'
   Vue.prototype.$motionUi = MotionUi
   ```

   This plugin will make sure that Motion UI runs on the client side only. We will cover plugins in more detail in Chapter 6, *Writing Plugins and Modules*.

2. Register the preceding Motion UI plugin in the `plugins` option in the Nuxt config file as follows:

   ```
   // nuxt.config.js
   export default {
     plugins: [
       '~/plugins/client-only/motion-ui.client.js',
     ],
   }
   ```

Adding UI Frameworks

3. Use the Motion UI functions in the template anywhere you like, for example:

```
// pages/motion-ui.vue
<template>
  <h1 data-animation="spin-in">Hello Motion UI</h1>
</template>

<script>
import $ from 'jquery'

export default {
  mounted () {
    $('h1').click(function() {
      var $animation = $('h1').data('animation')
      this.$motionUi.animateIn($('h1'), $animation)
    })
  }
}
</script>
```

In this page, we store the transition name `spin-in` in the `data` attribute in the element and then pass it to the Motion UI `animateIn` function to apply the animation when the element is clicked. Note that we use jQuery to get the data from the `data` attribute.

> If you want to find out the rest of the built-in transition names, please visit `https://get.foundation/sites/docs/motion-ui.html#built-in-transitions`.

It is cool, isn't it? It can be handy if you need CSS animations or transitions on your elements and you don't need to write tons of CSS lines yourself. This can keep your CSS styles small and focus on the main and custom presentation of your template. Talking of saving and not having to write genetic code yourself, it is worth mentioning the common icon font that's offered by Zurb Foundation as well – Foundation Icon Font 3. Let's find out how you can benefit from it in the next section.

> For more information about Motion UI, please visit `https://get.foundation/sites/docs/motion-ui.html`. As for Panini and Style Sherpa, please visit `https://get.foundation/sites/docs/panini.html` and `https://get.foundation/sites/docs/style-sherpa.html`.

Adding icons with Foundation Icon Fonts 3

Foundation Icon Fonts 3 is one of the useful icon font sets that we can use with CSS on projects for frontend development. It can save you from creating common icons yourself such as social media icons (Facebook, Twitter, YouTube), arrow icons (arrow up, arrow down, and so on), accessibility icons (wheelchair, elevator, and so on), e-commerce icons (shopping cart, credit card, and so on), and text editor icons (bold, italic, and so on). Let's find out how you can install it for your Nuxt project in the following steps:

1. Install Foundation Icon Fonts 3 via npm:

   ```
   $ npm i foundation-icon-fonts
   ```

2. Add the path of Foundation Icon Fonts globally in the Nuxt config file:

   ```
   // nuxt.config.js
   export default {
     css: [
       'foundation-icon-fonts/foundation-icons.css',
     ]
   }
   ```

3. Apply the icon to any `<i>` element using the icon name prefixed with `fi`, for example:

   ```
   <i class="fi-heart"></i>
   ```

   > You can find out the rest of the icon names at https://zurb.com/playground/foundation-icon-fonts-3.

Well done! In this section and in the previous sections on adding Foundation to your Nuxt project, you have managed to use the grid system to structure your layouts and Sass to create CSS animations with Motion UI. But adding a grid system and writing CSS animations is not enough for a building an app; we would need specific CSS to describe the presentation of HTML documents and Vue pages in our Nuxt app. We can just use Sass throughout our project to create custom styles that cannot be done by just using Foundation alone, but let's try another popular styling preprocessor and add it to your Nuxt project – **Less**. Let's find out in the next section.

> You can find all the example code that you have learned so far on Foundation in `/chapter-3/nuxt-universal/adding-foundation/` in our GitHub repository.

Adding Less (Leaner Style Sheets)

Less, standing for Leaner Style Sheets, is a language extension for CSS. It looks just like CSS, so it is extremely easy to pick it up in "less" time. Less only makes a few convenient additions to the CSS language, which is one of the reasons it can be learned so quickly. You can have variables, mixins, nesting, nested at-rules and bubbling, operations, functions, and so on in writing CSS with Less; for example, the following is what the variables look like:

```less
@width: 10px;
@height: @width + 10px;
```

These variables can be used just like those in other programming languages; for example, you can use the preceding variables in the following way in your ordinary CSS:

```less
#header {
  width: @width;
  height: @height;
}
```

The preceding code will be converted to the following CSS, which our browsers will understand:

```css
#header {
  width: 10px;
  height: 20px;
}
```

It is very easy and neat, isn't it? In Nuxt, you can use Less as your CSS preprocessor by using the `lang` attribute in the `<style>` block:

```html
<style lang="less">
</style>
```

This way is good and manageable if you want to apply local styles to specific pages or layouts. And you should add a `scoped` attribute before the `lang` attribute so that the local style is applied locally to the specific page and does not interfere with the styles in other pages. However, if you have multiple pages and layouts sharing a common style, then you should create the style globally in the `/assets/` directory in your project. So, let's find out how you can create global styles with Less in the following steps:

1. Install Less and its webpack loader via npm on your terminal:

```
$ npm i less --save-dev
$ npm i less-loader --save-dev
```

2. Create a `main.less` file in the `/assets/` directory and add the following styles:

```
// assets/less/main.less
@borderWidth: 1px;
@borderStyle: solid;

.cell {
  border: @borderWidth @borderStyle blue;
}

.row {
  border: @borderWidth @borderStyle red;
}
```

3. Install the preceding global styles in the Nuxt config file as follows:

```
// nuxt.config.js
export default {
  css: [
    'assets/lcss/main.less'
  ]
}
```

4. Apply the preceding styles anywhere in your project, for example:

```
// pages/index.vue
<template>
  <div class="row">
    <div class="grid-x">
      <div class="medium-6 cell">
        <img class="welcome" src="~/assets/images/sample-01.jpg">
      </div>
      <div class="medium-6 cell">
        <img class="welcome" src="~/assets/images/sample-02.jpg">
      </div>
    </div>
  </div>
</template>
```

You should see the borders that you just added to the CSS classes when you launch your app on the browser. These borders can be useful as guidelines when developing layouts because the grid lines underneath the grid system are "invisible" and it can be difficult to visualize them without any visible lines.

Adding UI Frameworks

> You can find the preceding code in `/chapter-3/nuxt-universal/adding-less/` in our GitHub repository.

Since we are covering the CSS preprocessor in this section, it is worth mentioning that we can use any preprocessor, whether in the `<style>` block, `<template>` block, or `<script>` block, for example:

- If you want to write JavaScript with CoffeeScript, you can do that as follows:

    ```
    <script lang="coffee">
    export default data: ->
      { message: 'hello World' }
    </script>
    ```

    > For more information about CoffeeScript, please visit https://coffeescript.org/.

- If you want to write HTML tags using Pug in Nuxt, you can do it as follows:

    ```
    <template lang="pug">
      h1.blue Greet {{ message }}!
    </template>
    ```

    > For more information about Pug, please visit https://coffeescript.org/.

- If you want to write CSS styles using Sass (Syntactically Awesome Style Sheets) or Scss (Sassy Cascaded Style Sheets) instead of Less, you can do that as follows:

    ```
    <style lang="sass">
    .blue
      color: blue
    </style>

    <style lang="scss">
    .blue {
      color: blue;
    }
    </style>
    ```

[74]

> For more information about Sass and Scss, please visit https://coffeescript.org/.

In this book, we use Less, vanilla HTML, and JavaScript (mostly ECMAScript 6 or ECMAScript 2015) throughout the chapters. But you are free to venture with any preprocessor we have mentioned. Now let's take a look at another way of adding effects and animations to the HTML elements in your Nuxt project – jQuery UI.

Adding jQuery UI

jQuery UI is a set of user interface (UI) interactions, effects, widgets, and utilities that are built on top of jQuery. It is a useful tool for designers and developers alike. Just like Motion UI and Foundation, jQuery UI helps you write less code and do more with the elements in your project. It can be added to a plain HTML page easily by using its CDN resources and jQuery as its dependency, for example:

```
<script src="https://code.jquery.com/jquery-3.5.1.min.js"></script>
<script src="https://code.jquery.com/ui/1.12.1/jquery-ui.js"></script>
<link rel="stylesheet"
href="https://code.jquery.com/ui/1.12.1/themes/base/jquery-ui.css">

<div id="accordion">...</div>

<script>
  $('#accordion').accordion()
</script>
```

Again, it is the same as Foundation. It is a bit complicated when you want to integrate jQuery UI with Nuxt. We can use the preceding CDN resources and add them to the `head` option in the Nuxt config file as follows:

```
// nuxt.config.js
export default {
  head: {
    script: [
      { src: 'https://cdnjs.cloudflare.com/.../jquery.min.js' },
      { src: 'https://code.jquery.com/.../jquery-ui.js' },
    ],
    link: [
      { rel: 'stylesheet', href:
        'https://code.jquery.com/.../jquery-ui.css' },
    ]
```

Adding UI Frameworks

```
  }
}
```

But still, just like integrating with Foundation, it is not encouraged to do it this way. Here is the proper way of doing it:

1. Install jQuery UI via npm on your terminal:

   ```
   $ npm i jquery-ui-bundle
   ```

2. Add the CSS source of jQuery UI from the `/node_modules/` folder to the `css` option in the Nuxt config file:

   ```
   // nuxt.config.js
   module.exports = {
     css: [
       'jquery-ui-bundle/jquery-ui.min.css'
     ]
   }
   ```

3. Create a file called `jquery-ui-bundle.js` in the `/plugins/` directory and import jQuery UI as follows:

   ```
   // plugins/client-only/jquery-ui-bundle.client.js
   import 'jquery-ui-bundle'
   ```

   Again, this plugin will make sure that jQuery UI runs on the client side only and we will cover plugins in more detail in `Chapter 6`, *Writing Plugins and Modules*.

4. Register the preceding jQuery UI plugin in the `plugins` option in the Nuxt config file as follows:

   ```
   // nuxt.config.js
   export default {
     plugins: [
       '~/plugins/client-only/jquery-ui-bundle.client.js',
     ],
   }
   ```

5. Now you can use jQuery UI anywhere you like, for example:

   ```
   // pages/index.vue
   <template>
     <div id="accordion">...</div>
   </template>

   <script>
   import $ from 'jquery'
   ```

[76]

```
export default {
  mounted () {
    $('#accordion').accordion()
  }
}
</script>
```

In this example, we use one of the widgets from jQuery UI, Accordion, for displaying collapsible content panels. You can find the details of the HTML code at `https://jqueryui.com/accordion/`.

Besides widgets, jQuery UI comes with effects such as animation easing effects. Let's find out how you can create animations with the easing effects in the following steps:

1. Create a new page, `animate.vue`, in the `/pages/` directory with the following element in the `<template>` block:

   ```
   // pages/animate.vue
   <h1>Hello jQuery UI</h1>
   ```

2. Create the animation using the jQuery `animate` function with the jQuery UI easing effect, as follows, in the `<template>` block:

   ```
   // pages/animate.vue
   import $ from 'jquery'

   export default {
     mounted () {
       var state = true
       $('h1').on('click', function() {
         if (state) {
           $(this).animate({
             color: 'red', fontSize: '10em'
           }, 1000, 'easeInQuint', () => {
             console.log('easing in done')
           })
         } else {
           $(this).animate({
             color: 'black', fontSize: '2em'
           }, 1000, 'easeOutExpo', () => {
             console.log('easing out done')
           })
         }
         state = !state
       })
     }
   }
   ```

Adding UI Frameworks

In this code, we use the `easeInQuint` easing effect when the element is clicked and the `easeOutExpo` easing effect when it is clicked again. The font size of the element is animated from `2em` to `10em` upon clicking and from `10em` to `2em` when it is clicked again. It is the same for the text color, which is animated between `red` and `black` when the element is clicked.

3. Refresh your browser and you should see that we have applied the animation and the easing effects to `H1`.

> For more easing effects, please visit https://api.jqueryui.com/easings/, while for more information about the jQuery animate function, please visit https://api.jquery.com/animate/.
>
> If you want to find out the rest of the effects, widgets, and utilities from jQuery UI, please visit https://jqueryui.com/.

Even though you can create animations and transitions with Motion UI using CSS, jQuery UI is another option for applying animations to your HTML elements using JavaScript. Besides jQuery and jQuery UI, there are other JavaScript libraries that we can benefit from to present our content interactively and interestingly in specific ways, such as animating our content when scrolling the page up or down and swiping in the contents from left or right. These last two animation tools that we will look into are AOS and Swiper. So, let's do that in the next section.

> You can find all the code we have used for this section in `/chapter-3/nuxt-universal/adding-jquery-ui/` in our GitHub repository.

Adding AOS

AOS is a JavaScript animation library that animates your DOM elements beautifully into view as you scroll down (or up) the page. It is a small library and very easy to use for triggering animations as you scroll a page without having to code them yourself. To animate an element, simply use the `data-aos` attribute:

```
<div data-aos="fade-in">...</div>
```

[78]

Just as simple as this, the element will fade in gradually as you scroll the page. You can even set how long in seconds for the animation to complete. So, let's find out how you can add this library to your Nuxt project in the following steps:

1. Install AOS via npm on your terminal:

   ```
   $ npm i aos
   ```

2. Add the following elements to `index.vue` as follows:

   ```
   // pages/index.vue
   <template>
     <div class="grid-x">
       <div class="medium-6 medium-offset-3 cell" data-aos="fade-up">
         <img src="~/assets/images/sample-01.jpg">
       </div>
       <div class="medium-6 medium-offset-3 cell" data-aos="fade-up">
         <img src="~/assets/images/sample-02.jpg">
       </div>
       <div class="medium-6 medium-offset-3 cell" data-aos="fade-up">
         <img src="~/assets/images/sample-03.jpg">
       </div>
     </div>
   </template>
   ```

   In this template, we use Foundation to add the grid structure to the elements and apply the AOS `fade-up` animation on each element by using the `data-aos` attribute.

3. Import the AOS JavaScript and CSS resources in the `<script>` block and initiate AOS when the Vue component is mounted:

   ```
   // pages/index.vue
   <script>
   import 'aos/dist/aos.css'
   import aos from 'aos'

   export default {
     mounted () {
       aos.init()
     }
   }
   </script>
   ```

When you refresh your screen, you should see the elements are fading in upward, one after another, in order, as you are scrolling down the page. It is wonderful that it allows you to present your content beautifully so effortlessly, isn't it?

Adding UI Frameworks

However, the way we have just applied AOS isn't good if you have multiple pages that you want to animate as well. You'd have to duplicate the preceding script to every page where you need the AOS animations. So, if you have more than one page that you want to animate with AOS, then you should register and initiate it globally. Let's find out how it can be done in the following steps:

1. Create an `aos.client.js` plugin in the `/plugins/` directory, import the AOS resources, and initiate AOS as follows:

    ```
    // plugins/client-only/aos.client.js
    import 'aos/dist/aos.css'
    import aos from 'aos'

    aos.init({
      duration: 2000,
    })
    ```

    In this plugin, we instruct AOS to take 2 seconds to animate our elements – globally. You can find out the rest of the setting options at https://github.com/michalsnik/aos#1-initialize-aos.

2. Register the preceding AOS plugin in the `plugins` option in the Nuxt config file as follows:

    ```
    // nuxt.config.js
    module.exports = {
      plugins: [
        '~/plugins/client-only/aos.client.js',
      ],
    }
    ```

    That's it. Now you can apply the AOS animations to multiple pages without duplicating the script.

Note that we import the CSS resource directly in the AOS plugin instead of importing it globally through the `css` option in the Nuxt config file, as opposed to what we did for Foundation and Motion UI in the past sections. So, if you want to do the same for Foundation, you can import its CSS resource to the plugin file directly as follows:

```
// plugins/client-only/foundation-site.client.js
import 'foundation-sites/dist/css/foundation.min.css'
import 'foundation-sites'
```

Then, you don't have to use the global `css` option in the Nuxt config file. This way is preferred if you want to keep your config file "thin" and keep the CSS and JavaScript resources of your UI frameworks in their plugin files.

> You can find the source code of this example Nuxt app in `/chapter-3/nuxt-universal/adding-aos/` from our GitHub repository.
>
> If you want to find out more information about AOS and the rest of its animation names, please visit https://michalsnik.github.io/aos/.

Now let's explore the last JavaScript helper that can help accelerate your frontend development – **Swiper**.

Adding Swiper

Swiper is a JavaScript touch slider that can be used in modern web apps (desktop or mobile) and mobile native or hybrid apps. It is part of Framework7 (https://framework7.io/) and Ionic Framework (https://ionicframework.com/) for building mobile hybrid apps. We can get Swiper set up for a web app easily using its CDN resources, just like we did with other frameworks and libraries in the past sections. But let's find out how you can install and use it in a proper way with Nuxt in the following steps:

1. Install Swiper in your Nuxt project via npm through your terminal:

    ```
    $ npm i swiper
    ```

2. Add the following HTML elements to create an image slider in the `<template>` block:

    ```
    // pages/index.vue
    <template>
      <div class="swiper-container">
        <div class="swiper-wrapper">
          <div class="swiper-slide"><img
           src="~/assets/images/sample-01.jpg">
          </div>
          <div class="swiper-slide"><img
           src="~/assets/images/sample-02.jpg">
          </div>
          <div class="swiper-slide"><img
           src="~/assets/images/sample-03.jpg">
          </div>
    ```

Adding UI Frameworks

```
    </div>
    <div class="swiper-button-next"></div>
    <div class="swiper-button-prev"></div>
  </div>
</template>
```

From these elements, we want to create an image slider with three images that can be slid into the view from left or right and two buttons – a next button and a previous button.

3. Import Swiper resources in the `<script>` block and create a new Swiper instance when the page is mounted:

```
// pages/index.vue
<script>
import 'swiper/swiper-bundle.css'
import Swiper from 'swiper/bundle'

export default {
  mounted () {
    var swiper = new Swiper('.swiper-container', {
      navigation: {
        nextEl: '.swiper-button-next',
        prevEl: '.swiper-button-prev',
      },
    })
  }
}
</script>
```

In this script, we provide the class name of our image slider to Swiper so that a new instance can be initiated. Also, we register our next and previous buttons to the new instance through Swiper's `pagination` option.

> You can find the rest of the setting options for initializing Swiper and the API that you can use to interact with the instantiated instance at https://swiperjs.com/api/.

4. Add the following CSS styles to customize the image slider in the `<style>` block:

```
// pages/index.vue
<style>
  .swiper-container {
    width: 100%;
    height: 100%;
  }
```

[82]

```
    .swiper-slide {
      display: flex;
      justify-content: center;
      align-items: center;
    }
</style>
```

In this style, we just want to make the slide occupy the screen fully by using 100% on the CSS `width` and `height` properties and to centralize the image in the slider container by using the CSS `flex` property.

5. Now you can run Nuxt and load the page on your browser and you should see an interactive image slider working nicely.

> You can find out about some great example slides from the Swiper official website at https://swiperjs.com/demos/.

Note that the way we just used Swiper is meant for a single page only. If you want to create sliders on multiple pages, then you can register Swiper globally through a plugin. So let's find out how to do that in the following steps:

1. Create a `swiper.client.js` plugin in the `/plugins/` directory, import Swiper resources, and create a property called `$swiper`. Attach Swiper to this property and inject it into the Vue instance as follows:

```
// plugins/client-only/swiper.client.js
import 'swiper/swiper-bundle.css'
import Vue from 'vue'
import Swiper from 'swiper/bundle'

Vue.prototype.$swiper = Swiper
```

2. Register this Swiper plugin in the `plugins` option in the Nuxt config file:

```
// nuxt.config.js
export default {
  plugins: [
    '~/plugins/client-only/swiper.client.js',
  ],
}
```

Adding UI Frameworks

3. Now you can create the new instance of Swiper in multiple pages in your app by calling the `$swiper` property through the `this` keyword, for example:

```
// pages/global.vue
<script>
export default {
  mounted () {
    var swiper = new this.$swiper('.swiper-container', { ... })
  }
}
</script>
```

Again, we have organized the CSS resource in the plugin file instead of registering it globally through the `css` option in the Nuxt config file. However, if you want to override some styles in any of these UI frameworks and libraries globally, then it is easier to override them by registering their CSS resources globally in the `css` option followed by your custom styles in a CSS file that's stored in the `/assets/` directory.

> You can download the source code of this chapter in `/chapter-3/nuxt-universal/adding-swiper/` from our GitHub repository. If you want to find out more information about Swiper, please visit `https://swiperjs.com/`.

Well done! You have managed to pick up some of the popular UI frameworks and libraries that we selected for you to accelerate your frontend development. We hope that they will be useful in the Nuxt projects you create in the future. We will use some of these frameworks and libraries occasionally in the coming chapters, especially in the final chapter – *Chapter 18*, *Creating a Nuxt App with CMS and GraphQL*. Right now, let's summarize what you have learned in this chapter.

Summary

In this chapter, you have installed Foundation as the main UI framework in your Nuxt project and used Foundation's grid system, JavaScript utilities, and plugins to create a simple grid layout, form, and navigation. You have used Motion UI from Foundation to create Sass animations and transitions and Foundation Icon Fonts 3, also from Foundation, for adding common and useful icons to your HTML page. You have installed Less as the styling preprocessor and created some variables in the Less style sheet.

You have installed jQuery UI, adding its Accordion widget to your app, and created an animation using its easing effects. You have installed AOS and used it to animate your elements into the viewport when scrolling the page down or up. Lastly, you have installed Swiper for creating a simple image slide. Last but not least, you have learned how to install these frameworks and libraries globally through the Nuxt config file or just using them locally on specific pages individually.

In the coming chapter, we will cover the view, routing, and transition in Nuxt. You will create custom pages, routes, and CSS transitions and learn how to use the /assets/ directory to serve assets like images and fonts. Also, you will learn how to customize the default layout and add new ones in the /layouts/ directory. You will be given a simple website example that uses all these Nuxt features so that you can grab a sense of concrete use of what you have learned from this book. So, let's explore Nuxt further in the next chapter!

Section 2: View, Routing, Components, Plugins, and Modules

In this section, we will start adding routes, pages, templates, components, plugins, modules, and Vue forms to make our Nuxt app more complicated and interesting.

This section comprises the following chapters:

- Chapter 4, *Adding Views, Routes, and Transitions*
- Chapter 5, *Adding Vue Components*
- Chapter 6, *Writing Plugins and Modules*
- Chapter 7, *Adding Vue Forms*

4
Adding Views, Routes, and Transitions

You created some simple pages, routes, and even layouts in the previous chapter for working with frontend UI frameworks and libraries, but they are just very basic ones. So, in this chapter, we will dive deeper into each of them, as well as templates in Nuxt. You will customize the default template and layout and create custom ones. You will also learn how to customize global meta tags and add specific ones to the individual pages of your appchild page. This is useful if the information of. You will create CSS and JavaScript transitions and animations for transitioning pages. So, by the end of this chapter, you will be able to deliver a simple yet fully functioning web app or website (with some dummy data) from what you will learn in this chapter and what you already learned in the previous chapter.

The topics we will cover in this chapter are as follows:

- Creating custom routes
- Creating custom views
- Creating custom transitions

Creating custom routes

If we are going to understand how a router works in Nuxt, we should first understand how it works in Vue. We can then understand how to implement it in our Nuxt app. Custom routes in a traditional Vue app are created via Vue Router. So, let's begin by understanding what Vue Router is.

Introducing Vue Router

Vue Router is a Vue plugin that allows you to create robust routes for navigating between pages in a single-page application (SPA) without having to refresh the page. A quick use is, for example, if we want to have a `User` component that is used for all users but with different user IDs. You can use this component as follows:

```
const User = {
  template: '<div>User {{ $route.params.id }}</div>'
}

const router = new VueRouter({
  routes: [
    { path: '/user/:id', component: User }
  ]
})
```

In this example, any `/user` route followed by an ID (for example, `/user/1` or `user/2`) will be directed to the `User` component, which will render the template with the ID. This is only possible when the Vue plugin is installed, so let's see how we can install it for Vue apps in the next section, before learning how it works in a Nuxt app.

> For more information about Vue Router, visit `https://router.vuejs.org/`.

Installing Vue Router

In Vue, you must *explicitly* install Vue Router to create routes in a traditional Vue app. Even if you are using Vue CLI (which we will cover in Chapter 11, *Writing Route Middlewares and Server Middlewares*), you must select **Manually select features** to pick **Router** from the options that you are prompted to select, to choose the features you need. So, let's take a look at how you can install it *manually* in this section. There are two options to install Vue Router:

- You can use npm:

    ```
    $ npm install vue-router
    ```

    Then, in the app root, explicitly import vue-router via Vue.use():

    ```
    import Vue from 'vue'
    import VueRouter from 'vue-router'

    Vue.use(VueRouter)
    ```

- Alternatively, you can use CDN or direct download:

    ```
    <script src="/path/to/vue.js"></script>
    <script src="/path/to/vue-router.js"></script>
    ```

If you are using CDN, simply add vue-router after the Vue core and the rest of the installation will be taken care of by itself. Once you are done installing Vue Router, you can use it to create routes.

Creating routes with Vue Router

If you are using the CDN option, then first of all, create a .html file in your project root with the following basic HTML structure and include the CDN links in the <head> block:

```
<!DOCTYPE html>
<html>
  <head>
    <script src="https://unpkg.com/vue/dist/vue.js"></script>
    <script src="https://unpkg.com/vue-router/dist/vue-router.js"></script>
  </head>
  <body>
    //...
  </body>
</html>
```

Adding Views, Routes, and Transitions

After that, you can get Vue Router started very quickly by following these steps:

1. Create the app base with the following markups in the `<body>` block:

   ```
   <div id="app">
     <h1>Hello App!</h1>
     <p>
       <router-link to="/about">About</router-link>
       <router-link to="/contact">Contact</router-link>
     </p>
     <router-view></router-view>
   </div>
   <script type="text/javascript">
   //...
   </script>
   ```

   The `<router-link>` component is used to specify the target location and will be rendered as the `<a>` tag with `href`, while the `<router-view>` component is used to render the requested content, which is the Vue component that we are going to create in the next step.

2. Define two Vue components in the `<script>` block:

   ```
   const About = { template: '<div>About</div>' }
   const Contact = { template: '<div>Contact</div>' }
   ```

3. Create a constant variable called `routes` and add the Vue component to the `component` property with the path that matches the link in `<router-link>`:

   ```
   const routes = [
     { path: '/about', component: About },
     { path: '/contact', component: Contact }
   ]
   ```

4. Create a router instance using the `new` operator and pass in the `routes` constant:

   ```
   const router = new VueRouter({
     routes
   })
   ```

   > Note that `route` in the preceding code block is a short form (shorthand property name) for `routes: routes` in ES6/ES2015. For more information about the shorthand property name, please visit https://developer.mozilla.org/en-US/docs/Web/JavaScript/Reference/Operators/Object_initializer.

[92]

5. Create a Vue instance using the `new` operator and pass in the `router` instance, and then mount the `#app` element to the root instance:

   ```
   const app = new Vue({
     router
   }).$mount('#app')
   ```

6. Run the app in your browser, then you should see the **About** and **Contact** links on your screen. When you navigate to `/about` and `/contact`, you should see that their components are successfully rendered as expected on your screen.

> You can find the code for the preceding the app in `/chapter-4/vue/vue-route/basic.html` in our GitHub repository and run it in your favorite browser to see how it works.

Now, let's explore how Nuxt generates the preceding routes for us via Vue Router. The process of creating routes in Nuxt is simpler because `vue-router` comes out of the box in Nuxt. That means that technically, you skip the preceding installation step in the traditional Vue app. You also skip the preceding JavaScript steps – *steps 3* to *5*. Nuxt will scan the `.vue` file tree in the `/pages/` directory and generate the routes for you automatically. So, let's explore how Nuxt creates and handles routes for you. We will first begin by creating basic routes.

Creating basic routes

Basic routes are created by simply adding `.vue` files with fixed filenames to the `/pages/` directory. You can also create sub-routes by organizing `.vue` files into different folders. Take the following example:

```
pages/
--| users/
-----| index.vue
-----| john-doe.vue
--| index.vue
```

Then, Nuxt will generate the following routes for you without you having to write any of them:

```
router: {
  routes: [
    {
      name: 'index',
```

```
      path: '/',
      component: 'pages/index.vue'
    },
    {
      name: 'users',
      path: '/users',
      component: 'pages/users/index.vue'
    },
    {
      name: 'users-john-doe',
      path: '/users/john-doe',
      component: 'pages/users/john-doe.vue'
    }
  ]
}
```

> You can find this example app in /chapter-4/nuxt-universal/routing/basic-routes/ in our GitHub repository.

You should be familiar with these basic routes from the previous chapter. This type of route is good for top-level pages, such as /about, /contact, and /posts. However, if you have multiple subpages in each of these top-level pages and they will increase dynamically over time, then you should use dynamic routes to handle the routes for these subpages. Let's find out how you can create dynamic routes in the next section.

Creating dynamic routes

Dynamic routes are generated by Nuxt when using underscores. Dynamic routes are useful and unavoidable in a more complex app. So, if you want to create dynamic routes, then just create a .vue file (or directory) with a prefixed underscore followed by the name of the file (or directory). Take the following example:

```
pages/
--| _slug/
-----| index.vue
--| users/
-----| _id.vue
--| index.vue
```

Then, you will get the following routes from Nuxt without you having to write any of them:

```
router: {
  routes: [
    {
      name: 'index',
      path: '/',
      component: 'pages/index.vue'
    },
    {
      name: 'users-id',
      path: '/users/:id?',
      component: 'pages/users/_id.vue'
    },
    {
      name: 'slug',
      path: '/:slug',
      component: 'pages/_slug/index.vue'
    }
  ]
}
```

> You can find this example app in /chapter-4/nuxt-universal/routing/dynamic-routes/ in our GitHub repository.

Dynamic routes are good for pages that share the same layout. For example, if you have the /about and /contact routes using the same layout (which is quite unlikely), then the /_slug/ directory in the preceding dynamic route example code is a good choice. So, just as with the subpages under the /users route that share the same layout, the /_id.vue file approach is a good choice for this scenario.

Besides using this (simple) dynamic route to create sub-routes for subpages under the /users route, we can also use more complex dynamic routes for them – nested routes. This is a case when you don't want the parent layout to be replaced completely by the child layout when rendering the subpages; in other words, when you want to render the subpage *inside* the parent layout. Let's find out how you can achieve this in the next section.

Creating nested routes

In a nutshell, routes generated from nested components are called nested routes. In some cases, you may want to compose components (child components) that are nested inside other components (parent components), and you will want to render these child components *inside* particular views of the parent components, instead of having the parent components replaced by the child components.

To do that in a Vue app, you will need to insert a `<router-view>` component inside the parent component for the child component. For example, say you have a `Users` parent component and you want the contents of the individual user to be loaded inside this parent when a specific user is called. Then, you can create a nested route for them with the following steps:

1. Create a parent component:

   ```
   const Users = {
     template: `
       <div class="user">
         <h2>Users</h2>
         <router-link to="/user/1">1</router-link>
         <router-link to="/user/2">2</router-link>
         <router-link to="/user/3">3</router-link>
         <router-view></router-view>
       </div>
     `
   }
   ```

   If you put the preceding code in a diagram, it can be visually explained, as follows:

   ```
   +-------------------+
   | users             |
   | +---------------+ |
   | | 1, 2, 3       | |
   | +---------------+ |
   | +---------------+ |
   | | <router-view> | |
   | +---------------+ |
   +-------------------+
   ```

2. Create a child component that will display the content or information of the individual user:

   ```
   const User = { template: '<div>User {{ $route.params.id }}</div>' }
   ```

[96]

3. Create the nested route with a `children` property, as follows:

```
const routes = [
  {
    path: '/users',
    component: Users,
    children: [
      {
        path: ':id',
        component: User,
        name: 'user-id'
      }
    ]
  }
]
```

4. Define the router instance and pass in the preceding nested routes, as follows, before injecting the router into the Vue root instance:

```
const router = new VueRouter({
  routes
})

const app = new Vue({
  router
}).$mount('#app')
```

Then, the preceding code will produce the following visual when a child link is clicked on; for example, child number `1` and `/users/1` will be dynamically generated as its route:

```
/users/1
+------------------+
| users            |
| +--------------+ |
| | 1, 2, 3      | |
| +--------------+ |
| +--------------+ |
| | User 1       | |
| +--------------+ |
+------------------+
```

5. But we are not finished yet because we still need to deal with the empty view in `/users` when no user has been called yet. So, to fix that, you will create an index child component, as follows:

```
const Index = { template: '<div>Users Index</div>' }
```

Adding Views, Routes, and Transitions

6. Add the preceding index component to the `children` block with an empty string, `''`, on the `path` key:

    ```
    const routes = [
      {
        path: '/users',
        component: Users,
        children: [
          {
            path: '',
            component: Index,
            name: 'user-index'
          },
          //...
        ]
      }
    ]
    ```

7. So now, if you navigate to `/users` in your browser, you should get the following result:

    ```
    /users
    +------------------+
    | users            |
    | +--------------+ |
    | | 1, 2, 3      | |
    | +--------------+ |
    | +--------------+ |
    | | Users Index  | |
    | +--------------+ |
    +------------------+
    ```

    You can see that the `children` option is just another array of route configuration objects, like the `routes` constant itself. Therefore, you can keep nesting views as much as you need. However, we should avoid deep nesting to keep our application simple as much as possible for better maintenance.

    > You can find the preceding example code in `/chapter-4/vue/vue-route/nested-route.html` in our GitHub repository.

It is the same in Nuxt; you can create the nested route by using the child routes of vue-router. If you want to define the parent component of a nested route, you only need to create a Vue file with the same name as the directory that contains your children views. Take the following example:

```
pages/
--| users/
-----| _id.vue
-----| index.vue
--| users.vue
```

Nuxt will automatically generate the following routes:

```
router: {
  routes: [
    {
      path: '/users',
      component: 'pages/users.vue',
      children: [
        {
          path: '',
          component: 'pages/users/index.vue',
          name: 'users'
        },
        {
          path: ':id',
          component: 'pages/users/_id.vue',
          name: 'users-id'
        }
      ]
    }
  ]
}
```

You can see that Nuxt generates the routes the same as you would in the Vue app. Note that in Nuxt, we include `<nuxt-child/>` in the parent component (the .vue file), while in Vue, we include `<router-view></router-view>` in the parent component, just as in the preceding User example. Let's understand this better with an exercise just like we did in the Vue app:

1. Create a parent component with a `<nuxt-child/>` component:

    ```
    // pages/users.vue
    <template>
      <div>
        <h1>Users</h1>
        <nuxt-child/>
    ```

Adding Views, Routes, and Transitions

```
      </div>
    </template>
```

2. Create an index child component to hold a list of users:

```
// pages/users/index.vue
<template>
  <ul>
    <li v-for="user in users" v-bind:key="user.id">
      <nuxt-link :to="`users/${user.id}`">
        {{ user.name }}
      </nuxt-link>
    </li>
  </ul>
</template>

<script>
import axios from 'axios'
export default {
  async asyncData () {
    let { data } = await
    axios.get('https://jsonplaceholder.typicode.com/users')
    return { users: data }
  }
}
</script>
```

> Note that we will cover the `asyncData` method in the upcoming section of this chapter and `axios` in Chapter 5, *Adding Vue Components*, so do not worry about them at this stage.

3. Create an individual child component with a link for returning to the child index page:

```
// pages/users/_id.vue
<template>
  <div v-if="user">
    <h2>{{ user.name }}</h2>
    <nuxt-link class="button" to="/users">
      Users
    </nuxt-link>
  </div>
</template>

<script>
import axios from 'axios'
export default {
```

```
    async asyncData ({ params }) {
      let { data } = await
      axios.get('https://jsonplaceholder.typicode.com/users/'
        + params.id)
      return { user: data }
    }
  }
</script>
```

You can see that Nuxt has saved you from configuring the nested routes that you have to do in Vue apps with use of the `children` property (as shown in *step 3* of the preceding Vue app example).

So, in this Nuxt app, the element of `<h1>Users</h1>` in `users.vue` will always be seen when a child page is rendered after it. The `<ul>` element containing the list elements will always be replaced by the child page. This is useful if the information of the parent is persistent throughout the subpages as you don't have to re-request the parent information whenever the subpage is rendered.

> You can find this example app in `/chapter-4/nuxt-universal/routes/nested-routes/` in our GitHub repository.

Since there are dynamic routes for "upgrading" the basic routes, you may ask, what about dynamic routes for the nested routes? Technically, yes, this is possible, and they are called dynamic nested routes. So, let's find out more about them in the next section.

Creating dynamic nested routes

We have seen how this works with dynamic routes and nested routes, respectively, so theoretically and technically, it is possible to combine these two options to create dynamic nested routes by having dynamic children (for example, `_subTopic`) in dynamic parents (for example, `_topic`). This is best illustrated in the following example structure:

```
pages/
--| _topic/
-----| _subTopic/
--------| _slug.vue
--------| index.vue
-----| _subTopic.vue
-----| index.vue
--| _topic.vue
--| index.vue
```

Adding Views, Routes, and Transitions

Nuxt will automatically generate the following routes:

```
router: {
  routes: [
    {
      path: '/',
      component: 'pages/index.vue',
      name: 'index'
    },
    {
      path: '/:topic',
      component: 'pages/_topic.vue',
      children: [
        {
          path: '',
          component: 'pages/_topic/index.vue',
          name: 'topic'
        },
        {
          path: ':subTopic',
          component: 'pages/_topic/_subTopic.vue',
          children: [
            {
              path: '',
              component: 'pages/_topic/_subTopic/index.vue',
              name: 'topic-subTopic'
            },
            {
              path: ':slug',
              component: 'pages/_topic/_subTopic/_slug.vue',
              name: 'topic-subTopic-slug'
            }
          ]
        }
      ]
    }
  ]
}
```

You can see that the routes are more complicated, which can make your application harder to develop just by reading and trying to understand the file directory tree because it is quite abstract, and it can be too abstract at some point if it grows "bigger." It is good practice to always design and structure our app to be as simple as possible. The following example routes are a good example of this type of route:

- Some examples for /_topic/ are as follows:

  ```
  /science
  /arts
  ```

- Some examples for /_topic/_subTopic/ are as follows:

  ```
  /science/astronomy
  /science/geology
  /arts/architecture
  /arts/performing-arts
  ```

- Some examples for /_topic/_subTopic/_slug.vue are as follows:

  ```
  /science/astronomy/astrophysics
  /science/astronomy/planetary-science
  /science/geology/biogeology
  /science/geology/geophysics
  /arts/architecture/interior-architecture
  /arts/architecture/landscape-architecture
  /arts/performing-arts/dance
  /arts/performing-arts/music
  ```

> You can find an example app for this type of route in /chapter-4/nuxt-universal/routing/dynamic-nested-routes/ in our GitHub repository.

Creating dynamic routes and pages always requires the parameters in the route (in other words, the route params) so that we can pass them (whether they are IDs or slugs) to the dynamic pages to be processed. But before processing and responding to the parameters, it is a good idea to validate them. So, let's take a look at how we can validate the route params in the next topic.

Validating route params

You can use a `validate` method in a component to validate the params of a dynamic route before any further data is processed or fetched asynchronously. This validation *should* always return `true` to move forward; Nuxt will stop the route and immediately throw a 404 error page if it gets a `false` Boolean. For example, you want to make sure the ID must be a number:

```
// pages/users/_id.vue
export default {
  validate ({ params }) {
    return /^\d+$/.test(params.id)
  }
}
```

So, you will get a 404 page with a `This page could not be found` message if you request the page with `localhost:3000/users/xyz`. If you want to customize the 404 message, you can use a `throw` statement to throw an exception with the `Error` object, as follows:

```
// pages/users/_id.vue
export default {
  validate ({ params }) {
    let test = /^\d+$/.test(params.id)
    if (test === false) {
      throw new Error('User not found')
    }
    return true
  }
}
```

You also can use `async` with the `validate` method for `await` operations:

```
async validate({ params }) {
  // ...
}
```

You also can use `return` promises in the `validate` method:

```
validate({ params }) {
  return new Promise(...)
}
```

> You can find the preceding example app on ID validation in `/chapter-4/nuxt-universal/routing/validate-route-params/` in our GitHub repository.

Validating the route params is one way of handling invalid or unknown routes, but another way of handling them is by using a _.vue file to catch them. So, let's find out how in the next section.

Handling unknown routes with _.vue files

Besides throwing a *general* 404 page with the `validate` method, you can use a _.vue file to throw a custom error page. Let's explore how this works with the following steps:

1. Create an empty _.vue file in the /pages/ directory, as follows:

   ```
   pages/
   --| _.vue
   --| index.vue
   --| users.vue
   --| users/
   -----| _id.vue
   -----| index.vue
   ```

2. Add any custom content to this _.vue file, as follows:

   ```
   // pages/_.vue
   <template>
     <div>
       <h1>Not found</h1>
       <p>Sorry, the page you are looking for is not found.</p>
     </div>
   </template>
   ```

3. Launch the app and navigate to the following routes, and you will see that Nuxt will call this _.vue file to handle these requests on any levels that do not match the correct routes:

   ```
   /company
   /company/careers
   /company/careers/london
   /users/category/subject
   /users/category/subject/type
   ```

[105]

4. If you want to throw a more specific 404 page on a specific level – for example, in the /users route only – then create another _.vue file in the /users/ folder, as follows:

```
pages/
--| _.vue
--| index.vuc
--| users.vue
--| users/
-----| _.vue
-----| _id.vue
-----| index.vue
```

5. Add custom content for this _.vue file, as follows:

```
// pages/users/_.vue
<template>
  <div>
    <h1>User Not found</h1>
    <p>Sorry, the user you are looking for is not found.</p>
  </div>
</template>
```

6. Navigate to the following routes again and you will see that Nuxt is no longer calling this /pages/_.vue file for unmatched requests:

```
/users/category/subject
/users/category/subject/type
```

Instead, Nuxt is now calling the /pages/users/_.vue file to handle them.

> You can find this example app in /chapter-4/nuxt-universal/routing/unknown-routes/ in our GitHub repository.

We hope that by now, you should know how to create routes in various ways that suit your app, but routes and pages are inextricably related and inseparable in Nuxt, so you also need to know how to create Nuxt pages, which are custom views. You will learn how to do that in the next topic.

Creating custom views

Every route you have created in the custom routes above will land on a "page" that has all the HTML markup and content that we want to show on the frontend. From a software architecture perspective, this HTML markup and content, including meta info, images, and fonts, are the view or presentation layer of your app. In Nuxt, we can create and customize our view easily. Let's discover what makes up a Nuxt view and how you can customize it.

Understanding the Nuxt view

The view structure in Nuxt consists of the app template, HTML head, layout, and page layers. You can use them to create views for your app routes. In a more complex app, you would populate them with data from an API, while in a simple app, you can just embed dummy data directly and manually into them. We will walk you through each of these layers in the upcoming sections. Before diving into that, please take a moment to study the following diagram, which will give you a complete view of the Nuxt view:

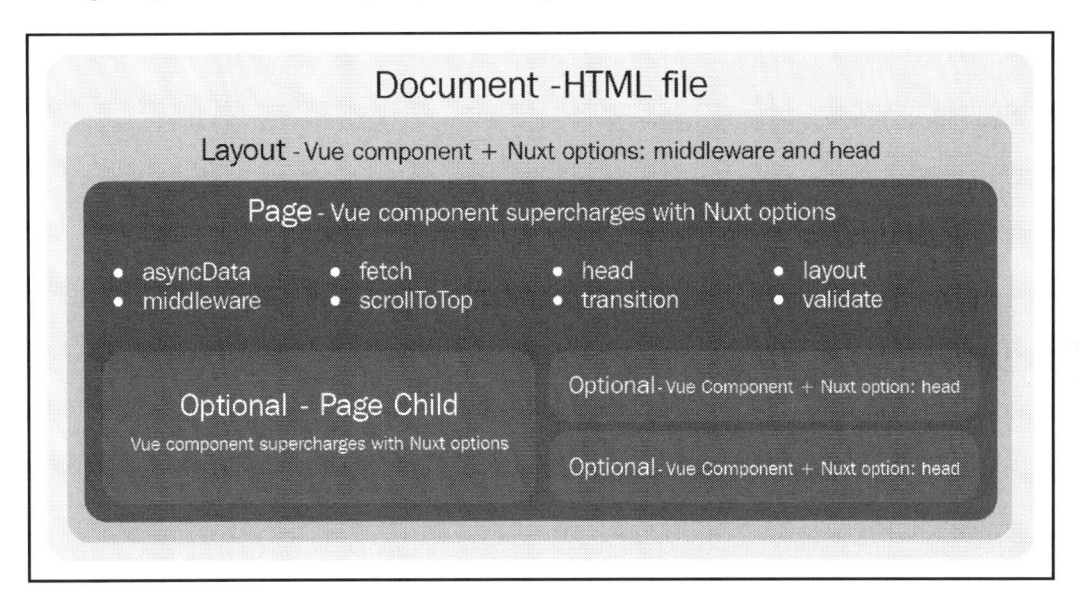

Reference source: https://nuxtjs.org/guide/views

You can see that the **Document - HTML** file is the outmost layer of the Nuxt view, followed by **Layout**, **Page**, and the optional **Page Child** and **Vue Component** layers. The **Document - HTML** file is the app template of your Nuxt app. Let's start by looking at this most basic layer first and learn how you can customize it in the next section.

Customizing the app template

Nuxt creates the HTML app template behind the scenes for you, so basically, you don't have to bother creating it. However, you still can customize it, such as by adding scripts or styles, if you want to. The default Nuxt HTML template is as simple as this:

```
<!DOCTYPE html>
<html {{ HTML_ATTRS }}>
 <head>
 {{ HEAD }}
 </head>
 <body {{ BODY_ATTRS }}>
 {{ APP }}
 </body>
</html>
```

If you want to change or override this default, simply create an `app.html` file in your root directory. Take the following example:

```
// app.html
<!DOCTYPE html>
<!--[if IE 9]><html lang="en-US" class="lt-ie9 ie9" {{ HTML_ATTRS }}><![endif]-->
<!--[if (gt IE 9)|!(IE)]><!--><html {{ HTML_ATTRS }}><!--<![endif]-->
  <head>
    {{ HEAD }}
  </head>
  <body {{ BODY_ATTRS }}>
    {{ APP }}
  </body>
</html>
```

Restart your app and you should see that your custom app HTML template has replaced the default one from Nuxt.

> You can find this example in `/chapter-4/nuxt-universal/view/app-template/` in our GitHub repository.

The next closest layer to the HTML document (which is an `<html>` element) is the HTML head, the `<head>` element, which contains important meta information and the scripts and styles of your page. We don't add or customize this data in the app template directly, but rather in the Nuxt config file and the files in the `/pages/` directory. So, let's find out how in the next section.

Creating a custom HTML head

An HTML `<head>` element consists of the `<title>`, `<style>`, `<link>`, and `<meta>` elements. It can be a tedious task to add these elements manually. So, Nuxt takes care of them for you in your app. In Chapter 2, *Getting Started with Nuxt*, you learned that they are generated for you by Nuxt from the data in the JavaScript objects, which are written with curly braces ({ }), in the Nuxt config file, as follows:

```
// nuxt.config.js
export default {
  head: {
    title: 'Default Title',
    meta: [
      { charset: 'utf-8' },
      { name: 'viewport', content: 'width=device-width, initial-scale=1' },
      { hid: 'description', name: 'description', content: 'parent' }
    ],
    link: [
      { rel: 'icon', type: 'image/x-icon', href: '/favicon.ico' }
    ]
  }
}
```

In this topic, we are interested in the `meta` block in the Nuxt config file and the pages inside the `/pages/` directory. Nuxt uses the Vue Meta plugin to manage these meta attributes. So, to understand how it works in Nuxt, we should first understand how Vue Meta works in a traditional Vue app.

Introducing Vue Meta

Vue Meta is a Vue plugin for managing and creating HTML metadata with built-in reactivity in Vue. You just have to add the `metaInfo` special property to any of your Vue components and it will automatically be rendered into HTML meta tags, as follows:

```
// Component.vue
export default {
  metaInfo: {
    meta: [
      { charset: 'utf-8' },
      { name: 'viewport', content: 'width=device-width, initial-scale=1' }
    ]
  }
}
```

Adding Views, Routes, and Transitions

The preceding block of JavaScript code will be rendered into the following HTML tags in your page:

```
<meta charset="utf-8">
<meta name="viewport" content="width=device-width, initial-scale=1">
```

> For more information about Vue Meta, visit https://vue-meta.nuxtjs.org/.

You can see that what you need to do is just provide the metadata in a JavaScript object. Now, let's get it installed and learn how to configure it for a Vue app.

Installing Vue Meta

Like all other Vue plugins, you can install Vue Meta and hook it up to your Vue app with the following steps:

1. Install Vue Meta via npm:

   ```
   $ npm i vue-meta
   ```

   Alternatively, you can install it via CDN with an `<script>` element, as follows:

   ```
   <script src="https://unpkg.com/vue-meta@1.5.8/lib/vue-meta.js"></script>
   ```

2. Import Vue Meta with Vue Router in your main application file, if you are writing an ES6 JavaScript app:

   ```
   //main.js
   import Vue from 'vue'
   import Router from 'vue-router'
   import Meta from 'vue-meta'

   Vue.use(Router)
   Vue.use(Meta)
   export default new Router({
     //...
   })
   ```

3. Then, you can use it in any Vue component, as follows:

```
// app.vue
var { data } = await axios.get(...)
export default {
  metaInfo () {
    return {
      title: 'Nuxt',
      titleTemplate: '%s | My Awesome Webapp',
      meta: [
        { vmid: 'description', name: 'description', content: 'My
          Nuxt portfolio' }
      ]
    }
  }
}
```

In this example, because we are using `axios` to fetch the data asynchronously, we must use the `metaInfo` method to inject the meta information from the async data, instead of using the `metaInfo` property. You can even add a template for your page title by using a `titleTemplate` option, just as in the preceding example. Next, we will create a simple Vue app with this plugin so that you can get a bigger picture of how to use it.

Creating metadata with Vue Meta in Vue apps

As usual, we can get a Vue app started and running on a single HTML page. Let's get it started:

1. Include the CND links in the `<head>` block:

```
<script src="https://unpkg.com/vue/dist/vue.js"></script>
<script src="https://unpkg.com/vue-router/dist/vue-router.js"></script>
<script src="https://unpkg.com/vue-meta@1.5.8/lib/vue-meta.js"></script>
```

2. Create the following components with the metadata in the `<script>` block:

```
const About = {
  name: 'about',
  metaInfo: {
    title: 'About',
    titleTemplate: null,
    meta: [
      { vmid: 'description', name: 'description', content: 'About
        my Nuxt...'
```

Adding Views, Routes, and Transitions

```
          }
        ]
      }
    }
    const Contact = {
      name: 'contact',
      metaInfo: {
        title: 'Contact',
        meta: [
          { vmid: 'description', name: 'description', content:
            'Contact me...' }
        ]
      }
    }
```

3. Then, add the default metadata in the root instance:

```
const app = new Vue({
  metaInfo: {
    title: 'Nuxt',
    titleTemplate: '%s | My Awesome Webapp',
    meta: [
      { vmid: 'description', name: 'description', content: 'My
        Nuxt portfolio'
      }
    ]
  },
  router
}).$mount('#app')
```

Note that we can override the default meta template in the component by simply adding `null` to the `titleTemplate` option in the child component, just like the preceding About component.

> You can find this example app in /chapter-4/vue/vue-meta/basic.html in our GitHub repository.

In this example, since we are not using `axios` to fetch the data asynchronously, we can use the `metaInfo` property directly, instead of using the `metaInfo` method to inject the meta information with the async data. Then, you will see the page title and meta information change in the browser when navigating around the routes you have just created. It is very easy to use this plugin in a Vue app, isn't it? Now, we should see how it works in a Nuxt app in the next section.

[112]

Customizing the default meta tags in Nuxt apps

Creating and customizing meta information in a Nuxt app is simpler because Vue Meta comes by default in Nuxt. That means you don't have to install it as you do in the Vue app. You just have to use the `head` property in the Nuxt config file to define the default `<meta>` tags for your app, as follows:

```
// nuxt.config.js
head: {
  title: 'Nuxt',
  titleTemplate: '%s | My Awesome Webapp',
  meta: [
    { charset: 'utf-8' },
    { name: 'viewport', content: 'width=device-width, initial-scale=1' },
    { hid: 'description', name: 'description', content: 'My
      Nuxt portfolio' }
  ]
}
```

However, the difference between Nuxt and the Vue apps is that the `hid` key must be used in Nuxt, while `vmid` is used in Vue. You should *always* use `hid` for your meta elements to prevent the duplication of meta tags when defining them (the meta tags) in child components. Also, notice that the `metaInfo` key is only used in Vue, whereas the `title` key is used in Nuxt, to add our meta information.

So, this is how you add and customize the title and meta tags for your Nuxt app. However, they are added globally, which means they are applied to all of the pages in your app. So, how do you add them specifically to a page and override the global ones in the Nuxt config file? Let's find out in the next section.

Creating custom meta tags for Nuxt pages

If you want to add custom meta tags for a specific page or to override the default meta tags in a Nuxt config file, simply use the `head` method on that specific page directly, which will return a JavaScript object that contains the data for the `title` and `meta` options, as follows:

```
// pages/index.vue
export default {
  head () {
    return {
      title: 'Hello World!',
      meta: [
        { hid: 'description', name: 'description', content: 'My
          Nuxt portfolio' }
```

Adding Views, Routes, and Transitions

```
      ]
    }
   }
 }
```

Then, you will get this output for this page:

```
<title data-n-head="true">Hello World! | My Awesome Webapp</title>
<meta data-hid="description" name="description" content="My Nuxt portfolio" data-n-head="true">
```

> You can find this example app in `/chapter-4/nuxt-universal/view/html-head/` in our GitHub repository.

So, that's it. That is all about the app template and the HTML head in Nuxt. The next inward layer in the Nuxt view is the layout and we will guide you on how to create custom ones in the next section. Let's get to it.

Creating custom layouts

Layouts are the backbone of your pages and components. You may want to have multiple different layouts in your app. There is a layout called `default.vue`, generated automatically in the `/layouts/` directory when you install your app using the `npx create-nuxt-app` scaffolding tool. Just like the app template, you can modify this default layout or create your own custom ones.

Modifying the default layout

The default layout is always used for pages that don't have a specific or custom layout. If you go to the `/layouts/` directory and open this layout, you should see that there are only three lines of code in it for rendering your page component:

```
// layouts/default.vue
<template>
  <nuxt/>
</template>
```

Let's modify this default layout, as follows:

```
// layouts/default.vue
<template>
```

```
    <div>
      <div>...add a navigation bar here...</div>
      <nuxt/>
    </div>
</template>
```

You should see whatever you added there – for example, a navigation bar across all the pages in your app. Note that whether you are modifying this layout or creating new ones, make sure you have the `<nuxt/>` component where you want Nuxt to import the page component. Let's explore how you can create custom layouts in the next section.

Creating new custom layouts

Sometimes, we need more than one layout for a more complex app. We may need different layouts for certain pages. For a case like this, you will need to create custom layouts. You can create custom layouts with .vue files and just put them in the /layouts/ directory. Take the following example:

```
// layouts/about.vue
<template>
  <div>
    <div>...add an about navigation bar here....</div>
    <nuxt/>
  </div>
</template>
```

Then, you can use the `layout` property in the page component to assign this custom layout to that page, as follows:

```
// pages/about.vue
export default {
  layout: 'about'
  // OR
  layout (context) {
    return 'about'
  }
}
```

Nuxt now will use this /layouts/about.vue file as the base layout for this page component. But what about the layout for displaying error pages for unknown and invalid routes? Let's find out how this is made in the next section.

Creating custom error pages

Every Nuxt app you install comes with a default error page stored inside the `@nuxt` package in the `/node_modules/` directory that Nuxt uses to display errors, such as 404, 500, and so on. You can customize it by adding an `error.vue` file to the `/layouts/` directory. Let's find out how you can achieve this with the following steps:

1. Create a custom error page, as follows, in the `/layouts/` directory:

    ```vue
    // layouts/error.vue
    <template>
      <div>
        <h2 v-if="error.statusCode === 404">Page not found</h2>
        <h2 v-else>An error occurred</h2>
        <nuxt-link to="/">Home page</nuxt-link>
      </div>
    </template>

    <script>
    export default {
      props: ['error']
    }
    </script>
    ```

    Note that the error page is a page component. At first, it seems counter-intuitive and confusing as it is placed inside the `/layouts/` directory instead of the `/pages/` directory. However, it should be treated as a page even though it is in the `/layouts/` directory.

2. Just like other page components, you can create a custom layout for this error page, as follows:

    ```vue
    // layouts/layout-error.vue
    <template>
      <div>
        <h1>Error!</h1>
        <nuxt/>
      </div>
    </template>
    ```

3. Then, simply add `layout-error` to the `layout` option on the error page:

```
// layouts/error.vue
<script>
export default {
  layout: 'layout-error'
}
</script>
```

4. Now, if you navigate to any of the following unknown routes, Nuxt will call this custom error page and the custom error layout:

```
/company
/company/careers
/company/careers/london
/users/category/subject
/users/category/subject/type
```

> You can find this 404 example in `/chapter-4/nuxt-universal/view/custom-layouts/404/` in our GitHub repository.

That's it. That is all about the layout in Nuxt. The next inward layer in the Nuxt view is pages, and you will learn how to create custom ones for your app in the next section. So, read on.

Creating custom pages

Pages are a part of the Nuxt view's layers, just like the app template, HTML head, and layout, which we have already covered. The `/pages/` directory is where you store your pages. You will spend most of your time working in this directory to create pages for your Nuxt app. However, creating pages is not something new – we created a simple error page in the `/layouts/` directory in the previous section, and many pages when we were learning how to create custom routes for our app. So, when you want to create a custom page for a specific route, simply create a `.vue` file in the `/pages/` directory; for example, we can create the following pages:

```
pages/
--| index.vue
--| about.vue
--| contact.vue
```

[117]

However, there is more than that required for creating a custom page. We need to know the attributes and functions on the page that come with Nuxt. Even though pages are an important part of Nuxt app development, while it is not emphasized in Vue app development, they are deeply related to the Vue component and work a bit differently from a component. So, to create a page and use it sufficiently, we need to understand what a page is in Nuxt first. Let's find out.

Understanding pages

A page is a Vue component in nature. What sets it apart from the standard Vue component is the attributes and functions that are added in Nuxt only. We use these special attributes and functions to set or fetch data before rendering the page, as follows:

```
<template>
  <p>{{ message }}!</p>
</template>

<script>
export default {
  asyncData (context) {
    return { message: 'Hello World' }
  }
}
</script>
```

In the preceding example, we used a function called `asyncData` to set the data in the message key. This `asyncData` function is one of the functions you will see and often use in Nuxt apps. Let's dive into the attributes and functions that are designed specifically for a page in Nuxt.

The asyncData method

The `asyncData` method is the most important function in a page component. Nuxt always calls this function *before* initiating the page component. That means every time you request a page, this function is called first before the page is rendered. It gets the Nuxt context as the first argument and it can be used asynchronously, as follows:

```
<h1>{{ title }}</h1>

export default {
  async asyncData ({ params }) {
    let { data } = await axios.get(
      'https://jsonplaceholder.typicode.com/posts/' + params.id)
```

```
        return { title: data.title }
    }
}
```

In this example, we use the ES6 destructuring assignment syntax to unpack the properties packed in the Nuxt context, and this particular property is params. In other words, { params } is shorthand for context.params. We also can use the destructuring assignment syntax to unpack the data property in the async result from axios. Note that if you have data set in the data function in your page component, it will always be merged with the data from asyncData. Then, the merged data can be used in the <template> block. Let's create a simple example to demonstrate how asyncData merges with the data function:

```
<h1>{{ title }}</h1>

export default {
    data () {
        return { title: 'hello world!' }
    },
    asyncData (context) {
        return { title: 'hey nuxt!' }
    }
}
```

You have two sets of data objects returned from the data and asynData methods, but the output you will get for the preceding code is as follows:

```
<h1>hey nuxt!</h1>
```

You can see that the data from the asyncData function will always *replace* the data in the data function if they are both using the *same* data keys. Also, note that we can't use the this keyword in the asyncData method because this method is called *before* the page component is initiated. So, you *cannot* use this.title = data.title with this method to update the data. We will cover asyncData more in Chapter 8, *Adding a Server-Side Framework*.

> For more information about the destructuring assignment, visit https://developer.mozilla.org/en-US/docs/Web/JavaScript/Reference/Operators/Destructuring_assignment.

The fetch method

The `fetch` method works the same as the `asyncData` method, except it is called *after* the `created` Vue lifecycle hook – in other words, after initiating the component. Like the `asyncData` method, it can be used asynchronously, too; for example, you also can use it to set the data in the page component:

```
// pages/users/index.vue
<li v-for="user in users" v-bind:key="user.id">
  <nuxt-link :to="`users/${user.id}`">
    {{ user.name }}
  </nuxt-link>
</li>

import axios from 'axios'
export default {
  data () {
    return { users: [] }
  },
  async fetch () {
    let { data } = await axios.get
    ('https://jsonplaceholder.typicode.com/users')
    this.users = data
  }
}
```

Note that the `data` method must be used with the `fetch` method to set the data. Since it is called after the page component is initiated, we can use the `this` keyword to access the object in the `data` method. We also can use this method to set the data in the Vuex store from a page component, as follows:

```
// pages/posts/index.vue
<li v-for="post in $store.state.posts" v-bind:key="post.id">
  <nuxt-link :to="`posts/${post.id}`">
    {{ post.title }}
  </nuxt-link>
</li>

import axios from 'axios'
export default {
  async fetch () {
    let { data } = await axios.get(
    'https://jsonplaceholder.typicode.com/posts')
    const { store } = this.$nuxt.context
    store.commit('setPosts', data)
  }
}
```

We will cover the fetch method more with the Vuex store in Chapter 10, *Adding a Vuex Store*.

> You can find the preceding code in this section in /chapter-4/nuxt-universal/view/custom-pages/fecth-method/ in our GitHub repository.
>
> For more information about the fetch method, please visit https://nuxtjs.org/api/pages-fetch and https://nuxtjs.org/blog/understanding-how-fetch-works-in-nuxt-2-12/.

The head method

The head method is used to set the <meta> tags on a page, which we covered previously in the *Creating a custom HTML head* section. It can also be used with the components in the /components/ directory.

The layout property

The layout key (or property) is used to specify a layout from the /layouts/ directory for a page, which we covered previously in the *Creating custom layouts* section.

The loading property

The loading property lets you disable the default loading progress bar or set a custom loading bar on a specific page. We covered it briefly in Chapter 2, *Getting Started with Nuxt*, so we know that we can configure the global default loading component in a Nuxt config file as follows:

```
// nuxt.config.js
export default {
  loading: {
    color: '000000'
  }
}
```

Adding Views, Routes, and Transitions

However, because we are on `localhost` and there is no need for much time to process the data, we usually won't be able to see this loading bar in action. For the sake of seeing it in action, let's demonstrate how this loading component works and looks by *delaying* the loading time of the data in the component with the following steps (but note that this demonstration *should not* be done in production):

1. Create an `index.vue` page in the `/pages/` directory with the following code:

```
// pages/index.vue
<template>
  <div class="container">
    <p>Hello {{ name }}!</p>
    <NuxtLink to="/about">
      Go to /about
    </NuxtLink>
  </div>
</template>

<script>
export default {
  asyncData () {
    return new Promise((resolve) => {
      setTimeout(function () {
        resolve({ name: 'world' })
      }, 1000)
    })
  }
}
</script>
```

2. Create another page called `about.vue` in the `/pages/` directory with the following code:

```
// pages/about.vue
<template>
  <div class="container">
    <p>About Page</p>
    <NuxtLink to="/">
      Go to /
    </NuxtLink>
  </div>
</template>

<script>
export default {
  asyncData () {
    return new Promise((resolve) => {
```

[122]

```
      setTimeout(function () {
        resolve({})
      }, 1000)
    })
  }
}
</script>
```

In these two pages, we use `setTimeout` to delay the data response by 1 second. So, when navigating across the pages, you should see the black loading bar appearing at the top of the page before the requested page is loaded.

> You can find this example in /chapter-4/nuxt-universal/view/custom-pages/loading-page/ in our GitHub repository.

3. Of course, we can create a custom loading bar or layer by creating a component in the /components/ directory. Take the following example:

```
// components/loading.vue
<template>
  <div v-if="loading" class="loading-page">
    <p>Loading...</p>
  </div>
</template>

<script>
export default {
  data () {
    return { loading: false }
  },
  methods: {
    start () { this.loading = true },
    finish () { this.loading = false },
  }
}
</script>

<style scoped>
.loading-page {
  position: fixed;
  //...
}
</style>
```

Adding Views, Routes, and Transitions

Note that the `start` and `finish` methods must be exposed in the custom loading component so that Nuxt can call your component and use these methods when a route is changed (the `start` method is called) and loaded (the `finish` method is called).

So, in this component, the loading element is always hidden as the `loading` property is set to `false` by default in the `data` method. The loading element only becomes visible when the `loading` property is set to `true` during the route changes. It then becomes hidden again when the `loading` property is set to `false` after the route has finished loading.

> For more information about these and other available methods, please visit https://nuxtjs.org/api/configuration-loading.

4. Include the path of the preceding custom component in the `loading` property in the Nuxt config file:

   ```
   // nuxt.config.js
   export default {
     loading: '~/components/loading.vue'
   }
   ```

   > You can find this example in `/chapter-4/nuxt-universal/view/custom-pages/loading-global-custom/` in our GitHub repository.

5. We also can configure the loading behavior on specific pages, as follows:

   ```
   // pages/about.vue
   export default {
     loading: false
   }
   ```

6. If the value of the `loading` key is `false` on a page, it will stop calling the `this.$nuxt.$loading.finish()` and `this.$nuxt.$loading.start()` methods automatically, and this allows you to control them *manually* in your script, as follows:

   ```
   // pages/about.vue
   <span class="link" v-on:click="goToFinal">
     click here
   </span>
   ```

```
export default {
  loading: false,
  mounted () {
    setTimeout(() => {
      this.$nuxt.$loading.finish()
    }, 5000)
  },
  methods: {
    goToFinal () {
      this.$nuxt.$loading.start()
      setTimeout(() => {
        this.$router.push('/final')
      }, 5000)
    }
  }
}
```

7. Then, create the `final.vue` page in the `/pages/` directory:

```
// pages/final.vue
<template>
  <div class="container">
    <p>Final Page</p>
    <NuxtLink to="/">
      Go to /
    </NuxtLink>
  </div>
</template>
```

In this example, you can see that you have the control on the loading bar manually with `this.$nuxt.$loading.finish()` and `this.$nuxt.$loading.start()`. It takes 5 seconds for the loading bar to finish in the `mounted` method. The loading bar starts immediately when you trigger the `goToFinal` method, and it takes 5 seconds to change the route to `/final`.

> You can find this example in `/chapter-4/nuxt-universal/view/custom-pages/loading-page/` in our GitHub repository.

The transition property

The `transition` property is used to specify the transition for a page. You can use a string, an object, or a function with this key, as follows:

```
// pages/about.vue
export default {
  transition: ''
  // or
  transition: {}
  // or
  transition (to, from) {}
}
```

We will cover the `transition` property in depth in the *Creating custom transitions* section later in this chapter.

The scrollToTop property

The `scrollToTop` key is used when you want the page in the nested routes to start at the top before it is rendered. By default, Nuxt scrolls to the top when you go to another page, but on the child pages in the nested routes, Nuxt stays at the same scroll position from the previous child route. So, if you want to tell Nuxt to scroll to the top for these pages, then set `scrollToTop` to `true`, as follows:

```
// pages/users/_id.vue
export default {
  scrollToTop: true
}
```

The validate method

The `validate` method is a validator for dynamic routes, and we have already covered it previously in the *Validating route params* section.

The middleware property

The `middleware` property is used to specify middleware for a page. The assigned middleware will always be executed before the page is rendered, as follows:

```
// pages/secured.vue
export default {
  middleware: 'auth'
}
```

In this example, `auth` is the filename of the middleware that you will create in the `/middleware/` directory, as follows:

```
// middleware/auth.js
export default function ({ route }) {
  //...
}
```

We will cover middleware in depth in `Chapter 11`, *Writing Route Middlewares and Server Middlewares*.

So, that's it. You have completed the sections on the Nuxt view, from the app template, HTML head, and layouts to pages. Well done! We will cover the Vue components in the next chapter. But right now, the next thing we should look at is creating custom transitions between pages in Nuxt because transitions and pages are closely related, just like the page `transition` property you have been briefly introduced to. So, let's move on to our final topic of this chapter, where you will learn about the creation of custom transitions.

Creating custom transitions

So far, you have managed to create multiple routes and pages for a Nuxt app and add a loading bar that shows up when switching between pages. This makes a pretty decent-looking app already. But that is not all that you can do with Nuxt. You can add more stunning effects and transitions *between pages*. This is where the `transition` properties in pages (for example, `/pages/about.vue`) come in, as well as the `pageTransition` and `layoutTransition` options in the Nuxt config file.

We can apply a transition *globally* through the Nuxt config file or *specifically* on certain pages. We will guide you through this topic. However, to understand how the transition works in Nuxt, we should first understand how it works in Vue, and then we can learn how to implement it on our pages when the route is changed. Let's get started.

Understanding Vue transitions

Vue relies on CSS transitions and uses the `<transition>` Vue component to wrap around an HTML element or a Vue component to add the CSS transitions, as follows:

```
<transition>
  <p>hello world</p>
</transition>
```

You can see how easy it is – you can just wrap any element with the `<transition>` component like a piece of cake. When that happens, Vue will apply the following CSS transition classes to that element by adding and removing them at appropriate timings:

- The `.v-enter` and `.v-leave` classes define how your element looks before the transition starts.
- The `.v-enter-to` and `.v-leave-to` classes are the "completed" states for your element.
- The `.v-enter-active` and `.v-leave-active` classes are the active states of the element.

These classes are where the CSS transitions take place. For example, a transition that you would do in an HTML page could look as follows:

```
.element {
  opacity: 1;
  transition: opacity 300ms;
}
.element:hover {
  opacity: 0;
}
```

If we "translate" the preceding transition into the Vue context, we will get the following:

```
.v-enter,
.v-leave-to {
  opacity: 0;
}
.v-leave,
.v-enter-to {
  opacity: 1;
}
.v-enter-active,
.v-leave-active {
  transition: opacity 300ms;
}
```

We can visualize these Vue transition classes as simply as with the following diagram:

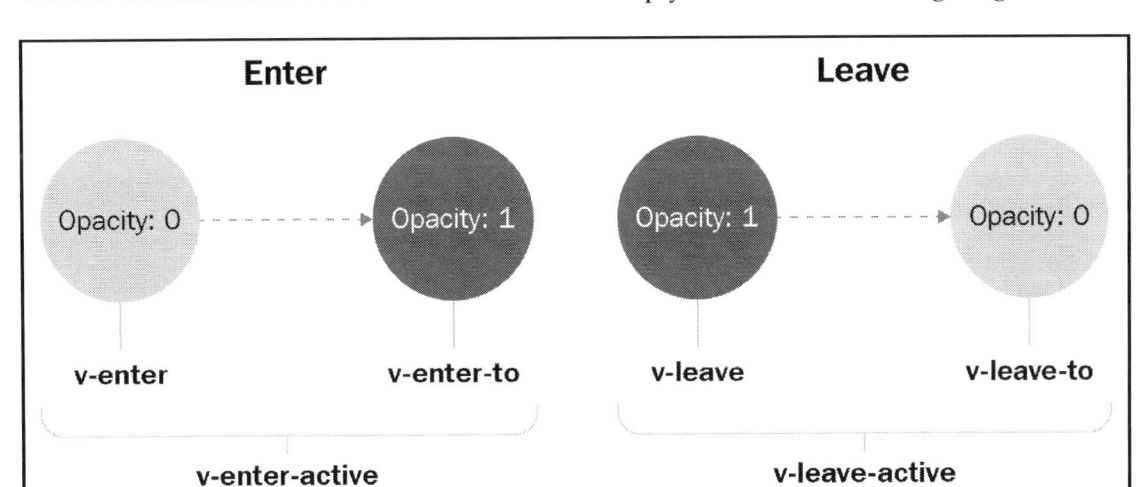

Reference source: https://vuejs.org/v2/guide/transitions.html

Vue prefixes the transition classes with `v-` by default, but if you want to change this prefix, then just use the `name` attribute on the `<transition>` component to specify a name – for example, `<transition name="fade">`; then, you can "refactor" your CSS transition classes, as follows:

```
.fade-enter,
.fade-leave-to {
  opacity: 0;
}
.fade-leave,
.fade-enter-to {
  opacity: 1;
}
.fade-enter-active,
.fade-leave-active {
  transition: opacity 300ms;
}
```

Let's apply the preceding transition to a simple Vue app with the following steps:

1. Create two simple routes and wrap the `<router-view>` component with a `<transition>` component, as follows:

```
<div id="app">
  <p>
    <router-link to="/about">About</router-link>
```

Adding Views, Routes, and Transitions

```
        <router-link to="/contact">Contact</router-link>
      </p>
      <transition name="fade" mode="out-in">
        <router-view></router-view>
      </transition>
    </div>
```

2. Add a `<style>` block with the preceding `fade-` CSS transition classes:

```
<style type="text/css">
  .fade-enter,
  //...
</style>
```

When you run the app on your browser, you can see that it takes 300 milliseconds to fade in and out the route component when switching between the routes.

> You can find this example in `/chapter-4/vue/transitions/basic.html` in our GitHub repository.

You can see that a transition requires a few CSS classes to make it work, but they are not difficult to master for a Vue app. Now, let's see how you can apply transitions in Nuxt in the next section.

Making transitions with the pageTransition property

In Nuxt, the `<transition>` component is not needed anymore. It is added for you by default, so you just have to create transitions in the `/assets/` directory or the `<style>` block on any specific page. The `pageTransition` property is used in the Nuxt config file to set the default properties of page transitions. The default values for the transition properties in Nuxt are as follows:

```
{
  name: 'page',
  mode: 'out-in'
}
```

So, Nuxt prefixes the transition classes with `page-` by default, as opposed to Vue, which uses `v-` as the prefix. The default transition mode is set to `out-in` in Nuxt. Let's see how transitions are done in Nuxt by creating a global transition for all pages and a local transition for a specific page with the following steps:

1. Create a `transition.css` file in the `/assets/` directory and add the following transition to it:

   ```
   // assets/css/transitions.css
   .page-enter,
   .page-leave-to {
     opacity: 0;
   }
   .page-leave,
   .page-enter-to {
     opacity: 1;
   }
   .page-enter-active,
   .page-leave-active {
     transition: opacity 300ms;
   }
   ```

2. Add the path of the preceding CSS transition resource to the Nuxt config file:

   ```
   // nuxt.config.js
   export default {
     css: [
       'assets/css/transitions.css'
     ]
   }
   ```

3. Remember that the default prefix is `page-`, so if you want to use a different prefix, we can use the `pageTransition` property in the Nuxt config file to change that prefix:

   ```
   // nuxt.config.js
   export default {
     pageTransition: 'fade'
     // or
     pageTransition: {
       name: 'fade',
       mode: 'out-in'
     }
   }
   ```

4. Then, change the prefix in all the default class names to `fade` in `transitions.css`, as follows:

```
// assets/css/transitions.css
.fade-enter,
.fade-leave-to {
  opacity: 0;
}
```

This example will apply the transition globally across all pages when the route is changed.

5. However, if we want to apply a different transition to a specific page or override the global transition in a page, we can set it in the `transition` property of that page, as follows:

```
// pages/about.vue
export default {
  transition: {
    name: 'fade-about',
    mode: 'out-in'
  }
}
```

6. Then, create the CSS transitions for `fade-about` in `transitions.css`:

```
// assets/css/transitions.css
.fade-about-enter,
.fade-about-leave-to {
  opacity: 0;
}
.fade-about-leave,
.fade-about-enter-to {
  opacity: 1;
}
.fade-about-enter-active,
.fade-about-leave-active {
  transition: opacity 3s;
}
```

In this example, it takes 3 seconds to fade in and out the `about` page, while it takes 300 milliseconds for the rest of the pages.

> You can find this page-specific example and the global example in `/chapter-4/nuxt-universal/transition/page-transition-property/` in our GitHub repository.

You can see that, once again, Nuxt has lifted some repetitive tasks for you and added the flexibility for you to create custom prefix class names for your transitions. What's more, you even can create transitions *between layouts*! Let's find out how in the next section.

Making transitions with the layoutTransition property

CSS transitions are not only applicable to page components but also to layouts. The default for this `layoutTransition` property is the following:

```
{
  name: 'layout',
  mode: 'out-in'
}
```

So, the prefix of the layout transition classes is `layout` by default and the default transition mode is `out-in`. Let's see how transitions can be done by creating a global transition for all layouts with the following steps:

1. Create the `about.vue` and `user.vue` layouts in the `/layouts/` directory, as follows:

   ```
   // layouts/about.vue
   <template>
     <div>
       <p>About layout</p>
       //...
       <nuxt />
     </div>
   </template>
   ```

2. Apply the preceding layouts to the `about.vue` and `users.vue` pages in the `/pages/` directory, as follows:

   ```
   // pages/about.vue
   <script>
   export default {
     layout: 'about'
   }
   </script>
   ```

3. Create a `transition.css` file in the `/assets/` directory and add the following transition to it:

   ```
   // assets/css/transitions.css
   .layout-enter,
   .layout-leave-to {
     opacity: 0;
   }
   .layout-leave,
   .layout-enter-to {
     opacity: 1;
   }
   .layout-enter-active,
   .layout-leave-active {
     transition: opacity .5s;
   }
   ```

4. Add the path of the preceding CSS transition resource to the Nuxt config file:

   ```
   // nuxt.config.js
   export default {
     css: [
       'assets/css/transitions.css'
     ]
   }
   ```

5. The default prefix is `layout-`, but if you want to use a different prefix, you can use the `layoutTransition` property in the Nuxt config file to change it:

   ```
   // nuxt.config.js
   export default {
     layoutTransition: 'fade-layout'
     // or
     layoutTransition: {
       name: 'fade-layout',
       mode: 'out-in'
     }
   }
   ```

6. Change the prefix in all the default class names to `fade-layout` in `transitions.css`, as follows:

   ```
   // assets/css/transitions.css
   .fade-layout-enter,
   .fade-layout-leave-to {
     opacity: 0;
   }
   ```

In this example, it takes 0.5 of a second to fade in and out of the *entire* layout (which includes the navigation). You will see this transition when you navigate between pages that use *different layouts*, but not the pages that use the same layouts; for example, if you navigate between / and /contact, you won't get the preceding layout transition because they both use the *same layout*, which is /layouts/default.vue.

> You can find this example in /chapter-4/nuxt-universal/transition/layout-transition-property/ in our GitHub repository.

Once again, you can see that it is very easy to create transitions for layouts, and you can customize their prefix class names, just like with the page transitions. Besides using CSS transitions for transitioning pages and layouts, we also can use CSS animations. So, let's find out how in the next section.

Making transitions with CSS animations

A CSS transition is an animation that is performed between **two states** only: a start and an end. But when you need more intermediate states, you should use CSS animation instead so that you can have more control by adding multiple keyframes with different percentages between the start and the end states. Take the following example:

```
@keyframes example {
  0% { // 1st keyframe or start state.
    background-color: red;
  }
  25% { // 2nd keyframe.
    background-color: yellow;
  }
  50% { // 3rd keyframe.
    background-color: blue;
  }
  100% { // 4th keyframe end state.
    background-color: green;
  }
}
```

`0%` is the start state while `100%` is the end state of your animation. You can add more intermediate states between these two states by adding incremental percentages – for example, `10%`, `20%`, `30%`, and so on. However, a CSS transition does not have this ability to add these keyframes. So, we can say that a CSS transition is a simple form of a CSS animation.

Because of the fact that CSS transitions are "actually" CSS animations, we can apply CSS animations just as we apply CSS transitions in the Vue/Nuxt app. Let's find out how with the following steps:

1. Add the following CSS animation code to the `transitions.css` file, just as you did in the previous section:

   ```
   // assets/css/transitions.css
   .bounce-enter-active {
     animation: bounce-in .5s;
   }
   .bounce-leave-active {
     animation: bounce-in .5s reverse;
   }
   @keyframes bounce-in {
     0% {
       transform: scale(0);
     }
     50% {
       transform: scale(1.5);
     }
     100% {
       transform: scale(1);
     }
   }
   ```

2. Change the global default `page-` prefix to `bounce-` in the Nuxt config file:

   ```
   // nuxt.config.js
   export default {
     pageTransition: 'bounce'
   }
   ```

Once you have added the preceding code, refresh your browser and you will see the page bounces in and out when switching between pages.

> You can find this example in `/chapter-4/nuxt-universal/transition/css-animations/` in our GitHub repository.

Depending on how complex and detailed you want to animate, as well as the level of your CSS animation skills, you can create very stunning transitions for your pages and layouts. You just have to focus on writing the code and register it through the Nuxt config file, then Nuxt will take care of the rest of the job of adding and removing the CSS animation classes at appropriate timings for you. But what about JavaScript? Can we use jQuery instead, or any other JavaScript animation libraries to create animations for transitioning our pages and layouts? The answer is yes, you can. Let's find out how in the next section.

Making transitions with JavaScript hooks

Besides making transitions with CSS, you can also do so with JavaScript by adding the following hooks to the `<transition>` component in a Vue app:

```
<transition
  v-on:before-enter="beforeEnter"
  v-on:enter="enter"
  v-on:after-enter="afterEnter"
  v-on:enter-cancelled="enterCancelled"
  v-on:before-leave="beforeLeave"
  v-on:leave="leave"
  v-on:after-leave="afterLeave"
  v-on:leave-cancelled="leaveCancelled"
>
  //..
</transition>
```

> Note that you also can declare the hook without adding `v-on` at the beginning. So, writing the hook as `:before-enter` is the same as writing `v-on:before-enter`.

Then, on the JavaScript side, you should have the following default methods in the `methods` property to correspond with the preceding hooks:

```
methods: {
  beforeEnter (el) { ... },
  enter (el, done) {
    // ...
    done()
  },
  afterEnter (el) { ... },
  enterCancelled (el) { ... },
  beforeLeave (el) { ... },
  leave (el, done) {
    // ...
```

Adding Views, Routes, and Transitions

```
      done()
    },
    afterLeave (el) { ... },
    leaveCancelled (el) { ... }
}
```

You can use these JavaScript hooks alone or together with the CSS transitions. If you are using them alone, the `done` callback must be used in the `enter` and `leave` hooks (methods), or these two methods will run synchronously and the animation or transition you are trying to apply this to will end immediately. Also, if they are used alone, you should use `v-bind:css="false"` on the `<transition>` wrapper as well so that Vue will ignore your element safely, just in case you have the CSS transition in your app as well but it is being used for other elements. Let's make a simple Vue app with these JavaScript hooks with the following steps:

1. Add the following CDN links to the HTML `<head>` block:

   ```
   <script src="https://unpkg.com/vue/dist/vue.js"></script>
   <script src="https://unpkg.com/vue-router/dist/vue-router.js"></script>
   <script src="https://code.jquery.com/jquery-3.3.1.min.js"></script>
   ```

2. Add the app markups and the `<transition>` component with the hooks to the `<body>` block:

   ```
   <div id="app">
     <p>
       <router-link to="/about">About</router-link>
       <router-link to="/contact">Contact</router-link>
     </p>
     <transition
       appear
       v-bind:css="false"
       v-on:before-enter="beforeEnter"
       v-on:enter="enter"
       v-on:leave="leave"
       v-on:after-leave="afterLeave">
       <router-view></router-view>
     </transition>
   </div>
   ```

[138]

3. Follow this with the `<script>` block with the following methods to coordinate with the preceding hooks:

```
const app = new Vue({
  name: 'App',
  methods: {
    beforeEnter (el) { $(el).hide() },
    enter (el, done) {
      $(el).fadeTo('slow', 1)
      done()
    },
    leave (el, done) {
      $(el).fadeTo('slow', 0, function () {
        $(el).hide()
      })
      done()
    },
    afterLeave (el) { $(el).hide() }
  }
}).$mount('#app')
```

In this example, we use the `fadeTo` method from jQuery to control the transition, instead of using pure CSS. You should see the route components fade in and out when switching between them, just like the `.v-enter` and `.v-leave` CSS transitions.

> You can find this example in `/chapter-4/vue/transition/js-hooks.html` in our GitHub repository.

In Nuxt, we don't need to define the JavaScript hooks to the `<transition>` component, just the JavaScript methods in `pageTransition` for the Nuxt config file and `transition` for any `.vue` files in the `/pages/` directory. Let's create a quick example in a Nuxt app with the following steps:

1. Install jQuery via npm on your terminal:

   ```
   $ npm i jquery
   ```

2. Since we are using jQuery in the Nuxt config file and other pages, we can load jQuery *globally* through webpack in the Nuxt config file:

   ```
   // nuxt.config.js
   import webpack from 'webpack'
   ```

Adding Views, Routes, and Transitions

```
export default {
  build: {
    plugins: [
      new webpack.ProvidePlugin({
        $: "jquery"
      })
    ]
  }
}
```

3. Create a global transition with jQuery in the `pageTransition` option in the Nuxt config file:

```
// nuxt.config.js
export default {
  pageTransition: {
    mode: 'out-in',
    css: false,
    beforeEnter: el => { $(el).hide() },
    enter: (el, done) => {
      $(el).fadeTo(1000, 1)
      done()
    },
    //...
  }
}
```

This example will apply the transition *globally* across all pages when the route is changed. Also, we have turned off the CSS transition by setting the `css` option to `false`.

> Note that we write the JavaScript functions with object keys as an alternative to associating with the attribute hooks in the transition component.

4. Create an `about.vue` page in the `/pages/` directory and apply a different transition to override the preceding global transition through the `transition` property on the `about.vue` page:

```
// pages/about.vue
export default {
  transition: {
    mode: 'out-in',
    css: false,
    beforeEnter: el => { $(el).hide() },
    enter: (el, done) => {
```

```
      $(el).fadeTo(3000, 1)
      done()
    },
    //...
  }
}
```

So, in this example, it will take 3 seconds for the transition to take place on this particular page, while it takes 1 second for other pages.

Note that you must import jQuery to the `.vue` page if it is not loaded in the Nuxt config file; for example, assume that you just want to set the transition on this particular page only:

```
// pages/about.vue
import $ from 'jquery'

export default {
  transition: {
    beforeEnter (el) { $(el).hide() },
    //...
  }
}
```

Once the code is in place, refresh your browser and you should see the page fade in and out as it does with the Vue app when the route is changed between pages.

> You can find this example in `/chapter-4/nuxt-universal/transition/js-hooks/` in our GitHub repository.

Well done; you have completed the sections on creating transitions in Nuxt! You can see that JavaScript is another great way for writing transitions and animations in your Nuxt app. But before ending this chapter, let's take a look at the transition modes that we have been seeing throughout these sections on transitions. So, let's find out what they are used for.

> Note that even though jQuery is not encouraged these days, it is used occasionally in this book because it is a dependency of Foundation, which you learned about in the previous chapter. So, we will be reusing it sometimes. Alternatively, you can use Anime.js to make JavaScript animations. For more information about this library, please visit https://animejs.com/.

Understanding transition modes

You have probably wondered what `mode="out-in"` (in Vue) or `mode: 'out-in'` (in Nuxt) is – for example, in our previous Vue apps with the `<div>about</div>` and `<div>contact</div>` components in them. They are there because the transition between `<div>about</div>` and `<div>contact</div>` is rendered simultaneously. This is the default behavior of `<transition>`: entering and leaving simultaneously. But sometimes, you may not want this kind of simultaneous transition, so Vue provides a solution with the following transition modes:

- **The `in-out` mode**

    This mode is used to let the new element transit in first until its transition is complete, then the current element will transit out.

- **The `out-in` mode**

    This mode is used to let the current element transit out first until its transition is complete, then the new element will transit in.

So, you can use these modes in the following ways:

- In a Vue.js app, use them as follows:

    ```
    <transition name="fade" mode="out-in">
      //...
    </transition>
    ```

- In a Nuxt app, use them as follows:

    ```
    export default {
      transition: {
        name: 'fade',
        mode: 'out-in'
      }
    }
    ```

- In JavaScript hooks, use them as follows:

    ```
    export default {
      methods: {
        enter (el, done) {
          done() // equivalent to mode="out-in"
        },
        leave (el, done) {
          done() // equivalent to mode="out-in"
    ```

```
        }
      }
}
```

We have come a long way on this topic on creating custom transitions for our Nuxt/Vue apps. You can now make some decent transitions and animations from what you have learned in this chapter. Hence, we won't cover too much more on this topic any further due to the limited space in this book, but for more information and further reading on Vue transitions and animations, please visit `https://vuejs.org/v2/guide/transitions.html`. Let's now summarise what you have learned in this chapter!

Summary

In this chapter, you learned what a page is in Nuxt and how to create different kinds of routes for your app. You learned how to customize the default app template and layout, as well as how to create new layouts and a 404 page. You learned how to use CSS transitions and animations, as well as JavaScript hooks and methods, to make the transition between your app pages interesting. If you have been following the guides from the start, you should be able to deliver a small project with a nice looking layout by now. You can find a website example in `/chapter-4/nuxt-universal/sample-website/` in our GitHub repository that has used what we have learned in this and previous chapters.

In the next chapter, we are going to explore the `/components/` directory. You will learn how to make use of it in Nuxt apps to refine the layouts and pages we have covered in this chapter by understanding Vue components in more detail, including passing data to them from the page and layout components, creating single-file Vue components, registering global and local Vue components, and so on. Also, you will learn how to write reusable code with mixins, using the naming convention from the Vue style guide to define component names so that your components are organized and standardized for better future maintenance. All of these things will be worth knowing and exploring. So, let's get going.

5
Adding Vue Components

As we stated in the previous chapter, Vue components are an **optional part** of the Nuxt view. You've already learned about various constituents of the Nuxt view: app template, HTML head, layout, and page. However, we haven't covered the smallest unit in Nuxt - **the Vue component**. So, in this chapter, you will learn how it works and how to make use of /components/ for creating custom components. You will then learn how to create global and local components, as well as basic and global mixins, and get to know some of the naming conventions for developing Vue or Nuxt apps. Most excitingly, you will discover how to pass data down from a parent component to a child component, as well as emit data up to the parent from the child.

In this chapter, we will cover the following topics:

- Understanding Vue components
- Creating single-file Vue components
- Registering global and local components
- Writing basic and global mixins
- Defining component names and using naming conventions

Let's get started!

Adding Vue Components

Understanding Vue components

We covered the `/components/` directory briefly in Chapter 2, *Getting Started with Nuxt*, but we haven't got hands-on with it yet. All we know so far is there is a `Logo.vue` component in this directory if you install your Nuxt project with the Nuxt scaffolding tool. All the components in this directory are **Vue components**, just like the page components in the `/pages/` directory. The main difference is that there is no `asyncData` method supported in these components in the `/components/` directory. Let's take the `copyright.vue` component in `/chapter-4/nuxt-universal/sample-website/` as an example:

```
// components/copyright.vue
<template>
  <p v-html="copyright"></p>
</template>

<script>
export default {
  data () {
    return { copyright: '&copy; Lau Tiam Kok' }
  }
}
</script>
```

Let's try replacing the `data` function in the preceding code with the `asyncData` function, as follows:

```
// components/copyright.vue
export default {
  asyncData () {
    return { copyright: '&copy; Lau Tiam Kok' }
  }
}
```

You will get a warning error stating **Property or method "copyright" is not defined...** on your browser's console. So, how can we get the data for copyright purposes dynamically? We can request data using the `fetch` method in the component directly with an HTTP client (for example, `axios`), as follows:

1. Install the `axios` package via npm in the project directory:

    ```
    $ npm i axios
    ```

[146]

2. Import `axios` and request the data in the `fetch` method, as follows:

```
// components/copyright.vue
import axios from 'axios'

export default {
  data () {
    return { copyright: null }
  },
  fetch () {
    const { data } = axios.get('http/path/to/site-info.json')
    this.copyright = data.copyright
  }
}
```

This method works fine, but it is not ideal to use an HTTP request to get a small piece of data from a payload, which is better off being requested once and then passing the pieces of data from a parent scope into its child components, like so:

```
// components/copyright.vue
export default {
  props: ['copyright']
}
```

In the preceding snippet, the child component is the `copyright.vue` file in the `/components/` directory. The magic in this solution is just using the `props` property in the component. It's simpler and neater, thus making it an elegant solution! But if we are going to understand how it works and how we can use it, we need to understand Vue's component system.

What is a component?

Components are single, self-contained, and reusable **Vue instances** with a custom name. We define components by using the Vue `component` method. For example, if we want to define a component called `post-item`, we would do this:

```
Vue.component('post-item', {
  data () {
    return { text: 'Hello World!' }
  },
  template: '<p>{{ text }}</p>'
})
```

Adding Vue Components

After doing this, we can use this component as `<post-item>` inside the HTML document when the root Vue instance is created with the `new` statement, as follows:

```
<div id="post">
  <post-item></post-item>
</div>

<script type="text/javascript">
  Vue.component('post-item', { ... }
  new Vue({ el: '#post' })
</script>
```

All components are essentially Vue instances. This means they possess the same options (`data`, `computed`, `watch`, `methods`, and so on) as `new Vue`, except a few root-specific options such as `el`. Also, components can be nested inside other components and become tree-like components eventually. However, when this happens, passing data around them becomes tricky. So, fetching the data directly in the specific component using the `fetch` method might be more suitable for this situation. Alternatively, you can use Vuex store, which you will discover in `Chapter 10`, *Adding a Vuex Store*.

However, we will put aside deeply nested components for a moment and focus on simple parent-child components in this chapter and learn how to pass data around them. Data can be passed either from the parent components to their children or from their children to the parents. But how can we do this? First, let's find out how we can pass data to the child components from their parents.

Passing data to child components with props

Let's create a small Vue app by starting with a child component called `user-item`, as shown here:

```
Vue.component('user-item', {
  template: '<li>John Doe</li>'
})
```

You can see that it is just a static component and doesn't do much; you can't abstract or reuse it at all. It only becomes reusable if we can pass data into the template dynamically, inside the `template` property. This can be done with a `props` property. Let's refactor the component, as follows:

```
Vue.component('user-item', {
  props: ['name'],
  template: '<li>{{ name }}</li>'
})
```

In a sense, `props` behave like variables and we set the data for them with the `v-bind` directive, as follows:

```
<ol>
  <user-item
    v-for="user in users"
    v-bind:name="user.name"
    v-bind:key="user.id"
  ></user-item>
</ol>
```

In this refactored component, we use a `v-bind` directive to bind `item.name` to `name`, as in `v-bind:name`. The props inside the component must accept `name` as the property for this component. However, in a more complex app, it is likely we will need to pass more data, and writing multiple props for every piece of data can be counter-productive. So, let's refactor the `<user-item>` component so that it accepts a single prop called `user` instead:

```
<ol>
  <user-item
    v-for="user in users"
    v-bind:user="user"
    v-bind:key="user.id"
  ></user-item>
</ol>
```

Now, we should refactor the component code once more, as follows:

```
Vue.component('user-item', {
  props: ['user'],
  template: '<li>{{ user.name }}</li>'
})
```

Let's put what we've done here into a single page HTML so that you can see the bigger picture:

1. Include the following CDN link in the `<head>` block:

    ```
    <script src="https://cdn.jsdelivr.net/npm/vue/dist/vue.js"></script>
    ```

2. Create the following markups in the `<body>` block:

    ```
    <div id="app">
      <ol>
        <user-item
          v-for="user in users"
          v-bind:user="user"
    ```

[149]

Adding Vue Components

```
        v-bind:key="user.id"
      ></user-item>
    </ol>
  </div>
```

3. Add the following code to the `<script>` block:

```
Vue.component('user-item', {
  props: ['user'],
  template: '<li>{{ user.name }}</li>'
})

new Vue({
  el: '#app',
  data: {
    users: [
      { id: 0, name: 'John Doe' },
      { id: 1, name: 'Jane Doe' },
      { id: 2, name: 'Mary Moe' }
    ]
  }
})
```

In this example, we have broken down the app into smaller units: a child and a parent. However, they are bound through the `props` property. Now, we can further refine them without the fear of them interfering with each other.

> You can find this example code in `/chapter-5/vue/component/basic.html` in this book's GitHub repository.

However, in a real and complex app, we should divide this app into separate files (single-file components) that are more manageable. We will show you how to create them in the *Creating single-file Vue components* section. But for now, let's discover how we can pass the data up to the parent from the child component.

[150]

Listening to child component events

So far, you've learned how to pass data down to child components from the parent using the `props` property. But what about passing data up to the parent from the child component? We can achieve this by using the `$emit` method with a custom event, as follows:

```
$emit(<event>)
```

You can choose any name for the custom event in the child component to be broadcasted. Then, the parent component can listen to this broadcasted event using the `v-on` directive and decide what to do next in this format:

```
v-on:<event>="<event-handler>"
```

So, if you are emitting a custom event called `done`, then the parent will be listing to this `done` event with the `v-on` directive as `v-on:done`, followed by an event handler. This event handler can be a plain JavaScript function, such as `v-on:done=handleDone`. Let's create a simple app to demonstrate this:

1. Create the app's markups, as follows:

    ```
    <div id="todos">
      <todo-item
        v-on:completed="handleCompleted"
      ></todo-item>
    </div>
    ```

2. Create a child component, as follows:

    ```
    Vue.component('todo-item', {
      template: '<button v-on:click="clicked">Task completed</button>',
      methods: {
        clicked () {
          this.$emit('completed')
        }
      }
    })
    ```

Adding Vue Components

3. Create a Vue root instance as the parent:

```
new Vue({
  el: '#todos',
  methods: {
    handleCompleted () {
      alert('Task Done')
    }
  }
})
```

In this example, the child component will emit a `completed` event when the `clicked` method in it is triggered. Here, the parent receives the event via `v-on` and then triggers the `handleCompleted` method on its side.

> You can find this example in `/chapter-5/vue/component/emit/emit-basic.html` in this book's GitHub repository.

Emitting a value with an event

However, emitting just an event is not enough sometimes. In some cases, it's more useful to emit the event with a value. We can do that by using the second parameter in the `$emit` method, as follows:

```
$emit(<event>, <value>)
```

Then, when the parent is listening to the event, it can access the emitted event's value with `$event` in this format:

```
v-on:<event>="<event-handler> = $event"
```

If the event handler is a method, then the value will be the first parameter for that method in this format:

```
methods: {
  handleCompleted (<value>) { ... }
}
```

So, now, we can simply modify the previous app, as follows:

```
// Child
clicked () {
  this.$emit('completed', 'Task done')
}
```

[152]

```
// Parent
methods: {
  handleCompleted (value) {
    alert(value)
  }
}
```

Here, you can see that it is fun and easy to pass the data down or up between the parent and child components. But if you have an `<input>` element in your child component, how can you pass the value in the input field up to the parent in a two-way data binding? This isn't as hard as it seems if we understand what is going on "under" the two-way data binding in Vue. We'll learn about this in the next section.

> You can find a simple example of this in `/chapter-5/vue/component/emit/value.html` and a more complex example in `/chapter-5/vue/component/emit/emit-value-with-props.html`, both of which can be found in this book's GitHub repository.

Creating custom input components with v-model

We also can use a component to create custom two-way binding inputs that work the same as a `v-model` directive for emitting events to the parent. Let's create a basic custom input component:

```
<custom-input v-model="newTodoText"></custom-input>

Vue.component('custom-input', {
  props: ['value'],
  template: `<input v-on:input="$emit('input', $event.target.value)">`,
})
```

How does it work? To understand this, we need to understand how `v-model` works under the hood. Let's use a simple `v-model` input:

```
<input v-model="handler">
```

The preceding `<input>` element is shorthand for the following:

```
<input
  v-bind:value="handler"
  v-on:input="handler = $event.target.value"
>
```

[153]

Adding Vue Components

So, writing `v-model="newTodoText"` in our custom input is shorthand for the following:

```
v-bind:value="newTodoText"
v-on:input="newTodoText = $event.target.value"
```

This means the component underneath this shorthand must have the `value` attribute in the `props` property to let the data be passed down from the top. It must emit an `input` event with `$event.target.value` in order to pass the data up to the top.

So, in this example, we emit the value when the user types in the `custom-input` child component, while the parent listens to the change via `v-model="newTodoText"` and updates the value of `newTodoText` in the `data` object:

```
<p>{{ newTodoText }}</p>

new Vue({
  el: '#todos',
  data: {
    newTodoText: null
  }
})
```

This makes perfect sense when you know the mechanism underneath the two-way data binding in Vue – the `v-model` directive – doesn't it? But what about the checkbox input and radio button elements, if you don't want to use their default values? In this situation, you'd want to send the custom ones to the parent component instead. We'll learn how to do this in the next section.

> You can find this simple example in `/chapter-5/vue/component/custom-inputs/basic.html` and a more complex example in `/chapter-5/vue/component/custom-inputs/props.html`, both of which can be found in this book's GitHub repository.

Customizing the model in custom input components

By default, the model in a custom input component uses the `value` property as the prop and `input` as the event. Using the `custom-input` component from our previous example, this can be written as follows:

```
Vue.component('custom-input', {
  props: {
    value: null
  },
```

```
    model: {
      prop: 'value', // <-- default
      event: 'input' // <-- default
    }
})
```

In this example, we don't need to specify the `prop` and `event` properties since they are the default behavior in this component's model. But this becomes useful when we don't want to use these defaults for some input types, such as checkboxes and radio buttons.

We may want to use the `value` attribute in these inputs for a different purpose, such as sending a specific value along with the checkbox's `name` to the server in the submitted data, as follows:

```
Vue.component('custom-checkbox', {
    model: {
      prop: 'checked',
      event: 'change'
    },
    props: {
      checked: Boolean
    },
    template: `
      <input
        type="checkbox"
        v-bind:checked="checked"
        v-on:change="changed"
        name="subscribe"
        value="newsletter"
      >
    `,
    methods: {
      changed ($event) {
        this.$emit('change', $event.target.checked)
      }
    }
})
```

In this example, we want to send these two pieces of data to the server:

```
name="subscribe"
value="newsletter"
```

We can also do this in JSON format after performing serialization with `JSON.stringify`:

```
[{
  "name":"subscribe",
  "value":"newsletter"
}]
```

So, let's say we don't set the following custom model in this component:

```
model: {
  prop: 'checked',
  event: 'change'
}
```

In this case, we can only send the following default data to the server:

```
[{
  "name":"subscribe",
  "value":"on"
}]
```

> You can find this example in `/chapter-5/vue/component/custom-inputs/checkbox.html` in this book's GitHub repository.

Again, it makes sense when you know what is underneath a Vue component as it can be customized with a bit of effort. The Vue components in the `/components/` directory work the same as the components you have just learned about. But before diving into writing the components for a Nuxt app, you should understand why the `key` attribute is important when using the `v-for` directive. Let's find out.

Understanding the key attribute in v-for loops

In many of this book's previous examples and exercises, you probably noticed a `key` attribute in all our `v-for` loops, as follows:

```
<ol>
  <user-item
    v-for="user in users"
    v-bind:user="user"
    v-bind:key="user.id"
  ></user-item>
</ol>
```

You may be wondering what it is and what it is for. The `key` attribute is a unique identity of each DOM node so that Vue can track their changes, and thus reuse and reorder existing elements. Tracking by the index is the default behavior of Vue to track nodes with `v-for`, so using `index` for the key attribute like so is redundant:

```
<div v-for="(user, index) in users" :key="index">
  //...
</div>
```

Hence, if we want Vue to track each item's identity accurately, we must bind each key attribute with a unique value by using the `v-bind` directive, as follows:

```
<div v-for="user in users" :key="user.id">
  //...
</div>
```

We can use a shorthand `:key` to bind the unique value, as shown in the previous example. Also, bear in mind that `key` is a reserved attribute. This means it cannot be used as a component prop:

```
Vue.component('user-item', {
  props: ['key', 'user']
})
```

Using `key` in the `props` property will result in the following error in the browser's console:

```
[Vue warn]: "key" is a reserved attribute and cannot be used as component prop.
```

The `key` attribute is always required when using `v-for` with a component. Thus, it is good practice to use `key` explicitly with `v-for` whenever possible, whether you're using it with a component or not.

To demonstrate this issue, let's create a Vue app where we'll be using an `index` as our `key`, along with a little help from jQuery:

1. Include the required CDN links in the `<head>` block, along with some CSS styles:

   ```
   <script src="https://cdn.jsdelivr.net/npm/vue/dist/vue.js"></script>
   <script src="http://code.jquery.com/jquery-3.3.1.js"></script>
   <style type="text/css">
     .removed {
       text-decoration: line-through;
     }
     .removed button {
       display: none;
   ```

Adding Vue Components

```
    }
</style>
```

2. Create the required app HTML markup in the `<body>` block:

```html
<div id="todo-list-example">
  <form v-on:submit.prevent="addNewTodo">
    <label for="new-todo">Add a todo</label>
    <input
      v-model="newTodoText"
      id="new-todo"
      placeholder="E.g. Feed the cat"
    >
    <button>Add</button>
  </form>
  <ul>
    <todo-item
      v-for="(todo, index) in todos"
      v-bind:key="index"
      v-bind:title="todo.title"
    ></todo-item>
  </ul>
</div>
```

3. Create the required component in the `<script>` block:

```js
Vue.component('todo-item', {
  template: `<li>{{ title }} <button v-
    on:click="remove($event)">Remove</button></li>`,
  props: ['title'],
  methods: {
    remove: function ($event) {
      $($event.target).parent().addClass('removed')
    }
  }
})
```

4. Create the required list of todo tasks, as follows:

```js
new Vue({
  el: '#todo-list-example',
  data: {
    newTodoText: '',
    todos: [
      { id: 1, title: 'Do the dishes' },
      //...
    ],
    nextTodoId: 4
```

```
    },
    methods: {
      addNewTodo: function () {
        this.todos.unshift({
          id: this.nextTodoId++,
          title: this.newTodoText
        })
        this.newTodoText = ''
      }
    }
  })
```

In this example, we added a new todo task to the top of the list as a result of an `unshift` occurring on our `todos` array. We remove a todo task by adding a `removed` class name to the `li` element. Then, we use CSS to add a strike-through to the removed todo task and hide the **Remove** button.

5. Let's remove `Do the dishes`. You will see the following:

    `Do the dishes`   (with a strike-through)

6. Now, add a new task called `Feed the cat`. You will see the following:

    `Feed the cat` (with a strike-through)

This is because `Feed the cat` has now taken over the index of `Do the dishes`, which is 0. Vue is just reusing the element instead of rendering a new one. In other words, whenever any changes are made to the items, Vue will just update the DOM elements according to their indexes in the array. This means we get an unintended outcome.

> You can find this example in `/chapter-5/vue/component/key/using-index.html` in this book's GitHub repository. Run it on your browser to see the issue for yourself. Then, compare it with the one using `id` as a key in `/chapter-5/vue/component/key/using-id.html`. You will see that you get the correct behavior.

Adding Vue Components

The issue of using an index as a key can also be explained by the following pseudo-code, in which a list of numbers is being generated with `index` set as the key for each of them:

```
let numbers = [1,2,3]

<div v-for="(number, index) in numbers" :key="index">
  // Which turns into number - index
  1 - 0
  2 - 1
  3 - 2
</div>
```

This looks great and works fine at first glance. But if you add number 4, the index information becomes useless. This is because each number now gets a new index:

```
<div v-for="(number, index) in numbers" :key="index">
  4 - 0
  1 - 1
  2 - 2
  3 - 3
</div>
```

As you can see 1, 2, and 3 have lost their states and have to be rerendered. This is why using a unique key is required for cases like this. It is important for each item to keep its index number and not be reassigned on every change:

```
<user-item
  v-for="(user, index) in users"
  v-bind:key="user.id"
  v-bind:name="user.name"
></user-item>
```

As a rule of thumb, whenever you manipulate a list in a way that results in a change of indexes, use a key so that Vue can update the DOM correctly afterward. These manipulations include the following:

- Adding an item to an array, in any position other than the end of the array
- Removing an item from an array, from any position other than the end of the array
- Reordering the array in any way

If your list is never changed during the lifetime of your component, or you only append items with a push function instead of the `unshift` function, as in the previous example, it is fine to use indexes as keys. But if you try and keep track of where you need one and where you don't, you will eventually end up with "bugs" as you may misinterpret what Vue does.

If you are unsure whether to use indexes as keys or not, then it probably better to use the `key` attribute with an immutable ID in the `v-for` loop. Using the `key` attribute with a unique value is not only important with the `v-for` directive but also in the `<input>` elements in an HTML form. We'll look at this in the next section.

Controlling reusable elements with key attributes

For the sake of providing better performance, we have discovered that Vue always reuses DOM nodes instead of rendering anew, and this can have some undesirable results, as demonstrated in the previous section. Here is another example without `v-for` to demonstrate why having the key attribute is rather important:

```html
<div id="app">
  <template v-if="type === 'fruits'">
    <label>Fruits</label>
    <input />
  </template>
  <template v-else>
    <label>Vegetables</label>
    <input />
  </template>
  <button v-on:click="toggleType">Toggle Type</button>
</div>

<script type="text/javascript">
  new Vue({
    el: '#app',
    data: { type: 'fruits' },
    methods: {
      toggleType: function () {
        return this.type = this.type === 'fruits' ? 'vegetables' : 'fruits'
      }
    }
  })
</script>
```

In this example, if you type in the name of a fruit and switch the type, you will still see the name you just entered in the `vegetables` input field. This is because Vue is trying to reuse the same `<input>` element as best as it can to get the fastest result. But this isn't always desirable. You can tell Vue not to reuse the same `<input>` element by adding the `key` attribute to each `<input>` element, along with a unique value, as follows:

```html
<template v-if="type === 'fruits'">
  <label>Fruits</label>
```

Adding Vue Components

```
    <input key="fruits-input"/>
  </template>
  <template v-else>
    <label>Vegetables</label>
    <input key="vegetables-input"/>
  </template>
```

So, if you refresh the page and test it again, the input fields should now work as expected, without "reusing" each other when you toggle them. This doesn't count for the `<label>` elements because there is no `key` attribute in them. However, visually, this is not a problem.

> You can find this example code in the `toggle-with-key.html` and `toggle-without-key.html` files inside the `/chapter-5/vue/component/key/` directory of this book's GitHub repository.

That's all you need to know about the basic nature of the Vue component. So, by now, you should have enough essential knowledge to get started with the next level of creating Vue components by using single-file components. Let's get going!

> If you want to find out more about Vue components and more in-depth parts of Vue components, such as slots, please visit https://vuejs.org/v2/guide/components.html.

Creating single-file Vue components

We have been writing Vue apps using single HTML pages for quickness and getting the outcomes we wanted to see. But in a real development project in Vue or Nuxt, we wouldn't want to write something like this:

```
const Foo = { template: '<div>foo</div>' }
const Bar = { template: '<div>bar</div>' }
```

In the preceding code, we have created two Vue components using JavaScript objects in one place (for example, in a single HTML page), but it is better to separate them and create each component in a separate `.js` file, like so:

```
// components/foo.js
Vue.component('page-foo', {
  data: function () {
    return { message: 'foo' }
```

```
  },
  template: '<div>{{ count }}</div>'
})
```

This can work very well for a simple component, where the HTML layout is simple. However, in more complex layouts that involve more complicated HTML markups, we would want to avoid coding our HTML inside a JavaScript file. This issue can be solved by single-file components with a .vue extension, as shown here:

```
// index.vue
<template>
  <p>{{ message }}</p>
</template>

<script>
export default {
  data () {
    return { message: 'Hello World!' }
  }
}
</script>

<style scoped>
p {
  font-size: 2em;
  text-align: center;
}
</style>
```

However, we can't just run that file on the browser without compiling it with build tools such as webpack or rollup. In this book, we're using webpack. This means that, from now on, we will no longer be using CDN or single HTML pages to create complex Vue apps. Instead, we will be using .vue and .js files with only one .html file to create our Vue apps. We will guide you through how to use webpack to help us to do that in the following section. Let's dive in.

Compiling single-file components with webpack

To compile `.vue` components, we need to install `vue-loader` and `vue-template-compiler` into the webpack build process. But before that, we must create a `package.json` file in our project directory that lists the Node.js packages our project relies on. You can check the details of the `package.json` fields at `https://docs.npmjs.com/creating-a-package-json-file`. The most basic and required are the `name` and `version` fields. Let's get started:

1. Create a `package.json` file in your project directory with the following required fields and values:

   ```
   // package.json
   {
     "name": "vue-single-file-component",
     "version": "1.0.0"
   }
   ```

2. Open a terminal, change the directory to your project, and install `vue-loader` and `vue-template-compiler`:

   ```
   $ npm i vue-loader --save-dev
   $ npm i vue-template-compiler --save-dev
   ```

   You should see a warning on your terminal since the Node.js packages you installed here require other Node.js packages, the most notable of which is the webpack package. In this book, we have set up a basic build process with webpack in `/chapter-5/vue/component-webpack/basic/` in this book's GitHub repository. We will be using this setup for most of our upcoming Vue apps. We have separated the webpack configuration file into three smaller config files:

   - `webpack.common.js` contains common webpack plugins and configurations that are shared in the development and production process.
   - `webpack.dev.js` contains plugins and configurations for the development process only.
   - `webpack.prod.js` contains plugins and configurations for the production process only.

The following code shows how we use these files in `script` commands, respectively:

```
// package.json
"scripts": {
  "start": "webpack-dev-server --open --config webpack.dev.js",
  "watch": "webpack --watch",
  "build": "webpack --config webpack.prod.js"
}
```

> Note that in this book, we are assuming that you already know how to use webpack to compile JavaScript modules in general. If you are new to webpack, please visit https://webpack.js.org/ for more information.

3. So, after installing `vue-loader` and `vue-template-compiler`, we will need to configure `module.rules` in `webpack.common.js` (or `webpack.config.js`, if you are using a single config file), as follows:

```
// webpack.common.js
const VueLoaderPlugin = require('vue-loader/lib/plugin')

module.exports = {
  mode: 'development',
  module: {
    rules: [
      {
        test: /\.vue$/,
        loader: 'vue-loader'
      },
      {
        test: /\.js$/,
        loader: 'babel-loader'
      },
      {
        test: /\.css$/,
        use: [
          'vue-style-loader',
          'css-loader'
        ]
      }
    ]
  },
  plugins: [
    new VueLoaderPlugin()
  ]
}
```

Adding Vue Components

4. We can then use the following commands we set in `package.json` to see our app in action:

    - `$ npm run start` for live reloading and development at `localhost:8080`
    - `$ npm run watch` for development at `/path/to/your/project/dist/`
    - `$ npm run build` for compiling our code at `/path/to/your/project/dist/`

That's it. You now have a basic build process to develop Vue apps with webpack. So, from now on, in more complex apps, we will be writing single-file components and using this method to compile them. We'll create a simple Vue app in the following section.

Passing data and listening to events in single-file components

So far, we have been using a single HTML page for our "todo" demonstrations. This time, we'll use single-file components with a simple "todo" grocery list. Let's begin:

1. Create an `index.html` file with a `"todos"` ID in the `<div>` element for Vue to run the Vue instance:

    ```
    // index.html
    <!doctype html>
    <html>
      <head>
        <title>Todo Grocery Application (Single File
          Components)</title>
      </head>
      <body>
        <div id="todos"></div>
      </body>
    </html>
    ```

2. Create a `/src/` directory in your project root and an `entry.js` file in it as the file entry point to indicate which modules webpack should use to start building out our app internal dependency graph. webpack will also use this file to figure out what other modules and libraries the entry point depends on (directly and indirectly):

    ```
    // src/entry.js
    'use strict'

    import Vue from 'vue/dist/vue.js'
    ```

[166]

```
import App from './app.vue'

new Vue({
  el: 'todos',
  template: '<App/>',
  components: {
    App
  }
})
```

3. Create a parent component that provides dummy data with a list of items in the `<script>` block:

```
// src/app.vue
<template>
  <div>
    <ol>
      <TodoItem
        v-for="thing in groceryList"
        v-bind:item="thing"
        v-bind:key="item.id"
        v-on:add-item="addItem"
        v-on:delete-item="deleteItem"
      ></TodoItem>
    </ol>
    <p><span v-html="&pound;"></span>{{ total }}</p>
  </div>
</template>

<script>
import TodoItem from './todo-item.vue'
export default {
  data () {
    return {
      cart: [],
      total: 0,
      groceryList: [
        { id: 0, text: 'Lentils', price: 2 },
        //...
      ]
    }
  },
  components: {
    TodoItem
  }
}
</script>
```

Adding Vue Components

In the preceding code, we simply `import` the child component as a `TodoItem` and generate a list of them from the data in `groceryList` with `v-for`.

4. Add the following methods to the `methods` object in order to add and delete items. Then, add a method to the `computed` object that sums up the total cost of the items in the shopping cart:

```
// src/app.vue
methods: {
  addItem (item) {
    this.cart.push(item)
    this.total = this.shoppingCartTotal
  },
  deleteItem (item) {
    this.cart.splice(this.cart.findIndex(e => e === item), 1)
    this.total = this.shoppingCartTotal
  }
},
computed: {
  shoppingCartTotal () {
    let prices = this.cart.map(item => item.price)
    let sum = prices.reduce((accumulator, currentValue) =>
     accumulator + currentValue, 0)
    return sum
  }
}
```

5. Create a child component that displays the item being passed down from the parent via `props`:

```
// src/todo-item.vue
<template>
  <li>
    <input type="checkbox" :name="item.id" v-model="checked"> {{
     item.text }}
    <span v-html="&pound;"></span>{{ item.price }}
  </li>
</template>

<script>
export default {
  props: ['item'],
  data () {
    return { checked: false }
  },
  methods: {
    addToCart (item) {
```

[168]

```
              this.$emit('add-item', item)
        }
      },
      watch: {
        checked (boolean) {
          if (boolean === false) {
            return this.$emit('delete-item', this.item)
          }
          this.$emit('add-item', this.item)
        }
      }
    }
</script>
```

In this component, we also have a `checkbox` button. This is used to emit the `delete-item` or `add-item` event and pass the item data up to the parent. Now, if you run the app with `$ npm run start`, you should see it load at `localhost:8080`.

Well done! You have managed to build a Vue app with single-file components using webpack, which is what Nuxt uses behind the scene to compile and build your Nuxt app. It is always useful to know what is running beneath an established system. When you know how to use webpack, you can use the webpack build setup that you just learned about for various JavaScript and CSS related projects.

> You can find this example in `/chapter-5/vue/component-webpack/todo/` in this book's GitHub repository.

In the next section, we'll apply what we learned in the previous sections to the sample website in `/chapter-5/nuxt-universal/local-components/sample-website/`, which can be found in this book's GitHub repository.

Adding Vue components in Nuxt

There are only two `.vue` files in the sample website that we can improve with Vue components: `/layouts/default.vue` and `/pages/work/index.vue`. First, we should improve `/layouts/default.vue`. There are only three things we need to improve in this file: the navigation, the social media links, and the copyright.

Adding Vue Components

Refactoring navigation and social links

We will begin by refactoring the navigation and social media links:

1. Create a navigation component in the /components/ directory, as follows:

```
// components/nav.vue
<template>
  <li>
    <nuxt-link :to="item.link" v-html="item.name">
    </nuxt-link>
  </li>
</template>

<script>
export default {
  props: ['item']
}
</script>
```

2. Create a social links component in the /components/ directory as well, as follows:

```
// components/social.vue
<template>
  <li>
    <a :href="item.link" target="_blank">
      <i :class="item.classes"></i>
    </a>
  </li>
</template>

<script>
export default {
  props: ['item']
}
</script>
```

3. Import them into the `<script>` block in the layout, as follows:

```
// layouts/default.vue
import Nav from '~/components/nav.vue'
import Social from '~/components/social.vue'

components: {
  Nav,
  Social
}
```

[170]

> Note that you can skip this step if you have the `components` option set to `true` in your Nuxt config file.

4. Remove the existing navigation and social links blocks from the `<template>` block:

   ```
   // layouts/default.vue
   <template v-for="item in nav">
     <li><nuxt-link :to="item.link" v-html="item.name">
     </nuxt-link></li>
   </template>

   <template v-for="item in social">
     <li>
       <a :href="item.link" target="_blank">
         <i :class="item.classes"></i>
       </a>
     </li>
   </template>
   ```

5. Replace them with the imported `Nav` and `Social` components, as follows:

   ```
   // layouts/default.vue
   <Nav
     v-for="item in nav"
     v-bind:item="item"
     v-bind:key="item.slug"
   ></Nav>

   <Social
     v-for="item in social"
     v-bind:item="item"
     v-bind:key="item.name"
   ></Social>
   ```

And with that, you're done!

Adding Vue Components

Refactoring the copyright component

We will now refactor the copyright component that we already have in the /components/ directory. Let's get started:

1. Remove the `data` function from the `<script>` block in the /components/base-copyright.vue file:

   ```
   // components/copyright.vue
   export default {
     data () {
       return { copyright: '&copy; Lau Tiam Kok' }
     }
   }
   ```

2. Replace the preceding `data` function with the `props` property, as follows:

   ```
   // components/copyright.vue
   export default {
     props: ['copyright']
   }
   ```

3. Add the copyright data in the `<script>` block to /layouts/default.vue instead:

   ```
   // layouts/default.vue
   data () {
     return {
       copyright: '&copy; Lau Tiam Kok',
     }
   }
   ```

4. Remove the existing `<Copyright />` component in the `<template>` block:

   ```
   // layouts/default.vue
   <Copyright />
   ```

5. Add a new `<Copyright />` component with the copyright data bound to it:

   ```
   // layouts/default.vue
   <Copyright v-bind:copyright="copyright" />
   ```

With that, you should have managed to pass the data down to the components (the children) from the default page (the parent) where you kept your data. Well done! That's it for /layouts/default.vue. We can also improve the work pages, which we have already done for you in /chapter-5/nuxt-universal/local-components/sample-website/, which can be found in this book's GitHub repository. If you install this sample website and run it on your local machine, you will see that we have finally applied our components beautifully. With this, you can see how easy it is to abstract the elements in layouts so that they become components once you have understood how Vue component system works. But what about passing the data up to the parent components? For this, we have created an example app with child components emitting events to the parent components in /chapter-5/nuxt-universal/local-components/emit-events/, which can be found in this book's GitHub repository. We have also added custom input and checkbox components to the app, so please check it out. The following is an example snippet:

```
// components/input-checkbox.vue
<template>
  <input
    type="checkbox"
    v-bind:checked="checked"
    v-on:change="changed"
    name="subscribe"
    value="newsletter"
  >
</template>

<script>
export default {
  model: {
    prop: 'checked',
    event: 'change'
  },
  props: { checked: Boolean },
  methods: {
    changed ($event) {
      this.$emit('change', $event.target.checked)
    }
  }
}
</script>
```

Adding Vue Components

Here, you can see that the component code we used in the Nuxt app is the same as what we wrote in the Vue app. These kinds of components are nested components. The `props` property and the `$emit` method are used to pass the data up and down between the parent and the child components. These nested components also are local because they are only available in the scope of the component (parent) that imports them. So, from another perspective, Vue components can be categorized into local components and global components. You've been learning about global components ever since the *What is a component?* section. However, you've only learned how to use them in a Vue app. In the next section, we will look at how to register global components for Nuxt apps. But before jumping into that, let's revisit Vue components from a holistic view: global components and local components.

Registering global and local components

We have created many components either using `Vue.component()`, plain JavaScript objects, or single-file components engines. Some of the components we've created have been global components, while some of them have been local components. For example, all the refactored components you just created in the `/components/` directory in the previous section are local ones, while the components you created in the *What is a component?* section are global ones. Whether they are local or global components, they have to be registered if you want to use them. Some of them are registered at the time of their creation, while some of them are registered manually. In the following sections, you will learn how to register them globally and locally. You will also learn about the two types of registration that will affect your app. We will be looking at registering Vue components, instead of passing around them.

Registering global components in Vue

Global components, just as their name suggests, are available globally throughout your application. They are globally registered when you create them using `Vue.component()`:

```
Vue.component('my-component-name', { ... })
```

Global components must be registered before the instantiation of the root Vue instance. After they've been registered, they can be used in the template of the root Vue instance, as follows:

```
Vue.component('component-x', { ... })
Vue.component('component-y', { ... })
Vue.component('component-z', { ... })
```

```
new Vue({ el: '#app' })

<div id="app">
  <component-x></component-x>
  <component-y></component-y>
  <component-z></component-z>
</div>
```

Here, you can see that it is very easy to register global components – you might not even realize the registration process while creating them. We will look into this type of registration for Nuxt shortly in the *Registering global components in Nuxt* section. But now, we'll learn how to register local components.

Registering local components in Vue/Nuxt

We have seen and used local components in the Vue and Nuxt apps in this chapter. These components are created by using plain JavaScript objects, as follows:

```
var ComponentX = { ... }
var ComponentY = { ... }
var ComponentZ = { ... }
```

Then, they can be registered through the `components` option, as follows:

```
new Vue({
  el: '#app',
  components: {
    'component-x': ComponentX,
    'component-y': ComponentY,
    'component-z': ComponentZ
  }
})
```

Adding Vue Components

Remember the Vue app we created at the beginning of the *Passing data to child components with props* section, in the `/chapter-5/vue/component/basic.html` file in this book's GitHub repository? The `user-item` component in that app is a global component. Now, let's refactor it and turn it into a local component:

1. Remove the following global component:

    ```
    Vue.component('user-item', {
      props: ['user'],
      template: '<li>{{ user.name }}</li>'
    })
    ```

2. Replace it with a local component, as follows:

    ```
    const UserItem = {
      props: ['user'],
      template: '<li>{{ user.name }}</li>'
    }
    ```

3. Register the local component using the `components` options:

    ```
    new Vue({
      el: '#app',
      data: {
        users: [
          { id: 0, name: 'John Doe' },
          //...
        ]
      },
      components: {
        'user-item': UserItem
      }
    })
    ```

The app will work the same way as it did previously. The only difference is that `user-item` is no longer available globally. This means it is not available in any other sub-components. For instance, if you want to make `ComponentX` available in `ComponentZ`, then you have to "attach" it manually:

```
var ComponentX = { ... }

var ComponentZ = {
  components: {
    'component-x': ComponentX
  }
}
```

[176]

If you are writing ES2015 modules using babel and webpack, you can make ComponentX a single-file component and then import it, as follows:

```
// components/ComponentZ.vue
import Componentx from './Componentx.vue'

export default {
  components: {
    'component-x': ComponentX
  }
}

<component-x
  v-for="item in items"
  ...
></component-x>
```

You also can omit component-x from the components option and use the ComponentX variable directly inside it, as follows:

```
// components/ComponentZ.vue
export default {
  components: {
    ComponentX
  }
}
```

Using variables such as ComponentX in a JavaScript object in ES2015+ is short form for ComponentX: ComponentX. Since component-x is never registered, so instead of using the component as <component-x>, you will need to use <ComponentX> in the template instead:

```
<ComponentX
  v-for="item in items"
  ...
></ComponentX>
```

Writing ES2015 in the preceding single-file component is the same as how we write .vue files in Nuxt. So by now, you should have realized that we have been writing local components in our Nuxt apps, such as /components/copyright.vue and /components/nav.vue. But how do we write global components in Nuxt apps? That's where the /plugins/ directory comes in. In the next section, you'll learn how to do this in Nuxt.

Adding Vue Components

> You can find the preceding app in `/chapter-5/vue/component/registering-local-components.html`, in this book's GitHub repository.

Registering global components in Nuxt

We learned about the directory structure in Chapter 2, *Getting Started with Nuxt*, and that the `/plugins/` directory is where we can create JavaScript files that we want to run before instantiating the root Vue app. Hence, this is the best place to register our global components.

Let's create our first global component:

1. Create a simple Vue component in the `/plugins/` directory, as follows:

    ```
    // components/global/sample-1.vue
    <template>
      <p>{{ message }}</p>
    </template>

    <script>
    export default {
      data () {
        return {
          message: 'A message from sample global component 1.'
        }
      }
    }
    </script>
    ```

2. Create a `.js` file in the `/plugins/` directory and import the preceding component, as follows:

    ```
    // plugins/global-components.js
    import Vue from 'vue'
    import Sample from '~/components/global/sample-1.vue'

    Vue.component('sample-1', Sample)
    ```

3. We can also create a second global component directly in `/plugins/global-components.js`, like this:

    ```
    Vue.component('sample-2', {
      render (createElement) {
    ```

[178]

```
        return createElement('p', 'A message from sample global
          component 2.')
    }
})
```

4. Tell Nuxt to run them first before instantiating the root app in the Nuxt config file, as follows:

   ```
   // nuxt.config.js
   plugins: [
     '~/plugins/global-components.js',
   ]
   ```

   Note that this component will be available on both the client and server sides of your Nuxt app. If you want to run this component on a specific side only, such as only on the client-side, then you can register it, as follows:

   ```
   // nuxt.config.js
   plugins: [
     { src: '~/plugins/global-components.js', mode: 'client' }
   ]
   ```

   Now, this component will only be available on the client-side. But if you just want to run it on the server side, simply use `server` in the preceding `mode` option.

5. We can use these global components anywhere we like without having to import them again manually, as shown in the following code:

   ```
   // pages/about.vue
   <sample-1 />
   <sample-2 />
   ```

6. Run the app on your browser. You should get the following output:

   ```
   <p>A message from sample global component 1.</p>
   <p>A message from sample global component 2.</p>
   ```

That's it! This is how you can register global components in Nuxt by involving various files. The bottom line of global registration is using `Vue.component`, just like we do in the Vue app. However, global registration is not often ideal, just like its "cousin", global mixins, which we will cover in the next section. For instance, globally registering components but not needing them in most cases can be unnecessary for both server and client sides. Now, let's move on and take a look at what mixins are and how to write them.

Adding Vue Components

> You can find this example in `/chapter-5/nuxt-universal/global-components/` in this book's GitHub repository.

Writing basic and global mixins

A mixin is just a JavaScript object that can be used to contain any component option, such as `created`, `methods`, `mounted`, and so on. They can be used to make these options reusable. We can do this by importing them into a component and "mixing" them with the other options in that component.

Using mixins can be useful in some situations, such as in Chapter 2, *Getting Started with Nuxt*. We know that when Vue Loader compiles the `<template>` blocks in single-file components, it converts any encountered asset URLs into webpack module requests, like so:

```
<img src="~/assets/sample-1.jpg">
```

The preceding image will be converted into the following JavaScript code:

```
createElement('img', {
  attrs: {
    src: require('~/assets/sample-1.jpg') // this is now a module request
  }
})
```

This isn't difficult if you insert the image manually. But in most cases, we'll want to insert images dynamically, as follows:

```
// pages/about.vue
<template>
  <img :src="'~/assets/images' + post.image.src" :alt="post.image.alt">
</template>

const post = {
  title: 'About',
  image: {
    src: '/about.jpg',
    alt: 'Sample alt 1'
  }
}

export default {
```

```
    data () {
      return { post }
    }
}
```

In this example, you will get a 404 error for the image on your console because Vue Loader never compiles it when it is used with a `:src` directive, and so webpack never compiles the image in the build process. To resolve this problem, we need to insert the module request into the `:sr` directive manually:

```
<img :src="require('~/assets/images/about.jpg')" :alt="post.image.alt">
```

However, this is no good either because a dynamic image solution is preferred. So, the solution here is as follows:

```
<img :src="loadAssetImage(post.image.src)" :alt="post.image.alt">
```

In this solution, we write a reusable `loadAssetImage` function so that it can be called in any Vue component where it is needed. Hence, mixins are what we need in this situation. There are a few ways of using mixins. We'll have a look at some common ways in the following sections.

Creating basic mixins/non-global mixins

In a non-single-file component Vue app, we can we define a mixin object like so:

```
var myMixin = {
  created () {
    this.hello()
  },
  methods: {
    hello () { console.log('hello from mixin!') }
  }
}
```

Then, we can "attach" it to a component using `Vue.extend()`:

```
const Foo = Vue.extend({
  mixins: [myMixin],
  template: '<div>foo</div>'
})
```

In this example, we only attached this mixin to `Foo`, so you will only see that `console.log` message when this component is called.

> You can find this example in `/chapter-5/vue/mixins/basic.html` in this book's GitHub repository.

For Nuxt apps, we create and keep the mixin object in the `/plugins/` directory, in a `.js` file. Let's demonstrate this:

1. Create a `mixin-basic.js` file in the `/plugins/` directory with a function that prints a message on the browser console when the Vue instance is created:

    ```
    // plugins/mixin-basic.js
    export default {
      created () {
        this.hello()
      },
      methods: {
        hello () {
          console.log('hello from mixin!')
        }
      }
    }
    ```

2. Import it whenever and wherever we need it, as follows:

    ```
    // pages/about.vue
    import Mixin from '~/plugins/mixin-basic.js'

    export default {
      mixins: [Mixin]
    }
    ```

In this example, you will only get the `console.log` message when you are on the `/about` route. This is how we create and use a non-global mixin. But in some cases, we need global mixins for all the components in our app. Let's take a look at how we can do that.

> You can find this example in `/chapter-5/nuxt-universal/mixins/basic/` in this book's GitHub repository.

Creating global mixins

We can create and apply a mixin globally by using `Vue.mixin()`:

```
Vue.mixin({
  mounted () {
    console.log('hello from mixin!')
  }
})
```

Global mixins must be defined before you instantiate the Vue instance:

```
const app = new Vue({
  //...
}).$mount('#app')
```

Now, every component you create will be affected and show that message. You can find this example in `/chapter-5/vue/mixins/global.html` in this book's GitHub repository. If you run it on your browser, you will see the `console.log` message appear on every route as it spreads across all the route components. In this way, we can see the potential harm that could be done if it's misused. In Nuxt, we create global mixins in the same way; that is, by using `Vue.mixin()`. Let's take a look:

1. Create a `mixin-utils.js` file in the `/plugins/` directory, along with the function for loading images from the `/assets/` directory:

    ```
    // plugins/mixin-utils.js
    import Vue from 'vue'

    Vue.mixin({
      methods: {
        loadAssetImage (src) {
          return require('~/assets/images' + src)
        }
      }
    })
    ```

2. Include the preceding global mixin path in the Nuxt config file:

    ```
    // nuxt.config.js
    module.exports = {
      plugins: [
        '~/plugins/mixin-utils.js'
      ]
    }
    ```

Adding Vue Components

3. Now, you can use the `loadAssetImage` function anywhere you like in your component, as follows:

```
// pages/about.vue
<img :src="loadAssetImage(post.image.src)" :alt="post.image.alt">
```

Note that we don't need to import global mixins like we import basic mixins because we already injected them globally through `nuxt.config.js`. But again, use them sparsely and carefully.

> You can find this mixin example in `/chapter-5/nuxt-universal/mixins/global/` in this book's GitHub repository.

Mixins are useful. Global mixins such as global Vue components are hard to manage when there are too many of them, thus making your app hard to predict and debug. So, use them wisely and sparsely. We hope that you now know how Vue components work and how to write them. However, knowing how they work and how to write them is not enough – we should know about the standard rules we need to comply with when writing them for readability and future manageability. Therefore, before we end this chapter, we will look at some of these rules.

Defining component names and using naming conventions

We have seen and created many components in this and the previous chapters. The more components we make, the more we need to follow naming conventions for our components. Otherwise, we will inevitably get confused and come across errors, bikeshedding, and anti-patterns. Our components will inevitably conflict with each other – even with the HTML elements. Luckily, there is an official Vue style guide that we can comply with to improve our app's readability. In this section, we'll go through a few that are specific to this book.

Multi-word component names

Our existing and future HTML elements are single words (for example, `article`, `main`, `body`, and so on), so to prevent conflicts from occurring, we should use multi-words when naming our components (except for the root app components). For example, the following is considered bad practice:

```
// .js
Vue.component('post', { ... })

// .vue
export default {
  name: 'post'
}
```

The component's name should be written as follows:

```
// .js
Vue.component('post-item', { ... })

// .vue
export default {
  name: 'PostItem'
}
```

Component data

We should always use the `data` function instead of the `data` property for our component data, except in the root Vue instance. For example, this is considered bad practice:

```
// .js
Vue.component('foo-component', {
  data: { ... }
})

// .vue
export default {
  data: { ... }
}
```

The data in the preceding components should be written as follows:

```
// .js
Vue.component('foo-component', {
  data () {
    return { ... }
```

Adding Vue Components

```
  }
})

// .vue
export default {
  data () {
    return { ... }
  }
}

// .js or .vue
new Vue({
  data: { ... }
})
```

But why? This is because when Vue initiates data, it creates a reference of `data` from `vm.$options.data`. So, if the data is an object and when there are many instances of a component, they will all use the same `data`. Changing the data in an instance will affect the other instances. This is not what we want. So, if `data` is a function, Vue will use a `getData` method to return a new object that only belongs to the current instance that you are initializing. Hence, the data in the root instance is shared across all the other components' instances, which contain their own data. You can access the root data from any component's instance by using `this.$root.$data`. You can check out some examples in `/chapter-5/vue/component-webpack/data/` and `/chapter-5/vue/data/basic.html`, both of which can be found in this book's GitHub repository.

> You can check out the Vue source code on how data is initiated at https://github.com/vuejs/vue/blob/dev/src/core/instance/state.js#L112.

Prop definitions

We should define properties in the `props` property so that they're as detailed as possible by specifying their types (at a minimum). It is only okay to not have detailed definitions when you're prototyping. For example, this is considered bad practice:

```
props: ['message']
```

This should be written as follows:

```
props: {
  message: String
}
```

Or, even better, it should be written as follows:

```
props: {
  message: {
    type: String,
    required: false,
    validator (value) { ... }
  }
}
```

Component files

We should always comply with the one file one component "policy"; that is, writing only one component in one file. This means that you should not have more than one component in a file. For example, this is considered bad practice:

```
// .js
Vue.component('PostList', { ... })

Vue.component('PostItem', { ... })
```

They should be split into multiple files, as follows:

```
components/
|- PostList.js
|- PostItem.js
```

This should be done as follows if you are writing the components in .vue:

```
components/
|- PostList.vue
|- PostItem.vue
```

Single-file component filename casing

We should only use PascalCase or kebab-case for the filenames for single-file components. For example, these are considered bad practice:

```
components/
|- postitem.vue

components/
|- postItem.vue
```

They should be written as follows:

```
// PascalCase
components/
|- PostItem.vue

// kebab-case
components/
|- post-item.vue
```

Self-closing components

We should use the self-closing format when there's no content in our single-file components, unless they are used in a DOM template. For example, these are considered bad practice:

```
// .vue
<PostItem></PostItem>

// .html
<post-item/>
```

They should be written as follows:

```
// .vue
<PostItem/>

// .html
<post-item></post-item>
```

These are only a few essential rules. There are more, such as rules for writing multi-attribute elements, directive shorthands, quoted attribute values, and so on. But the selected rules that we've highlighted here should be enough for you to complete this book. You can find the other rules and the full style guide at `https://vuejs.org/v2/style-guide/`.

Summary

Well done! In this chapter, you learned about the differences between global and local Vue components, how to register global components in Nuxt apps, and how to create local and global mixins. You also learned how to pass data to child components from the parent component using the `props` property, how to emit data to the parent from the child component using the `$emit` method, and how to create custom input components. You then learned the importance of using the `key` attribute for components. After that, you learned how to write single-file components with webpack. Last but not least, you were introduced to some rules that should be followed in Nuxt and Vue app development.

In the next chapter, we are going to explore the use of the `/plugins/` directory further for extending a Nuxt app by writing custom plugins in Vue and importing them. We'll also look at importing external Vue plugins from the Vue community, creating global functions by injecting them into Nuxt's `$root` and `context` components, writing basic/async modules and module snippets, and using external Nuxt modules from the Nuxt community. We will guide you through these thoroughly, so stay tuned!

6 Writing Plugins and Modules

Remember how you have been writing some simple plugins in the Nuxt apps since Chapter 3, *Adding UI Frameworks*? As we mentioned before, plugins are **JavaScript functions** by nature. You will always need to write custom functions to suit your situations in web development and we will create quite a few functions throughout this book. In this chapter, we will look into creating custom plugins in more detail for your Nuxt app, as well as custom modules. You will learn to create custom plugins in a Vue app and implement them in the Nuxt app. Then you will learn how to create custom Nuxt modules on top of plugins. You will also learn to import and install the existing Vue plugins and Nuxt modules, which are provided as contributions from the Vue and Nuxt communities, into your Nuxt app. It is important to learn and understand Vue plugins and Nuxt modules, whether they are custom ones or imported externally, because we will be using some of them quite often in the coming chapters.

The topics we will cover in this chapter are the following:

- Writing Vue plugins
- Writing global functions in Nuxt
- Writing Nuxt modules
- Writing async Nuxt modules
- Writing Nuxt module snippets

Writing Vue plugins

Plugins are global JavaScript functions encapsulated in `.js` files that can be installed in your app by using the `Vue.use` global method. We have used some Vue plugins in our past examples in Chapter 4, *Adding Views, Routes, and Transitions*, such as `vue-router` and `vue-meta`. These plugins must be installed through the `Vue.use` method before the root Vue is initiated with the `new` statement, as seen in the following example:

```
// src/entry.js
import Vue from 'vue'
import Meta from 'vue-meta'

Vue.use(Meta)
new VueRouter({ ... })
```

You can pass options into the plugin through `Vue.use` to configure the plugin in this format:

```
Vue.use(<plugin>, <options>)
```

For example, we can pass the following options into the `vue-meta` plugin:

```
Vue.use(Meta, {
  keyName: metaData, // default => metaInfo
  refreshOnceOnNavigation: true // default => false
})
```

Options are optional. That means you can use the plugin itself without passing in any of them. `Vue.use` also can prevent you from accidentally injecting the same plugin twice or more, so calling a plugin multiple times will only install it once.

> You can check out awesome-vue for a huge collection of community-contributed plugins and libraries
> at https://github.com/vuejs/awesome-vuecomponents--libraries.

Now let's explore how you can create your Vue plugins in the next section.

Writing a custom plugin in Vue

Writing a Vue plugin is rather easy. You just need to use an `install` method in your plugin to accept `Vue` as the first argument and `options` as the second argument:

```
// plugin.js
export default {
  install (Vue, options) {
    // ...
  }
}
```

Let's create a simple custom greeting plugin in different languages for a standard Vue app. The language can be configured through the `options` parameter; English will be used as the default language when no option is provided:

1. Create a `/plugins/` folder in the `/src/` directory with a `basic.js` file in it with the following code:

    ```
    // src/plugins/basic.js
    export default {
      install (Vue, options) {
        if (options === undefined) {
          options = {}
        }
        let { language } = options
        let languages = {
          'EN': 'Hello!',
          'ES': 'Hola!'
        }
        if (language === undefined) {
          language = 'EN'
        }
        Vue.prototype.$greet = (name) => {
          return languages[language] + ' ' + name
        }
        Vue.prototype.$message = 'Helló Világ!'
      }
    }
    ```

    In this simple plugin, we also added an instance property called `$message` with a default "Hello World!" value in Hungarian (`Helló Világ!`), which can be modified when this plugin is used in a component. Note that `{ language } = options` is the ES6 way of writing `language = options.language`. Also, we should prefix methods and properties with a `$` because it is a convention to do so.

Writing Plugins and Modules

2. Install and configure this plugin as follows:

   ```
   // src/entry.js
   import PluginSample from './plugins/basic'
   Vue.use(PluginBasic, {
     language: 'ES'
   })
   ```

3. Then we can use the plugin globally in any Vue component, as in the following example:

   ```
   // src/components/home.vue
   <p>{{ $greet('John') }}</p>
   <p>{{ $message }}</p>
   <p>{{ messages }}</p>

   export default {
     data () {
       let helloWorld = []
       helloWorld.push(this.$message)

       this.$message = 'Ciao mondo!'
       helloWorld.push(this.$message)

       return { messages: helloWorld }
     }
   }
   ```

So, when you run your app on a browser, you should get the following output on your screen:

```
Hola! John
Ciao mondo!
[ "Helló Világ!", "Ciao mondo!" ]
```

You also can use `component` or `directive` in the plugin, as in the following example:

```
// src/plugins/component.js
export default {
  install (Vue, options) {
    Vue.component('custom-component', {
      // ...
    })
  }
}

// src/plugins/directive.js
```

```
export default {
  install (Vue, options) {
    Vue.directive('custom-directive', {
      bind (el, binding, vnode, oldVnode) {
        // ...
      }
    })
  }
}
```

We also can use `Vue.mixin()` to inject a plugin to all components, as follows:

```
// src/plugins/plugin-mixin.js
export default {
  install (Vue, options) {
    Vue.mixin({
      // ...
    })
  }
}
```

> You can find the preceding example Vue app in `/chapter-6/vue/webpack/` in our GitHub repository.

That's it. It is pretty straightforward to create a Vue plugin that can be installed and used in Vue apps, isn't it? What about in Nuxt apps? How can we install the preceding custom Vue plugin in a Nuxt app? Let's find out in the next section.

Importing Vue plugins into Nuxt

The process works much the same in Nuxt apps. All plugins are to be run before the root Vue is initiated. So if we want to use a Vue plugin, as with the previous sample plugin, we need to set up the plugin before launching the Nuxt app. Let's copy our custom `basic.js` plugin into the `/plugins/` directory in our Nuxt app and then implement the following steps to install it:

1. Create a `basic-import.js` file to import `basic.js` in the `/plugins/` directory as follows:

    ```
    // plugins/basic-import.js
    import Vue from 'vue'
    import PluginSample from './basic'

    Vue.use(PluginSample)
    ```

    We skip the options this time when installing the plugin with the `Vue.use` method.

2. Add the file path of `basic-import.js` to the `plugins` option in the Nuxt config file as follows:

    ```
    export default {
      plugins: [
        '~/plugins/basic-import',
      ]
    }
    ```

3. Use this plugin in any pages you like – just like we did in the Vue app, for example:

    ```
    // pages/index.vue
    <p>{{ $greet('Jane') }}</p>
    <p>{{ $message }}</p>
    <p>{{ messages }}</p>

    export default {
      data () {
        let helloWorld = []
        helloWorld.push(this.$message)

        this.$message = 'Olá Mundo!'
        helloWorld.push(this.$message)

        return { messages: helloWorld }
    ```

            }
        }

4. Run the Nuxt app on the browser and you should get the following output on the screen:

   ```
   Hello! Jane
   Olá Mundo!
   [ "Helló Világ!", "Olá Mundo!" ]
   ```

We get an English version of "Hello!" for the `$greet` method this time because we did not set any language option when installing the plugin. Also, you will get "Olá Mundo!" for `$message` in the `<template>` block on this index page only; you will get "Helló Világ!" on other pages (for example, `/about`, `/contact`), because we only set this Portuguese version of "Hello World!" on the index page at `this.$message = 'Olá Mundo!'`.

As we mentioned at the beginning of this chapter, there is a huge collection of community-contributed Vue plugins that might be useful for your Nuxt app, but some plugins might work only in the browser because they lack SSR (server-side rendering) support. So in the next section, we will look into how we can resolve this type of plugins.

Importing external Vue plugins without SSR support

Some Vue plugins are already pre-installed for us in Nuxt, such as `vue-router`, `vue-meta`, `vuex`, and `vue-server-renderer`. The plugins that are not installed can be sorted easily following the steps that we used to install our custom Vue plugin in the previous section. Here is an example of how we can use `vue-notifications` in our Nuxt app:

1. Install the plugin using npm:

   ```
   $ npm i vue-notification
   ```

2. Import and inject the plugin just like we did with our custom one:

   ```
   // plugins/vue-notifications.js
   import Vue from 'vue'
   import VueNotifications from 'vue-notifications'

   Vue.use(VueNotifications)
   ```

3. Include the file path to the Nuxt config file:

```
// nuxt.config.js:
export default {
  plugins: ['~/plugins/vue-notifications']
}
```

For plugins that have no SSR support, or for when you just want to use this plugin on the client side only, you can use the `mode: 'client'` option in the `plugins` option to ensure this plugin is not executed on the server side, as in the following example:

```
// nuxt.config.js
export default {
  plugins: [
    { src: '~/plugins/vue-notifications', mode: 'client' }
  ]
}
```

As you can see, it only takes three steps to install a Vue plugin, whether they are external or your custom ones. So in a nutshell, Vue plugins are global JavaScript functions injected into the Vue instance by using the `Vue.use` method and by exposing an `install` method inside the plugin. But in Nuxt itself, there are other ways of creating global functions that can be injected into the Nuxt context (`context`) and the Vue instance (`$root`) without having to use the `install` method. We will look into these approaches in the coming sections.

> For more information about `vue-notifications`, please visit https://github.com/euvl/vue-notification.

Writing global functions in Nuxt

In Nuxt, we can create "plugins" or global functions by injecting them into the three following items:

- The Vue instance (on the client side):

```
// plugins/<function-name>.js
import Vue from 'vue'
Vue.prototype.$<function-name> = () => {
  //...
}
```

- The Nuxt context (on the server side):

    ```
    // plugins/<function-name>.js
    export default (context, inject) => {
      context.app.$<function-name> = () => {
        //...
      }
    }
    ```

- Both the Vue instance and the Nuxt context:

    ```
    // plugins/<function-name>.js
    export default (context, inject) => {
      inject('<function-name>', () => {
        //...
      })
    }
    ```

Using the preceding formats, you can write global functions easily for your app. In the coming sections, we will guide you through some example functions. So let's get started.

Injecting functions into the Vue instance

In this example, we will create a function for summing up two numbers, for example, 1 + 2 = 3. We will inject this function into the Vue instance with the following steps:

1. Create a .js file, import vue, and attach the function to vue.prototype in the /plugins/ directory:

    ```
    // plugins/vue-injections/sum.js
    import Vue from 'vue'
    Vue.prototype.$sum = (x, y) => x + y
    ```

2. Add the function file path to the plugins property in the Nuxt config file:

    ```
    // nuxt.config.js
    export default {
      plugins: ['~/plugins/vue-injections/sum']
    }
    ```

3. Use the function anywhere you like, such as the following, for example:

    ```
    // pages/vue-injections.vue
    <p>{{ this.$sum(1, 2) }}</p>
    <p>{{ sum }}</p>
    ```

Writing Plugins and Modules

```
export default {
  data () {
    return {
      sum: this.$sum(2, 3)
    }
  }
}
```

4. Run the page on the browser and you should get the following output on the screen (even when you refresh the page):

   ```
   3
   5
   ```

Injecting functions into the Nuxt context

In this example, we will create a function for squaring a number, for example, 5 * 5 = 25. We will inject this function into the Nuxt context via the following steps:

1. Create a .js file and attach the function to `context.app`:

   ```
   // plugins/ctx-injections/square.js
   export default ({ app }, inject) => {
     app.$square = (x) => x * x
   }
   ```

2. Add the function file path to the `plugins` option in the Nuxt config file:

   ```
   // nuxt.config.js
   export default {
     plugins: ['~/plugins/ctx-injections/square']
   }
   ```

3. Use the function on any page you like where you have the access to the context, for example, in the `asyncData` method:

   ```
   // pages/ctx-injections.vue
   <p>{{ square }}</p>

   export default {
     asyncData (context) {
       return {
         square: context.app.$square(5)
       }
     }
   }
   ```

[200]

4. Run the page on the browser and you should get the following output on the screen (even when you refresh the page):

   ```
   25
   ```

Note that `asyncData` is always called before the page component is initiated and that you cannot access `this` in this method. Therefore you cannot use the functions that you inject into the Vue instance (`$root`), like the `$sum` function we created in the previous example, inside the `asyncData` method (we will look into `asyncData` in more detail in Chapter 8, *Adding a Server-Side Framework*). Likewise, we cannot call the context-injected functions, like the `$square` function in this example, inside the Vue lifecycle hooks/methods (for example, `mounted`, `updated`, and so on). But, if you want a function that can be used from `this` and `context`, let's see how we can do that by injecting this kind of function into both the Vue instance and Nuxt context in the next section.

Injecting functions into both the Vue instance and the Nuxt context

In this example, we will create a function for multiplying two numbers, for example, 2 * 3 = 6. We will inject this function into both the Vue instances and the Nuxt context in the following steps:

1. Create a `.js` file and use the `inject` function to encapsulate your function:

   ```js
   // plugins/combined-injections/multiply.js
   export default ({ app }, inject) => {
     inject('multiply', (x, y) => x * y)
   }
   ```

   > Note that `$` is prefixed automatically to your function, so you don't have to worry about adding it to your function.

2. Add the function file path to the `plugins` property in the Nuxt config file:

   ```js
   // nuxt.config.js
   export default {
     plugins: ['~/plugins/combined-injections/multiply']
   }
   ```

Writing Plugins and Modules

3. Use the function on any page you like where you have access to `context` and `this` (the Vue instance), such as the following, for example:

   ```
   // pages/combined-injections.vue
   <p>{{ this.$multiply(4, 3) }}</p>
   <p>{{ multiply }}</p>

   export default {
     asyncData (context) {
       return { multiply: context.app.$multiply(2, 3) }
     }
   }
   ```

4. Run the page on the browser and you should get the following output on the screen (even when you refresh the page):

   ```
   12
   6
   ```

   You can use this function in any Vue lifecycle hook, such as the following, for example:

   ```
   mounted () {
     console.log(this.$multiply(5, 3))
   }
   ```

   You should get an output of 15 on your browser's console. Furthermore, you also can access this function from `this` in the `actions` and `mutations` objects/property in the Vuex store, which we will cover in Chapter 10, *Adding a Vuex Store*.

5. Create a `.js` file and encapsulate the following functions in the `actions` and `mutations` objects:

   ```
   // store/index.js
   export const state = () => ({
     xNumber: 1,
     yNumber: 3
   })

   export const mutations = {
     changeNumbers (state, newValue) {
       state.xNumber = this.$multiply(3, 8)
       state.yNumber = newValue
     }
   }
   ```

[202]

```
export const actions = {
  setNumbers ({ commit }) {
    const newValue = this.$multiply(9, 6)
    commit('changeNumbers', newValue)
  }
}
```

6. Use the preceding store `action` method, which is `setNumbers`, on any page you like, such as the following example:

   ```
   // pages/combined-injections.vue
   <p>{{ $store.state }}</p>
   <button class="button" v-on:click="updateStore">Update Store</button>

   export default {
     methods: {
       updateStore () {
         this.$store.dispatch('setNumbers')
       }
     }
   }
   ```

7. Run the page on the browser and you should get the following output on the screen (even when you refresh the page):

   ```
   { "xNumber": 1, "yNumber": 3 }
   ```

8. Click the **Update Store** button and the store default state with the preceding numbers will be changed as follows:

   ```
   { "xNumber": 24, "yNumber": 54 }
   ```

That is great. In this way, we can write a plugin that works on both the client and server sides. But sometimes, we need functions that can be used on either the server side or client side exclusively. To do this, we must instruct Nuxt how to run our functions specifically. So let's find out how you can do that in the next section.

Writing Plugins and Modules

Injecting client-only or server-only plugins

In this example, we will create a function for dividing two numbers, for example, 8 / 2 = 4, and another function for subtracting two numbers, for example, 8 - 2 = 6. We will inject the first function into the Vue instance and make it specifically for client-side use only, while the second one we inject into the Nuxt context and make it specifically for server-side use only:

1. Create two functions and append them with `.client.js` and `.server.js` as follows:

    ```js
    // plugins/name-conventions/divide.client.js
    import Vue from 'vue'
    Vue.prototype.$divide = (x, y) => x / y

    // plugins/name-conventions/subtract.server.js
    export default ({ app }, inject) => {
      inject('subtract', (x, y) => x - y)
    }
    ```

    The function file that is appended with `.client.js` will run on the client side only, while the function file that is appended with `.server.js` will run on the server side only.

2. Add the function file paths to the `plugins` property in the Nuxt config file:

    ```js
    // nuxt.config.js:
    export default {
      plugins: [
        '~/plugins/name-conventions/divide.client.js',
        '~/plugins/name-conventions/subtract.server.js'
      ]
    }
    ```

3. Use these plugins on any page you like, such as the following, for example:

    ```js
    // pages/name-conventions.vue
    <p>{{ divide }}</p>
    <p>{{ subtract }}</p>

    export default {
      data () {
        let divide = ''
        if (process.client) {
          divide = this.$divide(8, 2)
        }
        return { divide }
    ```

```
    },
    asyncData (context) {
      let subtract = ''
      if (process.server) {
        subtract = context.app.$subtract(10, 4)
      }
      return { subtract }
    }
  }
```

4. Run the page on the browser and you should get the following output on the screen:

   ```
   4
   6
   ```

Note that you will get the preceding result when you run the page on the browser for the first time, and even when you refresh the page. But after the first load, if you navigate to this page through `<nuxt-link>`, you will get the following output on the screen:

   ```
   4
   ```

Also, note that we must wrap the `$divide` method in the `process.client` if-condition because it is a function that only takes place on the client side. If you remove the `process.client` if-condition, you will get a server-side error in the browser:

   ```
   this.$divide is not a function
   ```

The same goes for the `$subtract` method: we must wrap it in the `process.server` if-condition because it is a function that only takes place on the server side. If you remove the `process.server` if-condition, you will get a client-side error on the browser:

   ```
   this.$subtract is not a function
   ```

It may not be ideal to wrap the function in the `process.server` or `process.client` if-condition blocks every time we use it. But you don't need to use the `process.client` if-condition on the Vue lifecycle hooks/methods that are called on the client side only, such as the `mounted` hook. So you can safely use your client-only function without the if-condition, as in the following example:

```
mounted () {
  console.log(this.$divide(8, 2))
}
```

[205]

Writing Plugins and Modules

You will get an output of 4 in your browser's console. The following table shows the eight Vue lifecycle hooks/methods and it is worth knowing that only two of them are called on both sides in a Nuxt app:

Server and Client	Client Only
• beforeCreate () • created ()	• beforeMount () • mounted () • beforeUpdate () • updated () • beforeDestroy () • destroyed ()

Note that the `data` method that we have been using in our Vue and Nuxt apps is called on both sides, just like the `asyncData` method. So, you can use the `$divide` method, which is made specifically for client-side use, without the if-condition in the hooks only under the list of **Client Only**. Whereas with the `$subtract` method, which is specifically made for server-side use only, you can safely it without the if-condition in the `nuxtServerInit` action only, as in the following example:

```
export const actions = {
  nuxtServerInit ({ commit }, context) {
    console.log(context.app.$subtract(10, 4))
  }
}
```

You will get an output of 6 when your app is running on the server side, even when you refresh a page (any page). It is worth knowing that the Nuxt context can be accessed through these methods only: `nuxtServerInit` and `asyncData`. The `nuxtServerInit` action gets to access the context as the second argument, while the `asyncData` method gets to access it as the first argument. We will cover the `nuxtServerInit` action in *Chapter 10, Adding a Vuex Store*, but instead, right now in the next section, we will look at the JavaScript functions that are injected into the Nuxt context after the `nuxtServerInit` action, but before the Vue instance and plugins, as well as before the `$root` and Nuxt context injected functions that you have just previously learned. This type of function is called a Nuxt module and you will know how to write these modules by the end of this chapter. Let's get going.

Writing Nuxt modules

A module is simply a top-level JavaScript function that is executed when Nuxt is started. Nuxt will call each module in order and wait for all modules to finish before continuing to call the Vue instance, the Vue plugins, and the global functions that are to be injected into `$root` and the Nuxt context. Because modules are called before them (i.e Vue instance, etc), we can use modules to override templates, configure webpack loaders, add CSS libraries, and perform other tasks that you need for your app. Besides this, modules can also be packaged into npm packages and shared with the Nuxt community. You can check out the following link for production-ready modules made by the Nuxt Community:

https://github.com/nuxt-community/awesome-nuxt#official

Let's give the Axios module a try, which is a module integrated with Axios (https://github.com/axios/axios) for Nuxt. It comes with features such as setting the base URL for the client and server sides automatically. We will discover some of its features in the coming chapters. If you want to find out more about this module, please visit https://axios.nuxtjs.org/. Right now, let's find out how we can use this module in the following steps:

1. Install it with npm:

    ```
    $ npm install @nuxtjs/axios
    ```

2. Configure it in the Nuxt config file:

    ```
    // nuxt.config.js
    module.exports = {
      modules: [
        '@nuxtjs/axios'
      ]
    }
    ```

3. Use it anywhere, for example, in the `asyncData` method on a page:

    ```
    // pages/index.vue
    async asyncData ({ $axios }) {
      const ip = await $axios.$get('http://icanhazip.com')
      console.log(ip)
    }
    ```

Writing Plugins and Modules

You also can use it in the `mounted` method (or `created`, `updated`, and so on) as follows:

```
// pages/index.vue
async mounted () {
  const ip = await this.$axios.$get('http://icanhazip.com')
  console.log(ip)
}
```

You should see your IP address on the browser's console every time you navigate to the /about page. You should notice that now you can send HTTP requests just like using vanilla Axios, without having to import it whenever you need it because it is now injected globally through the module. Wonderful, isn't it? Next, we will guide you through writing your modules by starting with a basic module.

Writing a basic module

As we have mentioned already, modules are functions, and they can be optionally packaged as npm modules. This is the very basic structure you need to create a module:

```
// modules/basic.js
export default function (moduleOptions) {
  // ....
}
```

You just need to create a /modules/ directory in your project root and then start writing the code for your module. Note that you must include this following line if you want to publish your module as an npm package:

```
module.exports.meta = require('./package.json')
```

If you want to create the module and publish it as an npm package, follow this template from the Nuxt community:

https://github.com/nuxt-community/module-template/tree/master/template

Whether you are creating a module for the Nuxt community or your own project only, each module can access the following things:

- **The module options:**

    We can pass some options in a JavaScript object to the module from the config file, for example:

    ```
    // nuxt.config.js
    export default {
      modules: [
        ['~/modules/basic/module', { language: 'ES' }],
      ]
    }
    ```

    Then you can access the preceding option as `moduleOptions` in the first argument of your module function, as follows:

    ```
    // modules/basic/module.js
    export default function (moduleOptions) {
      console.log(moduleOptions)
    }
    ```

    You will get the following options that you pass from the config file:

    ```
    {
      language: 'ES'
    }
    ```

- **The configuration options:**

    We also can create a custom option (for example, `token`, `proxy`, or `basic`) and pass some specific options to the module (this custom option can be used to share between modules), as in the following example:

    ```
    // nuxt.config.js
    export default {
      modules: [
        ['~/modules/basic/module'],
      ],
      basic: { // custom option
        option1: false,
        option2: true,
      }
    }
    ```

Then you can access the preceding custom option using `this.options`, as shown:

```
// modules/basic/module.js
export default function (moduleOptions) {
  console.log(this.options['basic'])
}
```

You will get the following options that you pass from the config file:

```
{
  option1: false,
  option2: true
}
```

We can then also combine `moduleOptions` and `this.options` as follows:

```
// modules/basic/module.js
export default function (moduleOptions) {
  const options = {
    ...this.options['basic'],
    ...moduleOptions
  }
  console.log(options)
}
```

You will get the following combined options that you pass from the config file:

```
{
  option1: false,
  option2: true
}
```

- **The Nuxt instance:**

  You can use `this.nuxt` to access the Nuxt instance. Please visit the following link for available methods (for example, the `hook` method, which we can use to create certain tasks on specific events when booting Nuxt):

  ```
  https://nuxtjs.org/api/internals-nuxt
  ```

- **The** `ModuleContainer` **instance:**

  You can use `this` to access the `ModuleContainer` instance. Please visit the following link for available methods (for example, the `addPlugin` method, which we use quite often in a module to register a plugin):

  https://nuxtjs.org/api/internals-module-container

- **The** `module.exports.meta` **code line:**

  If you are publishing your module as an npm package then this line is required, as we mentioned earlier. But in this book, we will guide you through the steps of creating modules for your project. Let's get started by creating a really basic module in the following steps:

1. Create a `module` file with the following code:

   ```
   // modules/basic/module.js
   const { resolve } = require('path')

   export default function (moduleOptions) {
     const options = {
       ...this.options['basic'],
       ...moduleOptions
     }

     // Add plugin.
     this.addPlugin({
       src: resolve(__dirname, 'plugin.js'),
       fileName: 'basic.js',
       options
     })
   }
   ```

2. Create a `plugin` file with the following code:

   ```
   // modules/basic/plugin.js
   var options = []

   <% if (options.option1 === true) { %>
     options.push('option 1')
   <% } %>

   <% if (options.option2 === true) { %>
     options.push('option 2')
   <% } %>
   ```

[211]

Writing Plugins and Modules

```
<% if (options.language === 'ES') { %>
  options.push('language ES')
<% } %>

const basic = function () {
  return options
}

export default ({ app }, inject) => {
  inject('basic', basic)
}
```

> Note that the `<%= %>` symbols are interpolation delimiters used by Lodash for interpolating data properties in the `template` function. We will cover them again later in this chapter. For more information about the Lodash `template` function, please visit https://lodash.com/docs/4.17.15#template.

3. Include the module file path (`/modules/basic/module.js`) only in the Nuxt config file and provide some options with the `basic` custom option as follows:

```
// nuxt.config.js
export default {
  modules: [
    ['~/modules/basic/module', { language: 'ES' }],
  ],

  basic: {
    option1: false,
    option2: true,
  }
}
```

4. Use it anywhere you like, such as the following, for example:

```
// pages/index.vue
mounted () {
  const basic = this.$basic()
  console.log(basic)
}
```

5. You should see the following output on the browser's console every time you visit the home page:

```
["option 2", "language ES"]
```

[212]

Notice how `module.js` handles high-level configuration details, such as languages and options. It is also responsible for registering the `plugin.js` file, which does the actual work. As you can see, the module is a wrapper around a plugin. We will study this more in the following sections.

> Note that if you are writing modules only for build time and development, then use the `buildModules` option in the Nuxt config file to register your modules, instead of using the `modules` option for the Node.js runtime. For more information about this option, please visit https://nuxtjs.org/guide/modules#build-only-modules and https://nuxtjs.org/api/configuration-modules.

Writing async Nuxt modules

If you need to use a `Promise` object in your module, for example, to fetch some async data from a remote API using an HTTP client, then Nuxt can perfectly support that. The following are some of the options you can write your async modules with.

Using async/await

You can use ES6 async/await in your module with Axios, the HTTP client that we have been using since `Chapter 4`, *Adding Views, Routes, and Transitions*, such as in the following example:

```
// modules/async-await/module.js
import axios from 'axios'

export default async function () {
  let { data } = await axios.get(
    'https://jsonplaceholder.typicode.com/posts')
  let routes = data.map(post => '/posts/' + post.id)
  console.log(routes)
}

// nuxt.config.js
modules: [
  ['~/modules/async-await/module']
]
```

[213]

Writing Plugins and Modules

In the preceding example, we use the `get` method from Axios to get all posts from the remote API, JSONPlaceholder (https://jsonplaceholder.typicode.com/). You should see the following output printed to your terminal when you boot your Nuxt app for the first time:

```
[
  '/posts/1',
  '/posts/2',
  '/posts/3',
  ...
]
```

Returning a Promise

You can use a promise chain in your module and return the `Promise` object, as in the following example:

```
// modules/promise-sample/module.js
import axios from 'axios'

export default function () {
  return axios.get('https://jsonplaceholder.typicode.com/comments')
    .then(res => res.data.map(comment => '/comments/' + comment.id))
    .then(routes => {
      console.log(routes)
    })
}

// nuxt.config.js
modules: [
  ['~/modules/promise-sample/module']
]
```

In this example, we use the `get` method from Axios to get all comments from the remote API. Then we use the `then` method to `chain` the `Promise` and print the result. You should see the following output printed to your terminal when you boot your Nuxt app for the first time:

```
[
  '/comments/1',
  '/comments/2',
  '/comments/3',
  ...
]
```

> You can find these two examples in `/chapter-6/nuxt-universal/modules/async/` in our GitHub repository.

With these two asynchronous options and the basic module writing skills that you have learned from the previous sections, you can start creating your Nuxt modules easily. We will look at more examples in the next section by writing small pieces of modules – **snippets**.

Writing Nuxt module snippets

In this topic, we are going to break down the custom modules we've created into small pieces – snippets.

> You can find all the following code in `/chapter-6/nuxt-universal/module-snippets/` in our GitHub repository.

Using top-level options

Remember the configuration options that we said can be passed into a module in the *Writing a basic module* section? Module options are top-level options for registering our modules in the Nuxt config file. We can even combine multiple options from the different modules and their options can be shared. Let's try an example of using `@nuxtjs/axios` and `@nuxtjs/proxy` together in the following steps:

1. Install these two modules together using npm:

   ```
   $ npm i @nuxtjs/axios
   $ npm i @nuxtjs/proxy
   ```

   These two modules are well integrated to prevent CORS problems, which we will see and discuss later in this book when developing cross-domain apps. It is not required to manually register the `@nuxtjs/proxy` module, but it does need to be in the dependencies in your `package.json` file.

Writing Plugins and Modules

2. Register the `@nuxtjs/axios` module and set the top-level options for these two modules in the Nuxt config file:

```js
// nuxt.config.js
export default {
  modules: [
    '@nuxtjs/axios'
  ],
  axios: {
    proxy: true
  },
  proxy: {
    '/api/': { target: 'https://jsonplaceholder.typicode.com/',
      pathRewrite: {'^/api/': ''} },
  }
}
```

The `proxy: true` option in the `axios` custom option tells Nuxt to use the `@nuxtjs/proxy` module as the proxy. The `/api/: {...}` option in the `proxy` custom option tells the `@nuxtjs/axios` module to use `https://jsonplaceholder.typicode.com/` as the target address for the API server, while the `pathRewrite` option tells the `@nuxtjs/axios` module to remove `/api/` from the address during the HTTP request because there is no route with `/api` in the target API.

3. Next, use them seamlessly in any component, as in the following example:

```vue
// pages/index.vue
<template>
  <ul>
    <li v-for="user in users">
      {{ user.name }}
    </li>
  </ul>
</template>

<script>
export default {
  async asyncData({ $axios }) {
    const users = await $axios.$get('/api/users')
    return { users }
  }
}
</script>
```

Using these two modules together, we now can just write shorter API addresses, such as `/api/users` instead of `https://jsonplaceholder.typicode.com/users`, in the request methods (for example, `get`, `post`, and `put`). This makes our code neater as we don't have to write the full URL on each call. Note that the `/api/` address that we configured in the Nuxt config file will be added to all requests to the API endpoint. So we use `pathRewrite`, as we already explained, to remove it when sending the request.

> You can find out more info and top-level options provided by these two modules at the following links:
> - `https://axios.nuxtjs.org/options` for `@nuxtjs/axios`
> - `https://github.com/nuxt-community/proxy-module` for `@nuxtjs/proxy`
>
> You can find the example module snippet we've just created in `/chapter-6/nuxt-universal/module-snippets/top-level/` in our GitHub repository.

Using the addPlugin helper

Remember the `ModuleContainer` instance and the `this.addPlugin` helper method that you can access via the `this` keyword that we covered in the *Writing a basic module* section? In this example, we will create a module that provides a plugin by using this helper, and that plugin is `bootstrap-vue`, which will be registered in the Vue instance. Let's create this module snippet with the following steps:

1. Install Bootstrap and BootstrapVue:

    ```
    $ npm i bootstrap-vue
    $ npm i bootstrap
    ```

2. Create a plugin file to import `vue` and `bootstrap-vue` and then register `bootstrap-vue` using the `use` method:

    ```
    // modules/bootstrap/plugin.js
    import Vue from 'vue'
    import BootstrapVue from 'bootstrap-vue/dist/bootstrap-vue.esm'

    Vue.use(BootstrapVue)
    ```

Writing Plugins and Modules

3. Create a module file to add the plugin file we just created using the `addPlugin` method:

   ```
   // modules/bootstrap/module.js
   import path from 'path'

   export default function (moduleOptions) {
     this.addPlugin(path.resolve(__dirname, 'plugin.js'))
   }
   ```

4. Add the file path of this `bootstrap` module in the Nuxt config file:

   ```
   // nuxt.config.js
   export default {
     modules: [
       ['~/modules/bootstrap/module']
     ]
   }
   ```

5. Start using `bootstrap-vue` on any component you like; for example, let's create a button to toggle an alert text in Bootstrap as follows:

   ```
   // pages/index.vue
   <b-button @click="toggle">
     {{ show ? 'Hide' : 'Show' }} Alert
   </b-button>
   <b-alert v-model="show">
     Hello {{ name }}!
   </b-alert>

   import 'bootstrap/dist/css/bootstrap.css'
   import 'bootstrap-vue/dist/bootstrap-vue.css'

   export default {
     data () {
       return {
         name: 'BootstrapVue',
         show: true
       }
     }
   }
   ```

With this module snippet, we don't have to import `bootstrap-vue` each time we need it on a component because it is already added globally via the preceding snippet module. We only need to import its CSS files. In the usage example, we use Bootstrap's custom `<b-button>` component to toggle Bootstrap's custom `<b-alert>` component. The `<b-button>` component will then toggle the text, **'Hide'** or **'Show'**, on that button.

[218]

> For more information on BootstrapVue, please visit `https://bootstrap-vue.js.org/`. You can find the example module snippet we just created in `/chapter-6/nuxt-universal/module-snippets/provide-plugin/` in our GitHub repository.

Using Lodash templates

Again, this is something we are familiar with from the custom module that we created in the *Writing a basic module* section – leveraging the Lodash templates to change the output of the registered plugin by using if-condition blocks. Again, Lodash templates are the blocks of code with which we can interpolate data properties with the `<%= %>` interpolation delimiters. Let's try another simple example in the following steps:

1. Create a plugin file to import `axios` and add the if-condition blocks to make sure the request URL is provided for `axios`, and to print the request result on the terminal when your Nuxt app is running in `dev` mode (`npm run dev`) for debugging:

    ```
    // modules/users/plugin.js
    import axios from 'axios'

    let users = []
    <% if (options.url) { %>
      users = axios.get('<%= options.url %>')
    <% } %>

    <% if (options.debug) { %>
      // Dev only code
      users.then((response) => {
        console.log(response);
      })
      .catch((error) => {
        console.log(error);
      })
    <% } %>

    export default ({ app }, inject) => {
      inject('getUsers', async () => {
        return users
      })
    }
    ```

Writing Plugins and Modules

2. Create a `module` file to add the plugin file we just created using the `addPlugin` method, with the `options` option to pass on the request URL and the Boolean value of `this.options.dev` to this plugin:

   ```
   // modules/users/module.js
   import path from 'path'

   export default function (moduleOptions) {
     this.addPlugin({
       src: path.resolve(__dirname, 'plugin.js'),
       options: {
         url: 'https://jsonplaceholder.typicode.com/users',
         debug: this.options.dev
       }
     })
   }
   ```

3. Add the file path of this module to the Nuxt config file:

   ```
   // nuxt.config.js
   export default {
     modules: [
         ['~/modules/users/module']
     ]
   }
   ```

4. Start using the `$getUsers` method on any component you like, as in the following example:

   ```
   // pages/index.vue
   <li v-for="user in users">
     {{ user.name }}
   </li>

   export default {
     async asyncData({ app }) {
       const { data: users } = await app.$getUsers()
       return { users }
     }
   }
   ```

In the preceding example, Nuxt will replace `options.url` with `https://jsonplaceholder.typicode.com/users` when copying the plugin to the project. The if-condition block of `options.debug` will be stripped off from the plugin code on production builds, so you won't see the `console.log` output on your terminal in the production mode (`npm run build` and `npm run start`).

> You can find the example module snippet we just created in `/chapter-6/nuxt-universal/module-snippets/template-plugin/` in our GitHub repository.

Adding a CSS library

In our module snippet example in the *Using the addPlugin helper* section, we created a module that allows us to use the `bootstrap-vue` plugin globally in our app without having to use the `import` statement to require this plugin, as in the following example:

```
// pages/index.vue
<b-button size="sm" @click="toggle">
  {{ show ? 'Hide' : 'Show' }} Alert
</b-button>

import 'bootstrap/dist/css/bootstrap.css'
import 'bootstrap-vue/dist/bootstrap-vue.css'
export default {
  //...
}
```

It looks quite neat as we don't have to import `bootstrap-vue` every time, instead only having to import the CSS styles. However, we still can save a couple of lines by adding the styles to the global CSS stack of our app through the module. Let's create a new example and see how we can do that in the following steps:

1. Create a module file with a `const` variable called `options` for passing the module and top-level options to the plugin file, and an if-condition block to determine whether to use the vanilla JavaScript `push` method to `push` the CSS files to the `css` options in the Nuxt config file:

   ```
   // modules/bootstrap/module.js
   import path from 'path'
   export default function (moduleOptions) {
     const options = Object.assign({}, this.options.bootstrap,
       moduleOptions)

     if (options.styles !== false) {
       this.options.css.push('bootstrap/dist/css/bootstrap.css')
       this.options.css.push('bootstrap-vue/dist/bootstrap-vue.css')
     }

     this.addPlugin({
   ```

Writing Plugins and Modules

```
      src: path.resolve(__dirname, 'plugin.js'),
      options
    })
  }
```

2. Create a plugin file with the registration of the `bootstrap-vue` plugin, and an if-condition Lodash-template block to print the options that are processed from the module file:

   ```
   // modules/bootstrap/plugin.js
   import Vue from 'vue'
   import BootstrapVue from 'bootstrap-vue/dist/bootstrap-vue.esm'

   Vue.use(BootstrapVue)

   <% if (options.debug) { %>
     <% console.log (options) %>
   <% } %>
   ```

3. Add the file path of the module to the Nuxt config file, with the module options specifying whether to disable the CSS files in the module file or not. Also, add the top-level options, `bootstrap`, to pass on the Boolean value to the `debug` option:

   ```
   // nuxt.config.js
   export default {
     modules: [
       ['~/modules/bootstrap/module', { styles: true }]
     ],

     bootstrap: {
       debug: process.env.NODE_ENV === 'development' ? true : false
     }
   }
   ```

4. Remove the CSS files from our component:

   ```
   // pages/index.vue
   <script>
   - import 'bootstrap/dist/css/bootstrap.css'
   - import 'bootstrap-vue/dist/bootstrap-vue.css'
   export default {
     //...
   }
   </script>
   ```

So, finally, we can use the `bootstrap-vue` plugin and its CSS files in our component without having to import all of them. Here's another quick example of pushing the Font Awesome `css` options to the Nuxt config file through the module snippet:

```
// modules/bootstrap/module.js
export default function (moduleOptions) {
  if (moduleOptions.fontAwesome !== false) {
    this.options.css.push('font-awesome/css/font-awesome.css')
  }
}
```

> If you want to find out more information about Font Awesome, please visit https://fontawesome.com/.
>
> You can find the example module snippet we just created in `/chapter-6/nuxt-universal/module-snippets/css-lib/` in our GitHub repository.

Registering custom webpack loaders

When we want to extend the webpack config in Nuxt, we usually do it in `nuxt.config.js` with `build.extend`. But we can do the same through a module by using `this.extendBuild` with the following module/loader template:

```
export default function (moduleOptions) {
  this.extendBuild((config, { isClient, isServer }) => {
    //...
  })
}
```

For example, let's say we want to extend our webpack config with `svg-transform-loader`, which is a webpack loader for adding or modifying tags and attributes in an SVG image. The main purpose of this loader is to allow us to use `fill`, `stroke`, and other manipulations on SVG images. We also can use it in CSS, Sass, Less, Stylus, or PostCSS; for example, if you want to fill an SVG image with the white color, you can use `fill` to add `fff` (the CSS color white code) to the image as follows:

```
.img {
  background-image: url('./img.svg?fill=fff');
}
```

Writing Plugins and Modules

If you want to `stroke` the SVG image by using a variable in Sass, you can do it as follows:

```
$stroke-color: fff;

.img {
  background-image: url('./img.svg?stroke={$stroke-color}');
}
```

Let's create an example module to register this loader to the Nuxt webpack default config so that we can manipulate the SVG images in our Nuxt app with the following steps:

1. Install the loader using npm:

   ```
   $ npm i svg-transform-loader
   ```

2. Create a module file using the module/loader template we provided previously as follows:

   ```
   // modules/svg-transform-loader/module.js
   export default function (moduleOptions) {
     this.extendBuild((config, { isClient, isServer }) => {
       //...
     })
   }
   ```

3. Inside the callback of `this.extendBuild`, add the following lines to find the file loader and remove `svg` from its existing rule test:

   ```
   const rule = config.module.rules.find(
     r => r.test.toString() === '/\\.(png|jpe?g|gif|svg|webp)$/i'
   )
   rule.test = /\.(png|jpe?g|gif|webp)$/i
   ```

4. Add the following block of code right after the preceding code block to `push` the `svg-transform-loader` loader into the default webpack config's module rules:

   ```
   config.module.rules.push({
     test: /\.svg(\?.)?$/, // match img.svg and img.svg?param=value
     use: [
       'url-loader',
       'svg-transform-loader'
     ]
   })
   ```

   The module is now completed and we can move on to *step 5*.

5. Add the file path of this module to the Nuxt config file:

```js
// nuxt.config.js
export default {
  modules: [
    ['~/modules/svg-transform-loader/module']
  ]
}
```

6. Start transforming any SVG images in our component, such as the following, for example:

```html
// pages/index.vue
<template>
  <div>
    <div class="background"></div>
    <img src="~/assets/bug.svg?stroke=red&stroke-
      width=4&fill=blue">
  </div>
</template>

<style lang="less">
.background {
   height: 100px;
   width: 100px;
   border: 4px solid red;
   background-image: url('~assets/bug.svg?stroke=red&stroke-
     width=2');
}
</style>
```

You can find out more information about `svg-transform-loader` at https://www.npmjs.com/package/svg-transform-loader. If you want to learn more about the rule test, and to see the full content of the Nuxt default webpack config, please visit the following links:

- https://webpack.js.org/configuration/module/ruletest for the webpack rule test
- https://github.com/nuxt/nuxt.js/blob/dev/packages/webpack/src/config/base.js for the Nuxt default webpack configuration

You can find the example module snippet we just created in /chapter-6/nuxt-universal/module-snippets/webpack-loader/ in our GitHub repository.

[225]

Writing Plugins and Modules

Registering custom webpack plugins

Nuxt modules not only allow us to register webpack loaders but also webpack plugins by using `this.options.build.plugins.push` in the following module/plugin architecture:

```
export default function (moduleOptions) {
  this.options.build.plugins.push({
    apply(compiler) {
      compiler.hooks.<hookType>.<tap>('<PluginName>', (param) => {
        //...
      })
    }
  })
}
```

The `<tap>` depends on the hook type; it can be `tapAsync`, `tapPromise`, or just `tap`. Let's create a very simple "Hello World" webpack plugin through a Nuxt module in the following steps:

1. Create a module file using the module/plugin architecture we've provided for printing "Hello World!" as follows:

    ```
    // modules/hello-world/module.js
    export default function (moduleOptions) {
      this.options.build.plugins.push({
        apply(compiler) {
          compiler.hooks.done.tap('HelloWordPlugin', (stats) => {
            console.log('Hello World!')
          })
        }
      })
    }
    ```

    Note that `stats` (statistics) is passed as the argument when the `done` hook is tapped.

2. Add the file path of this module to the Nuxt config file:

    ```
    // nuxt.config.js
    export default {
     modules: [
      ['~/modules/hello-world/module']
     }
    ```

3. Run your Nuxt app with `$ npm run dev`, you should see "Hello World!" on your terminal.

[226]

Note that the `apply` method, `compiler`, `hooks`, and the taps are all key parts of building a webpack plugin.

> If you are new to webpack plugins and want to learn more about how to develop plugins for webpack, please visit https://webpack.js.org/contribute/writing-a-plugin/.
>
> You can find the example module snippet we just created in /chapter-6/nuxt-universal/module-snippets/webpack-plugin/ in our GitHub repository.

Creating tasks on specific hooks

If you need to do certain tasks on a specific life cycle event (for example, when all modules have finished loading) when Nuxt is being booted, you can create a module and use the `hook` method to listen on that event and then do the task. Consider the following examples:

- If you want to do something when all modules have finished loading, try the following:

  ```
  export default function (moduleOptions) {
    this.nuxt.hook('modules:done', moduleContainer => {
      //...
    })
  }
  ```

- If you want to do something after the renderer has been created, try the following:

  ```
  export default function (moduleOptions) {
    this.nuxt.hook('render:before', renderer => {
      //...
    })
  }
  ```

- If you want to do something before the compiler (webpack is the default) starts, try the following:

  ```
  export default function (moduleOptions) {
    this.nuxt.hook('build:compile', async ({ name, compiler }) => {
      //...
    })
  }
  ```

Writing Plugins and Modules

- If you want to do something before Nuxt generates your pages, try the following:

  ```
  export default function (moduleOptions) {
    this.nuxt.hook('generate:before', async generator => {
      //...
    })
  }
  ```

- If you want to do something when Nuxt is ready, try the following:

  ```
  export default function (moduleOptions) {
    this.nuxt.hook('ready', async nuxt => {
      //...
    })
  }
  ```

Let's create a simple module to listen on the `modules:done` hook/event in the following steps:

1. Create a module file for printing `'All modules are loaded'` when all modules are loaded:

   ```
   // modules/tasks/module.js
   export default function (moduleOptions) {
     this.nuxt.hook('modules:done', moduleContainer => {
       console.log('All modules are loaded')
     })
   }
   ```

2. Create a few more modules for printing `'Module 1'`, `'Module 2'`, `'Module 3'`, and so on, as follows:

   ```
   // modules/module1.js
   export default function (moduleOptions) {
     console.log('Module 1')
   }
   ```

3. Add the file path of the hook module and other modules to the Nuxt config file:

   ```
   // nuxt.config.js
   export default {
     modules: [
       ['~/modules/tasks/module'],
       ['~/modules/module3'],
       ['~/modules/module1'],
       ['~/modules/module2']
     ]
   }
   ```

[228]

4. Run your Nuxt app with `$ npm run dev` and you should see the following output on your terminal:

```
Module 3
Module 1
Module 2
All modules are loaded
```

You can see that the hook module is always printed last, while the rest are printed according to their orders in the `modules` option.

Hook modules can be asynchronous, whether you are using `async/await` functions or returning a `Promise`.

> For more information about the preceding hooks and other hooks in the Nuxt's life cycle events, please visit the following links:
>
> - https://nuxtjs.org/api/internals-module-containerhooks for Nuxt's module life cycle event (the `ModuleContainer` class)
> - https://nuxtjs.org/api/internals-builderhooks for Nuxt's build life cycle event (the `Builder` class)
> - https://nuxtjs.org/api/internals-generatorhooks for Nuxt's generate life cycle event (the `Generator` class)
> - https://nuxtjs.org/api/internals-rendererhooks for Nuxt's render life cycle event (the `Renderer` class)
> - https://nuxtjs.org/api/internals-nuxthooks for the life cycle events in Nuxt itself (the `Nuxt` class)
>
> You can find the example module snippet we just created in `/chapter-6/nuxt-universal/module-snippets/hooks/` in our GitHub repository.

Summary

In this chapter, we have successfully covered plugins and modules in Nuxt. You have learned that they are technically JavaScript functions that you can create for your project, or import them from an external source. Also, you have learned to create global functions in the Nuxt environment by injecting them into the Vue instance or the Nuxt context, or both, for your Nuxt apps, as well as creating client-only and server-only functions. Finally, you have learned to create module snippets for adding JavaScript libraries by using the `addPlugin` helper, adding CSS libraries globally, using Lodash templates to conditionally change the output of a registered plugin, adding webpack loaders and plugins to the Nuxt default webpack configuration, and creating tasks with the Nuxt lifecycle event hooks, such as `modules:done`.

In the coming chapter, we are going to explore Vue forms and adding them to Nuxt apps. You will understand how `v-model` works in HTML elements such as `text`, `textarea`, `checkbox`, `radio`, and `select`. You will learn how to validate these elements in Vue apps, binding default and dynamic data, and using modifiers such as `.lazy` and `.trim` to modify or enforce the input value. You will also learn to validate them using the Vue plugin, `vee-validate`, and then apply them to Nuxt apps. We will guide you through all these areas smoothly. So stay tuned.

7
Adding Vue Forms

In this chapter, you will create forms with `v-model` and `v-bind`. You will learn to validate forms on the client side before sending the form data to the server. You will create forms with basic elements, binding dynamic values and using modifiers to modify the input element's behavior. You will also learn to use the `vee-validate` plugin for validating forms and applying it to Nuxt apps. It is important to learn and understand how to use `v-model` and `v-bind` with Vue forms in this chapter because we will use forms in the coming chapters, such as in Chapter 10, *Adding a Vuex Store*, and Chapter 12, *Creating User Logins and API Authentication*.

The topics we will cover in this chapter are the following:

- Understanding `v-model`
- Validating forms with basic data bindings
- Making dynamic value bindings
- Validating forms with `vee-validate`
- Applying Vue forms in Nuxt

Understanding v-model

`v-model` is a Vue directive (a custom built-in Vue HTML attribute) that allows us to create a two-way binding on the form's `input`, `textarea`, and `select` elements. You can bind a form input with the Vue data so that the data can be updated when the users interact with the input field. `v-model` will always skip the initial value you set on the form elements but treats the Vue data as the source of truth. So you should declare the initial value on the Vue side, inside the `data` option or function.

Adding Vue Forms

`v-model` will pick the appropriate way to update the element based on the input type, which means that if you use it on the form input with `type="text"`, it will use `value` as the property and `input` as the event to perform the two-way binding for you. Let's look at what falls under this directive in the coming sections.

Using v-model in text and textarea elements

Remember the two-way binding that we implemented with `v-model` to create custom input components in Chapter 5, *Adding Vue Components*? In the *Creating custom input components* section of that chapter, we learned that the `v-model` syntax for inputs – `<input v-model="username">` – is shorthand for the following:

```
<input
  v-bind:value="username"
  v-on:input="username = $event.target.value"
>
```

This text `input` element, behind the scene, binds the `value` attribute that gets the value from a handler, `username`, which gets its value from the `input` event. And so, a custom text input component, too, must always use the `value` prop and the `input` event in the `model` property as follows:

```
Vue.component('custom-input', {
  props: {
    value: String
  },
  model: {
    prop: 'value',
    event: 'input'
  },
  template: `<input v-on:input="$emit('input', $event.target.value)">`,
})
```

This is just because of the nature of a `v-model` input being made of `v-bind:value` and `v-on:input`. This is also the same when using the `v-model` directive in a `textarea` element, as in the following example:

```
<textarea v-model="message"></textarea>
```

[232]

This `v-model textarea` element is shorthand for the following:

```
<textarea
  v-bind:value="message"
  v-on:input="message = $event.target.value"
></textarea>
```

This `textarea` input element, behind the scene, binds the `value` attribute that gets the value from the handler, `message`, which gets its value from the `input` event. And so, a custom `textarea` component, too, must always comply with the nature of the `v-model textarea` element by using the `value` prop and the `input` event in the `model` property as follows:

```
Vue.component('custom-textarea', {
  props: {
    value: null
  },
  model: {
    prop: 'value',
    event: 'input'
  }
})
```

In short, the `v-model` text input element and the `v-model textarea` input element always bind the `value` attribute with a handler for getting the new value on the input event, and so must the custom input components by adopting the same attribute and event. What about `v-model` in checkboxes and radio buttons elements then? Let's dive into them in the next section.

Using v-model in checkbox and radio elements

On the other hand, `v-model checkbox` and `radio` button input elements always bind the `checked` attribute with a Boolean value that is updated on the `change` event, as in the following example:

```
<input type="checkbox" v-model="subscribe" value="yes" name="subscribe">
```

The `v-model checkbox` input element in the preceding code snippet is indeed shorthand for the following:

```
<input
  type="checkbox"
  name="subscribe"
  value="yes"
```

Adding Vue Forms

```
  v-bind:checked="false"
  v-on:change="subscribe = $event.target.checked"
>
```

And so, a custom checkbox input element, too, must always comply with the nature of the v-model checkbox input element (shown in the preceding code block) by adopting the checked prop and the change event in the model property as follows:

```
Vue.component('custom-checkbox', {
  props: {
    checked: Boolean,
  },
  model: {
    prop: 'checked',
    event: 'change'
  }
})
```

The same applies to the v-model radio button input elements, as follows:

```
<input type="radio" v-model="answer" value="yes" name="answer">
```

The preceding v-model element is another shorthand for the following:

```
<input
  type="radio"
  name="answer"
  value="yes"
  v-bind:checked="answer == 'yes'"
  v-on:change="answer = $event.target.value"
>
```

And so, a custom radio button input element, too, must always comply with the nature of the v-model element as follows:

```
Vue.component('custom-radio', {
  props: {
    checked: String,
    value: String
  },
  model: {
    prop: 'checked',
    event: 'change'
  }
})
```

In short, as the v-model checkbox and radio button input elements always bind the value attribute and are updated on the change event, so must the custom input components by adopting the same attribute and event. Now, let's take a look at how v-model works in select elements in the next section.

Using v-model in select elements

Not surprisingly, v-model select input elements always bind the value attribute with a handler for getting its selected value on the change event, as in the following example:

```
<select
  v-model="favourite"
  name="favourite"
>
  //...
</select>
```

The preceding v-model checkbox input element is just another shorthand for the following:

```
<select
  v-bind:value="favourite"
  v-on:change="favourite = $event.target.value"
  name="favourite"
>
  //...
</select>
```

And so, a custom checkbox input element, too, must always comply with the nature of the v-model element by using the value prop and the change event in the model property as follows:

```
Vue.component('custom-select', {
  props: {
    value: String
  },
  model: {
    prop: 'value',
    event: 'change'
  }
})
```

Adding Vue Forms

As you can see, `v-model` is syntactic sugar on top of `v-bind`, which binds a value to the markup, and `v-on`, which updates data on the user input events, which can be either `change` or `input` events. In short, `v-model` combines `v-bind` and `v-on` under the hood – but it is important to understand what lies underneath the syntax as a Vue/Nuxt apps developer.

> You can find the examples we've covered in this section in `/chapter-7/vue/html/` in our GitHub repository.

Now that you have discovered how the `v-model` directive works in the form's input elements, let's use these `v-model` elements on a form and validate them in the next section.

Validating forms with basic data bindings

A form is a document for collecting information. The HTML `<form>` element is a form where the data or information can be collected from the web user. This element requires `<input>` elements in it to specify what data we want to collect. But before accepting the data, we usually would want to validate and filter it so that we get genuine and correct data from the user.

Vue allows us to validate the data easily from the `v-model` input elements, so let's get started with a single-file components (SFC) Vue app and webpack, which you learned about in Chapter 5, *Adding Vue Components*, in the *Compiling single-file components with webpack* section. First, we will create a very simple form with a `submit` button and the markups for displaying the error message in the `<template>` block as follows:

```
// src/components/basic.vue
<form v-on:submit.prevent="checkForm" action="/" method="post">
  <p v-if="errors.length">
    <b>Please correct the following error(s):</b>
    <ul>
      <li v-for="error in errors">{{ error }}</li>
    </ul>
  </p>
  <p>
    <input type="submit" value="Submit">
  </p>
</form>
```

We will add the rest of the input elements inside `<form>` later. Now, let's set up the basic structure and understand what we will need. We use `v-on:submit.prevent` to prevent the browser from sending the form data by default because we will handle the submission with the `checkForm` method in the Vue instance in the `<script>` block:

```
// src/components/basic.vue
export default {
  data () {
    return {
      errors: [],
      form: {...}
    }
  },
  methods:{
    checkForm (e) {
      this.errors = []
      if (!this.errors.length) {
        this.processForm(e)
      }
    },
    processForm (e) {...}
  }
}
```

On the JavaScript side, we define an array to hold the errors that we might get in the validation process. The `checkForm` logic validates the required fields that we will add later in this section. If the required field fails to pass the validation then we push the error message to `errors`. When the form is filled in correctly and/or no error is found, it will be passed to the `processForm` logic, where we can do something further with the form data before sending it to the server.

Validating text elements

Let's get started by adding an `<input>` element for single-line text:

```
// src/components/basic.vue
<label for="name">Name</label>
<input v-model="form.name" type="text">

export default {
  data () {
    return {
      form: { name: null }
    }
  },
```

Adding Vue Forms

```
methods:{
  checkForm (e) {
    this.errors = []
    if (!this.form.name) {
      this.errors.push('Name required')
    }
  }
}
```

In the `<script>` block, we define a `name` property in the `data` function that holds the initial `null` value and will be updated on the `input` event from the `<input>` element. We validate the `name` data in the `if` condition block when you hit the `submit` button; if it has no data provided, then we `push` the error message to `errors`.

Validating textarea elements

The next element we are adding is `<textarea>` for multi-line text, which works the same way as `<input>`:

```
// src/components/basic.vue
<label for="message">Message</label>
<textarea v-model="form.message"></textarea>

export default {
  data () {
    return {
      form: { message: null }
    }
  },
  methods:{
    checkForm (e) {
      this.errors = []
      if (!this.form.message) {
        this.errors.push('Message required')
      }
    }
  }
}
```

In the `<script>` block, we define a `message` property in the `data` function that holds the initial `null` value and will be updated on the `input` event from the `<textarea>` element. We validate the `message` data in the `if` condition block when you hit the `submit` button; if it has no data provided, then we `push` the error message to `errors`.

Validating checkbox elements

The next element is a single checkbox `<input>` element that will hold the default Boolean value:

```
// src/components/basic.vue
<label class="label">Subscribe</label>
<input type="checkbox" v-model="form.subscribe">

export default {
  data () {
    return {
      form: { subscribe: false }
    }
  },
  methods:{
    checkForm (e) {
      this.errors = []
      if (!this.form.subscribe) {
        this.errors.push('Subscription required')
      }
    }
  }
}
```

We also will add the following multiple checkbox `<input>` elements that are bound to the same array, that is, `books: []`:

```
// src/components/basic.vue
<input type="checkbox" v-model="form.books" value="On the Origin of Species">
<label for="On the Origin of Species">On the Origin of Species</label>

<input type="checkbox" v-model="form.books" value="A Brief History of Time">
<label for="A Brief History of Time">A Brief History of Time</label>

<input type="checkbox" v-model="form.books" value="The Selfish Gene">
<label for="The Selfish Gene">The Selfish Gene</label>

export default {
  data () {
    return {
      form: { books: [] }
    }
  },
  methods:{
```

Adding Vue Forms

```
    checkForm (e) {
      this.errors = []
      if (this.form.books.length === 0) {
        this.errors.push('Books required')
      }
    }
  }
}
```

In the `<script>` block, we define a `subscribe` property in the `data` function that holds the initial Boolean `false` value and will be updated on the `change` event from the checkbox `<input>` element. We validate the `subscribe` data in the `if` condition block when you hit the `submit` button; if it has no data provided or it is `false`, then we `push` the error message to `errors`.

We do the same for the multiple checkbox `<input>` elements by defining a `books` property that holds the initial empty array and will be updated on the `change` event from the checkbox `<input>` element. We validate the `books` data in the `if` condition block; if its length is 0 then we `push` the error message to `errors`.

Validating radio elements

The next element is multiple radio button `<input>` elements that are bound to the same property name, that is, `gender`:

```
// src/components/basic.vue
<label for="male">Male</label>
<input type="radio" v-model="form.gender" value="male">

<label for="female">Female</label>
<input type="radio" v-model="form.gender" value="female">

<label for="other">Other</label>
<input type="radio" v-model="form.gender" value="other">

export default {
  data () {
    return {
      form: { gender: null }
    }
  },
  methods:{
    checkForm (e) {
      this.errors = []
```

[240]

```
      if (!this.form.gender) {
        this.errors.push('Gender required')
      }
    }
  }
}
```

In the `<script>` block, we define a `gender` property in the `data` function that holds the initial `null` value and will be updated on the `change` event from the selected `<input>` radio button element. We validate the `gender` data in the `if` condition block when you hit the `submit` button. If it has no data provided, then we `push` the error message to `errors`.

Validating select elements

The next element is a single `<select>` element with multiple `<option>` elements as follows:

```
// src/components/basic.vue
<select v-model="form.favourite">
  <option disabled value="">Please select one</option>
  <option value="On the Origin of Species">On the Origin of
    Species</option>
  <option value="A Brief History of Time">A Brief History of Time</option>
  <option value="The Selfish Gene">The Selfish Gene</option>
</select>

export default {
  data () {
    return {
      form: { favourite: null }
    }
  },
  methods:{
    checkForm (e) {
      this.errors = []
      if (!this.form.favourite) {
        this.errors.push('Favourite required')
      }
    }
  }
}
```

Adding Vue Forms

And the last one is multiple `<select>` elements with multiple `<option>` elements that are bound to the same `Array`, that is, `favourites: []`:

```
// src/components/basic.vue
<select v-model="form.favourites" multiple >
  <option value="On the Origin of Species">On the Origin of
    Species</option>
  <option value="A Brief History of Time">A Brief History of Time</option>
  <option value="The Selfish Gene">The Selfish Gene</option>
</select>

export default {
  data () {
    return {
      form: { favourites: [] }
    }
  },
  methods:{
    checkForm (e) {
      this.errors = []
      if (this.form.favourites.length === 0) {
        this.errors.push('Favourites required')
      }
    }
  }
}
```

In the `<script>` block, we define a `favourites` property in the `data` function that holds the initial `null` value and will be updated on the `change` event from the `<select>` element. We validate the `favourites` data in the `if` condition block when you hit the `submit` button. If it has no data provided, then we `push` the error message to `errors`. We do the same for the multiple `<select>` elements by defining a `favourites` property that holds the initial empty array and will be updated on the `change` event from the `<select>` element. We validate the `favourites` data in the `if` condition block; if its length is `0` then we push the error message to `errors`.

Then we will finish up this form with the `processForm` logic, which is called only when no error is found in the `checkForm` logic. We use a Node.js package, `qs`, to stringify the `this.form` object so we can send the data to the server in the following format:

```
name=John&message=Hello%20World&subscribe=true&gender=other
```

Let's install `qs` with npm:

```
$ npm i qs
```

Then we can use it as follows:

```
import axios from 'axios'
import qs from 'qs'

processForm (e) {
  var data = qs.stringify(this.form)
  axios.post('../server.php', data)
  .then((response) => {
    // success callback
  }, (response) => {
    // error callback
  })
}
```

We send the data using `axios` and get the response (usually in JSON format) back from the server, then you can do something with the response data, such as displaying a "success" or "failed" message on the server side.

> For more information about `qs`, visit https://www.npmjs.com/package/qs, and for `axios`, please visit https://github.com/axios/axios.
>
> You can find the preceding example app in /chapter-7/vue/webpack/ in our GitHub repository.

However, we are not quite finished yet, because we may want to bind dynamic values to the form inputs sometimes, instead of getting the default ones from `v-model`. For example, we only get the Boolean value for the `subscribe` property with a single checkbox `<input>` element in our example app, but we want to use a string value with `yes` or `no` instead. We will explore how we can change the default values in the coming section.

Making dynamic value bindings

In our example app in the previous section, we either get strings or Boolean values for the `radio`, `checkbox`, and `select` options by using `v-model` alone. We can change this default value by using `true-value`, `false-value`, and `v-bind`. Let's dive in.

Replacing Boolean – checkbox elements

We can bind our custom value to the **single** `checkbox` elements by using `true-value` and `false-value`. For example, we can bind the `yes` value to replace the default `true` Boolean value with `true-value` and `no` to replace the default `false` Boolean value with `false-value`:

```
// src/components/dynamic-values.vue
<input
  type="checkbox"
  v-model="form.subscribe"
  true-value="yes"
  false-value="no"
>

export default {
  data () {
    return {
      form: { subscribe: 'no' }
    }
  },
  methods:{
    checkForm (e) {
      this.errors = []
      if (this.form.subscribe !== 'yes') {
        this.errors.push('Subscription required')
      }
    }
  }
}
```

Now, you get a response of `yes` or `no` when you send the value of the `subscribe` input to the server. In the `<script>` block, we now declare `no` as the initial value on the `subscribe` property and validate it in the `if` condition block to make sure it is always `yes` when you hit the `submit` button, otherwise we push the error message to `errors`.

Replacing strings with dynamic properties – radio elements

As for the radio button `<input>` elements, we can bind their values to the dynamic property in the Vue instance by using `v-bind`:

```
// src/components/dynamic-values.vue
<input type="radio" v-model="form.gender" v-bind:value="gender.male">

export default {
  data () {
    return {
      gender: {
        male: 'm',
        female: 'f',
        other: 'o',
      },
      form: { gender: null }
    }
  }
}
```

Now you get m when this radio button is picked and the validation is the same as before.

Replacing strings with objects – select options elements

We also can use `v-bind` **non-string** values such as `Object` to the form inputs. See the following example:

```
// src/components/dynamic-values.vue
<select v-model="form.favourite">
  <option v-bind:value="{ title: 'On the Origin of Species' }">On
    the Origin of Species</option>
</select>

export default {
  data () {
    return {
      form: {
        favourite: null
      }
    }
```

Adding Vue Forms

```
    }
  }
```

Now when this option is selected, you get `object` for `typeof this.favourite` and `On the Origin of Species` for `this.favourite.title`. There is no change in the validation logic.

We also can render `<option>` elements dynamically with dynamic values and `v-for`:

```
// src/components/dynamic-values.vue
<select v-model="form.favourites" name="favourites_array[]" multiple >
  <option v-for="book in options.books" v-bind:value="book.value">
    {{ book.text }}
  </option>
</select>

data () {
  return {
    form: { favourites: [] },
    options: {
      books: [
        { value: { title: 'On the Origin of Species' }, text: 'On the
          Origin of Species'},
        { value: { title: 'A Brief History of Time' }, text: 'A Brief
          History of Time'},
        { value: { title: 'The Selfish Gene' }, text: 'The Selfish Gene'}
      ]
    }
  }
}
```

Now we don't have to hardcode the `<option>` elements anymore. We can pull the `books` data from elsewhere, such as an API.

Besides binding dynamic values to form inputs, we also can modify the default behavior of `v-model` on the input elements. For example, instead of syncing the input with the data, we can use the `change` event on them. Let's discover how you can do this in the next topic.

Using modifiers

Vue provides these three modifiers, `.lazy`, `.number`, and `.trim`, that we can use with `v-model` to change the default events or to add extra functionality to the form input. Let's dive in.

Adding .lazy

We can use `.lazy` with `v-model` to change the `input` event to a `change` event on the `<input>` and `<textarea>` elements. See the following example:

```
// src/components/modifiers.vue
<input v-model.lazy="form.name" type="text">
```

Now the input with the data is synced after `change`, instead of the `input` event, which is the default.

Adding .number

We can use `.number` with `v-model` to change the default typecast of `string` to `number` on `<input>` elements with `type="number"`. See the following example:

```
// src/components/modifiers.vue
<input v-model.number="form.age" type="number">
```

Now you get `number` for `typeof this.form.age` instead of `string` without having `.number`.

Adding .trim

We can use `.trim` with `v-model` to trim off the whitespace from the user input. See the following example:

```
// src/components/modifiers.vue
<textarea v-model.lazy.trim="form.message"></textarea>
```

Now the text from the user is trimmed automatically. Any extra whitespace at the beginning and end of the text will be trimmed off.

While writing custom validation logic is possible, there is already a great plugin that helps validate inputs easily and displays the corresponding errors. This plugin is called VeeValidate and is a template-based validation framework for Vue. Let's discover how we can leverage this plugin in the next section.

Adding Vue Forms

Validating forms with VeeValidate

With VeeValidate, we will use VeeValidate's components to validate our HTML forms and Vue's scoped slots to expose the error messages. For example, this is a `v-model` input element that we are already familiar with:

```
<input v-model="username" type="text" />
```

If you want to validate it with VeeValidate, you just have to wrap the input with a `<ValidationProvider>` component:

```
<ValidationProvider name="message" rules="required" v-slot="{ errors }">
  <input v-model="username" name="username" type="text" />
  <span>{{ errors[0] }}</span>
</ValidationProvider>
```

In general, we use the `<ValidationProvider>` component to validate `<input>` elements. We can attach validation rules to this component using the `rules` attribute and display errors with the `v-slot` directive. Let's discover how you can make use of this plugin to speed up the validation process in the following steps:

1. Install VeeValidate with npm:

    ```
    $ npm i vee-validate
    ```

2. Create a `.js` file in the `/src/` directory and add rules by using the `extend` function from VeeValidate:

    ```
    // src/vee-validate.js
    import { extend } from 'vee-validate'
    import { required } from 'vee-validate/dist/rules'

    extend('required', {
      ...required,
      message: 'This field is required'
    })
    ```

    VeeValidate provides many built-in validation rules in separate bundles, such as `required`, `email`, `min`, `regex`, and so on, so we can import the specific rules that we only need for our apps. So in the preceding code, we import the `required` rule and install it through the `extend` function, and then add our custom message in the `message` property.

[248]

3. Import `/src/vee-validate.js` into the main entry file where the Vue instance is initiated:

   ```
   // src/main.js
   import Vue from 'vue'
   import './vee-validate'
   ```

4. Import the `ValidationProvider` component locally into a page and start validating the input fields on that page:

   ```
   // src/components/vee-validation.vue
   <ValidationProvider name="name" rules="required|min:3" v-slot="{ errors }">
     <input v-model.lazy="name" type="text" name="name">
     <span>{{ errors[0] }}</span>
   </ValidationProvider>

   import { ValidationProvider } from 'vee-validate'

   export default {
     components: {
       ValidationProvider
     }
   }
   ```

   We also can register `ValidationProvider` globally in `/src/main.js` or `/src/plugins/vee-validate.js`:

   ```
   import Vue from 'vue'
   import { ValidationProvider, extend } from 'vee-validate'

   Vue.component('ValidationProvider', ValidationProvider)
   ```

   But this is probably not a good idea if you don't need this component on every page in your app. So if you just need it on a page, then import it locally.

5. Import the `ValidationObserver` component locally and add the `passes` object to the `v-slot` directive. So let's refactor the JavaScript code from *step 4* as follows:

   ```
   // src/components/vee-validation.vue
   <ValidationObserver v-slot="{ passes }">
     <form v-on:submit.prevent="passes(processForm)" novalidate="true">
       //...
       <input type="submit" value="Submit">
     </form>
   ```

Adding Vue Forms

```
    </ValidationObserver>

    import {
      ValidationObserver,
      ValidationProvider
    } from 'vee-validate'

    export default {
      components: {
        ValidationObserver,
        ValidationProvider
      },
      methods:{
        processForm () {
          console.log('Posting to the server...')
        }
      }
    }
```

We use the `<ValidationObserver>` component to wrap the `<form>` element to tell whether it is valid or not before submitting. We also use the `passes` property in the object of the scoped slot on the `<ValidationObserver>` component, which is used to prevent the form from submitting if it is invalid. Then we pass our `processForm` method to the `passes` function in the `v-on:submit` event on the form element. Our `processForm` method will not be called if the form is invalid.

That's it. We are done. You can see that we no longer need the `checkForm` method on the `v-on:submit` event in the `methods` property because VeeValidate has done the heavy lifting on validating the elements for us and now our JavaScript code is shortened. We only need to wrap around our input fields with `<ValidationProvider>` and `<ValidationObserver>` components.

> If you want to find out more about the Vue slots and VeeValidate, please visit the following links:
>
> - `https://logaretm.github.io/vee-validate/` for VeeValidate
> - `https://vuejs.org/v2/guide/components-slots.html` for Vue slots
>
> You can find the example of our preceding Vue app in `/chapter-7/vue/cli/` in our GitHub repository.

Next, we will find out how we can apply VeeValidate in Nuxt apps in the following section.

Applying custom validation to a Nuxt application

Let's apply the custom validation to the **Contact** page in the sample website that we already have. You have probably noticed that the existing contact form has already installed the validation from Foundation (Zurb). Using Foundation's form validation is another great way to spice up our HTML form validation.

> If you are interested in knowing more about Foundation, you can find out more from their official guide at https://foundation.zurb.com/sites/docs/abide.html.

But if we want to do the custom validation with VeeValidate, which we have just learned for use in the Vue app, then let's install and set up what we need for Nuxt in the following steps:

1. Install VeeValidate via npm:

   ```
   $ npm i vee-validate
   ```

2. Create a plugin file in the /plugins/ directory and add the rules we need, as follows:

   ```js
   // plugins/vee-validate.js
   import { extend } from 'vee-validate'
   import {
     required,
     email
   } from 'vee-validate/dist/rules'

   extend('required', {
     ...required,
     message: 'This field is required'
   })

   extend('email', {
     ...email,
     message: 'This field must be a valid email'
   })
   ```

   Everything in this file is the same as the file we did in the Vue app.

Adding Vue Forms

3. Include the plugin path in the `plugins` option in the Nuxt config file:

   ```
   // nuxt.config.js
   plugins: [
     '~/plugins/vee-validate'
   ]
   ```

4. Add an exception for the `/vee-validate/dist/rules.js` file in the `build` option in the Nuxt config file:

   ```
   // nuxt.config.js
   build: {
     transpile: [
       "vee-validate/dist/rules"
     ],
     extend(config, ctx) {}
   }
   ```

   In Nuxt, the `/node_modules/` folder is excluded from transpilation by default, and you will get an error reading `Unexpected token export` when using vee-validate, so we must add `/vee-validate/dist/rules.js` for transpilation before running the Nuxt app.

5. Import the `ValidationObserver` and `ValidationProvider` components just as we did for the Vue app:

   ```
   // pages/contact.vue
   import {
     ValidationObserver,
     ValidationProvider
   } from 'vee-validate'

   export default {
     components: {
       ValidationObserver,
       ValidationProvider
     }
   }
   ```

6. Remove Foundation's `data-abide` attribute from the `<form>` element, but wrap it with the `<ValidationObserver>` component and bind the `submit` event with the `passes` and `processForm` methods to the `<form>` element as follows:

   ```
   // pages/contact.vue
   <ValidationObserver v-slot="{ passes }" ref="observer">
     <form v-on:submit.prevent="passes(processForm)" novalidate>
     //...
   ```

```
        </form>
    </option>
```

This step is also the same as what we did with the Vue app, but we added `ref="observer"` in this example as we will need it in *step 8*.

7. Start refactoring all the `<input>` elements inside the `<form>` element with the `<ValidationProvider>` component, as follows:

```
// pages/contact.vue
<ValidationProvider name="name" rules="required|min:3" v-slot="{
errors, invalid, validated }">
  <label v-bind:class="[invalid && validated ? {'is-invalid-label':
    '{_field_}'} : '']">Name
    <input
      type="text"
      name="name"
      v-model.trim="name"
      v-bind:class="[invalid && validated ? {'is-invalid-input':
        '{_field_}'} : '']"
    >
    <span class="form-error">{{ errors[0] }}</span>
  </label>
</ValidationProvider>
```

This step is also the same as what we did with the Vue app, but in this example, we added two scoped slot data properties, `invalid` and `validated`, in the `v-slot` directive for binding classes conditionally to the `<label>` and `<input>` elements. So if we get `true` for both `invalid` and `validated`, then we will bind the `is-invalid-label` and `is-invalid-input` classes to the elements, respectively.

> For more information about the Validation Provider's scoped slot data properties, please visit `https://vee-validate.logaretm.com/v2/guide/components/validation-provider.html#scoped-slot-data`.

8. Refactor the `data` function in the `<script>` block by adding the following data properties to sync up with the `v-model` input elements. We also will add two methods in the `methods` option, as follows:

```
// pages/contact.vue
export default {
  data () {
    return {
```

Adding Vue Forms

```
      name: null,
      email: null,
      subject: null,
      message: null
    }
  },
  methods:{
    clear () {
      this.name = null
      this.email = null
      this.subject = null
      this.message = null
    },
    processForm (event) {
      alert('Processing!')
      console.log('Posting to the server...')
      this.clear()
      this.$refs.observer.reset()
    }
  }
}
```

This step is also the same as what we did with the Vue app, but in this example, we added the `clear` method and the `reset` method in `processForm` for the `methods` options. The `<ValidationObserver>` component does not reset the state of the form after submitting so we have to do it manually, by passing the observer as a reference in *step 6*, and then we can access it from the Vue instance with `this.$refs`.

9. Add these three scoped slot data properties, `dirty`, `invalid`, and `validated`, to the `<ValidationObserver>` component for toggling the alert and success messages, then let's refactor this component as follows:

```
// pages/contact.vue
<ValidationObserver v-slot="{ passes, dirty, invalid, validated }"
ref="observer">
  <div class="alert callout" v-if="invalid && validated">
    <p><i class="fi-alert"></i> There are some errors in your
      form.</p>
  </div>
  //...
  <div class="success callout" v-if="submitted && !dirty">
    <p><i class="fi-like"></i>  Thank you for contacting
      me.</p>
  </div>
</ValidationObserver>
```

[254]

```
export default {
  data () {
    return {
      submitted: false
      //...
    }
  },
  methods:{
    processForm (event) {
      console.log('Posting to the server...')
      this.submitted = true
      //...
    }
  }
}
```

In this last step, we added a `submitted` data property with a `false` Boolean by default, which will be set to `true` when the form is submitted in the `processForm` method. On the other hand, the alert message block will be visible when `invalid` and `validated` from the scoped slot are both `true`, and the success message block will be visible when both the `submitted` property is `true` and the `dirty` scoped slot data property is `false`. We get a `true` Boolean from the `dirty` property if one of the input fields is "dirty" – in other words, when a letter is present in the input field.

You can see that the refactored code in our Nuxt app is quite similar to what we did in the Vue standard app. But in the Nuxt app, we added more complex logic to the form such as toggling the alert and success messages, binding classes conditionally to the `<label>` and `<input>` elements, and resetting the `<ValidationObserver>` component whenever the form is submitted. The refactoring process is the same for the rest of the input elements, which you can find in the book's GitHub repository at `/chapter-7/nuxt-universal/sample-website/`.

Summary

In this chapter, we have covered Vue form validation with `v-model` on the various form inputs. You have learned basic and dynamic value binding, and how to use modifiers to change the default input event and typecast. You also have learned to use the `vee-validate` plugin to make the validation easier. Finally, we managed to apply these to the Nuxt app.

In the next chapter, we are going to explore how to add a server-side framework in Nuxt apps. You will learn to create a simple API with Koa and integrate it with Nuxt, and request the API data using `asyncData` with the HTTP client, Axios. Also, you will be introduced to a minimalistic build system based on webpack, called Backpack, which will simplify the custom webpack configuration that we have been using for the single-file component Vue apps. You will learn how to use this build system in Nuxt apps, too. So, stay tuned!

Section 3: Server-Side Development and Data Management

In this section, we will start adding a server-side framework and database system to the Nuxt project so that we can manage and fetch data from the server side. We will also add a Vuex store for managing global data in Nuxt.

This section comprises the following chapters:

- `Chapter 8`, *Adding a Server-Side Framework*
- `Chapter 9`, *Adding a Server-Side Database*
- `Chapter 10`, *Adding a Vuex Store*

8 Adding a Server-Side Framework

In this chapter, you will learn how to configure Nuxt with a server-side framework, and how to use the `asyncData` method to fetch the data from the server-side framework, such as Koa or Express. Setting up a server-side framework with Nuxt is fairly easy. We only need to pick a framework as the first-class citizen and use Nuxt as the middleware. We can use `npx create-nuxt-app <project-name>` to set that up for us, but we will walk you through how to do that manually so that you have a better understanding of how these two apps work together. Additionally, in this chapter, we will use **Backpack** as the build system for our app.

The topics we will cover in this chapter are as follows:

- Introducing Backpack
- Introducing Koa
- Integrating Koa with Nuxt
- Understanding async data
- Accessing context in asyncData
- Fetching async data with Axios

Introducing Backpack

Backpack is a build system for building modern Node.js apps with zero or minimal configuration. It supports the latest JavaScript and handles the file watching, live reloading, transpiling, and bundling that we have been doing with webpack in the previous chapters. We can think of it as a **wrapper** of webpack, a simplified version of the webpack configuration that we have been using in this book so far. You can find out more info about Backpack at `https://github.com/jaredpalmer/backpack`. Now, let's find out how we can use it to speed up our app development in the coming sections.

Installing and configuring Backpack

Creating a modern Node.js app with Backpack can be as easy as implementing the following steps:

1. Install Backpack via npm:

   ```
   $ npm i backpack-core
   ```

2. Create a /src/ directory and a package.json file in the project root with backpack in the dev script as follows:

   ```
   {
     "scripts": {
       "dev": "backpack"
     }
   }
   ```

   > Note that you must provide the /src/ as the **default entry directory** of your app.

3. Create a Backpack config file in your project root with a function to configure webpack as follows:

   ```
   // backpack.config.js
   module.exports = {
     webpack: (config, options, webpack) => {
       // ....
       return config
     }
   }
   ```

   This step is optional, but it is useful if you want to change the default entry directory (which is the /src/ directory that you created in *step 2*) of your app to a different one, for example, a /server/ directory, this can be done as follows:

   ```
   webpack: (config, options, webpack) => {
     config.entry.main = './server/index.js'
     return config
   }
   ```

4. Start your app in development mode with the following command:

   ```
   $ npm run dev
   ```

Then you can develop the source code of your app in the /server/ directory and browse to the app on the browser at whatever port you have set it to. Let's create a simple Express app with Backpack in the next section.

Creating a simple app using Backpack

Creating an Express app with Backpack can be as easy as implementing the following steps:

1. Install Express via npm:

   ```
   $ npm i express
   ```

2. Add `build` and `start` scripts after the `dev` script in the `package.json` file:

   ```
   // package.json
   "scripts": {
     "dev": "backpack",
     "build": "backpack build",
     "start": "cross-env NODE_ENV=production node build/main.js"
   }
   ```

3. Create the Backpack config file and use /server/ as the entry folder of your app, just as we have walked you through in the previous section:

   ```
   // backpack.config.js
   module.exports = {
     webpack: (config, options, webpack) => {
       config.entry.main = './server/index.js'
       return config
     }
   }
   ```

4. Create a simple route with a `'Hello World'` message:

   ```
   // server/index.js
   import express from 'express'
   const app = express()
   const port = 3000

   app.get('/', (req, res) =>
     res.send('Hello World')
   )
   ```

```
app.listen(port, () =>
  console.log(Example app listening on port ${port}!)
)
```

5. Run your app in development mode:

   $ npm run dev

You can now browse to your app on a browser at `127.0.0.1:3000`. You should see **Hello World** on the screen. You can find this example in `/chapter-8/backpack/` in our GitHub repository. Next, let's use Koa as the server-side framework that allows us to write ES2015 code and async functions in fewer lines than Express in the next section.

Introducing Koa

Koa is a Node.js web framework designed by the same team that brought you Express. The main goal of this framework is to be a smaller and more expressive foundation for web apps and APIs. If you have ever worked on Express and have gotten tired of callback hell when the app gets larger, Koa allows you to ditch the callbacks and greatly increase error handling by leveraging async functions. Another cool thing in Koa is **cascading** – the middleware you add will be running "downstream," and then flowing back "upstream," which gives you more predictable controls. We will demonstrate this later in this chapter.

> If you want to find out more info about Koa, please visit `https://koajs.com/`.

Installing and configuring Koa

Now, let's create a Koa app with the Backpack default configuration (without creating the Backpack config file) as follows:

1. Install Koa via npm:

   $ npm i koa

2. Use `/src/` as the Backpack default entry directory and create an entry file in this directory with minimal code in Koa style as follows:

   ```
   // src/index.js
   const Koa = require('koa')
   ```

```
const app = new Koa()

app.use(async ctx => {
  ctx.body = 'Hello World'
})
app.listen(3000)
```

3. Run the Koa app in development mode:

   $ npm run dev

You should see **Hello World** on the screen when browsing the app on a browser at `127.0.0.1:3000`. If you have been using Express to create your Node.js apps, you can see that Koa is an alternative that can be used to do the same thing with neater code. Next, let's learn what a Koa context is and how cascading works in Koa in the following sections.

What is ctx?

You may have wondered what that `ctx` is in the minimal code we created in the previous section and where the `req` and `res` objects are, because they are there in the Express app. They are not gone in Koa. They are just encapsulated in a single object in Koa, which is the Koa context, referred to as `ctx`. We can access the `request` and `response` objects as follows:

```
app.use(async ctx => {
  ctx.request
  ctx.response
})
```

So, you can see that we can easily use `ctx.request` to access the Node.js `request` object and `ctx.response` for the Node.js `response` object. These two important HTTP objects are not gone in Koa! They are just tucked away in the Koa context – `ctx`. Next, let's find out how cascading works in Koa in the next section.

Understanding how Koa cascading works

In a nutshell, the cascading in Koa works by invoking middleware downstream sequentially and then controlling them to flow back upstream sequentially. It is best to create a simple Koa app to demonstrate this great feature in Koa:

1. Create an `index.js` file in the `/src/` directory, just like we did in the previous section:

   ```
   // src/index.js
   const Koa = require('koa')
   const app = new Koa()

   app.use(async ctx => {
     console.log('Hello World')
     ctx.body = 'Hello World'
   })
   app.listen(3000)
   ```

2. Create three pieces of middleware just before the `Hello World` middleware as follows, so that we can run them first:

   ```
   app.use(async (ctx, next) => {
     console.log('Time started at: ', Date.now())
     await next()
   })

   app.use(async (ctx, next) => {
     console.log('I am the first')
     await next()
     console.log('I am the last')
   })

   app.use(async (ctx, next) => {
     console.log('I am the second')
     await next()
     console.log('I am the third')
   })
   ```

3. Run the app in development mode and you should get the following output on the terminal:

   ```
   Time started at: 1554647742894
   I am the first
   I am the second
   Hello World
   I am the third
   I am the last
   ```

In this demonstration, the request flows through `Time started at:` to `I am the first`, `I am the second`, and reaching `Hello World`. When there is no more middleware to be executed downward (downstream), each middleware will be unwound and resumed upward (upstream) in the following sequence: `I am the third`, `I am the last`.

> You can find this example in `/chapter-8/koa/cascading/` in our GitHub repository.

Next, we will walk you through some dependencies that you should install for developing a full stack Koa app so that it works just like Express apps.

Installing dependencies for Koa apps

Koa is minimalistic. It is barebones by nature. Hence, it does not have any middleware within its core. Express comes with a router, which, by default, Koa does not have. This can be a challenge when writing an app in Koa as you need to choose a third-party package or pick one of the packages listed on their GitHub main page at https://github.com/koajs. You may test out a few and find out they don't work as you want. There are a few Koa packages that can be used for routing; `koa-router` is mostly used in this book, alongside other essential dependencies for developing our API with Koa. Let's discover what they are and what they do by installing them and creating a skeleton app, as follows:

1. Install the `koa-router` module and use it as follows:

   ```
   $ npm i koa-router
   ```

   Import `koa-router` in the entry file with a home route, `/`, as follows:

   ```
   // src/index.js
   const Router = require('koa-router')
   const router = new Router()
   ```

Adding a Server-Side Framework

```
router.get('/', (ctx, next) => {
  ctx.body = 'Hello World'
})

app
  .use(router.routes())
  .use(router.allowedMethods())
```

You can find more information about this middleware at https://github.com/koajs/koa-router from Koa's GitHub repository. This module is forked from ZijianHe/koa-router (https://github.com/ZijianHe/koa-router). It is the most widely used router module in the Koa community. It provides Express-style routing using `app.get`, `app.put`, `app.post`, and so on. It also supports other important features, such as multiple route middleware and multiple and nestable routers.

2. Install the `koa-bodyparser` module and use it as follows:

   ```
   $ npm i koa-bodyparser
   ```

   Import `koa-bodyparser` in the entry file, register it, and create a home route, `/post`, as follows:

   ```
   // src/index.js
   const bodyParser = require('koa-bodyparser')
   app.use(bodyParser())

   router.post('/post', (ctx, next) => {
     ctx.body = ctx.request.body
   })
   ```

   You can find more information about this middleware at https://github.com/koajs/bodyparser from Koa's GitHub repository. You may wonder: what is a body parse anyway? When we are dealing with HTML forms, we use `application/x-www-form-urlencoding` or `multipart/form-data` to transact data between the client and server sides, for example:

   ```
   // application/x-www-form-urlencoding
   <form action="/update" method="post">
     //...
   </form>

   // multipart/form-data
   <form action="/update" method="post" encrypt="multipart/form-data">
     //...
   </form>
   ```

[266]

The default type for HTML forms is `application/x-www-urlencoded`, and if we want to read the data of HTTP `POST`, `PATCH`, and `PUT`, we use a body parser, which is a middleware that parses the incoming request, assembles the **chunks** containing the form data, and then creates a body object filled with the form data so that we can access them from the request object in the `ctx` object as follows:

```
ctx.body = ctx.request.body
```

3. Install the `koa-favicon` module and use it as follows:

   $ npm i koa-favicon

   Import `koa-favicon` in the entry file and register it with a path to `favicon` as follows:

   ```
   // src/index.js
   const favicon = require('koa-favicon')
   app.use(favicon('public/favicon.ico'))
   ```

   You can find more information about this middleware at https://github.com/koajs/favicon from Koa's GitHub repository. It is a middleware that serves a `favicon`, so let's create a `favicon.ico` file and keep it in the `/public` folder in the project root. You should see the `favicon` on your browser tab when you refresh the home page.

4. Install the `koa-static` module and use it as follows:

   $ npm i koa-static

   Import `koa-static` in the entry file and register it with the following paths as follows:

   ```
   const serve = require('koa-static')
   app.use(serve('.'))
   app.use(serve('static/fixtures'))
   ```

You can find more information about this middleware at https://github.com/koajs/static from Koa's GitHub repository. Koa, by default, doesn't allow you to serve static files. So this middleware will allow you to serve static files from your API. For example, the paths we just set will let us access the following files from the `/static` folder in the project root:

- GET `/package.json` at `127.0.0.1:3000/package.json`.
- GET `/hello.txt` at `127.0.0.1:3000/hello.txt`.

Adding a Server-Side Framework

We will use this skeleton in future chapters when creating APIs with Koa. Now, let's discover how we can integrate Koa with Nuxt in the next section.

> You can find this skeleton app at `/chapter-8/koa/skeleton/` in our GitHub repository.

Integrating Koa with Nuxt

Integrating Koa and Nuxt can be done on a single port for single-domain apps, or on separate ports for cross-domain apps. In this chapter, we will do the single-domain integration and then we will guide you through the cross-domain integration in Chapter 12, *Creating User Logins and API Authentication*. We will use the Koa skeleton that we have developed in the previous section for these two types of integration. The single-domain integration requires some configurations in the following steps. Let's get started:

1. Create a `/server/` directory in the Nuxt project's root and structure the server-side directory as follows after creating the project with the `create-nuxt-app` scaffolding tool:

   ```
   ├── package.json
   ├── nuxt.config.js
   ├── server
   │   ├── config
   │   │   └── ...
   │   ├── public
   │   │   └── ...
   │   ├── static
   │   │   └── ...
   │   └── index.js
   └── pages
       └── ...
   ```

2. Modify the default scripts to use Backpack in the default `package.json` file that comes with the scaffolding tool as follows:

   ```
   // package.json
   "scripts": {
     "dev": "backpack",
     "build": "nuxt build && backpack build",
     "start": "cross-env NODE_ENV=production node build/main.js",
     "generate": "nuxt generate"
   }
   ```

[268]

3. Create a Backpack config file in the root directory (where we have the Nuxt config file) for changing the Backpack default entry directory to the /server/ directory we just created:

   ```
   // backpack.config.js
   module.exports = {
     webpack: (config, options, webpack) => {
       config.entry.main = './server/index.js'
       return config
     }
   }
   ```

4. Create an `index.js` file in the /server/ directory to import Koa (make sure you have Koa installed already) as the main app and Nuxt as middleware in Koa as follows:

   ```
   // server/index.js
   import Koa from 'koa'
   import consola from 'consola'
   import { Nuxt, Builder } from 'nuxt'
   const app = new Koa()
   const nuxt = new Nuxt(config)

   async function start() {
     app.use((ctx) => {
       ctx.status = 200
       ctx.respond = false
       ctx.req.ctx = ctx
       nuxt.render(ctx.req, ctx.res)
     })
   }
   start()
   ```

   Notice that we create an async function to use Nuxt as middleware so that we can use the `await` statement in the next step for running the Nuxt build process.

   > Note that Consola is a console logger and you must install it via npm before using it. For more information about this package, please visit https://github.com/nuxt-contrib/consola.

5. Before registering Nuxt as the middleware, import the Nuxt configuration for the build process in development mode:

   ```
   // server/index.js
   let config = require('../nuxt.config.js')
   config.dev = !(app.env === 'production')
   ```

[269]

```
if (config.dev) {
  const builder = new Builder(nuxt)
  await builder.build()
} else {
  await nuxt.ready()
}
```

6. Run the app by listening to its port and host and log the server status with Consola as follows:

```
app.listen(port, host)
consola.ready({
  message: `Server listening on http://${host}:${port}`,
  badge: true
})
```

7. Launch the app in development mode:

   $ npm run dev

Our Nuxt and Koa apps are now running as a single app. You probably have realized that Nuxt is now running under Koa as a middleware. All our Nuxt pages are still running the same as before at `localhost:3000`, but we will configure `localhost:3000/api` as the API main endpoint in the coming section.

Adding routes and other essential middleware

We established the integration and structured the server-side directory in the previous section. Now let's refine some API routes and other middleware on our API in the following steps:

1. Install the Koa Router and Koa Static packages via npm:

   $ npm i koa-route
   $ npm i koa-static

2. Create a server-side config file:

```
// server/config/index.js
export default {
  static_dir: {
    root: '../static'
  }
}
```

3. Create a `routes.js` file in the `/server/` directory for defining routes that we will expose to the public with some dummy user data:

```
// server/routes.js
import Router from 'koa-router'
const router = new Router({ prefix: '/api' })

const users = [
  { id: 1, name: 'Alexandre' },
  { id: 2, name: 'Pooya' },
  { id: 3, name: 'Sébastien' }
]

router.get('/', async (ctx, next) => {
  ctx.type = 'json'
  ctx.body = {
    message: 'Hello World!'
  }
})

router.get('/users', async (ctx, next) => {
  ctx.type = 'json'
  ctx.body = users
})

router.get('/users/:id', async (ctx, next) => {
  const id = parseInt(ctx.params.id)
  const found = users.find(function (user) {
    return user.id == id
  })
  if (found) {
    ctx.body = found
  } else {
    ctx.throw(404, 'user not found')
  }
})
```

4. Import other middleware in a separate `middlewares.js` file and import the routes and config files from *steps 1* and *2*:

```
// server/middlewares.js
import serve from 'koa-static'
import bodyParser from 'koa-bodyparser'
import config from './config'
import routes from './routes'

export default (app) => {
  app.use(serve(config.static_dir.root))
```

Adding a Server-Side Framework

```
    app.use(bodyParser())
    app.use(routes.routes(), routes.allowedMethods())
}
```

We will not use `koa-favicon` in the API because we are exporting our data in JSON format and the image of `favicon.ico` will not be shown on the browser tab. Besides, Nuxt has already handled `favicon.ico` for us in the Nuxt config file, so we can remove the `koa-favicon` middleware from our skeleton. Instead, we will create a middleware to decorate our JSON data into these two final JSON outputs

- The format for 200 output:

    ```
    {"status":<status code>,"data":<data>}
    ```

- The format for all error outputs (for example, 400, 500):

    ```
    {"status":<status code>,"message":<error message>}
    ```

5. Add the following code just before the `app.use(serve(config.static_dir.root))` line to create the preceding formats:

```
app.use(async (ctx, next) => {
  try {
    await next()
    if (ctx.status === 404) {
      ctx.throw(404)
    }
    if (ctx.status === 200) {
      ctx.body = {
        status: 200,
        data: ctx.body
      }
    }
  } catch (err) {
    ctx.status = err.status || 500
    ctx.type = 'json'
    ctx.body = {
      status: ctx.status,
      message: err.message
    }
    ctx.app.emit('error', err, ctx)
  }
})
```

So now, with this middleware, instead of getting an output such as `{"message":"Hello World!"}`, we will get the decorated output as follows:

```
{"status":200,"data":{"message":"Hello World!"}}
```

6. Import this `middlewares.js` file in the main `index.js` file before registering Nuxt:

```js
// server/index.js
import middlewares from './middlewares'

middlewares(app)
app.use(ctx => {
  ...
  nuxt.render(ctx.req, ctx.res)
})
```

7. Rerun the app in development mode:

    $ npm run dev

8. Then, if you visit the app at `localhost:3000/api`, you will get the following output on the screen:

```
{"status":200,"data":{"message":"Hello World!"}}
```

If you visit the user index page at `localhost:3000/api/users`, you will get the following output on the screen:

```
{"status":200,"data":[{"id":1,"name":"Alexandre"},{"id":2,"name":"Pooya"},{"id":3,"name":"Sébastien"}]}
```

You also can use `localhost:3000/api/users/<id>` to get a specific user. For example, if you use `/api/users/1`, you will get the following output on the screen:

```
{"status":200,"data":{"id":1,"name":"Alexandre"}}
```

> You can find this integrated example app in `/chapter-8/nuxt-universal/skeletons/koa/` in our GitHub repository.

Next, we will look at how we can request the preceding API data with the `asyncData` method on the client side from the Nuxt pages in the coming section.

[273]

Understanding async data

The `asyncData` method allows us to fetch data asynchronously and render it on the server side before the component is initiated. It is an additional method that's only available in Nuxt. That means you can't use it in Vue because Vue does not have this default method. Nuxt always executes this method before rendering the page component. It is executed once on the server side on the page that uses this method and then will be executed on the client side when revisiting that page through the routes generated with the `<nuxt-link>` component. Nuxt will merge the returned data from the `asyncData` method with the component data from the `data` method or the `data` property. This method receives the `context` object as the first argument, as follows:

```
export default {
  asyncData (context) {
    // ...
  }
}
```

Bear in mind that this method is always executed before the page component is initiated, so we have no access to the component instance through the `this` keyword inside this method. There are two different ways of using it; let's explore them in the upcoming sections.

Returning a promise

We can use the `Promise` object in the `asyncData` method by returning `Promise`, for example:

```
// pages/returning-promise.vue
asyncData (context) {
  const promise = new Promise((resolve, reject) => {
    setTimeout(() => {
      resolve('Hello World by returning a Promise')
    }, 1000)
  })

  return promise.then((value) => {
    return { message: value }
  })
}
```

In the preceding code, Nuxt will wait for 1 second for the promise to be resolved before rendering the page component with `'Hello World by returning a Promise'`.

Using async/await

We also can use an `async/await` statement with the `asyncData` method, for example:

```
// pages/using-async.vue
async asyncData (context) {
  const promise = new Promise((resolve, reject) => {
    setTimeout(() => {
      resolve('Hello World by using async/await')
    }, 2000)
  })

  const result = await promise
  return { message: result }
}
```

In the preceding code, Nuxt will wait for 2 seconds for the promise to be resolved before rendering the page component with the `'Hello World by using async/await'` message. Using the `async/await` statement is a new way of writing asynchronous JavaScript code. It is built on top of the `Promise` object and makes our asynchronous code more readable. We will use this statement often throughout the book.

Merging the data

As we mentioned before, the asynchronous data from the `asyncData` method will be merged with the component data from the `data` method or the `data` property. That means that if you have set some default data in your component data with the same object keys in the `asyncData` method, they will be overwritten by the `asyncData` method as a result. Here's an example:

```
// pages/merging-data.vue
<p>{{ message }}</p>

export default {
  data () {
    return { message: 'Hello World' }
  },
  asyncData (context) {
    return { message: 'Data Merged' }
  }
}
```

In the preceding code, Nuxt will merge the two sets of data and you will get the following result on your screen:

```
<p>Data Merged</p>
```

> You can find the examples in `/chapter-8/nuxt-universal/koa-nuxt/understanding-asyncdata/` in our GitHub repository.

Next, we will look at how we can make use of the `context` object that we can access from the `asyncData` method in the coming section.

Accessing context in asyncData

We can access a bunch of useful stuff from the Nuxt context for fetching data. They stored inside the context object as the following keys:

• app	• req	• isDev
• route	• res	• isHMR
• store	• redirect	• beforeNuxtRender(fn)
• params	• error	• from
• query	• env	• nuxtState

They are provided additionally and especially in Nuxt only, so we won't find them in Vue. We can access them either with `context.<key>` or `{ <key> }`. So let's explore some of these keys and see how we can leverage them in the following sections.

> For more information about the Nuxt context, please visit `https://nuxtjs.org/api/context`.

[276]

Accessing the req/res objects

We can access the `req` and `res` objects when the `asyncData` method is executed on the server side. They contain useful information of the HTTP request sent from the user. But we should always check with an `if` condition before accessing them:

```
// pages/index.vue
<p>{{ host }}</p>

export default {
  asyncData ({ req, res }) {
    if (process.server) {
     return { host: req.headers.host }
    }
    return { host: '' }
  }
}
```

In the preceding code, we use the `if` condition to make sure that the `asyncData` method is called on the server side before obtaining the information of the request headers. These two objects are unavailable on the client side, so you will get `undefined` when accessing them on the client side. So the result we will get from the preceding code is `localhost:3000` when the page is loaded on the browser for the first time, but you will not see that piece of information again when revisiting this page by the route generated from the `<nuxt-link>` component unless you refresh that page.

Accessing the dynamic route data

We can access the dynamic route data through the `params` key when we have dynamic routes in our app. For example, if we have an `_id.vue` file in the `/pages/` directory, then we can access the value of the route parameter via `context.params.id` as follows:

```
// pages/users/_id.vue
<p>{{ id }}</p>

export default {
  asyncData ({ params }) {
    return { id: params.id }
  }
}
```

In the preceding code, you will get 1 for the `id` when calling `users/1` on the browser.

Listening to the query changes

By default, the `asyncData` method is not executed over changes on the query string. For example, if you are using queries such as /users?id=<id> on your route with the `<nuxt-link>` component, `asyncData` will not be called when changing from one query to another through the `<nuxt-link>` component routes. This is because watching the query changes is disabled by default in Nuxt to improve performance. If you want to override this default behavior, you can use the `watchQuery` property to listen to the specific parameters:

```
// pages/users/index.vue
<p>{{ id }}</p>
<ul>
  <li>
    <nuxt-link :to="'users?id=1'">1</nuxt-link>
    <nuxt-link :to="'users?id=2'">2</nuxt-link>
  </li>
</ul>

export default {
  asyncData ({ query }) {
    return { id: query.id }
  },
  watchQuery: ['id']
}
```

In the preceding code, we are listening to the `id` parameter, so you will get 1 for navigating to /users?id=1 and 2 for /users?id=2. If you want to set up a watcher for all query strings, just simply set `watchQuery` to `true`.

Handling errors

We can use the `error` method from the `context` object to call the Nuxt default error page and display the error. You can pass the error code and message through the default `params.statusCode` and `params.message` properties:

```
// pages/users/error.vue
export default {
  asyncData ({ error }) {
    return error({
      statusCode: 404,
      message: 'User not found'
    })
  }
}
```

If you want to change the default properties that you pass to the `error` method, you can create a custom error page, which you learned about in Chapter 4, *Adding Views, Routes, and Transitions*. Let's create these custom error properties and layout in the following steps:

1. Create a page that you want to throw the custom properties to:

```
// pages/users/error-custom.vue
export default {
  asyncData ({ error }) {
    return error({
      status: 404,
      text: 'User not found'
    })
  }
}
```

2. Create a custom error page in the `/layouts/` directory:

```
// layouts/error.vue
<template>
  <div>
    <h1>Custom Error Page</h1>
    <h2>{{ error.status }} Error</h2>
    <p>{{ error.text }}</p>
    <nuxt-link to="/">Home page</nuxt-link>
  </div>
</template>

<script>
export default {
  props: ['error'],
  layout: 'layout-error'
}
</script>
```

3. Create a custom layout page for this error page:

```
// layouts/layout-error.vue
<template>
  <nuxt />
</template>
```

You should see the custom properties and layout when visiting `/users/error-custom`.

> You can see all the examples in `/chapter-8/nuxt-universal/koa-nuxt/accessing-context/` in our GitHub repository.

Next, we will look at how we can use Axios, an HTTP client, with the `asyncData` method for requesting API data in the coming section.

Fetching async data with Axios

We have created a simple API with Koa and exposed some public routes for its data being accessed, such as `/api/users` and `/api/users/1`. We also have integrated this API with Nuxt into a single app in which Nuxt performs as middleware. You have also learned how the `asyncData` method works and how we can make use of the Nuxt context. Now, let's bring all these three parts together in the final step by using Axios with the `asyncData` method for requesting the API data.

Installing and configuring Axios

Axios is a promised-based HTTP client for Node.js apps. We worked with vanilla promises with the `asyncData` method in the previous section. We can simplify our code further and save some lines with Axios, which is powered by asynchronous JavaScript and XML (AJAX) to make asynchronous HTTP requests. Let's get it started in the following steps:

1. Install Axios via npm:

    ```
    $ npm i axios
    ```

    We should always use a full path when making HTTP requests with Axios:

    ```
    axios.get('https://jsonplaceholder.typicode.com/posts')
    ```

    But it can be repetitive to include `https://jsonplaceholder.typicode.com/` in the path for every request. Besides, this base URL can change over time. So we should abstract it and simplify the request:

    ```
    axios.get('/posts')
    ```

2. Create an Axios instance in the `/plugins/` directory:

    ```
    // plugins/axios-api.js
    import axios from 'axios'
    ```

```
export default axios.create({
  baseURL: 'http://localhost:3000'
})
```

3. Import this plugin whenever we need it on the component:

```
import axios from '~/plugins/axios-api'
```

After this installation and configuration, we are ready to fetch the async data in the next section.

Fetching data with Axios and asyncData

Let's create the pages that need to have the data rendered in the following steps:

1. Create an index user page to list all users:

```
// pages/users/index.vue
<li v-for="user in users" v-bind:key="user.id">
  <nuxt-link :to="'users/' + user.id">
    {{ user.name }}
  </nuxt-link>
</li>

<script>
import axios from '~/plugins/axios-api'
export default {
  async asyncData({error}) {
    try {
      let { data } = await axios.get('/api/users')
      return { users: data.data }
    } catch (e) {
      // handle error
    }
  }
}
</script>
```

On this page, we use the `get` method from Axios to call the API endpoint of `/api/users`, which will be transformed to `localhost:3000/api/users`, where the list of users can be output as follows:

```
{"status":200,"data":[{"id":1,"name":"Alexandre"},{"id":2,"name":"Pooya"},{"id":3,"name":"Sébastien"}]}
```

We then unpack the `data` key in the output by using JavaScript's destructuring assignment with `{ data }`. It is a good practice to wrap your code in `try/catch` blocks when using the `async/await` statements. Next, we will need to request a single user's data.

2. Create a single user page for rendering individual user data:

```
// pages/users/_id.vue
<h2>
  {{ user.name }}
</h2>

<script>
import axios from '~/plugins/axios-api'
export default {
  name: 'id',
  async asyncData ({ params, error }) {
    try {
      let { data } = await axios.get('/api/users/' + params.id)
      return { user: data.data }
    } catch (e) {
      // handle error
    }
  }
}
</script>
```

On this page, again, we use the `get` method from Axios to call the API endpoint of `/api/users/<id>`, which will be transformed to `localhost:3000/api/users/<id>`, to fetch the data of a single user:

```
{"status":200,"data":{"id":1,"name":"Alexandre"}}
```

And again, we unpack the `data` key in the output by using JavaScript's destructuring assignment with `{ data }` and wrap the `async/await` code in `try/catch` blocks.

In the next section, we want to achieve the same result as in this section, that is, to fetch a list of users and the data of a specific user. But we will do it on a single page with the `watchQuery` property, which you learned about in the previous section.

Listening on the query change

In this section, we will create a page for listening to the change in the query string and fetching the single-user data. To do this, we only require a .vue page to list all users and watch the query, and if there is any change in the query, we will get the id from the query and fetch the user with that id using Axios in the asyncData method. Let's get started:

1. Create a users-query.vue page in the /pages/ directory and add the following template to the <template> block:

```
// pages/users-query.vue
<ul>
  <li v-for="user in users" v-bind:key="user.id">
    <nuxt-link :to="'users-query?id=' + user.id">
      {{ user.name }}
    </nuxt-link>
  </li>
</ul>
<p>{{ user }}</p>
```

In this template, we use the v-for directive to loop through each user in users and add the query of each user to the <nuxt-link> component. The data of an individual user will be rendered inside the <p> tag after the <ul> tag.

2. Add the following code to the <script> block:

```
// pages/users-query.vue
import axios from '~/plugins/axios-api'

export default {
  async asyncData ({ query, error }) {
    var user = null
    if (Object.keys(query).length > 0) {
      try {
        let { data } = await axios.get('/api/users/' + query.id)
        user = data.data
      } catch (e) {
        // handle error
      }
    }

    try {
      let { data } = await axios.get('/api/users')
      return {
        users: data.data,
        user: user
```

Adding a Server-Side Framework

```
      }
    } catch (e) {
      // handle error
    }
  },
  watchQuery: true
}
```

This piece of code is the same as `/pages/users/index.vue`; we only add a `query` object to `asyncData` and fetch the user data based on the information in the query. And, of course, we add `watchQuery: true` or `watchQuery: ['id']` to watch the change in the query. So, in the browser, when you click a user from the list, such as `users-query?id=1`, the data of that user will be rendered inside the `<p>` tag as follows:

```
{ "id": 1, "name": "Alexandre" }
```

Well done! You have reached the end of this chapter. We hope that it was a simple and easy chapter for you to follow. Besides using Axios to make HTTP requests to the API backend, we can use one of these Nuxt modules: Axios and HTTP. We focus on vanilla Axios and the Axios module in this book. Do you remember that we covered the Axios module in Chapter 6, *Writing Plugins and Modules*? We will use this module often in the coming chapters. Now, let's summarize what you have learned in this chapter.

> You can find the preceding code in `/chapter-8/nuxt-universal/koa-nuxt/using-axios/axios-vanilla/` in our GitHub repository. If you want to find out more about the Nuxt HTTP module, please visit https://http.nuxtjs.org/.

Summary

In this chapter, you have learned how to configure Nuxt with a server-side framework, which is Koa in this book. You have installed Koa with the dependencies that we need to create an API. And then you used `asyncData` and Axios to query and fetch the data from the API. Also, you learned about the properties in the Nuxt context that you can destructure and access from the `asyncData` method, such as `params`, `query`, `req`, `res`, and `error`. Last but not least, you started using Backpack as a minimalist build tool in your apps.

In the next chapter, you will learn how to set up MongoDB and write some basic MongoDB queries, how to add data to a MongoDB database, how to integrate it with the server-side framework, Koa, which you have just learned about in this chapter, and then, finally, how to integrate it with Nuxt pages. We will guide you through everything that you will have to learn in order to make a more complete API. So, stayed tuned.

9
Adding a Server-Side Database

We added Koa as the server-side framework for our Nuxt app in the previous chapter with some dummy data. In this chapter, we will set up MongoDB as the server-side database to replace that dummy data. We will write some MongoDB CRUD queries, add data to the database, and use `asyncData` to fetch the data from the database.

The topics we will cover in this chapter are as follows:

- Introducing MongoDB
- Writing basic MongoDB queries
- Writing MongoDB CRUD operations
- Injecting data with MongoDB CRUD queries
- Integrating MongoDB with Koa
- Integrating with Nuxt pages

Introducing MongoDB

MongoDB is an open source document-oriented database management system (DBMS) that stores data in JSON-like documents called Binary JSON (BSON) – a binary representation of MongoDB's JSON-like documents that can be parsed more quickly than ordinary JSON. It is one of the most popular NoSQL database systems since 2009 that does not use tables and rows, in contrast with relational database management systems (RDBMSes). Every record of your data in MongoDB is a document composed of name-value pairs (or field and value pairs) that are similar to JSON objects but binary encoded to support data types that are outside the scope of JSON, such as ObjectId, Date, and Binary data (https://docs.mongodb.com/manual/reference/bson-types/). Hence, it is called Binary JSON. For example, a document of `{"hello":"world"}` will be stored in a `.bson` file as follows:

```
1600 0000 0268 656c 6c6f 0006 0000 0077
6f72 6c64 0000
```

In practice, the encoded data in BSON is not human-readable, but we don't have to worry much about it when working with MongoDB because they will be encoded and decoded by the MongoDB driver for you out of the box. You just need to use the MongoDB syntax, methods, operations, and selectors with the JSON document that you are familiar with when constructing the document for BSON storage. Let's get MongoDB installed and start writing.

Installing MongoDB

There are a few ways to install MongoDB depending on the edition (Community Edition or Enterprise) and the platform (Windows, Ubuntu, or macOS). You can follow the links provided here:

- **MongoDB Community Edition:**
  https://docs.mongodb.com/manual/installation/#mongodb-community-edition-installation-tutorials
- **MongoDB Enterprise:**
  https://docs.mongodb.com/manual/installation/#mongodb-enterprise-edition-installation-tutorial
- **Install MongoDB Community Edition on Ubuntu:**
  https://docs.mongodb.com/manual/tutorial/install-mongodb-on-ubuntu/

Installing on Ubuntu 20.04

In this book, we will install MongoDB 4.2 (Community Edition) on Ubuntu 20.04 (Focal Fossa). It works the same, too, if you are on Ubuntu 19.10 (Eoan Ermine). If you are using other older versions of Ubuntu, such as 14.04 LTS (Trusty Tahr), 16.04 LTS (Xenial Xerus), or 18.04 LTS (Bionic Beaver), please follow the MongoDB Community Edition on Ubuntu link in the previous section. So, let's get started:

1. Import the public key from `mongodb.org`:

    ```
    $ wget -qO - https://www.mongodb.org/static/pgp/server-4.2.asc | sudo apt-key add -
    ```

    You should get an `OK` in the response.

2. Create a list file for MongoDB:

   ```
   $ echo "deb [ arch=amd64 ] https://repo.mongodb.org/apt/ubuntu
   bionic/mongodb-org/4.2 multiverse" | sudo tee
   /etc/apt/sources.list.d/mongodb-org-4.2.list
   ```

3. Update all the local packages in your system:

   ```
   $ sudo apt-get update
   ```

4. Install the MongoDB packages:

   ```
   $ sudo apt-get install -y mongodb-org
   ```

Starting MongoDB

Once you have the MongoDB packages installed, the next thing you should do is see whether you can start and connect the MongoDB server from your terminal. So, let's begin:

1. Start MongoDB manually or automatically at boot time in the following commands:

   ```
   $ sudo systemctl start mongod
   $ sudo systemctl enable mongod
   ```

2. Verify it by checking its version:

   ```
   $ mongo --version
   ```

   You should get a similar output to this on your terminal:

   ```
   MongoDB shell version v4.2.1
   git version: edf6d45851c0b9ee15548f0f847df141764a317e
   OpenSSL version: OpenSSL 1.1.1d 10 Sep 2019
   allocator: tcmalloc
   modules: none
   build environment:
       distmod: ubuntu1804
       distarch: x86_64
       target_arch: x86_64
   ```

3. Optionally, check the MongoDB server status with the following command:

   ```
   $ sudo service mongod status
   ```

Adding a Server-Side Database

You should get the similar output to this on your terminal:

```
● mongod.service - MongoDB Database Server
    Loaded: loaded (/lib/systemd/system/mongod.service; enabled;
       vendor preset: enabled)
    Active: active (running) since Fri 2019-08-30 03:37:15 UTC;
       29s ago
      Docs: https://docs.mongodb.org/manual
  Main PID: 31961 (mongod)
    Memory: 68.2M
    CGroup: /system.slice/mongod.service
            └─31961 /usr/bin/mongod --config /etc/mongod.conf
```

4. Optionally, check whether MongoDB has been started on port 27017 with the `netstat` command:

    ```
    $ sudo netstat -plntu
    ```

    You should see the following similar output:

    ```
    Active Internet connections (only servers)
    Proto Recv-Q Send-Q Local Address Foreign Address State PID/Program
    name
    tcp 0 0 127.0.0.1:27017 0.0.0.0: LISTEN 792/mongod
    ```

5. Connect to the MongoDB Shell:

    ```
    $ mongo
    ```

6. Exit the MongoDB Shell (when you want to):

    ```
    > exit
    ```

If, for any reason, you want to remove MongoDB completely from your system, then use this command:

```
$ sudo apt-get purge mongodb-org*
```

In the next section, you will start writing some basic queries from the MongoDB Shell you have just learned about. Let's get right to it.

Writing basic MongoDB queries

Before you can write MongoDB queries and inject some data, first you must connect to MongoDB, so open a terminal and type the following:

```
$ mongo
```

Then you can list the databases that you have in the MongoDB system:

```
> show dbs
```

You should get the following output:

```
admin 0.000GB
config 0.000GB
```

These two databases (`admin` and `config`) are the default ones from MongoDB. However, we should create new databases according to our needs and purposes.

Creating a database

As soon as you have logged in the MongoDB shell, you can create a fresh database in MongoDB by using the `use` command:

```
> use nuxt-app
```

You should get the following result:

```
switched to db nuxt-app
```

However, note that it is the same when you want to select an existing database:

```
> use admin
```

You should get the following result:

```
switched to db admin
```

If you want to drop a database, first select the database using the `use` command, for example, `use nuxt-app`, followed by the `dropDatabase` function:

```
> db.dropDatabase()
```

You should get the following result:

```
{ "dropped" : "nuxt-app", "ok" : 1 }
```

Adding a Server-Side Database

The next thing we will learn is how to create or add collections to the database that we have created.

Creating a new collection

What is a MongoDB collection? If you are familiar with RDBMSes, a collection is akin to an RDBMS table, which can consist of different fields, except the enforcement of schema. We use the `createCollection` method to create a collection with the following format:

```
> db.createCollection(<name>, <options>)
```

The `<name>` parameter is the name of the collection, such as user, article, or whatever. The `<options>` parameter is optional, and is used to specify fields for creating a fixed-sized collection, or a collection that validates updates and inserts. For more information about these options, please visit https://docs.mongodb.com/manual/reference/method/db.createCollection/. Let's create a document and see what else you can do with the document in the following steps:

1. Create a collection without any options:

   ```
   > db.createCollection("users", {})
   ```

   You should get the following result:

   ```
   { "ok" : 1 }
   ```

2. List all collections in the database with the `getCollectionNames` method:

   ```
   > db.getCollectionNames()
   ```

   You should get the following result:

   ```
   [ "users" ]
   ```

3. Drop the `users` collection with the `drop` method:

   ```
   > db.users.drop()
   ```

   You should get the following result:

   ```
   true
   ```

Now that we know how to create a collection, the next thing you should know is how to add documents to the collection. Let's get to it in the next section.

Writing MongoDB CRUD operations

When it comes to managing and manipulating data in a database system, we are bound to create, read, update, and delete (CRUD) documents. We can use MongoDB's CRUD operations for this. You can read more information about MongoDB CRUD operations at `https://docs.mongodb.com/manual/crud/`. In this book, we will just see a simple example of how we can use each of these:

- **The Create operations**:
  We can use the following methods to create or insert fresh documents to a collection:

    ```
    db.<collection>.insertOne(<document>)
    db.<collection>.insertMany([<document>, <document>, <document>, ...])
    ```

    Note that if the collection does not exist in your database, these `insert` operations will create it for you automatically.

- **The Read operations**:
  We can use the following method to fetch documents from a collection:

    ```
    db.<collection>.find(<query>, <projection>)
    ```

- **The Update operations**:
  We can use the following methods to modify the existing documents in a collection:

    ```
    db.<collection>.updateOne(<filter>, <update>, <options>)
    db.<collection>.updateMany(<filter>, <update>, <options>)
    db.<collection>.replaceOne(<filter>, <replacement>, <options>)
    ```

- **The Delete operations**:
  We can use the following methods to remove documents from a collection:

    ```
    db.<collection>.deleteOne(<filter>, <options>)
    db.<collection>.deleteMany(<filter>, <options>)
    ```

With these simplified CRUD operations, you can start injecting data to the database in the next section, and then you are another step closer to create a fully functional API. Let's get going!

Injecting data with MongoDB CRUD

We will inject some data in the nuxt-app database with the MongoDB CRUD operations that you have learned about in the previous section.

Inserting documents

We can insert new documents by using the `insertOne` or `insertMany` methods as follows:

- **Insert a single document**: We can insert a new document like this:

    ```
    > db.<collection>.insertOne(<document>)
    ```

    Let's insert one document with the following code:

    ```
    db.user.insertOne(
      {
        name: "Alexandre",
        age: 30,
        slug: "alexandre",
        role: "admin",
        status: "ok"
      }
    )
    ```

    You should get a similar result to this:

    ```
    {
      "acknowledged" : true,
      "insertedId" : ObjectId("5ca...")
    }
    ```

- **Insert multiple documents**: We can insert multiple new documents like this:

    ```
    >
    db.<collection>.insertMany([<document>,<document>,<document>,...])
    ```

    Let's insert two documents with the following code:

    ```
    > db.user.insertMany([
      {
        name: "Pooya",
        age: 25,
        slug: "pooya",
        role: "admin",
        status: "ok"
    ```

```
    },
    {
      name: "Sébastien",
      age: 22,
      slug: "sebastien",
      role: "writer",
      status: "pending"
    }
])
```

You should get a similar result to this:

```
{
  "acknowledged" : true,
  "insertedIds" : [
    ObjectId("5ca..."),
    ObjectId("5ca...")
  ]
}
```

After adding documents to the user collection, we would like to fetch them, and that can be done simply by using the read operations in the next section.

Querying documents

We can fetch documents by using the find method as follows:

- **Selecting all documents in a collection**: We can fetch all the documents from a collection like this:

    ```
    > db.<collection>.find()
    ```

    This operation is the same as the following SQL statement:

    ```
    SELECT  FROM <table>
    ```

    Let's fetch all the documents from the user collection as follows:

    ```
    > db.user.find()
    ```

Adding a Server-Side Database

You should get a similar result to this:

```
{ "_id" : ObjectId("5ca..."), "name" : "Alexandre", "slug" :
 "alexandre", ... }
{ "_id" : ObjectId("5ca..."), "name" : "Pooya", "slug" : "pooya",
 ... }
{ "_id" : ObjectId("5ca..."), "name" : "Sébastien", "slug" :
 "sebastien", ... }
```

- **Specifying equality condition**: We can fetch specific documents from a collection like this:

    ```
    > db.<collection>.find(<query>, <projection>)
    ```

You can see that we use the same `find` method as the previous example but pass in the options in the `<query>` parameter to filter the documents that match the specific queries. For example, the following line selects the document where the `status` equals `ok`:

```
> db.user.find( { status: "ok" } )
```

This operation is the same as the following SQL statement:

```
SELECT  FROM user WHERE status = "ok"
```

You should get a similar result to this:

```
{ "_id" : ObjectId("5ca..."), "name" : "Alexandre", ... "status" :
"ok" }
{ "_id" : ObjectId("5ca..."), "name" : "Pooya", ... "status" : "ok"
}
```

- **Specifying conditions using query operators**: We also can use MongoDB query selectors, such as $eq, $gt, or $in, in the `find` method's `<query>` parameter. For example, the following line fetches documents where the `status` equals either `ok` or `pending`:

    ```
    > db.user.find( { status: { $in: [ "ok", "pending" ] } } )
    ```

This operation is the same as the following SQL statement:

```
SELECT  FROM user WHERE status in ("ok", "pending")
```

> You can find out more information about the query selectors at https://docs.mongodb.com/manual/reference/operator/query/query-selectors.

[296]

- **Specifying AND conditions**: You also can mix filters with query selectors. For example, the following line fetches documents where the `status` equals ok **and** the `age` is less than ($lt) 30:

    ```
    > db.user.find( { status: "ok", age: { $lt: 30 } } )
    ```

    You should get a similar result to this:

    ```
    { "_id" : ObjectId("5ca..."), "name" : "Pooya", "age" : 25, ... }
    ```

    This operation is the same as the following SQL statement:

    ```
    SELECT  FROM user WHERE status = "ok" AND age < 30
    ```

- **Specifying OR conditions**: You also can create OR conditions by using the `$or` selector to fetch the documents that match at least one condition. For example, the following line fetches documents where the `status` equals ok **or** the `age` is less than ($lt) 30:

    ```
    > db.user.find( { $or: [ { status: "ok" }, { age: { $lt: 30 } } ] } )
    ```

    This operation is the same as the following SQL statement:

    ```
    SELECT  FROM user WHERE status = "ok" OR age < 30
    ```

    You should get a similar result to this:

    ```
    { "_id" : ObjectId("5ca..."), "name" : "Pooya", "age" : 25, ... }
    ```

> You can find out more about the query and projection operators at `https://docs.mongodb.com/manual/reference/operator/query/` and the `$or` selector at `https://docs.mongodb.com/manual/reference/operator/query/logical`.

Now, the next thing we are interested in is updating existing documents, so let's move on to the next section.

Updating documents

We can update the existing documents by using the `updateOne` and `updateMany` methods as follows:

- **Updating a single document**:
  We can update an existing document like this:

  ```
  > db.<collection>.updateOne(<filter>, <update>, <options>)
  ```

  Let's update the document where the `name` equals Sébastien in the `<filter>` parameter with the update data using the `$set` operator in the `<update>` parameter, as follows:

  ```
  > db.user.updateOne(
     { name: "Sébastien" },
     {
       $set: { status: "ok" },
       $currentDate: { lastModified: true }
     }
  )
  ```

  You should get the following result:

  ```
  { "acknowledged" : true, "matchedCount" : 1, "modifiedCount" : 1 }
  ```

  The `$set` operator is used to replace the value of a field with the new value. It takes the following format:

  ```
  { $set: { <field1>: <value1>, ... } }
  ```

  The `$currentDate` operator is used to set the value of a field to the current date. The value it returns can be a human-readable date (which is the default), for example 2013-10-02T01:11:18.965Z or a timestamp, such as 1573612039.

  > You can find out more information about the `$set` operator at https://docs.mongodb.com/manual/reference/operator/update/set/. You can find out more information about `$currentDate` at https://docs.mongodb.com/manual/reference/operator/update/currentDate/.

- **Updating multiple documents**:
  We can update multiple existing documents like this:

  ```
  > db.<collection>.updateMany(<filter>, <update>, <options>)
  ```

Let's update documents where the `status` is `ok`:

```
> db.user.updateMany(
    { "status": "ok" },
    {
      $set: { status: "pending" },
      $currentDate: { lastModified: true }
    }
)
```

You should get the following result:

```
{ "acknowledged" : true, "matchedCount" : 3, "modifiedCount" : 3 }
```

> You can find out more information about the update operators at https://docs.mongodb.com/manual/reference/operator/update/.

- **Replacing a document**:
  We can replace the content of existing documents, except the `_id` field, like this:

  ```
  > db.<collection>.replaceOne(<filter>, <replacement>, <options>)
  ```

  Let's replace the document where `name` equals `Pooya` with a completely new document in the `<replacement>` parameter as follows:

  ```
  > db.user.replaceOne(
      { name: "Pooya" },
      {
        name: "Paula",
        age: "31",
        slug: "paula",
        role: "admin",
        status: "ok"
      }
  )
  ```

  You should get the following result:

  ```
  { "acknowledged" : true, "matchedCount" : 1, "modificdCount" : 1 }
  ```

After learning how to update existing documents, the next thing you should learn is how to delete existing documents. Let's dive into the next section.

Adding a Server-Side Database

Deleting documents

We can delete existing documents by using the `deleteOne` and `deleteMany` methods as follows:

- **Deleting only one document that matches a condition**:
  We can delete an existing document like this:

  ```
  > db.<collection>.deleteOne(<filter>, <options>)
  ```

  Let's delete the document where the `status` field equals `pending` as follows:

  ```
  > db.user.deleteOne( { status: "pending" } )
  ```

  You should get the following result:

  ```
  { "acknowledged" : true, "deletedCount" : 3 }
  ```

- **Deleting documents that match a condition**:
  We can delete multiple existing documents like this:

  ```
  > db.<collection>.deleteMany(<filter>, <options>)
  ```

  Let's delete documents where the `status` field equals `ok`:

  ```
  > db.user.deleteMany({ status : "ok" })
  ```

  You should get the following result:

  ```
  { "acknowledged" : true, "deletedCount" : 2 }
  ```

- **Deleting all documents**:
  We can delete all documents in a collection by passing an empty filter to the `deleteMany` method as follows:

  ```
  > db.<collection>.deleteMany({})
  ```

  Let's delete all documents from the `user` collection with the following code:

  ```
  > db.user.deleteMany({})
  ```

  You should get the following result:

  ```
  { "acknowledged" : true, "deletedCount" : 1 }
  ```

[300]

Well done! You have managed to complete the MongoDB CRUD operations in these sections. You can find out more other methods at https://docs.mongodb.com/manual/reference/method/js-collection/. In the next section, we will guide you through how to integrate CRUD operations with the server-side framework by using the MongoDB Driver. Let's get going.

Integrating MongoDB with Koa

We have studied a handful of MongoDB queries for performing CRUD operations through the MongoDB Shell. Now we only need the MongoDB driver to help us to connect to the MongoDB server and perform the same CRUD operations that we did with the MongoDB Shell. We will install this driver in our app as a dependency in our server-side framework – Koa.

Installing the MongoDB driver

The official MongoDB driver is mongodb for Node.js apps. It is a high-level API, built on top of the MongoDB Core driver, mongodb-core, a low-level API. The former is made for end users, while the latter is made for MongoDB library developers. mongodb contains abstractions and helpers that make MongoDB connections, CRUD operations, and authentication easy, while mongodb-core only contains the basic management of MongoDB topology connections, core CRUD operations, and authentication.

For more information about these two packages, visit the following sites:

- https://www.npmjs.com/package/mongodb for the MongoDB driver
- https://www.npmjs.com/package/mongodb-core for the MongoDB Core driver
- http://mongodb.github.io/node-mongodb-native/3.0/api/ for the MongoDB driver API

We can install the MongoDB driver with npm:

```
$ npm i mongodb
```

Next, we will look into how we can use it with a quick example in the coming section.

Creating a simple app with the MongoDB driver

Let's set up a simple app with the MongoDB driver to perform a simple connection check. In this test, we will use the Backpack build system that we covered in the previous chapter to run our test. So, let's get it started with the following steps:

1. Install the MongoDB driver as shown in the previous section, followed by Backpack and cross-env:

    ```
    $ npm i backpack-core
    $ npm i cross-env
    ```

2. Create a /src/ folder as the default entry directory and create an index.js file in it, and then import the MongoDB driver and the Assert module from Node.js as follows:

    ```
    // src/index.js
    import { MongoClient } from 'mongodb'
    import assert from 'assert'

    const url = 'mongodb://localhost:27017'
    const dbName = 'nuxt-app'
    ```

    In this step, we should also provide the MongoDB connection details: the MongoDB server default address, which is mongodb://localhost:27017, and the database that we want to connect to, which is nuxt-app.

    > Note that Assert is a Node.js built-in module that comes with a set of assertion functions for unit testing your code, so we don't have to install this module. If you want to find out more about this module, please visit https://nodejs.org/api/assert.html#assert_assert.

3. Next, establish the connection to the database in the MongoDB server and use Assert to confirm the connection as follows:

```
// src/index.js
MongoClient.connect(url, {
  useUnifiedTopology: true,
  useNewUrlParser: true
}, (err, client) => {
  assert.equal(null, err)
  console.log('Connected to the MongoDB server')

  const db = client.db(dbName)
  client.close()
})
```

In this example, we have used the `equal` method from the `assert` module to make sure that the `err` callback is `null`, before creating a database instance with the `client` callback. We should always close the connection with the `close` method whenever we finish a task.

4. If you run this connection test on your terminal with `npm run dev`, you should get the following output on your terminal:

```
Connected successfully to server
```

> You can find this simple example in `/chapter-9/mongo-driver/` in our GitHub repository.

Notice that we are connecting to MongoDB with any authentication because we have not secured our MongoDB yet. You will learn how to set up a new administrative user to secure your MongoDB in the last chapter of this book – *Chapter 18, Creating a Nuxt App with CMS and GraphQL*. To flatten your learning curve and to speed up the development process in the coming sections in this chapter, we will opt out of securing MongoDB. Now, let's take a deeper look at how we can configure the MongoDB driver in the next section.

Configuring the MongoDB driver

From the code in the previous section, you can see that we should always import `MongoClient`, providing the MongoDB server URL, database name, and so on whenever performing a MongoDB CRUD task. This can be tedious and counter-productive. Let's abstract the preceding MongoDB connection code into a class in the following steps:

1. Abstract the database connection details into a file:

    ```js
    // server/config/mongodb.js
    const database = {
      host: 'localhost',
      port: 27017,
      dbname: 'nuxt-app'
    }

    export default {
      host: database.host,
      port: database.port,
      dbname: database.dbname,
      url: 'mongodb://' + database.host + ':' + database.port
    }
    ```

2. Create a `class` function to construct the database connection so that we don't have to repeat this process whenever we perform the CRUD operations. We also construct an `objectId` property in our `class` function for storing the `ObjectId` method that we will need in order to parse the ID data coming from the client side so that this ID data will become an object from a string:

    ```js
    // server/mongo.js
    import mongodb from 'mongodb'
    import config from './config/mongodb'

    const MongoClient = mongodb.MongoClient

    export default class Mongo {
      constructor () {
        this.connection = null
        this.objectId = mongodb.ObjectId
      }

      async connect () {
        this.connection = await MongoClient.connect(config.url, {
          useUnifiedTopology: true,
          useNewUrlParser: true
        })
    ```

```
      return this.connection.db(config.dbname)
    }

    close () {
      this.connection.close()
    }
  }
```

3. Import the `class` and instantiate it with the `new` statement as follows:

```
import Mongo from './mongo'
const mongo = new Mongo()
```

For example, we can import it in our API routes where we need to connect to the MongoDB database to perform CRUD operations as follows:

```
// server/routes.js
import Router from 'koa-router'
import Mongo from './mongo'
const mongo = new Mongo()
const router = new Router({ prefix: '/api' })

router.post('/user', async (ctx, next) => {
  //...
})
```

Before creating the CRUD operations with the MongoDB driver and our server-side framework, Koa, we should understand `ObjectId` and the `ObjectId` method. Let's get into it.

Understanding ObjectId and the ObjectId method

`ObjectId` is a fast-generated and probably unique value that MongoDB uses as a primary key in a collection. It consists of 12 bytes; a timestamp takes the first 4 bytes to record the time when the `ObjectId` value is created. It is stored in a unique `_id` field for each document in a collection. This `_id` field will be automatically generated if it is not declared when a document is injected. On the other hand, `ObjectId(<hexadecimal>)` is a MongoDB method that we can use to return a new `ObjectId` value, and to parse an `ObjectId` value from a string to become an object. Here's an example:

```
// Pseudo code
var id = '5d2ba2bf089a7754e9094af5'
console.log(typeof id) // string
console.log(typeof ObjectId(id)) // object
```

Adding a Server-Side Database

In the preceding pseudocode, you can see that we use the `getTimestamp` method from the object created by the `ObjectId` method to obtain the timestamp from the `ObjectId` value. Here's an example:

```
// Pseudo code
var object = ObjectId(id)
var timestamp = object.getTimestamp()
console.log(timestamp) // 2019-07-14T21:46:39.000Z
```

For more information about `ObjectId` and the `ObjectId` method, check out the following links:

- https://docs.mongodb.com/manual/reference/bson-types/#objectid for `ObjectId`
- https://docs.mongodb.com/manual/reference/method/ObjectId/ for `ObjectId()`

Now, let's write some CRUD operations with the MongoDB driver in the coming sections. Firstly, we will write the operation of injecting a document.

Injecting one document

Before we start, we should look at the code structure that we need for every route that we will be creating:

```
// server/routes.js
router.get('/user', async (ctx, next) => {
  let result
  try {
    const connection = await mongo.connect()
    const collectionUsers = connection.collection('users')
    result = await collectionUsers...
    mongo.close()
  } catch (err) {
    ctx.throw(500, err)
  }
  ctx.type = 'json'
  ctx.body = result
})
```

Let's discuss the structure:

- **Catching and throwing errors**:
  When we use the `async/await` statement instead of the `Promise` object for an asynchronous operation, we must always wrap them in `try/catch` blocks to handle errors:

  ```
  try {
    // async/await code
  } catch (err) {
    // handle error
  }
  ```

- **Connecting to MongoDB databases and collections**:
  Before performing any CRUD operation, we must establish the connection and connect to the specific collection that we want to manipulate. In our case, the collection is `users`:

  ```
  const connection = await mongo.connect()
  const collectionUsers = connection.collection('users')
  ```

- **Performing the CRUD operation**:
  This is where we use the MongoDB API methods to read, inject, update, and delete users:

  ```
  result = await collectionUsers...
  ```

- **Closing the MongoDB connection**:
  We must make sure to close the connection after the CRUD operation:

  ```
  mongo.close()
  ```

Now let's use the preceding code structure to inject new users in the following steps:

1. Create a route with the `post` method to inject a new user document:

   ```
   // server/routes.js
   router.post('/user', async (ctx, next) => {
     let result
     //...
   })
   ```

Adding a Server-Side Database

2. Inside the `post` route, perform checks on the keys and values we receive from the client side before performing a CRUD operation with MongoDB:

   ```
   let body = ctx.request.body || {}
   
   if (body.name === undefined) {
     ctx.throw(400, 'name is undefined')
   }
   if (body.slug === undefined) {
     ctx.throw(400, 'slug is undefined')
   }
   if (body.name === '') {
     ctx.throw(400, 'name is required')
   }
   if (body.slug === '') {
     ctx.throw(400, 'slug is required')
   }
   ```

3. Before allowing a new document to be injected into the `user` collection, we want to make sure the `slug` value does not exist yet. To do that, we need to use the `findOne` API method with the `slug` key. If the result is positive, that means the `slug` value has been taken by other user documents, so we throw an error to the client:

   ```
   const found = await collectionUsers.findOne({
     slug: body.slug
   })
   if (found) {
     ctx.throw(404, 'slug has been taken')
   }
   ```

4. If the `slug` is unique, then we use the `insertOne` API method to inject a new document with the provided data:

   ```
   result = await collectionUsers.insertOne({
     name: body.name,
     slug: body.slug
   })
   ```

After injecting the document, the next thing we will need is to fetch and view the documents we have injected, which we'll do in the next section.

Fetching all documents

After adding the users to the `users` collection, we can retrieve all or just one of them through the routes that we created in Chapter 8, *Adding a Server-Side Framework*. Now we just have to refactor them using the same code structure as in the previous section for fetching real data from the database:

1. Refactor the route for listing all user documents with the `get` method:

   ```
   // server/routes.js
   router.get('/users', async (ctx, next) => {
     let result
     //...
   })
   ```

2. Inside the `get` router, fetch all documents from the `user` collection by using the `find` API method:

   ```
   result = await collectionUser.find({
   }, {
     // Exclude some fields
   }).toArray()
   ```

   If you want to exclude the fields from the query result, use the `projection` key and a value of `0` for the field you don't want to show in the result. For example, if you don't want the `_id` field on each document in the result, do this:

   ```
   projection:{ _id: 0 }
   ```

3. Refactor the route for fetching a user document with the `get` method:

   ```
   // server/routes.js
   router.get('/users/:id', async (ctx, next) => {
     let result
     //...
   })
   ```

Adding a Server-Side Database

4. Fetch a single document by using the `findOne` method with `_id`. We must parse the `id` string with the `ObjectId` method, which we have a copy of in our `constructor` function in the `class` function as `objectId`:

```
const id = ctx.params.id
result = await collectionUsers.findOne({
  _id: mongo.objectId(id)
}, {
  // Exclude some fields
})
```

The `mongo.objectId(id)` method parses the `id` string into an `ObjectID` object, and then we can use it to query the document from the collection. Now that we can fetch the documents we have created, the next thing we need to do is update them. Let's get to it in the next section.

Updating one document

After adding the users to the `users` collection, we also can update them using the same code structure as in the previous section in the following steps:

1. Create a route with the `put` method for updating the existing user document as follows:

```
// server/routes.js
router.put('/user', async (ctx, next) => {
  let result
  //...
})
```

2. Before updating a document, we want to make sure the `slug` value is unique. So, inside the `put` route, we search for a match with the `findOne` API with `$ne` to exclude the document that we are updating. If there is no match, then we go on updating the document with the `updateOne` API method:

```
const found = await collectionUser.findOne({
  slug: body.slug,
  _id: { $ne: mongo.objectId(body.id) }
})
if (found) {
  ctx.throw(404, 'slug has been taken')
}

result = await collectionUser.updateOne({
```

```
            _id: mongo.objectId(body.id)
}, {
    $set: { name: body.name, slug: body.slug },
    $currentDate: { lastModified: true }
})
```

We use three operators in this CRUD operation: the `$set` operator, the `$currentDate` operator, and the `$ne` selector. These are some of the update operators and query selectors that you will frequently use for updating documents:

- **The update operators**:
  The `$set` operator is used to replace the value of a field with the new specified value in the following format:

  ```
  { $set: { <field1>: <value1>, ... } }
  ```

  The `$currentDate` operator is used to set the current date to a specified field, either as a BSON Date type (the default) or a BSON Timestamp type, in the following format:

  ```
  { $currentDate: { <field1>: <typeSpecification1>, ... } }
  ```

  > For more information about these two and other update operators, please visit https://docs.mongodb.com/manual/reference/operator/update/.

- **The query selectors**:
  The `$ne` selector is used to select documents where the value of the field is not equal to the specified value, including those do not contain the field. Here's an example:

  ```
  db.user.find( { age: { $ne: 18 } } )
  ```

  This query will select all documents in the `user` collection where the `age` field value does not equal `18`, including those documents that do not contain the `age` field.

  > For more information about this and other query selectors, please visit https://docs.mongodb.com/manual/reference/operator/query/.

Now, let's take a look at how we can delete the document we have created in the next section.

Deleting one document

Lastly, we also will be using the same code structure as in the previous section to delete existing users from the `users` collection in the following steps:

1. Create a route with the `del` method to delete an existing user document:

   ```
   // server/routes.js
   router.del('/user', async (ctx, next) => {
     let result
     //...
   })
   ```

2. Before deleting the document with the `deleteOne` API method, inside the `del` route, as always, we use the `findOne` API method to find this document to make sure we have it in the `user` collection first:

   ```
   let body = ctx.request.body || {}
   const found = await collectionUser.findOne({
     _id: mongo.objectId(body.id)
   })
   if (!found) {
     ctx.throw(404, 'no user found')
   }

   result = await collectionUser.deleteOne({
     _id: mongo.objectId(body.id)
   })
   ```

Well done! You have managed to get through writing MongoDB CRUD operations and integrating them into the API (Koa). The final part of this chapter involves integrating these operations with Nuxt pages. Let's get to this in the next section.

Integrating with Nuxt Pages

We have the server side ready, and now we need a user interface on the client side so we can send and fetch data. We will create three new pages in the /pages/users/ directory. This is our structure:

```
users
├── index.vue
├── _id.vue
├── add
│   └── index.vue
├── update
│   └── _id.vue
└── delete
    └── _id.vue
```

As soon as we have the structure in place, we are ready to create pages and write the CRUD tasks from the Nuxt side (the client) in the following sections. Let's start with the *create* CRUD task in the next section.

Creating an add page for adding new users

We will create this page to communicate with the server-side POST route, /api/user/, to add a new user in the following steps:

1. Create a form to collect the new user data in the <template> block as follows:

   ```
   // pages/users/add/index.vue
   <form v-on:submit.prevent="add">
     <p>Name: <input v-model="name" type="text" name="name"></p>
     <p>Slug: <input v-model="slug" type="text" name="slug"></p>
     <button type="submit">Add</button>
     <button v-on:click="cancel">Cancel</button>
   </form>
   ```

2. Create an add method to send the data to the server and a cancel method to cancel the form in the <script> block as follows:

   ```
   // pages/users/add/index.vue
   export default {
     methods: {
       async add () {
         let { data } = await axios.post('/api/user/', {
           name: this.name,
           slug: this.slug,
   ```

Adding a Server-Side Database

```
      })
    },
    cancel () {
      this.$router.push('/users/')
    }
  }
}
```

With these two steps, we have established the *create* CRUD task successfully on the client side (Nuxt) with the server side (API). So now you add new users to the database from the client side at `localhost:3000/users/add` by using the form you have just created to collect the user data and send them to the API's POST route at `localhost:3000/api/user/`. After being able to add new users, we should move on to the *update* CRUD task on the client side. Let's get to it.

Creating an update page for updating existing users

The update page is basically quite similar to the add page. This page will communicate with the server-side PUT route, `/api/user/`, to update the existing user with the following steps:

1. Create a form to display the existing data and to collect the new data in the `<template>` block. The difference in the update page is the method that we bind to the `<form>` element:

   ```
   // pages/users/update/_id.vue
   <form v-on:submit.prevent="update">
     //...
     <button type="submit">Update</button>
   </form>
   ```

2. Create an `update` method to send the data to the server in the `<script>` block. We will use the `asyncData` method to fetch the existing data as follows:

   ```
   // pages/users/update/_id.vue
   export default {
     async asyncData ({ params, error }) {
       let { data } = await axios.get('/api/users/' + params.id)
       let user = data.data
       return {
         id: user._id,
         name: user.name,
   ```

```
        slug: user.slug,
      }
    },
    methods: {
      async update () {
        let { data } = await axios.put('/api/user/', {
          name: this.name,
          slug: this.slug,
          id: this.id,
        })
      }
    }
  }
```

Again, we have established the update CRUD task successfully in these two steps on the client side (Nuxt) with the server side (API). So now you can update the existing users in the database from the client side at `localhost:3000/users/update` by using the form to collect the user data and send them to the API's PUT route at `localhost:3000/api/user/`. After being able to update the user, we should now move on to the *delete* CRUD task on the client side. Let's get to it.

Creating a delete page for deleting existing users

This page will communicate with the server-side DELETE route, `/api/user/`, to delete the existing user:

1. Create a `<button>` element that we can use to delete the document in the `<template>` block. We don't need a form to send the data because we can collect the data (which is only the document `_id` data) in the `remove` method. We only need the button to trigger this method as follows:

   ```
   // pages/users/delete/_id.vue
   <button v-on:click="remove">Delete</button>
   ```

2. Create the `remove` method to send the data to the server as we explained in the `<script>` block. But first, we will need to use the `asyncData` method to fetch the existing data:

   ```
   // pages/users/delete/_id.vue
   export default {
    async asyncData ({ params, error }) {
       // Fetch the existing user
       // Same as in update page
     },
   ```

Adding a Server-Side Database

```
      methods: {
        async remove () {
          let payload = { id: this.id }
          let { data } = await axios.delete('/api/user/', {
            data: payload,
          })
        }
      }
    }
```

Finally, we have established the *delete* CRUD task successfully in these two steps on the client side (Nuxt) with the server side (API). Now you can remove the existing users from the database from the client side at `localhost:3000/users/delete` by sending the user data, which is an ID only, and send it to the API's DELETE route at `localhost:3000/api/user/`. So if you launch the app with `npm run dev`, you should see it running at `localhost:3000`.

Navigate to the following routes to add, update, read, and delete users:

- `localhost:3000/users` for reading/listing all users
- `localhost:3000/users/add` for injecting a new user
- `localhost:3000/users/update/<id>` for updating an existing user by their ID
- `localhost:3000/users/delete/<id>` for deleting an existing user by their ID

Well done! You have finally managed to get through the milestones we set in this chapter. MongoDB can be an overwhelming subject to pick up as a beginner, but if you have followed through the guides and milestones we set in this chapter, you can create a pretty decent API with little effort. Use the links we provided when you need to venture beyond the CRUD operations that we have explained in this book. Let's now summarize what you have learned in this chapter.

> You can find the code we have created for this chapter in `/chapter-9/nuxt-universal/koa-mongodb/axios/` in our GitHub repository.

Summary

In this chapter, you have learned how to install MongoDB on your local machine, and you have used some basic MongoDB queries for CRUD operations on the MongoDB Shell. You also learned how to install and use the MongoDB driver to connect to MongoDB from the server-side framework, and you have written the code to perform CRUD operations in the Koa environment. Finally, you have created the front pages from the client side, Nuxt, for adding new users to the MongoDB database, and for updating and deleting existing users by communicating with the API that you have developed with Koa.

In the next chapter, we will explore the Vuex store and use it in Nuxt apps. You will learn about the Vuex architecture before installing it and writing a simple Vuex store in a Vue app. You will also learn about the Vuex core concepts, including the state, getters, actions, and modules, before writing a Vuex store in a Nuxt app with these concepts. We will guide you through them, so stay tuned.

10 Adding a Vuex Store

Having a database system such as MongoDB to manage our data is great, as we can use it to remotely request data for our routes whenever required. However, occasionally, we need to share some data across pages or components, and we don't want to make additional and unnecessary HTTP requests for this kind of data. Ideally, we would like to have a central place in our local app where we can store this "omnipresent" and centralized data. Fortunately, we have a system called Vuex to store this kind of data for us, and that is what you will explore in this chapter. So, in this chapter, you will learn how to use Vuex for state management (centralized data management) in your apps. You will learn about the Vuex architecture, its core concepts, and the suggested directory structure for managing modular Vuex stores. Lastly, you will learn how to activate and use a Vuex store in Nuxt apps.

The topics we will cover in this chapter are as follows:

- Understanding the Vuex architecture
- Getting started with Vuex
- Understanding Vuex core concepts
- Structuring Vuex store modules
- Handling forms in a Vuex store
- Using a Vuex store in Nuxt

Understanding the Vuex architecture

Before learning how to use a Vuex store in Nuxt apps, we should understand how it works in standard Vue apps. But what is Vuex? Let's find out in the upcoming section.

What is Vuex?

In a nutshell, Vuex is a centralized data (also referred as state) management system with some rules (which we will look into later) to ensure that the state can only be mutated predictably from multiple (distant) components that need to access the common data. This idea of information centralization is common with tools such as Redux in React. They all share a similar state management pattern with Vuex. Let's take a look at what this pattern is in the next section.

State management pattern

To understand the state management pattern in Vuex, let's take a look at a simple Vue app that we are already familiar with:

```
<div id="app"></div>

new Vue({
  // state
  data () {
    return { message: '' }
  },

  // view
  template: `
    <div>
      <p>{{ message }}</p>
      <button v-on:click="greet">Greet</button>
    </div>
  `,

  // actions
  methods: {
    greet () {
      this.message = 'Hello World'
    }
  }
}).$mount('#app')
```

This simple app has the following parts:

- `state`, which holds the source of the app
- `view`, which maps the state
- `actions`, which can be used to mutate the state from the view

They work perfectly and are easy to manage in a small app like this, but this simplicity becomes unsustainable and problematic when we have two or more components sharing the same state, or when we want to mutate the state with actions from different views.

Passing props can be the solution that pops into your mind, but this is tedious for deeply nested components. That's where Vuex comes in, extracting the common state and managing it globally in a specific location, called a store, so that any component can access it from anywhere, regardless of how deep it is nested.

Thus, separation using state management with some enforced rules can maintain the independence of the views and the state. Using this, we can make our code more structured and maintainable. Let's take a look at the architecture of Vuex in the following diagram:

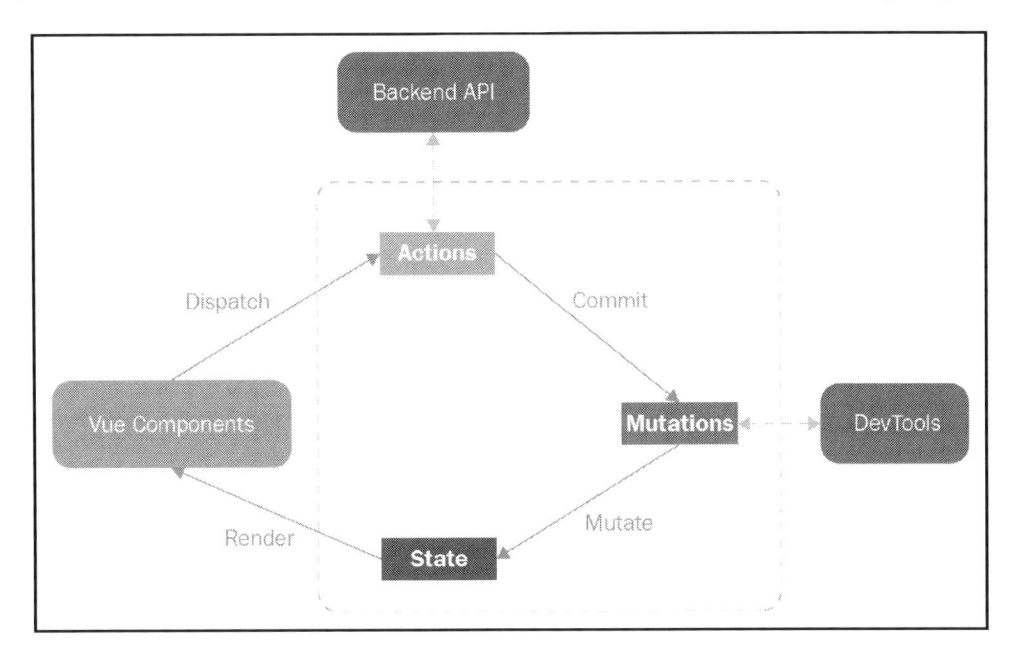

Reference Source: https://vuex.vuejs.org/

In a nutshell, Vuex consists of actions, mutations, and the state. The state is always mutated through mutations, while mutations are always committed through the actions in the Vuex lifecycle. The mutated state is then rendered to the components and, at the same time, the actions are (usually) dispatched from the components. Communication with the backend API usually occurs in the actions. Let's get started with Vuex in the next section and dive into its constitutions.

Adding a Vuex Store

Getting started with Vuex

As we mentioned in the previous section, all Vuex activities happen in a store, which can be created simply in your project root. However, while it seems simple, a Vuex store is different from a plain JavaScript object because a Vuex store is reactive, just like the two-way binding on an `<input>` element with the `v-model` directive. So, any state data you access in Vue components is *reactively* updated when it is changed in the store. The data in the store's state must be *explicitly* committed through mutations, just like we explained in the diagram in the previous section.

For this exercise, we will use a single-file component skeleton to build some simple Vue apps with Vuex. We will put all our sample code in `/chapter-10/vue/vuex-sfc/` in our GitHub repository. Let's get started.

Installing Vuex

Before we can create a Vuex store, we must install Vuex and import it using the following steps:

1. Install Vuex by using npm:

   ```
   $ npm i vuex
   ```

2. Import and register it by using the `Vue.use()` method:

   ```
   import Vue from 'vue'
   import Vuex from 'vuex'

   Vue.use(Vuex)
   ```

Remember that the preceding installation steps are meant to use Vuex with a module system, which is what we are going for in this chapter. But before jumping into a module system app, we should take a look at how we can create the Vuex app by using CDN or a direct download in the next section.

> Note that Vuex requires Promise support. If your browser does not support Promise, please check out how you can install a polyfill library for your apps at `https://vuex.vuejs.org/installation.html#promise`.

Creating a simple store

We can start with a simple store by using CDN or direct download with the following steps:

1. Install Vue and Vuex with the HTML `<script>` blocks:

   ```
   <script src="/path/to/vue.js"></script>
   <script src="/path/to/vuex.js"></script>
   ```

2. Activate the Vuex store in the HTML `<body>` block:

   ```
   <script type="text/javascript">
     const store = new Vuex.Store({
       state: { count: 0 },
       mutations: {
          increment (state) { state.count++ }
       }
     })
     store.commit('increment')
     console.log(store.state.count) // -> 1
   </script>
   ```

   You can see from this code that you just need to create the Vuex state in a JavaScript object, a mutation method, and then you can access the state object with the store's `state` key and trigger the change in the state with the store's `commit` method, as follows:

   ```
   store.commit('increment')
   console.log(store.state.count)
   ```

In this simple example, we have complied with one of the enforced rules in Vuex, which is changing the state data by committing the mutation instead of changing it directly. Let's dive into the core concepts of Vuex and other rules by creating module system apps in the next section.

Understanding Vuex core concepts

There are five core concepts in Vuex that we will guide you through in this section. They are state, getters, mutations, actions, and modules. We will start by looking into the state concept first in the following section.

The state

The state is the heart of a Vuex store. It is the source of the "global" data that we can manage and maintain in a structured and predictable way in Vuex. A state in Vuex is a single state tree–a single JavaScript object that contains all the app state data. So, you will usually have one store per app. Let's take a look at how we can get the state into components in the following sections.

Accessing the state

As we mentioned in the previous section, Vuex stores are reactive, but if we want to access the reactive value in the view, we should use the `computed` property instead of the `data` method, as follows:

```
// vuex-sfc/state/basic/src/app.vue
<p>{{ number }}</p>

import Vue from 'vue/dist/vue.js'
import Vuex from 'vuex'
Vue.use(Vuex)

const store = new Vuex.Store({
  state: { number: 1 }
})

export default {
  computed: {
    number () {
      return store.state.number
    }
  }
}
```

So now, the `number` field in the `<template>` block is reactive and the `computed` property will re-evaluate and update the DOM whenever `store.state.number` changes. But this pattern causes a coupling issue and is against the extracting idea of Vuex. So, let's refactor the preceding code with the following steps:

1. Extract the store to the root component:

    ```
    // vuex-sfc/state/inject/src/entry.js
    import Vue from 'vue/dist/vue.js'
    import App from './app.vue'

    import Vuex from 'vuex'
    ```

```
Vue.use(Vuex)

const store = new Vuex.Store({
  state: { number: 0 }
})

new Vue({
  el: 'app',
  template: '<App/>',
  store,
  components: {
    App
  }
})
```

2. Remove the store from the child component but keep the computed property as it is:

```
// vuex-sfc/state/inject/src/app.vue
<p>{{ number }}</p>

export default {
  computed: {
    number () {
      return this.$store.state.number
    }
  }
}
```

In the updated code, the store is now injected into the child component and you can access it by using `this.$store` from the component. However, this pattern can get repetitive and verbose when you have lots of store state properties that you need to compute with the computed property. In this case, we can use the mapState helper to lift the burden. Let's take a look at how we can use it in the next section.

The mapState helper

We can use the mapState helper to help us generate the computed state functions to save some lines and keystrokes with the following steps:

1. Create a store with multiple state properties:

```
// vuex-sfc/state/mapstate/src/entry.js
const store = new Vuex.Store({
  state: {
    experience: 1,
```

Adding a Vuex Store

```
      name: 'John',
      age: 20,
      job: 'designer'
    }
  })
```

2. Import the `mapState` helper from Vuex and pass the state properties as an array to the `mapState` method:

   ```
   // vuex-sfc/state/mapstate/src/app.vue
   import { mapState } from 'vuex'

   export default {
     computed: mapState([
       'experience', 'name', 'age', 'job'
     ])
   }
   ```

This works perfectly as long as the name of a mapped computed property is the same as a state property name. However, it is better to use it with the object spread operator so that we can mix multiple `mapState` helpers in the `computed` property:

```
computed: {
  ...mapState({
    // ...
  })
}
```

For example, you may want to compute the state data with the data in the child component, as follows:

```
// vuex-sfc/state/mapstate/src/app.vue
import { mapState } from 'vuex'

export default {
  data () {
    return { localExperience: 2 }
  },
  computed: {
    ...mapState([
      'experience', 'name', 'age', 'job'
    ]),
    ...mapState({
      experienceTotal (state) {
        return state.experience + this.localExperience
      }
```

```
    })
  }
}
```

You also can pass a string value to make an alias for the `experience` state property, as follows:

```
...mapState({
  experienceAlias: 'experience'
})
```

3. Add the computed state properties to `<template>`, as follows:

```
// vuex-sfc/state/mapstate/src/app.vue
<p>{{ name }}, {{ age }}, {{ job }}</p>
<p>{{ experience }}, {{ experienceAlias }}, {{ experienceTotal }}</p>
```

You should get the following result on your browser:

```
John, 20, designer
1, 1, 3
```

You may be wondering that since we can compute the state data in the child component, can we compute the state data in the store itself? The answer is yes, we can do so with getters, which we will cover in the next section. Let's get to it.

Getters

You can define getter methods in the `getters` property in the store to compute the state before it is used in the view by the child components. Just like the `computed` property, the computed result in a getter is reactive, but it is cached and will be updated whenever its dependencies are changed. A getter takes the state as its first argument and `getters` as the second argument. Let's create some getters and use them in the child component with the following steps:

1. Create a store with a `state` property with a list of items and some getters for accessing these items:

```
// vuex-sfc/getters/basic/src/entry.js
const store = new Vuex.Store({
  state: {
    fruits: [
      { name: 'strawberries', type: 'berries' },
      { name: 'orange', type: 'citrus' },
```

Adding a Vuex Store

```
      { name: 'lime', type: 'citrus' }
    ]
  },
  getters: {
    getCitrus: state => {
      return state.fruits.filter(fruit => fruit.type === 'citrus')
    },
    countCitrus: (state, getters) => {
      return getters.getCitrus.length
    },
    getFruitByName: (state, getters) => (name) => {
      return state.fruits.find(fruit => fruit.name === name)
    }
  }
})
```

In this store, we created the `getCitrus` method to get all the items with a type of `citrus` and the `countCitrus` method to depend on the result in the `getCitrus` method. The third method, `getFruitByName`, is used to get a specific item in the list by citrus name.

2. Create some methods in the `computed` property to execute the getters in the store, as follows:

```
// vuex-sfc/getters/basic/src/app.vue
export default {
  computed: {
    totalCitrus () {
      return this.$store.getters.countCitrus
    },
    getOrange () {
      return this.$store.getters.getFruitByName('orange')
    }
  }
}
```

3. Add the computed state properties to `<template>`, as follows:

```
// vuex-sfc/getters/basic/src/app.vue
<p>{{ totalCitrus }}</p>
<p>{{ getOrange }}</p>
```

You should get the following result in your browser:

```
2
{ "name": "orange", "type": "citrus" }
```

The same as the `mapState` helper, we can use the `mapGetters` helper in the `computed` properties, which saves us some lines and keystrokes. Let's get to it in the next section.

The mapGetters helper

Just like the `mapState` helper, we can use the `mapGetters` helper to map the store getters in the `computed` properties. Let's see how we can use it with the following steps:

1. Import the `mapGetters` helper from Vuex and pass the getters as an array to the `mapGetters` method with the object spread operator so that we can mix multiple `mapGetters` helpers in the `computed` property:

   ```
   // vuex-sfc/getters/mapgetters/src/app.vue
   import { mapGetters } from 'vuex'

   export default {
     computed: {
       ...mapGetters([
         'countCitrus'
       ]),
       ...mapGetters({
         totalCitrus: 'countCitrus'
       })
     }
   }
   ```

   In the preceding code, we created an alias for the `countCitrus` getter by passing the string value to the `totalCitrus` key. Note that with the object spread operator, we also can mix other vanilla methods in the `computed` property. So, let's add a vanilla `getOrange` getter method to the `computed` option on top of these `mapGetters` helpers, as follows:

   ```
   // vuex-sfc/getters/mapgetters/src/app.vue
   export default {
     computed: {
       // ... mapGetters
       getOrange () {
         return this.$store.getters.getFruitByName('orange')
       }
     }
   }
   ```

[329]

Adding a Vuex Store

2. Add the computed state properties to `<template>`, as follows:

```
// vuex-sfc/getters/mapgetters/src/app.vue
<p>{{ countCitrus }}</p>
<p>{{ totalCitrus }}</p>
<p>{{ getOrange }}</p>
```

You should get the following result in your browser:

```
2
2
{ "name": "orange", "type": "citrus" }
```

So far, you have learned how to access the state in the store by using the computed methods and getters. What about changing the state? Let's get to it in the next section.

Mutations

Just as we mentioned in the previous sections, the store state must be explicitly committed through mutations. A mutation is simply a function just like any other function you have learned about in the store properties, but it must be defined in the `mutations` property in the store. It always takes the state as the first argument. Let's create some mutations and use them in the child component with the following steps:

1. Create a store with a `state` property and some mutation methods that we can use to mutate the state, as follows:

```
// vuex-sfc/mutations/basic/src/entry.js
const store = new Vuex.Store({
  state: { number: 1 },
  mutations: {
    multiply (state) {
      state.number = state.number * 2
    },
    divide (state) {
      state.number = state.number / 2
    },
    multiplyBy (state, n) {
      state.number = state.number * n
    }
  }
})
```

2. Create the following methods in the component to add a call to commit the mutation by using `this.$store.commit`:

   ```
   // vuex-sfc/mutations/basic/src/app.js
   export default {
     methods: {
       multiply () {
         this.$store.commit('multiply')
       },
       multiplyBy (number) {
         this.$store.commit('multiply', number)
       },
       divide () {
         this.$store.commit('divide')
       }
     }
   }
   ```

Like getter methods, you also can use the `mapMutations` helper on mutation methods, so let's get to it in the next section.

The mapMutations helper

We can use the `mapMutations` helper to map the component methods to the mutation methods with object spread operators so that we can mix multiple `mapMutations` helpers in the `method` property. Let's see how we can do it with the following steps:

1. Import the `mapMutations` helper from Vuex and pass the mutations as an array to the `mapMutations` method with object spread operators, as follows:

   ```
   // vuex-sfc/mutations/mapmutations/src/app.vue
   import { mapMutations } from 'vuex'

   export default {
     computed: {
       number () {
         return this.$store.state.number
       }
     },
     methods: {
       ...mapMutations([
         'multiply',
         'multiplyBy',
         'divide'
       ]),
       ...mapMutations({
   ```

Adding a Vuex Store

```
      square: 'multiply'
    })
  }
}
```

2. Add the computed state property and the methods to `<template>`, as follows:

```
// vuex-sfc/mutations/mapmutations/src/app.vue
<p>{{ number }}</p>
<p>
  <button v-on:click="multiply">x 2</button>
  <button v-on:click="divide">/ 2</button>
  <button v-on:click="square">x 2 (square)</button>
  <button v-on:click="multiplyBy(10)">x 10</button>
</p>
```

You should see that the `number` state is reactively being multiplied or divided on your browser when you click on the preceding buttons. In this example, we have managed to change the state value through mutations, which is one of the rules in Vuex. Another rule is that we *must not* make asynchronous calls in mutations. In other words, *mutations must be synchronous* so that every mutation can be logged by the DevTool for debugging. If you want to make asynchronous calls, use actions, which we will walk you through in the next section. Let's get to it.

Actions

Actions are functions just like mutations, except they are not used for mutating the state but committing the mutations. Unlike mutations, actions *can be asynchronous*. We create action methods in the `actions` property in the store. An action method takes the context object as its first argument, your custom parameters as the second argument, and so forth. You can use `context.commit` to commit a mutation, `context.state` to access the state, and `context.getters` to access the getters. Let's add some action methods with the following steps:

1. Create a store with a `state` property and the action methods, as follows:

```
// vuex-sfc/actions/basic/src/entry.js
const store = new Vuex.Store({
  state: { number: 1 },
  mutations: { ... },
  actions: {
    multiplyAsync (context) {
      setTimeout(() => {
        context.commit('multiply')
```

[332]

```
      }, 1000)
    },
    multiply (context) {
      context.commit('multiply')
    },
    multiplyBy (context, n) {
      context.commit('multiplyBy', n)
    },
    divide (context) {
      context.commit('divide')
    }
  }
})
```

In this example, we used the same mutations from the previous section and created the action methods, one of them making an asynchronous action method to demonstrate why we need actions for asynchronous calls, even though they seem tedious at first.

Note that if you prefer, you can destructure `context` with an ES6 JavaScript destructuring assignment and import the `commit` property directly, as follows:

```
divide ({ commit }) {
  commit('divide')
}
```

2. Create a component and dispatch the preceding actions with `this.$store.commit`, as follows:

```
// vuex-sfc/actions/basic/src/app.js
export default {
  methods: {
    multiply () {
      this.$store.dispatch('multiply')
    },
    multiplyAsync () {
      this.$store.dispatch('multiplyAsync')
    },
    multiplyBy (number) {
      this.$store.dispatch('multiply', number)
    },
    divide () {
      this.$store.dispatch('divide')
    }
  }
}
```

Adding a Vuex Store

Like mutation and getter methods, you also can use the `mapActions` helper on action methods, so let's get to it in the next section.

The mapActions helper

We can use the `mapActions` helper to map the component methods to the action methods with object spread operators so that we can mix multiple `mapActions` helpers in the `method` property. Let's see how we can do so with the following steps:

1. Import the `mapActions` helper from Vuex and pass the mutations as an array to the `mapActions` method with object spread operators, as follows:

    ```
    // vuex-sfc/actions/mapactions/src/app.vue
    import { mapActions } from 'vuex'

    export default {
      methods: {
        ...mapActions([
          'multiply',
          'multiplyAsync',
          'multiplyBy',
          'divide'
        ]),
        ...mapActions({
          square: 'multiply'
        })
      }
    }
    ```

2. Add the computed state property and bind the methods to `<template>`, as follows:

    ```
    // vuex-sfc/mapactions/src/app.vue
    <p>{{ number }}</p>
    <p>
      <button v-on:click="multiply">x 2</button>
      <button v-on:click="square">x 2 (square)</button>
      <button v-on:click="multiplyAsync">x 2 (multiplyAsync)</button>
      <button v-on:click="divide">/ 2</button>
      <button v-on:click="multiplyBy(10)">x 10</button>
    </p>

    export default {
      computed: {
        number () {
          return this.$store.state.number
    ```

[334]

```
      }
    },
  }
```

You should see that the number state is reactively being multiplied or divided on your browser when you click on the preceding buttons. In this example, again, we have managed to change the state value by committing mutations through actions that can only be dispatched by using the store dispatch method. These are the enforced rules that we must comply with when applying a store to our app.

However, when the store and the app grow, we might want to separate the state, mutations, and actions into groups. In this case, we will need the last concept in Vuex–modules–which is covered in the next section we will walk you through. Let's get to it.

Modules

We can divide our store into modules to scale the app. Each module can have a state, mutations, actions, and getters, as follows:

```
const module1 = {
  state: { ... },
  mutations: { ... },
  actions: { ... },
  getters: { ... }
}

const module2 = {
  state: { ... },
  mutations: { ... },
  actions: { ... },
  getters: { ... }
}

const store = new Vuex.Store({
  modules: {
    a: module1,
    b: module2
  }
})
```

You can then access each module's state or other properties, as follows:

```
store.state.a
store.state.b
```

Adding a Vuex Store

When writing modules for your store, you should understand the local state, the root state, and the namespacing in the store's modules. Let's look at them in the following sections.

Understanding the local state and root state

The mutations and getters in each module will receive the module's local state as their first argument, as follows:

```
const module1 = {
  state: { number: 1 },
  mutations: {
    multiply (state) {
      console.log(state.number)
    }
  },

  getters: {
    getNumber (state) {
      console.log(state.number)
    }
  }
}
```

In this code, the state in the mutation and getter methods is the local module state, so you will get 1 for `console.log(state.number)`, while in each module's actions, you will get the context as the first argument, which you can use to access the local state and root state as `context.state` and `context.rootState`, as follows:

```
const module1 = {
  actions: {
    doSum ({ state, commit, rootState }) {
      //...
    }
  }
}
```

The root state is also available in each module's getters as the third argument, as follows:

```
const module1 = {
  getters: {
    getSum (state, getters, rootState) {
      //...
    }
  }
}
```

The local state from the modules and the root state from the store root can get mixed up and become confusing when we have multiple modules. This brings us to namespacing, which can make our modules more self-contained and less likely to conflict with each other. Let's get to it in the next section.

Understanding namespacing

By default, the `actions`, `mutations`, and `getters` properties in each module are registered under the global namespace, so the key or method name in each of these properties must be unique. In other words, a method name cannot be repeated in two different modules, as follows:

```
// entry.js
const module1 = {
  getters: {
    getNumber (state) {
      return state.number
    }
  }
}

const module2 = {
  getters: {
    getNumber (state) {
      return state.number
    }
  }
}
```

For the preceding example, you will see the following error due to using the same method name in the getters:

```
[vuex] duplicate getter key: getNumber
```

So, to avoid duplication, the method name must be explicitly named for each module, as follows:

```
getNumberModule1
getNumberModule2
```

Adding a Vuex Store

Then, you can access these methods in the child component and map them, as follows:

```
// app.js
import { mapGetters } from 'vuex'

export default {
  computed: {
    ...mapGetters({
      getNumberModule1: 'getNumberModule1',
      getNumberModule2: 'getNumberModule2'
    })
  }
}
```

These methods also can be written as follows if you don't want to use `mapGetters` as in the preceding code:

```
// app.js
export default {
  computed: {
    getNumberModule1 (state) {
      return this.$store.getters.getNumberModule1
    },
    getNumberModule2 (state) {
      return this.$store.getters.getNumberModule2
    }
  }
}
```

However, this pattern may look verbose as we have to write `this.$store.getters` or `this.$store.actions` repetitively for every method we create in the store. It is the same for accessing the state of each module, as follows:

```
// app.js
export default {
  computed: {
    ...mapState({
      numberModule1 (state) {
        return this.$store.state.a.number
      }
    }),
    ...mapState({
      numberModule2 (state) {
        return this.$store.state.b.number
      }
    })
  }
}
```

So, the solution for a situation like this is to use namespacing for each module by setting the `namespaced` key in each module to `true`, as follows:

```
const module1 = {
  namespaced: true
}
```

When the module is registered, all of its getters, actions, and mutations will be automatically namespaced based on the path the module is registered at. Take the following example:

```
// entry.js
const module1 = {
  namespaced: true
  state: { number:1 }
}

const module2 = {
  namespaced: true
  state: { number:2 }
}

const store = new Vuex.Store({
  modules: {
    a: module1,
    b: module2
  }
})
```

Now, you can access the state of each module with less code that is more easily readable, as follows:

```
// app.js
import { mapState } from 'vuex'

export default {
  computed: {
    ...mapState('a', {
      numberModule1 (state) {
        return state.number
      }
    }),
    ...mapState('b', {
      numberModule2 (state) {
        return state.number
      }
    })
```

Adding a Vuex Store

```
    }
}
```

For the preceding example code, you will get 1 for `numberModule1` and 2 for `numberModule2`. Besides, you can also eliminate the error of "duplicate getter keys" by using namespacing. So now, you can have more "abstract" names for methods, as follows:

```
// entry.js
const module1 = {
  getters: {
    getNumber (state) {
      return state.number
    }
  }
}

const module2 = {
  getters: {
    getNumber (state) {
      return state.number
    }
  }
}
```

Now, you can call and map these methods precisely with the namespaces that they are registered under, as follows:

```
// app.js
import { mapGetters } from 'vuex'

export default {
  computed: {
    ...mapGetters('a', {
      getNumberModule1: 'getNumber',
    }),
    ...mapGetters('b', {
      getNumberModule2: 'getNumber',
    })
  }
}
```

We have been writing the store in the root file, `entry.js`. Whether you are writing to a modular store or not, this root file will get bloated when the state properties and the methods in mutations, getters, and actions grow over time. So, this brings us to the next section, where you will learn how to separate and structure these methods and state properties in single files of their own. Let's get to it.

[340]

Structuring Vuex store modules

In a Vue app, as long as you comply with the enforced rules we went through in the previous sections, there are no strict restrictions on how you should structure your store. Depending on how complex your store is, there are two recommended structures in this book that you can use in the following sections. Let's get started.

Creating a simple store module structure

In this simple module structure, you can have a /store/ directory that contains a /modules/ directory that keeps all the modules in this folder. Here are the steps to create this simple project structure:

1. Create a /store/ directory with a /modules/ directory in it with the store modules, as follows:

```
// vuex-sfc/structuring-modules/basic/
├── index.html
├── entry.js
├── components
│   ├── app.vue
│   └── ...
└── store
    ├── index.js
    ├── actions.js
    ├── getters.js
    ├── mutations.js
    └── modules
        ├── module1.js
        └── module2.js
```

In this simple structure, /store/index.js is where we assemble modules from the /modules/ directory and export the store, along with the root's state, actions, getters, and mutations, as follows:

```
// store/index.js
import Vue from 'vue'
import actions from './actions'
import getters from './getters'
import mutations from './mutations'
import module1 from './modules/module1'
import module2 from './modules/module2'

import Vuex from 'vuex'
```

[341]

Adding a Vuex Store

```
Vue.use(Vuex)

export default new Vuex.Store({
  state: {
    number: 3
  },
  actions,
  getters,
  mutations,
  modules: {
    a: module1,
    b: module2
  }
})
```

2. Split the root's actions, mutations, and getters into separate files and assemble them in the root index file, as follows:

```
// store/mutations.js
export default {
  mutation1 (state) {
    //...
  },
  mutation2 (state, n) {
    //...
  }
}
```

3. Create modules in `.js` files with their states, actions, mutations, and getters just like you have learned in the previous sections, as follows:

```
// store/modules/module1.js
export default {
  namespaced: true,
  state: {
    number: 1
  },
  mutations: { ... },
  getters: { ... },
  actions: { ... }
}
```

If a module file gets too big, we can split the module's state, actions, mutations, and getters into separate files. This brings us to an advanced store module structure, which we will look at in the next section. Let's have a look.

Creating an advanced store module structure

In this advanced module structure, you can have a `/store/` directory that contains a `/modules/` directory that keeps all modules in subfolders of this folder. We can split a module's state, actions, mutations, and getters into separate files and then keep them in the module folder with the following steps:

1. Create a `/store/` directory that contains a `/modules/` directory for the store modules, as follows:

   ```
   // vuex-sfc/structuring-modules/advanced/
   ├── index.html
   ├── entry.js
   ├── components
   │   └── app.vue
   └── store
       ├── index.js
       ├── action.js
       └── ...
           ├── module1
           │   ├── index.js
           │   ├── state.js
           │   ├── mutations.js
           │   └── ...
           └── module2
               ├── index.js
               ├── state.js
               ├── mutations.js
               └── ...
   ```

   In this more complex project structure, `/store/module1/index.js` is where we assemble `module1`, while `/store/module2/index.js` is where we assemble `module2`, as follows:

   ```
   // store/module1/index.js
   import state from './state'
   import getters from './getters'
   import actions from './actions'
   import mutations from './mutations'

   export default {
     namespaced: true,
     state,
     getters,
     actions,
     mutations
   }
   ```

Adding a Vuex Store

We also can split a module state into a single file, as follows:

```
// store/module1/state.js
export default () => ({
  number: 1
})
```

2. Split the module's actions, mutations, and getters into separate files to assemble them in the preceding module index file, as follows:

```
// store/module1/mutations.js
export default {
  mutation1 (state) {
    //...
  },
  mutation2 (state, n) {
    //...
  }
}
```

3. Import the module index files to the store root where we assemble modules and export the store, as follows:

```
// store/index.js
import module1 from './module1'
import module2 from './module2'
```

4. Switch on strict mode to ensure that the store state is only mutated in the `mutations` property, as follows:

```
const store = new Vuex.Store({
  strict: true,
  ...
})
```

Using strict mode is good practice to remind us to mutate any state inside the `mutations` property. So, an error will be thrown during development whenever the store state is mutated outside of the `mutations` property. However, we should disable it for production because it can impair performance when there are a large number of state mutations in the store. So, we can dynamically turn it off with the build tools, as follows:

```
// store/index.js
const debug = process.env.NODE_ENV !== 'production'

const store = new Vuex.Store({
  strict: debug,
```

```
    ...
})
```

However, there is a caveat to using strict mode for handling forms in the store, which we will cover in the next section.

Handling forms in a Vuex store

When we use two-way data binding with a `v-model` in a Vue app, the data in the Vue instance is synchronized with the v-model input field. So, when you type anything into the input field, the data will be updated immediately. However, this will create a problem in a Vuex store because we *must not* mutate the store state (data) outside the `mutations` property. Let's take a look at a simple two-way data binding in a Vuex store:

```
// vuex-non-sfc/handling-forms/v-model.html
<input v-model="user.message" />

const store = new Vuex.Store({
  strict: true,
  state: {
    message: ''
  }
})

new Vue({
  el: 'demo',
  store: store,
  computed: {
    user () {
      return this.$store.state.user
    }
  }
})
```

For this example, you will see the following error message in your browser's debug tool when typing a message in the input field:

```
Error: [vuex] do not mutate vuex store state outside mutation handlers.
```

This is because the `v-model` attempts to mutate `message` in the store state directly when you type, so it results in an error in the strict mode. Let's see what options we have to resolve this in the following sections.

Using v-bind and v-on directives

In most cases, two-way binding is not always suitable. It makes more sense to use one-way binding and explicit data updates in Vuex by binding `<input>` with the `value` attribute on the `input` or `change` events. You can get this working easily with the following steps:

1. Create a method for mutating the state in the `mutations` property just as you learned in the previous sections:

   ```
   // vuex-sfc/form-handling/value-event/store/index.js
   export default new Vuex.Store({
     strict: true,
     state: {
       message: ''
     },
     mutations: {
       updateMessage (state, message) {
         state.message = message
       }
     }
   })
   ```

2. Bind the `<input>` element with the `value` attribute and the `input` event with the methods, as follows:

   ```
   // vuex-sfc/form-handling/value-event/components/app.vue
   <input v-bind:value="message" v-on:input="updateMessage" />

   import { mapState } from 'vuex'

   export default {
     computed: {
       ...mapState({
         message: state => state.message
       })
     },
     methods: {
       updateMessage (e) {
         this.$store.commit('updateMessage', e.target.value)
       }
     }
   }
   ```

In this solution, we use the `updateMessage` method in the child component to commit the mutation method, `updateMessage`, in the store and pass the value from the input event. By only committing the mutation *explicitly* like this, we are not going against the enforced rule in Vuex that we must comply with. So, adopting this solution means you cannot use the v-model to handle forms for the Vuex store. However, you can still use it if you are using the computed getter and setter from Vue itself. Let's look at this in the next section.

Using a two-way computed property

We can use Vue's built-in, two-way computed property with a setter for handling forms with a v-model with the help of the following steps:

1. Create a method for mutating the state in the `mutations` property, just as in the previous section.
2. Apply the `get` and `set` methods to the `message` key, as follows:

   ```
   // vuex-sfc/form-handling/getter-setter/components/app.vue
   <input v-model="message" />

   export default {
     computed: {
       message: {
         get () {
           return this.$store.state.message
         },
         set (value) {
           this.$store.commit('updateMessage', value)
         }
       }
     }
   }
   ```

However, this probably works well for simple computed properties. If you have a deep level object with more than 10 keys to update, you will need 10 sets of two-way computed properties (the getter and setter). The code will eventually get more repetitive and verbose than the event-based solution.

Well done! You have managed to get through the foundation and concept of a Vuex store. You have learned how to use a store in a Vue app. Now, it is time to move on to applying a store in Nuxt. So, let's get to it in the next section.

Adding a Vuex Store

> If you want to find out more information about Vuex, please visit https://vuex.vuejs.org/.

Using a Vuex store in Nuxt

In Nuxt, Vuex is already installed for you. You only need to be sure that the /store/ directory is present in the project root. If you are installing your Nuxt project using create-nuxt-app, this directory is autogenerated for you during project installation. In Nuxt, you can create your store in two different modes:

- Module
- Classic (deprecated)

Since the classic mode is deprecated, we will only focus on the module mode in this book. So, let's get started in the following section.

> You can find the source code for all of the following Nuxt examples in /chapter-10/nuxt-universal/ in our GitHub repository.

Using module mode

Unlike Vue apps, in Nuxt, the namespaced key is set to true by default for each module, as well as the root module. Also, in Nuxt, you do not need to assemble modules in the store root; you just need to export the state *as a function*, and the mutations, getters, and actions *as objects* in the root and module files. Let's get things going with the following steps:

1. Create a store root, as follows:

    ```js
    // store/index.js
    export const state = () => ({
      number: 3
    })

    export const mutations = {
      mutation1 (state) { ... }
    }
    ```

[348]

```
export const getters = {
  getter1 (state, getter) { ... }
}

export const actions = {
  action1 ({ state, commit }) { ... }
}
```

In Nuxt, Vuex's strict mode is set to `true` by default during development and turned off automatically in production mode, but you can disable that during development, as follows:

```
// store/index.js
export const strict = false
```

2. Create a module, as follows:

```
// store/module1.js
export const state = () => ({
  number: 1
})

export const mutations = {
  mutation1 (state) { ... }
}

export const getters = {
  getter1 (state, getter, rootState) { ... }
}

export const actions = {
  action1 ({ state, commit, rootState }) { ... }
}
```

Then, just as we did it *manually* in a Vue app in the previous section, the store will be autogenerated, as follows:

```
new Vuex.Store({
  state: () => ({
    number: 3
  }),
  mutations: {
    mutation1 (state) { ... }
  },
  getters: {
    getter1 (state, getter) { ... }
  },
  actions: {
```

Adding a Vuex Store

```
      action1 ({ state, commit }) { ... }
    },
    modules: {
      module1: {
        namespaced: true,
        state: () => ({
          number: 1
        }),
        mutations: {
          mutation1 (state) { ... }
        }
        ...
      }
    }
  })
```

3. Map all the store states, getters, mutations, and actions in the `<script>` block of any page, as follows:

```
// pages/index.vue
import { mapState, mapGetters, mapActions } from 'vuex'

export default {
  computed: {
    ...mapState({
      numberRoot: state => state.number,
    }),
    ...mapState('module1', {
      numberModule1: state => state.number,
    }),
    ...mapGetters({
      getNumberRoot: 'getter1'
    }),
    ...mapGetters('module1', {
      getNumberModule1: 'getter1'
    })
  },
  methods: {
    ...mapActions({
      doNumberRoot:'action1'
    }),
    ...mapActions('module1', {
      doNumberModule1:'action1'
    })
  }
}
```

4. Display the computed properties with methods to commit mutations in the `<template>` block, as follows:

```
// pages/index.vue
<p>{{ numberRoot }}, {{ getNumberRoot }}</p>
<button v-on:click="doNumberRoot">x 2 (root)</button>

<p>{{ numberModule1 }}, {{ getNumberModule1 }}</p>
<button v-on:click="doNumberModule1">x 2 (module1)</button>
```

You should see the following initial results on your screen, and they will be mutated when you click on the preceding buttons that are displayed on the screen from the template:

```
3, 3
1, 1
```

As we mentioned earlier, you do not need to assemble modules in the store root in Nuxt because they are "assembled" for you by Nuxt, only if you use the following structure:

```
// chapter-10/nuxt-universal/module-mode/
└── store
    ├── index.js
    ├── module1.js
    ├── module2.js
    └── ...
```

But if you were to use the structure that we used to assemble modules manually in the store root as we did for a Vue app, as follows:

```
// chapter-10/vuex-sfc/structuring-modules/basic/
└── store
    ├── index.js
    ├── ...
    └── modules
        ├── module1.js
        └── module2.js
```

You will get the following errors in the Nuxt app:

```
ERROR [vuex] module namespace not found in mapState(): module1/
ERROR [vuex] module namespace not found in mapGetters(): module1/
```

To fix these errors, you need to tell Nuxt *explicitly* where these modules are kept:

```
export default {
  computed: {
    ...mapState('modules/module1', {
```

[351]

Adding a Vuex Store

```
      numberModule1: state => state.number,
    }),
    ...mapGetters('modules/module1', {
      getNumberModule1: 'getter1'
    })
  },
  methods: {
    ...mapActions('modules/module1', {
      doNumberModule1:'action1'
    })
  }
}
```

Just as with Vuex in Vue apps, we can split the state, actions, mutations, and getters into separate files in a Nuxt app, too. Let's see how we can do that and what the differences with Nuxt are in the next section.

Using module files

We can split big files in our modules into separate files – `state.js`, `actions.js`, `mutations.js`, and `getters.js` – for the store root and each module. So, let's do so with the following steps:

1. Create separate files of the state, actions, mutations, and getters for the store root, as follows:

    ```
    // store/state.js
    export default () => ({
      number: 3
    })

    // store/mutations.js
    export default {
      mutation1 (state) { ... }
    }
    ```

2. Create separate files of the state, actions, mutations, and getters for the module, as follows:

    ```
    // store/module1/state.js
    export default () => ({
      number: 1
    })

    // store/module1/mutations.js
    ```

```
export default {
  mutation1 (state) { ... }
}
```

Again, in Nuxt, we do not need to assemble these separate files with index.js as we do in a Vue app. Nuxt will do this for us as long as we use the following structure:

```
// chapter-10/nuxt-universal/module-files/
└── store
    ├── state.js
    ├── action.js
    └── ...
        ├── module1
        │   ├── state.js
        │   ├── mutations.js
        │   └── ...
        └── module2
            ├── state.js
            ├── mutations.js
            └── ...
```

We can compare this to the following structure that we used for the Vue app, where we needed an index.js file for the store root and each module to assemble the state, actions, mutations, and getters from the separate files:

```
// chapter-10/vuex-sfc/structuring-modules/advanced/
└── store
    ├── index.js
    ├── action.js
    └── ...
        ├── module1
        │   ├── index.js
        │   ├── state.js
        │   ├── mutations.js
        │   └── ...
        └── module2
            ├── index.js
            ├── state.js
            ├── mutations.js
            └── ...
```

So, the store comes out of the box in Nuxt and it saves you some lines of code for assembling files and registering modules. Sweet, isn't it? Now, let's venture a bit further to see how we can *fill the store state dynamically* in Nuxt with the fetch method in the next section.

Using the fetch method

We can use the `fetch` method to fill the store state before a page is rendered. It works the same as the `asyncData` method, which we have already covered – it is called each time before a component is loaded. It is called on the server side once and then on the client side when navigating to other routes. Just like `asyncData`, we can use `async/await` with the `fetch` method for asynchronous data. It is called after the component is created, so we can access the component instance through `this` in the `fetch` method. So, we can access the store through `this.$nuxt.context.store`. Let's create a simple Nuxt app using this method with the following steps:

1. Request the list of users from a remote API asynchronously with the `fetch` method in any page, as follows:

   ```
   // pages/index.vue
   import axios from 'axios'

   export default {
     async fetch () {
       const { store } = this.$nuxt.context
       await store.dispatch('users/getUsers')
     }
   }
   ```

2. Create a user module with the state, mutations, and actions, as follows:

   ```
   // store/users/state.js
   export default () => ({
     list: {}
   })

   // store/users/mutations.js
   export default {
     setUsers (state, data) {
       state.list = data
     },
     removeUser (state, id) {
       let found = state.list.find(todo => todo.id === id)
       state.list.splice(state.list.indexOf(found), 1)
     }
   }

   // store/users/actions.js
   export default {
     setUsers ({ commit }, data) {
       commit('setUsers', data)
   ```

```
    },
    removeUser ({ commit }, id) {
      commit('removeUser', id)
    }
  }
}
```

The `setUsers` methods in the mutations and actions are used to set the list of users to the state, while the `removeUser` methods are used to remove users from the state one at a time.

3. Map the methods from the state and actions to the page, as follows:

```
// pages/index.vue
import { mapState, mapActions } from 'vuex'

export default {
  computed: {
    ...mapState ('users', {
      users (state) {
        return state.list
      }
    })
  },
  methods: {
    ...mapActions('users', {
      removeUser: 'removeUser'
    })
  }
}
```

4. Loop and display the list of users in the `<template>` block, as follows:

```
// pages/index.vue
<li v-for="(user, index) in users" v-bind:key="user.id">
  {{ user.name }}
  <button class="button" v-
on:click="removeUser(user.id)">Remove</button>
</li>
```

You should see the list of users on the screen when you load the app in a browser, and you can click to remove a user with the **Remove** button. We can also use `async/await` in the actions to fetch the remote data, as follows:

```
// store/users/actions.js
import axios from 'axios'

export const actions = {
  async getUsers ({ commit }) {
```

Adding a Vuex Store

```
    const { data } = await
axios.get('https://jsonplaceholder.typicode.com/users')
    commit('setUsers', data)
  }
}
```

Then, we can just dispatch the `getUsers` action, as follows:

```
// pages/index.vue
export default {
  async fetch () {
    const { store } = this.$nuxt.context
    await store.dispatch('users/getUsers')
  }
}
```

Besides fetching and populating the state with the `fetch` method in Nuxt, we also can use the `nuxtServerInit` action, which is only available in Nuxt. Let's move on to look at it in the next section.

Using the nuxtServerInit action

Unlike the `asyncData` method, which is only available in page-level components, and the `fetch` method, which is available in all Vue components (including page-level components), the `nuxtServerInit` action is a reserved store action method available only in the Nuxt store if it is defined. It only can be defined in the `index.js` file in the store root and will be called on the server side only, before the Nuxt app is initiated. Unlike the `asyncData` and `fetch` methods, which are called on the server side and then the client side on the subsequent routes, the `nuxtServerInit` action method is only called on the server side *once*, unless you refresh *any page* of the app in the browser. Also, unlike the `asyncData` method, which gets the Nuxt context object as its first argument, the `nuxtServerInit` action method gets it as its second argument. The first argument it receives is the store context object. Let's put these context objects into the following table:

First argument	Second argument
• dispatch • commit • getters • state • rootGetters • rootState	• isStatic • isDev • isHMR • app • req • res • ...

So, the `nuxtServerInit` action method is very useful when we want to get the data from the server side from any page in our app and then populate the store state with the server data–for example, the authenticated user data that we store in the session on the server side when a user has logged into our app. This session data can be stored as `req.session.authUser` in Express or `ctx.session.authUser` in Koa. Then, we can pass `ctx.session` to `nuxtServerInit` through the `req` object.

Let's create a simple user login app with this method action and use Koa as the server-side API, which you learned about in Chapter 8, *Adding a Server-Side Framework*. We just need a bit of modification on the server side before we can inject any data into the session and create a store with the `nuxtServerIni` action method, which we can do with the following steps:

1. Install the session package, `koa-session`, using npm:

    ```
    $ npm install koa-session
    ```

2. Import and register the session package as a middleware, as follows:

    ```
    // server/middlewares.js
    import session from 'koa-session'

    app.keys = ['some secret hurr']
    app.use(session(app))
    ```

3. Create two routes on the server side, as follows:

    ```
    // server/routes.js
    router.post('/login', async (ctx, next) => {
      let request = ctx.request.body || {}
      if (request.username === 'demo' && request.password === 'demo') {
        ctx.session.authUser = { username: 'demo' }
        ctx.body = { username: 'demo' }
      } else {
        ctx.throw(401)
      }
    })

    router.post('/logout', async (ctx, next) => {
      delete ctx.session.authUser
      ctx.body = { ok: true }
    })
    ```

    In the preceding code, we use the `/login` route to inject the authenticated user data, `authUser`, into the Koa context, `ctx`, with the session, while `/logout` is used to unset the authenticated data.

Adding a Vuex Store

4. Create the store state with an `authUser` key to hold the authenticated data:

   ```
   // store/state.js
   export default () => ({
     authUser: null
   })
   ```

5. Create a mutation method to set the data to the `authUser` key in the preceding state:

   ```
   // store/mutations.js
   export default {
     setUser (state, data) {
       state.authUser = data
     }
   }
   ```

6. Create an `index.js` file in the store root with the following actions:

   ```
   // store/index.js
   export const actions = {
     nuxtServerInit({ commit }, { req }) {
       if (req.ctx.session && req.ctx.session.authUser) {
         commit('setUser', req.ctx.session.authUser)
       }
     },
     async login({ commit }, { username, password }) {
       const { data } = await axios.post('/api/login', { username,
         password })
       commit('setUser', data.data)
     },
     async logout({ commit }) {
       await axios.post('/api/logout')
       commit('setUser', null)
     }
   }
   ```

   In the preceding code, the `nuxtServerInit` action method is used to access the session data from the server and populate the store state by committing the `setUser` mutation method. The `login` and `logout` action methods are used to authenticate the user login credentials and unset them. Note that the session data is stored inside `req.ctx` as this book is using Koa as the server API. If you are using Express, use the following code:

   ```
   actions: {
     nuxtServerInit ({ commit }, { req }) {
       if (req.session.user) {
   ```

[358]

```
        commit('user', req.session.user)
      }
    }
  }
```

Just like the `asyncData` and `fetch` methods, the `nuxtServerInit` action method can be asynchronous, too. You just have to return a Promise, or use an `async/await` statement for the Nuxt server to wait for the action to be completed asynchronously, as follows:

```
actions: {
  async nuxtServerInit({ commit }) {
    await commit('setUser', req.ctx.session.authUser)
  }
}
```

7. Create a form to use the store's action methods, as follows:

```
// pages/index.vue
<form v-on:submit.prevent="login">
  <input v-model="username" type="text" name="username" />
  <input v-model="password" type="password" name="password" />
  <button class="button" type="submit">Login</button>
</form>

export default {
  data() {
    return {
      username: '',
      password: ''
    }
  },
  methods: {
    async login() {
      await this.$store.dispatch('login', {
        username: this.username,
        password: this.password
      })
    },
    async logout() {
      await this.$store.dispatch('logout')
    }
  }
}
```

Adding a Vuex Store

> We have simplified the preceding code and the code in *step 6* to fit this page, but you can find the complete versions for them from our GitHub repository in `/chapter-10/nuxt-universal/nuxtServerInit/`.

Well done! You have finally made it through one of the exciting features of Nuxt and Vue–Vuex stores. This was a long chapter, but it is a very important one as we will need to come back to Vuex and use it often in the upcoming chapters. Now, let's summarize what you have learned in this chapter.

Summary

We have come a long way. In this chapter, you learned about the architecture, core concepts, module structures, and form handling in Vuex stores. At this point, you should know that a Vuex store simply relates to state (or data) centralization and management with some enforced rules that you must comply with. So, for any state property that you may have in your store, the correct way of accessing it is by computing it in the `computed` property in your components. If you want to change the value of the state property, you must mutate it through mutations, which must be synchronous. If you want to make asynchronous calls to mutate the state, then you must use actions to commit the mutations by dispatching the actions in your components.

You have also learned that creating a store in Nuxt apps is easier and simpler than in Vue apps because Vuex is preinstalled on Nuxt by default. Also, in Nuxt, you do not need to assemble modules and all their methods manually because they are done for you by default. Additionally, in Nuxt, you can use the `fetch` and `nuxtServerInit` methods to populate the store state with a server-side API before rendering the page components and initiating your Nuxt app. Lastly, you have managed to create a simple user login app using a Vuex store with the `nuxtServerInit` action method, and this has paved the way for creating user logins and API authentication in the upcoming chapters.

In the next chapter, we will look at middleware in Nuxt – specifically, route middleware and server middleware. You will learn to differentiate between these two types of Nuxt middleware. You will create some route middleware with navigation guards in Vue apps, before making middleware in Nuxt apps. Then, you will write some Nuxt server middleware in the `serverMiddleware` configuration option as an alternative server API to the server-side API that you learned to create in `Chapter 8`, *Adding a Server-Side Framework*. Last but not least, you will learn how to use Vue CLI to create Vue apps as opposed to the Vue apps we have been making with the custom webpack configuration. So, let's get to it.

Section 4: Middleware and Security

In this section, we will learn about middleware – more specifically, route middleware and server middleware. We will then learn how to add authentication with middleware to create a user login session.

This section comprises the following chapters:

- `Chapter 11`, *Writing Route Middleware and Server Middleware*
- `Chapter 12`, *Creating User Logins and API Authentication*

11 Writing Route Middlewares and Server Middlewares

Remember when you created a middleware on the server side using Koa in Chapter 8, *Adding a Server-Side Framework*? Middlewares are both useful and powerful, as you will have noted in cascading with Koa apps, where you can predict and control the flow of your entire app sequentially. So, what about in Nuxt? Well, there are two types of middleware we should explore in Nuxt: route middleware and server middleware. In this chapter, you will learn how to differentiate between them and create some basic middlewares before moving on to the next chapter on authentication, where middlewares are very much needed. We will also use middlewares in the chapters after the next one. So, in this chapter, just like in many of the previous chapters, you will create some middlewares in a Vue app with navigation guards so that you can grasp the middleware mechanism in the Vue/Nuxt system before creating the route middlewares and server middlewares in a Nuxt app.

In this chapter, we will cover the following topics:

- Writing middlewares with Vue Router
- Introducing Vue CLI
- Writing route middlewares in Nuxt
- Writing Nuxt server middlewares

Writing middlewares with Vue Router

Before learning how middleware works in a Nuxt app, we should understand how it works in a standard Vue app. Additionally, before creating middlewares in the Vue app, let's first understand what they are.

What is middleware?

Put simply, a middleware is a software layer situated between two or more pieces of software. This is an old concept in software development. Middleware is a term that has been in use since 1968. It gained popularity in the 1980s as a solution to the problem of how to link newer apps to older legacy systems. There are many definitions for it, such as (from *Google Dictionary*) "[middleware is a] software that acts as a bridge between an operating system or database and apps, especially on a network."

In the web development world, server-side software or apps, such as Koa and Express, take in a request and output a response. The middlewares are programs or functions that are executed in the middle after the incoming request, and they produce an output that could either be the final output or be used by the next middleware until the cycle is completed. This also means that we can have **more** than one middleware, and they will execute in the order they are declared:

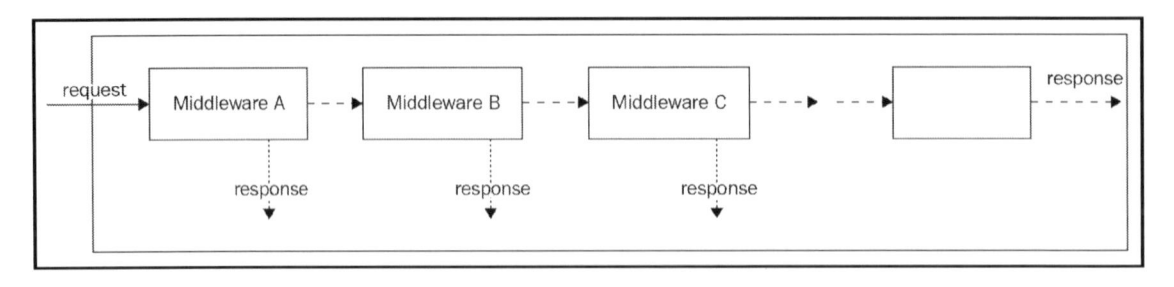

Furthermore, middleware is not only limited to server-side technologies. It is also very common on the client side when you have routing in your app. Vue Router by Vue.js is a good example of using this middleware concept. We have studied and used Vue Router already in `Chapter 4`, *Adding Views, Routes, and Transitions*, to create the router for our Vue apps. Now, let's dive deeper into the advanced usage of Vue Router – navigation guards.

Installing Vue Router

If you have followed the chapters of this book from the beginning, you should already know how to install Vue Router from `Chapter 4`, *Adding Views, Routes, and Transitions*. However, here is a quick recap.

Follow these steps to download Vue Router directly:

1. Click on the following link and download the source code:

    https://unpkg.com/vue-router/dist/vue-router.js

2. Include the router after Vue so that it can be installed automatically by itself:

    ```
    <script src="/path/to/vue.js"></script>
    <script src="/path/to/vue-router.js"></script>
    ```

Alternatively, you can install Vue Router via npm:

1. Install the router to your project using npm:

    ```
    $ npm i vue-router
    ```

2. Register the router explicitly using the `use` method:

    ```
    import Vue from 'vue'
    import VueRouter from 'vue-router'

    Vue.use(VueRouter)
    ```

3. Once you have the router in place, you can start creating middlewares using the navigation guards that come with Vue Router:

    ```
    const router = new VueRouter({ ... })
    router.beforeEach((to, from, next) => {
      // ...
    })
    ```

The `beforeEach` navigation guard in the preceding example is a global navigation guard that is called when navigating to any route. Apart from global guards, there are navigation guards for specific routes too, and that is what we are going to explore in more detail in the next section. So, let's get going!

> If you want to find out more information about Vue Router, please visit https://router.vuejs.org/.

Using navigation guards

Navigation guards are used to guard the navigation in your app. These guards allow us to call functions before entering, updating, and leaving a route. When certain conditions are not met, they can either redirect or cancel the route. There are several ways in which to hook into the route navigation process: globally, per-route, or in-component. Let's explore the global guard in the next section.

> Note that you can find all of the following examples in /chapter-11/vue/non-sfc/ from our GitHub repository.

Creating global guards

There are two global guards offered by Vue Router – global before guards and global after guards. Let's learn how to use them before applying them to our app:

- **Global before guards**: Global before guards are called when a route is being entered. They are called in a specific order and can be asynchronous. The navigation is always in wait until all the guards are resolved. We can register these guards using the `beforeEach` method from Vue Router, as follows:

  ```
  const router = new VueRouter({ ... })
  router.beforeEach((to, from, next) => { ... })
  ```

- **Global after guards**: Global after guards are called after a route has been entered. Unlike global before guards, global after guards do not have the `next` function, and so they do not affect navigation. We can register these guards using the `afterEach` method from Vue Router, as follows:

  ```
  const router = new VueRouter({ ... })
  router.afterEach((to, from) => { ... })
  ```

Let's create a Vue app with a simple HTML page and use these guards in the following steps:

1. Create two routes with the `<router-link>` elements, as follows:

   ```
   <div id="app">
     <p>
       <router-link to="/page1">Page 1</router-link>
       <router-link to="/page2">Page 2</router-link>
     </p>
     <router-view></router-view>
   </div>
   ```

2. Define the components (`Page1` and `Page2`) for the routes, and pass them to the router instance in the `<script>` block:

   ```
   const Page1 = { template: '<div>Page 1</div>' }
   const Page2 = { template: '<div>Page 2</div>' }

   const routes = [
     { path: '/page1', component: Page1 },
     { path: '/page2', component: Page2 }
   ]

   const router = new VueRouter({
     routes
   })
   ```

3. Declare the global before guard and the global after guard **after** the route instance, as follows:

   ```
   router.beforeEach((to, from, next) => {
     console.log('global before hook')
     next()
   })

   router.afterEach((to, from,) => {
     console.log('global after hook')
   })
   ```

4. Mount the root instance after the guards and run our app:

   ```
   const app = new Vue({
     router
   }).$mount('#app')
   ```

5. Run the app in your browser, and you should get the following logs in the browser console when you switch between the routes:

```
global before hook
global after hook
```

Global guards can be useful when you want to apply something common to all routes. However, sometimes, we need something specific for certain routes only. For this, you should use per-route guards. Let's learn how to deploy them in the next section.

Creating per-route guards

We can create per-route guards by using `beforeEnter` as a method or property directly on the configuration object of a route. For example, take a look at the following:

```
beforeEnter: (to, from, next) => { ... }
// or:
beforeEnter (to, from, next) { ... }
```

Let's duplicate our previous Vue app and change the configuration of the routes to use these per-route guards, as follows:

```
const routes = [
  {
    path: '/page1',
    component: Page1,
    beforeEnter: (to, from, next) => {
      console.log('before entering page 1')
      next()
    }
  },
  {
    path: '/page2',
    component: Page2,
    beforeEnter (to, from, next) {
      console.log('before entering page 2')
      next()
    }
  }
]
```

You should get the `before entering page 1` log on your browser's console when you navigate to /page1 and the `before entering page 2` log when you are on /page2. So, since we can apply a guard to the route of a page, what about applying guards to the route component itself? The answer is yes, we can. Let's move on to the next section and learn how to use in-component guards to guard a specific component.

Creating in-component guards

We can use the following methods individually or together inside a route component to create the navigation guards for a specific component.

The beforeRouteEnter guard:

Just like in the global before guard and the `beforeEnter` per-route guard, the `beforeRouteEnter` guard is called before the route renders the component, but it is applied to the component itself. We can register this type of guard using the `beforeRouteEnter` method, as follows:

```
beforeRouteEnter (to, from, next) { ... }
```

Because it is called before the component instance, it does not have access to the Vue component via the `this` keyword. But this can be resolved by passing a callback of the Vue component to the `next` argument:

```
beforeRouteEnter (to, from, next) {
  next(vueComponent => { ... })
}
```

The beforeRouteLeave guard:

In comparison, the `beforeRouteLeave` guard is called when the component that is rendered by the route is about to navigate away from it. Since it is called when the Vue component is rendered, it can access the Vue component via the `this` keyword. We can register this type of guard using the `beforeRouteLeave` method, as follows:

```
beforeRouteLeave (to, from, next) { ... }
```

Usually, this type of guard is best used to prevent the user from leaving the route accidentally. So, the navigation can be canceled by calling `next(false)`:

```
beforeRouteLeave (to, from, next) {
  const confirmed = window.confirm('Are you sure you want to leave?')
  if (confirmed) {
    next()
```

Writing Route Middlewares and Server Middlewares

```
    } else {
      next(false)
    }
  }
```

The beforeRouteUpdate guard:

The `beforeRouteUpdate` guard is called when the component that is rendered by the route has changed but the component is reused in the new route; for example, if you have subroute components that use the same route component: `/page1/foo` and `/page1/bar`. So, navigating from `/page1/foo` to `/page1/bar` will trigger this method. And since it is called when the component is rendered, it has access to the Vue component via the `this` keyword. We can register this type of guard using the `beforeRouteUpdate` method:

```
beforeRouteUpdate (to, from, next) { ... }
```

Note that the `beforeRouteEnter` method is the only guard that supports a callback in the `next` method. The Vue component is already available before calling the `beforeRouteUpdate` and `beforeRouteLeave` methods. Therefore, using a callback in the `next` method in either of them is unsupported because it is unnecessary. So, just use the `this` keyword if you want to access the Vue component:

```
beforeRouteUpdate (to, from, next) {
  this.name = to.params.name
  next()
}
```

Now, let's create a Vue app with a simple HTML page using the following guards:

1. Create a page component with the `beforeRouteEnter`, `beforeRouteUpdate`, and `beforeRouteLeave` methods all together, as follows:

```
const Page1 = {
  template: '<div>Page 1 {{ $route.params.slug }}</div>',
  beforeRouteEnter (to, from, next) {
    console.log('before entering page 1')
    next(vueComponent => {
      console.log('before entering page 1: ',
        vueComponent.$route.path)
    })
  },
  beforeRouteUpdate (to, from, next) {
    console.log('before updating page 1: ', this.$route.path)
    next()
  },
```

```
    beforeRouteLeave (to, from, next) {
      console.log('before leaving page 1: ', this.$route.path)
      next()
    }
  }
```

2. Create another page component with just the `beforeRouteEnter` and `beforeRouteLeave` methods, as follows:

```
  const Page2 = {
    template: '<div>Page 2</div>',
    beforeRouteEnter (to, from, next) {
      console.log('before entering page 2')
      next(vueComponent => {
        console.log('before entering page 2: ',
          vueComponent.$route.path)
      })
    },
    beforeRouteLeave (to, from, next) {
      console.log('before leaving page 2: ', this.$route.path)
      next()
    }
  }
```

3. Define the main routes and the subroute before initiating the router instance, as follows:

```
  const routes = [
    {
      path: '/page1',
      component: Page1,
      children: [
        {
          path: ':slug'
        }
      ]
    },
    {
      path: '/page2',
      component: Page2
    }
  ]
```

Writing Route Middlewares and Server Middlewares

4. Create the navigation links with the `<router-link>` Vue component, as follows:

```
<div id="app">
  <ul>
    <li><router-link to="/">Home</router-link></li>
    <li><router-link to="/page1">Page 1</router-link></li>
    <li><router-link to="/page1/foo">Page 1: foo</router-link></li>
    <li><router-link to="/page1/bar">Page 1: bar</router-link></li>
    <li><router-link to="/page2">Page 2</router-link></li>
  </ul>
  <router-view></router-view>
</div>
```

5. Run the app in your browser, and you should get the following logs in the browser console when switching between the routes:

- When navigating from `/` to `/page1`, you should see the following:

```
before entering page 1
before entering page 1: /page1
```

- When navigating from `/page1` to `/page2`, you should see the following:

```
before leaving page 1: /page1
before entering page 2
before entering page 2: /page2
```

- When navigating from `/page2` to `/page1/foo`, you should see the following:

```
before leaving page 2: /page2
before entering page 1
before entering page 1: /page1/foo
```

- When navigating from `/page1/foo` to `/page1/bar`, you should see the following:

```
before updating page 1: /page1/foo
```

- When navigating from `/page1/bar` to `/`, you should see the following:

```
before leaving page 1: /page1/bar
```

As you can see, the navigation guards in Vue are simply JavaScript functions that allow us to create middlewares with some default arguments. Now, let's take a closer look at the arguments (`to`, `from`, and `next`) that each guard method gets in the next section.

Understanding the navigation guard arguments: to, from, and next

You have already seen these arguments in the navigation guards used in the previous sections, but we haven't walked you through them yet. All guards, except the `afterEach` global guard, use these three arguments: `to`, `from`, and `next`.

The `to` argument:

This argument is the route object that you navigate to (hence, it is called the *to* argument). This object holds the parsed information of the URL and the route:

name	query
meta	params
path	fullPath
hash	matched

If you want to know more about each of these object properties, please visit https://router.vuejs.org/api/the-route-object.

The `from` argument:

This argument is the current route object that you navigate from. Again, this object holds the parsed information of the URL and the route:

name	query
meta	params
path	fullPath
hash	matched

The `next` argument:

This argument is a function you must call to move on to the next guard (middleware) in the queue. If you want to abort the current navigation, you can pass a `false` Boolean to this function:

```
next(false)
```

Writing Route Middlewares and Server Middlewares

If you want to redirect to a different location, you can use the following line:

```
next('/')
// or
next({ path: '/' })
```

If you want to abort the navigation with an instance of `Error`, you can use the following lines:

```
const error = new Error('An error occurred!')
next(error)
```

Then, you can catch the error from the root:

```
router.onError(err
  => { ... })
```

Now, let's create a Vue app with a simple HTML page and experiment with the next function in the following steps:

1. Create the following page components with the `beforeRouteEnter` method, as follows:

    ```
    const Page1 = {
      template: '<div>Page 1</div>',
      beforeRouteEnter (to, from, next) {
        const error = new Error('An error occurred!')
        error.statusCode = 500
        console.log('before entering page 1')
        next(error)
      }
    }

     const Page2 = {
      template: '<div>Page 2</div>',
      beforeRouteEnter (to, from, next) {
        console.log('before entering page 2')
        next({ path: '/' })
      }
    }
    ```

    In the preceding code, we pass the `Error` instance to the next function for `Page1` while redirecting the route to the home page for `Page2`.

2. Define the routes before initiating the router instance, as follows:

```
const routes = [
  {
    path: '/page1',
    component: Page1
  },
  {
    path: '/page2',
    component: Page2
  }
]
```

3. Create an instance of the router and *listen* to the error using the `onError` method:

```
const router = new VueRouter({
  routes
})

router.onError(err => {
  console.error('Handling this error: ', err.message)
  console.log(err.statusCode)
})
```

4. Create the following navigation links with the `<router-link>` Vue component:

```
<div id="app">
  <ul>
    <li><router-link to="/">Home</router-link></li>
    <li><router-link to="/page1">Page 1</router-link></li>
    <li><router-link to="/page2">Page 2</router-link></li>
  </ul>
  <router-view></router-view>
</div>
```

5. Run the app in your browser, and you should get the following logs in the browser console when switching between the routes:

- When navigating from / to /page1, you should see the following:

  ```
  before entering page 1
  Handling this error: An error occurred!
  500
  ```

- When navigating from /page1 to /page2, you should see the following:

  ```
  before entering page 2
  ```

You will also notice that you are directed to / when navigating from /page1 to /page2 because of this line of code: `next({ path: '/' })`.

So far, we have created middlewares in a single HTML page. However, in a real-life project, we should try creating them with the Vue Single-File Component (SFC) that you learned about in previous chapters. So, in the next section, you will learn to create middlewares in the Vue SFC with Vue CLI, as opposed to the custom webpack build process that you have learned so far. So, let's get to it.

Introducing Vue CLI

We have used webpack to create our custom Vue SFC apps in Chapter 5, *Adding Vue Components*. As a developer, it is useful to know how to peer into the mechanism of a complex thing, and we must also understand how to use common and standard patterns to work with others collaboratively. Therefore, these days, we are inclined to use frameworks. Vue CLI is the standard tooling for Vue app development. It does what our webpack custom tool does and more. If you don't want to create your own Vue SFC developing tool, Vue CLI is a great choice. It supports Babel, ESLint, TypeScript, PostCSS, PWA, unit testing, and end-to-end testing out of the box. To read more about Vue CLI, please visit https://cli.vuejs.org/.

Installing Vue CLI

It is very easy to get started with Vue CLI. Perform these steps:

1. Use npm to install it globally:

    ```
    $ npm i -g @vue/cli
    ```

2. Create a project when you want to:

    ```
    $ vue create my-project
    ```

3. You will be prompted to pick a preset – `default` or `manually select features`, as follows:

    ```
    Vue CLI v4.4.6
    ? Please pick a preset: (Use arrow keys)
    > default (babel, eslint)
      Manually select features
    ```

4. Choose the `default` preset as we can install what we need manually later on. You should see something similar to the last part of the following output in your terminal when the installation is complete:

   ```
   Successfully created project my-project.
   Get started with the following commands:

   $ cd my-project
   $ npm run serve
   ```

5. Change your directory to `my-project` and start the development process:

   ```
   $ npm run serve
   ```

   You should get something similar to this:

   ```
   DONE Compiled successfully in 3469ms

   App running at:
   - Local:   http://localhost:8080/
   - Network: http://199.188.0.44:8080/

   Note that the development build is not optimized.
   To create a production build, run npm run build.
   ```

In the following sections, we are going to transform the navigation guards that you learned about in the previous sections into proper middlewares using Vue CLI. That means we will separate all of the hooks and guards into separate .js files and keep them in a common folder called `middlewares`. However, before we do that, we should first understand the project directory structure that Vue CLI generates for us and then add our own required directories. Let's get to it.

Understanding Vue CLI's project structure

After creating the project with Vue CLI, if you take a look inside the project directory, you'll see that it provides us with a barebones structure, as follows:

```
├── package.json
├── babel.config.js
├── README.md
├── public
│   ├── index.html
│   └── favicon.ico
└── src
```

[377]

Writing Route Middlewares and Server Middlewares

```
├── App.vue
├── main.js
├── router.js
├── components
│   └── HelloWorld.vue
└── assets
    └── logo.png
```

From this basic structure, we can build and grow our app. So, let's develop our app in the /src/ directory and add the following directories to it using a router file:

```
└── src
    ├── middlewares/
    ├── store/
    ├── routes/
    └── router.js
```

We will create two route components, login and secured, as SFC pages, and make the secured page a 403 protected page, which will require the user to log in to provide their name and age to access the page. The following are the files and the structure inside the /src/ directory that we will need for this simple Vue app:

```
└── src
    ├── App.vue
    ├── main.js
    ├── router.js
    ├── components
    │   ├── secured.vue
    │   └── login.vue
    ├── assets
    │   └── ...
    ├── middlewares
    │   ├── isLoggedIn.js
    │   └── isAdult.js
    ├── store
    │   ├── index.js
    │   ├── mutations.js
    │   └── actions.js
    └── routes
        ├── index.js
        ├── secured.js
        └── login.js
```

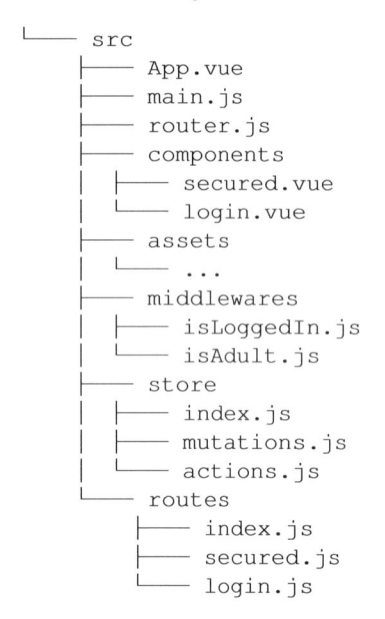

We now have an idea of what directories and files we need for our app. Next, we will move on to writing the code for these files.

Writing middlewares and a Vuex store with Vue CLI

If you take a look at `package.json`, you will see that the default dependencies that come with Vue CLI are very basic and minimal:

```
// package.json
"dependencies": {
  "core-js": "^2.6.5",
  "vue": "^2.6.10"
}
```

So, we will install our project dependencies and write the code we need in the following steps:

1. Install the following packages via npm:

   ```
   $ npm i vuex
   $ npm i vue-router
   $ npm i vue-router-multiguard
   ```

   > Note that Vue does not support multiple guards per route. So, if you want to create more than one guard for a route, Vue Router Multiguard allows you to do this. For more information about this package, please visit https://github.com/atanas-dev/vue-router-multiguard.

2. Create the state, actions, and mutations to store the authenticated user details in the Vuex store so that these details can be accessed by any component:

   ```
   // src/store/index.js
   import Vue from 'vue'
   import Vuex from 'vuex'

   import actions from './actions'
   import mutations from './mutations'

   Vue.use(Vuex)

   export default new Vuex.Store({
     state: { user: null },
     actions,
     mutations
   })
   ```

Writing Route Middlewares and Server Middlewares

For the sake of readability and simplicity, we will separate the store's actions into a separate file, as follows:

```js
// src/store/actions.js
const actions = {
  async login({ commit }, { name, age }) {
    if (!name || !age) {
      throw new Error('Bad credentials')
    }
    const data = {
      name: name,
      age: age
    }
    commit('setUser', data)
  },

  async logout({ commit }) {
    commit('setUser', null)
  }
}
export default actions
```

We will also separate the store's mutations into a separate file, as follows:

```js
// src/store/mutations.js
const mutations = {
  setUser (state, user) {
    state.user = user
  }
}
export default mutations
```

3. Create a middleware to ensure the user has logged in:

```js
// src/middlewares/isLoggedIn.js
import store from '../store'

export default (to, from, next) => {
  if (!store.state.user) {
    const err = new Error('You are not connected')
    err.statusCode = 403
    next(err)
  } else {
    next()
  }
}
```

[380]

4. Create another middleware to ensure the user is over 18 years old:

```js
// src/middlewares/isAdult.js
import store from '../store'

export default (to, from, next) => {
  if (store.state.user.age < 18) {
    const err = new Error('You must be over 18')
    err.statusCode = 403
    next(err)
  } else {
    next()
  }
}
```

5. Import these two middlewares in the secured route by using `vue-router-multiguard` to insert multiple middlewares in `beforeEnter`:

```js
// src/routes/secured.js
import multiguard from 'vue-router-multiguard'
import secured from '../components/secured.vue'
import isLoggedIn from '../middlewares/isLoggedIn'
import isAdult from '../middlewares/isAdult'

export default {
  name: 'secured',
  path: '/secured',
  component: secured,
  beforeEnter: multiguard([isLoggedIn, isAdult])
}
```

6. Create a client-side authentication with a simple login page. Here are the basic input fields we need for the `login` and `logout` methods:

```html
// src/components/login.vue
<form @submit.prevent="login">
  <p>Name: <input v-model="name" type="text" name="name"></p>
  <p>Age: <input v-model="age" type="number" name="age"></p>
  <button type="submit">Submit</button>
</form>

export default {
  data() {
    return {
      error: null,
      name: '',
      age: ''
    }
```

[381]

```
    },
    methods: {
      async login() { ... },
      async logout() { ... }
    }
  }
```

7. Complete the preceding `login` and `logout` methods by dispatching the `login` and `logout` action methods in the `try` and `catch` blocks, as follows:

```
async login() {
  try {
    await this.$store.dispatch('login', {
      name: this.name,
      age: this.age
    })
    this.name = ''
    this.age = ''
    this.error = null
  } catch (e) {
    this.error = e.message
  }
},
async logout() {
  try {
    await this.$store.dispatch('logout')
  } catch (e) {
    this.error = e.message
  }
}
```

8. Import the completed login component into the login route, as follows:

```
// src/routes/login.js
import Login from '../components/login.vue'

export default {
  name: 'login',
  path: '/',
  component: Login
}
```

Note that we name this route `login` because we will need this name later to redirect the navigation route when we get the authentication error from the preceding middlewares.

9. Import the `login` and `secured` routes to the index route, as follows:

```
// src/routes/index.js
import login from './login'
import secured from './secured'

const routes = [
  login,
  secured
]

export default routes
```

10. Import the preceding index route into the Vue Router instance and catch the route errors using `router.onError`, as follows:

```
// src/router.js
import Vue from 'vue'
import VueRouter from 'vue-router'
import Routes from './routes'

Vue.use(VueRouter)

const router = new VueRouter({
  routes: Routes
})

router.onError(err => {
  alert(err.message)
  router.push({ name: 'login' })
})

export default router
```

In this step, we use `router.onError` to handle the `Error` object that passed from the middlewares, and `router.push` to redirect the navigation route to the login page when the authentication conditions are not met. The name of the object must be the same as the login route in *step 7*, which is *login*.

11. Import the router and store it in the `main` file:

```
// src/main.js
import Vue from 'vue'
import App from './App.vue'
import router from './router'
import store from './store'
```

Writing Route Middlewares and Server Middlewares

```
new Vue({
  router,
  store,
  render: h => h(App),
}).$mount('#app')
```

12. Run the project with `npm run serve`, and you should see that the app is loaded at `localhost:8080`. If you type a name and a number less than 18 into the input fields on the home page and then click on the login button, you should get an alert saying that "You must be over 18" when trying to access the secured page. On the other hand, if you type in a number higher than 18, you should see the name and the number on the secured page:

    ```
    Name: John
    Age: 20
    ```

> You can find the entire code for this app in `/chapter-11/vue/vue-cli/basic/` from our GitHub repository. You can also find the app with the custom webpack in `/chapter-11/vue/webpack/`.

Well done! You have managed to get through all of the sections on middleware for Vue projects. Now, let's apply what you have just learned about Nuxt projects in the upcoming section.

Writing route middlewares in Nuxt

As always, once we understand how middleware works in Vue, it will then be easier to work with it in Nuxt as Nuxt has taken care of Vue Router for us. In the coming sections, we will learn how to work with global and per-route middlewares for Nuxt apps.

In Nuxt, all middleware should be kept in the `/middleware/` directory, and the middleware filename will be the name of the middleware. For example, `/middleware/user.js` is the user middleware. A middleware gets the Nuxt context as its first argument:

```
export default (context) => { ... }
```

Additionally, middleware can be asynchronous:

```
export default async (context) => {
    const { data } = await axios.get('/api/path')
}
```

In universal mode, middlewares are called on the server side once (for example, when first requesting the Nuxt app or when refreshing a page) and then on the client side when navigating to other routes. On the other hand, middlewares are always called on the client side whether you are requesting the app for the first time or when you are navigating to further routes after the first request. Middlewares are executed in the Nuxt configuration file first, then in layouts, and, finally, in pages. We will now start writing some global middlewares in the next section.

Writing global middlewares

Adding global middlewares is very straightforward; you just have to declare them in the `middleware` key in the `router` option of the `config` file. For example, take a look at the following:

```
// nuxt.config.js
export default {
  router: {
    middleware: 'auth'
  }
}
```

Now, let's create some global middleware in the following steps. In this exercise, we want to to get the information of the user agent from the HTTP request header and to track the routes the user is navigating to:

1. Create two middlewares in the /middleware/ directory, one for obtaining the user agent information and the other for obtaining the route path information that the user is navigating to:

    ```
    // middleware/user-agent.js
    export default (context) => {
      context.userAgent = process.server ? context.req.headers[
        'user-agent'] : navigator.userAgent
    }

    // middleware/visits.js
    export default ({ store, route, redirect }) => {
      store.commit('addVisit', route.path)
    }
    ```

2. Declare the preceding middlewares in the `middleware` key in the `router` option, as follows:

```
// nuxt.config.js
module.exports = {
  router: {
    middleware: ['visits', 'user-agent']
  }
}
```

> Note that, in Nuxt, we do not need a third-party package like we do in the Vue app to call multiple guards.

3. Create the store's state and mutations for storing the visited route:

```
// store/state.js
export default () => ({
  visits: []
})

// store/mutations.js
export default {
  addVisit (state, path) {
    state.visits.push({
      path,
      date: new Date().toJSON()
    })
  }
}
```

4. Use the `user-agent` middleware in the `about` page:

```
// pages/about.vue
<p>{{ userAgent }}</p>

export default {
  asyncData ({ userAgent }) {
    return {
      userAgent
    }
  }
}
```

5. As for `visits` middleware, we want to use it on a component and then inject this component into our layout, that is, the `default.vue` layout. First, create the `visits` component in the `/components/` directory:

```
// components/visits.vue
<li v-for="(visit, index) in visits" :key="index">
  <i>{{ visit.date | dates }} | {{ visit.date | times }}</i> - {{
    visit.path }}
</li>

export default {
  filters: {
    dates(date) {
      return date.split('T')[0]
    },
    times(date) {
      return date.split('T')[1].split('.')[0]
    }
  },
  computed: {
    visits() {
      return this.$store.state.visits.slice().reverse()
    }
  }
}
```

So, we have created two filters in this component. The `date` filter is used to obtain the date from a string. For example, we will get `2019-05-24` from `2019-05-24T21:55:44.673Z`. In comparison, the `time` filter is used to obtain the time from a string. For example, we will get `21:55:44` from `2019-05-24T21:55:44.673Z`.

6. Import the `visits` component into our layout:

```
// layouts/default.vue
<template>
  <Visits />
</template>

import Visits from '~/components/visits.vue'
export default {
  components: {
    Visits
  }
}
```

We should get the following results in our browser when we navigate around the routes:

```
2019-06-06 | 01:55:44 - /contact
2019-06-06 | 01:55:37 - /about
2019-06-06 | 01:55:30 - /
```

Additionally, we should get the information of the user agent from the request headers when you are on the about page:

```
Mozilla/5.0 (X11; Linux x86_64) AppleWebKit/537.36 (KHTML, like Gecko) Chrome/73.0.3683.75 Safari/537.36
```

> You can find the preceding source code in /chapter-11/nuxt-universal/route-middleware/global/ in our GitHub repository.

That's all for global middleware. Now, let's move on to per-route middlewares in the next section.

Writing per-route middlewares

Adding per-route middlewares is also very straightforward; you just have to declare them in the middleware key in the specific layout or page. For example, take a look at the following:

```
// pages/index.vue or layouts/default.vue
export default {
  middleware: 'auth'
}
```

So, let's create some per-route middlewares in the following steps. In this exercise, we will use sessions and JSON Web Tokens (JWTs) to access restricted pages or a secured API. Although in real life, we can either just use a session or a token for an authentication system, we will use both for our exercise so that we know how to use them together for potentially more complex production systems. In our exercise, we will want the user to log in and get the token from the server. The user will be not able to access the secured routes when the token is expired or invalid.

Additionally, the user will be logged out when the session time is over:

1. Create an `auth` middleware to check whether the state in our store has any data. If there is no authenticated data, then we use the `error` function in the Nuxt context to send the error to the front:

    ```
    // middleware/auth.js
    export default function ({ store, error }) {
      if (!store.state.auth) {
        error({
          message: 'You are not connected',
          statusCode: 403
        })
      }
    }
    ```

2. Create a `token` middleware to ensure the token is in the store; otherwise, it sends the error to the front. If the token is present in the store, we set `Authorization` with the token to the default `axios` header:

    ```
    // middleware/token.js
    export default async ({ store, error }) => {
      if (!store.state.auth.token) {
        error({
          message: 'No token',
          statusCode: 403
        })
      }
      axios.defaults.headers.common['Authorization'] = `Bearer: ${store.state.auth.token}`
    }
    ```

3. Add these two preceding middlewares to the `middleware` key on the secured page:

    ```
    // pages/secured.vue
    <p>{{ greeting }}</p>

    export default {
      async asyncData ({ redirect }) {
        try {
          const { data } = await axios.get('/api/private')
          return {
            greeting: data.data.message
          }
        } catch (error) {
          if(process.browser){
    ```

[389]

```
        alert(error.response.data.message)
      }
      return redirect('/login')
    }
  },
  middleware: ['auth', 'token']
}
```

After setting the Authorization header with the JWT in the headers, we can access the secured API routes, which are guarded by a server-side middleware (we will learn more about this in Chapter 12, *Creating User Logins and API Authentication*). We will get the data from the secured API route that we want to access and will be prompted with the error message if the token is incorrect or has expired.

4. Create the store's state, mutations, and actions in the /store/ directory to store the authenticated data:

```
// store/state.js
export default () => ({
  auth: null
})

// store/mutations.js
export default {
  setAuth (state, data) {
    state.auth = data
  }
}

// store/actions.js
export default {
  async login({ commit }, { username, password }) {
    try {
      const { data } = await axios.post('/api/public/users/login',
      { username, password })
      commit('setAuth', data.data)
    } catch (error) {
      // handle error
    }
  },

  async logout({ commit }) {
    await axios.post('/api/public/users/logout')
    commit('setAuth', null)
  }
}
```

[390]

A known and expected behavior is that, when the page is refreshed, the state of the store is reset to default. There are a few solutions that we can use if we want to persist in the state:

1. localStorage
2. sessionStorage
3. vuex-persistedstate (a Vuex plugin)

In our case, however, since we use the session to store the authenticated information, we can actually retrace our data from the session via the following:

1. req.ctx.session (Koa) or req.session (Express)
2. req.headers.cookie

Once we have decided which solution or option we want to go for (let's say `req.headers.cookie`), then we can refill the state as follows:

```
// store/index.js
const cookie = process.server ? require('cookie') : undefined

export const actions = {
  nuxtServerInit({ commit }, { req }) {
    var session = null
    var auth = null
    if (req.headers.cookie && req.headers.cookie.indexOf('koa:sess') > -1) {
      session = cookie.parse(req.headers.cookie)['koa:sess']
    }
    if (session) {
      auth = JSON.parse(Buffer.from(session, 'base64'))
      commit('setAuth', auth)
    }
  }
}
```

> You can find the preceding source code in /chapter-11/nuxt-universal/route-middleware/per-route/ in our GitHub repository.

When all the preceding steps are followed and the middlewares are created, we can run this simple authentication app with `npm run dev` to see how it works. We will get to server-side authentication in the next chapter. Right now, we just have to focus on the middleware and understand how it works, which will help us in the next chapter. Now, let's move on to the final part of this chapter – server middlewares.

[391]

Writing Nuxt server middlewares

Put simply, server middlewares are server-side apps that are used as middlewares in Nuxt. We have been running our Nuxt apps under a server-side framework such as Koa since Chapter 8, *Adding a Server-Side Framework*. If you are using Express, this is the `scripts` object in your `package.json` file:

```
// package.json
"scripts": {
  "dev": "cross-env NODE_ENV=development nodemon server/index.js --watch
    server",
  "build": "nuxt build",
  "start": "cross-env NODE_ENV=production node server/index.js",
  "generate": "nuxt generate"
}
```

In this npm script, the `dev` and `start` scripts instruct the server to run your app from `/server/index.js`. This might not be ideal as we have coupled Nuxt and the server-side framework tightly, and it results in extra work in the configuration. However, we can tell Nuxt not to attach to the server-side framework's configurations in `/server/index.js` and keep our original Nuxt run scripts as they are shown here:

```
// package.json
"scripts": {
  "dev": "nuxt",
  "build": "nuxt build",
  "start": "nuxt start",
  "generate": "nuxt generate"
}
```

On the contrary, we can have the server-side framework running under Nuxt instead, by using the `serverMiddleware` property in the Nuxt configuration file. For example, take a look at the following:

```
// nuxt.config.js
export default {
  serverMiddleware: [
    '~/api'
  ]
}
```

Unlike route middlewares, which are called before each route on the client side, server middlewares are always called on the server side before `vue-server-renderer`. Therefore, server middlewares can be used for server-specific tasks, just like we did with Koa or Express in previous chapters. So, let's explore how to use Express and Koa as our server middleware in the next sections.

Using Express as Nuxt's server middleware

Let's create a simple authentication app using Express as Nuxt's server middleware. We will be still using the client-side code from the authentication exercise along with the per-route middlewares that you learned about in the preceding section, where the user is required to provide a username and password to access a secured page. Additionally, we will be using a Vuex store to centralize the authenticated user data just like before. The major difference in this exercise is that our Nuxt app will be *moved out* of the server-side app as a middleware, and, instead, the server-side app will be *moved into* the Nuxt app as middleware. So, let's get started by following these steps:

1. Install `cookie-session` and `body-parser` as server middlewares, and add the path of our API after them in the Nuxt `config` file, as follows:

   ```
   // nuxt.config.js
   import bodyParser from 'body-parser'
   import cookieSession from 'cookie-session'

   export default {
     serverMiddleware: [
       bodyParser.json(),
       cookieSession({
         name: 'express:sess',
         secret: 'super-secret-key',
         maxAge: 60000
       }),
       '~/api'
     ]
   }
   ```

   Note that cookie-session is a cookie-based session middleware for Express that stores the session in a cookie on the client side. In comparison, body-parser is a body-parsing middleware for Express, just like the `koa-bodyparser` for Koa that you learned about in Chapter 8, *Adding a Server-Side Framework*.

Writing Route Middlewares and Server Middlewares

> For more information about `cookie-session` and `body-parser` for Express, please visit https://github.com/expressjs/cookie-session and https://github.com/expressjs/body-parser.

2. Create an `/api/` directory using an `index.js` file, in which Express is imported and exported as another server middleware:

   ```js
   // api/index.js
   import express from 'express'
   const app = express()

   app.get('/', (req, res) => res.send('Hello World!'))

   // Export the server middleware
   export default {
     path: '/api',
     handler: app
   }
   ```

3. Run the app using `npm run dev`, and you should get the "Hello World!" message in `localhost:3000/api`.

4. Add the `login` and `logout` post methods in `/api/index.js`, as follows:

   ```js
   // api/index.js
   app.post('/login', (req, res) => {
     if (req.body.username === 'demo' && req.body.password === 'demo') {
       req.session.auth = { username: 'demo' }
       return res.json({ username: 'demo' })
     }
     res.status(401).json({ message: 'Bad credentials' })
   })

   app.post('/logout', (req, res) => {
     delete req.session.auth
     res.json({ ok: true })
   })
   ```

   In the preceding code, we store the authenticated payload to the Express session as `auth` in the HTTP request object when the user has logged in successfully. Then, we will clear the `auth` session by deleting it when the user has logged out.

[394]

5. Create a store with `state.js` and `mutations.js`, just like you did for writing a per-route middleware, as follows:

```
// store/state.js
export default () => ({
  auth: null,
})

// store/mutations.js
export default {
  setAuth (state, data) {
    state.auth = data
  }
}
```

6. Just as with writing per-route middleware, create the `login` and `logout` action methods in the `actions.js` file in the store, as follows:

```
// store/actions.js
import axios from 'axios'

export default {
  async login({ commit }, { username, password }) {
    try {
      const { data } = await axios.post('/api/login', { username,
        password })
      commit('setAuth', data)
    } catch (error) {
      // handle error...
    }
  },

  async logout({ commit }) {
    await axios.post('/api/logout')
    commit('setAuth', null)
  }
}
```

7. Add a `nuxtServerInit` action to `index.js` in the store to repopulate the state from the Express session in the HTTP request object when refreshing pages:

```
// store/index.js
export const actions = {
  nuxtServerInit({ commit }, { req }) {
    if (req.session && req.session.auth) {
      commit('setAuth', req.session.auth)
    }
```

```
      }
    }
```

8. Finally, just like in per-route middleware authentication, create a login page in the `/pages/` directory with a form. Use the same `login` and `logout` methods you did before to dispatch the `login` and `logout` action methods in the store:

   ```
   // pages/index.vue
   <form v-if="!$store.state.auth" @submit.prevent="login">
     <p v-if="error" class="error">{{ error }}</p>
     <p>Username: <input v-model="username" type="text"
       name="username"></p>
     <p>Password: <input v-model="password" type="password"
       name="password"></p>
     <button type="submit">Login</button>
   </form>

   export default {
     data () {
       return {
         error: null,
         username: '',
         password: ''
       }
     },
     methods: {
       async login () { ... },
       async logout () { ... }
     }
   }
   ```

9. Run the app with `npm run dev`. You should have an authentication app that works just like before, but it is no longer running from `/server/index.js`.

> You can find the preceding source code in `/chapter-11/nuxt-universal/server-middleware/express/` in our GitHub repository.

Using the `serverMiddleware` property allows our Nuxt app to look neat and feel light again by freeing it from the server-side app, don't you think? With this approach, we can make it more flexible too, as we can use any server-side framework or app. For example, instead of using Express, we can use Koa, which we will look at in the next section.

Using Koa as Nuxt's server middleware

Just like Koa and Express, Connect is a simple framework that is used to glue together various middlewares for handling HTTP requests. Nuxt internally uses Connect as a server, so most Express middleware works with Nuxt's server middleware. In comparison, it is a bit harder for Koa middleware to work as Nuxt's server middleware because the `req` and `res` objects are *tucked away* and kept inside `ctx` in Koa. We can compare these three frameworks with a simple "Hello World" message, as follows:

```
// Connect
const connect = require('connect')
const app = connect()
app.use((req, res, next) => res.end('Hello World'))

// Express
const express = require('express')
const app = express()
app.get('/', (req, res, next) => res.send('Hello World'))

// Koa
const Koa = require('koa')
const app = new Koa()
app.use(async (ctx, next) => ctx.body = 'Hello World')
```

Notice that `req` is a Node.js HTTP request object, while `res` is a Node.js HTTP response object. They can be named anything you like, for example, *request* instead of *req* and *response* instead of *res*. From the preceding comparisons, you can see how Koa handles these two objects differently from the other frameworks. So, we can't use Koa as Nuxt's server middleware like in Express, and we can't define any Koa middleware in the `serverMiddleware` property but just add the path of the directory where the Koa API is kept. Rest assured, it is not difficult to get them working as middleware in our Nuxt app. Let's proceed with the following steps:

1. Add the path where we want to create our API with Koa, as follows:

    ```
    // nuxt.config.js
    export default {
      serverMiddleware: [
        '~/api'
      ]
    }
    ```

Writing Route Middlewares and Server Middlewares

2. Import `koa` and `koa-router`, create a `Hello World!` message with the router, and then export them to the `index.js` file inside the `/api/` directory:

    ```js
    // api/index.js
    import Koa from 'koa'
    import Router from 'koa-router'

    router.get('/', async (ctx, next) => {
      ctx.type = 'json'
      ctx.body = {
        message: 'Hello World!'
      }
    })

    app.use(router.routes())
    app.use(router.allowedMethods())

    // Export the server middleware
    export default {
      path: '/api',
      handler: app.listen()
    }
    ```

3. Import `koa-bodyparser` and `koa-session`, and register them as middlewares in the Koa instance in the `/api/index.js` file, as follows:

    ```js
    // api/index.js
    import bodyParser from 'koa-bodyparser'
    import session from 'koa-session'

    const CONFIG = {
      key: 'koa:sess',
      maxAge: 60000,
    }

    app.use(session(CONFIG, app))
    app.use(bodyParser())
    ```

4. Create the `login` and `logout` routes using the Koa router, as follows:

    ```js
    // api/index.js
    router.post('/login', async (ctx, next) => {
      let request = ctx.request.body || {}
      if (request.username === 'demo' && request.password === 'demo') {
        ctx.session.auth = { username: 'demo' }
        ctx.body = {
          username: 'demo'
        }
    ```

```
    } else {
      ctx.throw(401, 'Bad credentials')
    }
  })

  router.post('/logout', async (ctx, next) => {
    ctx.session = null
    ctx.body = { ok: true }
  })
```

In the preceding code, just like in the Express example in the previous section, we store the authenticated payload to the Koa session as `auth` in the Koa context object when the user has logged in successfully. Then, we will clear the `auth` session by setting the session to `null` when the user has logged out.

5. Create a store with the state, mutations, and actions just like you did in the Express example. Additionally, create `nuxtServerInit` in the `index.js` file in the store just like you did when writing per-route middlewares:

```
// store/index.js
export const actions = {
  nuxtServerInit({ commit }, { req }) {
    // ...
  }
}
```

6. Just like before, create the form `login` and `logout` methods in the `/pages/` directory to dispatch the action methods from the store:

```
// pages/index.vue
<form v-if="!$store.state.auth" @submit.prevent="login">
  //...
</form>

export default {
  methods: {
    async login () { ... },
    async logout () { ... }
  }
}
```

7. Run the app with `npm run dev`. You should have an authentication app that works just like the one in Express in the previous section, but it is no longer running from `/server/index.js`.

Writing Route Middlewares and Server Middlewares

> You can find the entire source code for this example in `/chapter-11/nuxt-universal/server-middleware/koa/` in our GitHub repository.

Depending on your preference, you can use Express or Koa as Nuxt's server middleware in your next project. In this book, we mostly use Koa for its simplicity. You even can create custom server middleware without needing either of them. Let's take a look at how to create custom server middleware in the next section.

Creating custom server middleware

Since Nuxt internally uses Connect as the server, we can add our custom middlewares without the need for an external server such as Koa or Express. You can develop a complex Nuxt server middleware just like we did with Koa and Express in the previous sections. However, let's not endlessly repeat what we have already done. Let's create a very basic custom middleware that prints a "Hello World" message to confirm the feasibility of building a complex one from a basic middleware in the following steps:

1. Add the path where we want to create our custom middleware:

    ```
    // nuxt.config.js
    serverMiddleware: [
      { path: '/api', handler: '~/api/index.js' }
    ]
    ```

2. Add the API routes to the `index.js` file inside the `/api/` directory:

    ```
    // api/index.js
    export default function (req, res, next) {
      res.end('Hello world!')
    }
    ```

3. Run the app with `npm run dev` and navigate to `localhost:3000/api`. You should see the "Hello World!" message printed on your screen.

> You can refer to the Connect documentation at https://github.com/senchalabs/connect for more information. Additionally, you can find the source code for this example in `/chapter-11/nuxt-universal/server-middleware/custom/` in our GitHub repository.

Well done! You have managed to get through another big chapter on Nuxt. Before moving on to the next chapter, let's summarize what you have learned so far.

Summary

In this chapter, you learned the distinction between route middleware and server middleware. You used navigation guards from Vue Router to create middlewares for Vue apps. You also used Vue CLI to develop a simple Vue authentication app. Taking what you learned about Vue apps, you implemented the same concept (of route middleware) in Nuxt apps with global and per-route middlewares. After that, you managed to learn about Nuxt's server middleware and how to use Express and Koa as server middlewares. Middlewares are important and useful, especially for authentication and security. We have already made a few authentication apps, and we are going to study and understand them in more detail in the next chapter.

In the next chapter, you will learn, in detail, about developing user logins and authentication APIs to improve the authentication apps that you have created in this chapter. We will walk you through session-based authentication and token-based authentication. While you have created an authentication app using these two technologies, we haven't explained what they are yet. But rest assured, you will understand them better in the next chapter. Besides this, you will learn how to create backend and frontend authentication and signing in with Google OAuth for your Nuxt app. So, stay tuned!

12
Creating User Logins and API Authentication

In the last two chapters, we started working on session and **JSON Web Token** (**JWT**) authentication in Nuxt apps. We used sessions for authentication in Chapter 10, *Adding a Vuex Store*, to exercise `nuxtServerInit`. Then we used sessions and tokens together for authentication in Chapter 11, *Writing Route Middlewares and Server Middlewares*, to exercise per-route middleware, for example:

```
// store/index.js
nuxtServerInit({ commit }, { req }) {
  if (req.ctx.session && req.ctx.session.authUser) {
    commit('setUser', req.ctx.session.authUser)
  }
}

// middleware/token.js
export default async ({ store, error }) => {
  if (!store.state.auth.token) {
    // handle error
  }
  axios.defaults.headers.common['Authorization'] = Bearer:
${store.state.auth.token}
}
```

They may seem overwhelming if you are new to web authentication but fear not. In a nutshell, authentication is the process of verifying who you are. An authentication system allows you to access a resource when your credentials match the credentials in a database or a data authentication server. There are several authentication methods. Session-based and token-based authentication are the most common, or a combination of these two. So, let's dive into them.

The topics we will cover in this chapter are as follows:

- Understanding session-based authentication
- Understanding token-based authentication
- Creating backend authentication
- Creating frontend authentication
- Signing in with Google OAuth

Understanding session-based authentication

HyperText Transfer Protocol (HTTP) is stateless. Hence, all HTTP requests are stateless. That means it does not remember anything or any user we have authenticated, and our application wouldn't know whether it is the same person from the previous request. So, we would have to authenticate again on the next request. This is not ideal.

So, session-based and cookie-based authentication (usually referred to only as session-based authentication) were introduced to store user data between HTTP requests to put away the stateless nature of HTTP requests. They make the authentication process "stateful." That means an authenticated record or session is stored on both the server and client sides. The server can keep the active sessions in a database or the server memory, thus it is known as session-based authentication. The client can create a cookie to hold the session identifier (session ID), so it is known as cookie-based authentication.

But what are sessions and cookies anyway? Let's jump into them in the following sections.

What are sessions and cookies?

A session is a piece of temporary information interchanged between two or more communicating devices, or between a computer and user. It is established at a certain time and then expires at a future time. It also expires when the user closes the browser or when leaving a website. When a session is established, a file is created in a temporary directory (or in a database or the server memory) on the server to store the registered session values. This data is then available throughout the website during the visit, and the browser receives a session ID, which is to be sent back, either by a cookie or by the `GET` variable, to the server for validation.

In short, cookies and sessions are just data. Cookies are only stored on the client-side machine, while sessions get stored on the client as well as on the server. Sessions are considered more secure than cookies because the data can be kept solely on the server. Cookies are often created when the session is established and they are saved on the client computer. They can be the name, age, or ID of the authenticated user and they are sent back to the server by the browser to identify the user. Let's take a look at how they work in the next section with an example flow.

The session authentication flow

Session-based and cookie-based authentication can be understood in the following example authentication flow:

1. The user sends their credentials, for example, username and password, from the client app on their browser to the server.
2. The server checks the credentials and sends a unique token (session ID) to the client. Also, this token will be saved in a database or memory on the server side.
3. The client app stores the token in cookies on the client side and will use it in every HTTP request and send it back to the server.
4. The server receives the token and authenticates the user and then returns the requested data to the client application.
5. The client app destroys the token when the user logs out. Before logging out, the client can also send a request to the server to remove the session, or the session will end by itself depending on the expiration time that has been set.

In session-based authentication, the server does all the heavy lifting. It is stateful. It associates the session identifier with the user account (for example, in a database). The disadvantage of session-based authentication is the scalability when there is a large number of users using the system at the same time because sessions are stored in the server's memory, so it involves large memory usage. Also, cookies work great on a single domain or subdomains but are disabled by the browser normally on cross-domain sharing (cross-origin resource sharing). So, this causes an issue for the client when making API requests that are served from a different domain. But this issue can be overcome with token-based authentication, which we will walk through in the next section.

Understanding token-based authentication

Token-based authentication is simpler. There are a few implementations of tokens, however, JSON Web Tokens is the most common one. Token-based authentication is stateless. That means no session is persisted on the server side because the state is stored inside the token on the client side. The responsibility of the server is only to create a JWT with a secret and send it to the client. The client stores the JWT in local storage, or a client-side cookie, and includes it in the header whenever making a request. The server then validates the JWT and sends a response.

But what is a JWT and how does it work? Let's find out in the next section.

What are JSON Web Tokens?

To understand how a JWT works, we should understand what it is first. In short, a JWT is a string of a hashed JSON object composed of a header, a payload, and a signature. A JWT is generated with the following format:

```
header.payload.signature
```

The header typically consists of two parts: type and algorithm. The type is JWT, and the algorithm can be HMAC, SHA256, or RSA, which is a hashing algorithm that uses a secret key to sign the token, for example:

```
{
  "typ": "JWT",
  "alg": "HS256"
}
```

The payload is the part where the information (or claims) is stored inside a JWT, for example:

```
{
  "userId": "b08f86af-35da-48f2-8fab-cef3904660bd",
  "name": "Jane Doe"
}
```

In this example, we only include two claims in the payload. You can put as many claims as you like. The more claims you include, the bigger the JWT size, which may affect performance. There are other optional claims, such as `iss` (issuer), `sub` (subject), and `exp` (expiration time).

Chapter 12

> If you want to find out more details about the JWT standard fields, please visit `https://tools.ietf.org/html/rfc7519`.

The signature is computed using the encoded header, the encoded payload, a secret, and the algorithm specified in the header. Whatever algorithm you choose in the header part, you must use that algorithm to encrypt the first two parts of the JWT: `base64(header) + '.' + base64(payload)`, for example, in this pseudocode:

```
// signature algorithm
data = base64urlEncode(header) + '.' + base64urlEncode(payload)
hashedData = hash(data, secret)
signature = base64urlEncode(hashedData)
```

The signature is the only part of the JWT that is not publicly readable because it is encrypted with a secret key. Unless someone has the secret key, they cannot decrypt this information. So, the example output from the preceding pseudocode is three Base64-URL strings separated by dots that can be passed easily in HTTP requests:

```
// JWT Token
eyJ0eXAiOiJKV1QiLCJhbGciOiJIUzI1NiJ9.eyJ1c2VySWQiOiJiMDhmODZhZi0zNWRhLTQ4ZjItOGZhYi1jZWYzOTA0NjYwYmQifQ.-xN_h82PHVTCMA9vdoHrcZxH-x5mb11y1537t3rGzcM
```

Let's take a look at how this token authentication works in the next section, with an example flow.

The token authentication flow

Token-based authentication can be understood with the following example authentication flow:

1. The user sends their credentials, for example, username and password, from the client app on their browser to the server.
2. The server checks the username and password and returns a signed token (the JWT) if the credentials are correct.
3. This token is stored on the client side. It can be stored in local storage, session storage, or in a cookie.
4. The client app generally includes this token as an additional header on any subsequent request to the server.

5. The server receives and decodes the JWT and then allows request access if the token is valid.
6. The token is destroyed on the client side when the user logs out and no further interaction with the server is needed.

In token-based authentication, generally, you should not include any sensitive information in the payload and the token should not be kept over a long period. The additional header that you use to include the token should be in this format:

```
Authorization: Bearer <token>
```

Scalability in token-based authentication is not an issue because the token is stored on the client side. Cross-domain sharing is not an issue either because JWT is a string with all the necessary information, included in the request header, that is checked on each request made by the client to the server. In Node.js apps, we can use one of the Node.js modules, such as `jsonwebtoken`, to generate the token for us. Let's take a look at how we can use this Node.js module in the next section.

Using Node.js modules for JWT

As we mentioned previously, `jsonwebtoken` can be used to generate JWTs on the server side. You can use this module synchronously or asynchronously in the following simplified steps:

1. Install `jsonwebtoken` via npm:

    ```
    $ npm i jsonwebtoken
    ```

2. Import and sign a token on the server side:

    ```
    import jwt from 'jsonwebtoken'
    var token = jwt.sign({ name: 'john' }, 'secret', { expiresIn: '1h' })
    ```

3. Asynchronously verify the token coming from the client side:

    ```
    try {
      var verified = jwt.verify(token, 'secret')
    } catch(err) {
      // handle error
    }
    ```

> If you want to find out more information about this module, please visit https://github.com/brianloveswords/node-jws.

So, now you have a basic understanding of session-based and token-based authentication, we will guide you on how to apply them in server-side and client-side apps that use Koa and Nuxt. In this chapter, we will use token-based authentication to create two authentication options in our apps: local authentication and Google OAuth authentication. Local authentication is the option where we authenticate the user within our apps internally and locally, while Google OAuth authentication is the option where we authenticate the user using Google OAuth. So, let's find out in the coming sections!

Creating backend authentication

In previous exercises in Chapter 10, *Adding a Vuex Store*, and Chapter 11, *Writing Route Middlewares and Server Middlewares*, we used a dummy user for our backend authentication, particularly in /chapter-11/nuxt-universal/route-middleware/per-route/ for per-route middlewares, for example:

```
// server/modules/public/user/_routes/login.js
router.post('/login', async (ctx, next) => {
  let request = ctx.request.body || {}

  if (request.username === 'demo' && request.password === 'demo') {
    let payload = { id: 1, name: 'Alexandre', username: 'demo' }
    let token = jwt.sign(payload, config.JWT_SECRET, { expiresIn: 1 * 60 })
    //...
  }
})
```

But in this chapter, we are going to use a database with some user data for authentication. Also, in Chapter 9, *Adding a Server-Side Database*, we used MongoDB as our database server. But this time, let's try a different database system for the sake of diversity – **MySQL**. So, let's get started.

Creating User Logins and API Authentication

Using MySQL as the server database

Be sure you have the MySQL server installed on your local machine. The latest MySQL version is 5.7 at the time of writing this book. Depending on what operating system you are using, you can find out the specific guidelines for your system at `https://dev.mysql.com/doc/mysql-installation-excerpt/5.7/en/installing.html`. If you are using Linux, you can find out the installation guide for your Linux distribution at `https://dev.mysql.com/doc/mysql-installation-excerpt/5.7/en/linux-installation.html`. If you are on Linux Ubuntu and using the APT repository, you can follow the guide at `https://dev.mysql.com/doc/mysql-apt-repo-quick-guide/en/apt-repo-fresh-install`.

Alternatively, you can install the MariaDB server instead of the MySQL server to use the **relational database management system (DBMS)** in your projects. Again, depending on what operating system you are using, you can find out the specific guidelines for your system at `https://mariadb.com/downloads/`. If you are using Linux, you can find the guide for your specific Linux distribution at `https://downloads.mariadb.org/mariadb/repositories/`. If you are on Linux Ubuntu 19.10, you can follow the guide at `https://downloads.mariadb.org/mariadb/repositories/#distro=Ubuntu&distro_release=eoan--ubuntu_eoan&mirror=bm&version=10.4`.

Whichever you choose, it is convenient to have an administration tool to manage your MySQL databases from a browser. You can use phpMyAdmin or Adminer (`https://www.adminer.org/latest.php`); both require PHP installed on your machine. If you are new to PHP, you can use the installation guide in Chapter 16, *Creating a Framework-Agnostic PHP API for Nuxt*. Adminer is preferred in this book. You can download the program at `https://www.phpmyadmin.net/downloads/`. If you want to use phpMyAdmin, please visit `https://www.phpmyadmin.net/` to find out more. As soon as you have the administration tool, take the following steps to set up the database that we will need throughout this chapter:

1. Create a database, for example, "nuxt-auth", using Adminer.

2. Insert the following table and sample data in the database:

   ```
   DROP TABLE IF EXISTS users;
   CREATE TABLE users (
     id int(11) NOT NULL AUTO_INCREMENT,
     name varchar(255) NOT NULL,
     email varchar(255) NOT NULL,
     username varchar(255) NOT NULL,
     password varchar(255) NOT NULL,
     created_on datetime NOT NULL,
     last_on datetime NOT NULL,
     PRIMARY KEY (id),
   ```

```
    UNIQUE KEY email (email),
    UNIQUE KEY username (username)
) ENGINE=InnoDB DEFAULT CHARSET=utf8;

INSERT INTO users (id, name, email, username, password, created_on,
last_on) VALUES
(1, 'Alexandre', 'demo@gmail.com', 'demo',
'$2a$10$pyMYtPfIvE.PAboF3cIx9.IsyW73voMIRxFINohzgeV0I2BxwnrEu',
'2019-06-17 00:00:00', '2019-01-21 23:32:58');
```

The user password in the preceding sample data is `123123` and is bcrypted as `$2a$10$pyMYtPfIvE.PAboF3cIx9.IsyW73voMIRxFINohzgeV0I2BxwnrEu`. We will install and use the `bcryptjs` Node.js module to hash and validate this password on the server side. But before jumping to `bcryptjs`, let's take a look at the structure for the app that we will create in the next section.

> You can find a copy of the database we have exported as `nuxt-auth.sql` in `/chapter-12/` in our GitHub repository.

Structuring cross-domain app directories

We have been making Nuxt apps for single domains. Our server-side APIs have been tightly coupled with Nuxt since Chapter 8, *Adding a Server-Side Framework*, in which we used Koa as the server-side framework and API for handling and serving data for the Nuxt apps. If you take a look back in `/chapter-8/nuxt-universal/koa-nuxt/` in our GitHub repository, you should remember we have kept our server-side programs and files in the `/server/` directory. We have also kept our package/module dependencies in one `package.json` file and installed them in the same `/node_modules/` directory. It can be confusing eventually, when our apps get larger, mixing the module dependencies for two frameworks (Nuxt and Koa) in the same `package.json` file. It can make the debugging process harder too. So separating our single app that's made of Nuxt and Koa (or any other server-side frameworks, such as Express) into two individual apps probably is better for scalability and maintenance. Now, it is time to make a cross-domain Nuxt app. We will reuse and restructure our Nuxt apps from Chapter 8, *Adding a Server-Side Framework*. Let's call our Nuxt app a frontend app and the Koa app a backend app. We will add new modules separately in these two apps as we go along.

Creating User Logins and API Authentication

The backend app will do the backend authentication, while the frontend app will do the frontend authentication separately, but they will act as one eventually. And to make this learning and restructuring process easier for you, we will use JWT only for authentication. So, let's create our new working directories in the following steps:

1. Create a project directory and name it anything you like with two subdirectories in it. One is called `frontend` and the other is called `backend`, as follows:

   ```
   <project-name>
   ├── frontend
   └── backend
   ```

2. Install the Nuxt app with the scaffolding tool, `create-nuxt-app`, in the `/frontend/` directory so you get the Nuxt directories that you are already familiar with, as follows:

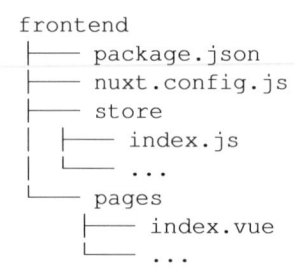

   ```
   frontend
   ├── package.json
   ├── nuxt.config.js
   ├── store
   │   ├── index.js
   │   └── ...
   └── pages
       ├── index.vue
       └── ...
   ```

3. Create a `package.json` file, a `backpack.config.js` file, a `/static/` folder, and an `/src/` folder in the `/backend/` directory, followed by other files and subfolders (we will go through them in more detail in the upcoming section) in the `/src/` folder as follows:

   ```
   backend
   ├── package.json
   ├── backpack.config.js
   ├── assets
   │   └── ...
   ├── static
   │   └── ...
   └── src
       ├── index.js
       ├── ...
       ├── modules
       │   └── ...
       └── core
           └── ...
   ```

The backend directory is where our API is, which can be made using Express or Koa. We will still use Koa, which you are already familiar with. We will install server-side dependencies in this directory, such as `mysql`, `bcryptjs`, and `jsonwebtoken` so that they don't get mixed up with the frontend modules for the Nuxt app.

As you can see, in this new structure, we managed to separate and decouple our API from the Nuxt app completely. There are benefits of this for debugging and development. Technically, we will now develop and test an app at a time. Developing two apps in a single environment can be confusing and it can be difficult to collaborate when the apps get larger – just as we mentioned earlier.

Before looking into how we can use JWT on the server side, let's first take a deeper look at how we can structure the API routes and modules in the `/src/` directory in the next section.

Creating API public/private routes and their modules

Note that it is **not** mandatory to follow the directory structure suggested here in this book. There are no arbitrary or official rules for how we should structure our app with Koa. There are some skeletons, boilerplates, and frameworks contributed by the Koa community, which you can take a look at by visiting `https://github.com/koajs/koa/wiki`. Now let's take a closer look at the directory structure in the `/src/` directory, where we will develop our API source code, in the following steps:

1. Create the following folders and empty `.js` files in the `/src/` directory as follows:

```
└── src
    ├── index.js
    ├── middlewares.js
    ├── routes-private.js
    ├── routes-public.js
    ├── config
    │   └── index.js
    ├── core
    │   └── database
    ├── middlewares
    │   ├── authenticate.js
    │   ├── errorHandler.js
```

Creating User Logins and API Authentication

```
    └── ...
└── modules
    └── ...
```

Inside the /src/ directory, the /middlewares/ directory is where all middlewares are kept, such as authenticate.js, which we want to register with the Kao app.use method, while the /modules/ directory is where all the groups of API endpoints are kept, such as home, user, and login.

2. Create two main directories, private and public, with subdirectories in each of them as follows:

```
└── modules
    ├── private
    │   └── home
    └── public
        ├── home
        ├── user
        └── login
```

The /public/ directory is used for public access without JWT, such as the login route, while the /private/ directory is used for access that requires JWT to protect the modules. As you can see, we have separated API routes into two main groups, so the /private/ group will be handled in routes-private.js, and the /public/ group will be handled in routes-public.js. We have the /config/ directory to keep all config files, and the /core/ directory to keep the abstract programs or modules that can be shared and used throughout the app, such as the mysql connection pool that you will discover later in this chapter. So, from the preceding directory tree, we will use these public modules in our API: home, user, login, and one private module: home.

3. In each module, for example, in the user module, create a /_routes/ directory to configure all the routes (or endpoints) that belong to this particular module (or group):

```
└── user
    ├── index.js
    └── _routes
        ├── index.js
        └── fetch-user.js
```

[414]

In this `user`, module, the `/user/index.js` file is where all routes of this module are assembled and grouped in the module route, for example:

```
// src/modules/public/user/index.js
import Router from 'koa-router'
import fetchUsers from './_routes'
import fetchUser from './_routes/fetch-user'

const router = new Router({
  prefix: '/users'
})
const routes = [fetchUsers, fetchUser]

for (var route of routes) {
  router.use(route.routes(), route.allowedMethods())
}
```

The value of `/users` that is set to the `prefix` key is the module route for this user module. Inside each imported child route is where we develop our code, such as the code for the login route.

4. In each `.js` file in each module, for example, in the `user` module, add the following basic code structure for building our code in the later stages:

```
// src/modules/public/user/_routes/index.js
import Router from 'koa-router'
import pool from 'core/database/mysql'

const router = new Router()

router.get('/', async (ctx, next) => {
  // code goes here....
})
export default router
```

5. Let's create the `home` module, which will return a response with a `'Hello World!'` message as follows:

```
// src/modules/public/home/_routes/index.js
import Router from 'koa-router'
const router = new Router()

router.get('/', async (ctx, next) => {
  ctx.type = 'json'
  ctx.body = {
    message: 'Hello World!'
  }
```

Creating User Logins and API Authentication

```
})
export default router
```

6. It is only one route from the `home` module, but we still need to assemble this route in an `index.js` file in this module so that we can keep our code consistent with other modules, as follows:

```
// src/modules/public/home/index.js
import Router from 'koa-router'
import index from './_routes'

const router = new Router() // no prefix
const routes = [index]

for (var route of routes) {
  router.use(route.routes(), route.allowedMethods())
}
export default router
```

> Note that there is no prefix added to this `home` module, so we can access its only route directly at `localhost:4000/public`.

7. Create the `routes-public.js` file in the `/src/` directory and import all the public routes from the public modules in the `/modules/` directory as follows:

```
// src/routes-public.js
import Router from 'koa-router'

import home from './modules/public/home'
import user from './modules/public/user'
import login from './modules/public/login'

const router = new Router({ prefix: '/public' })
const modules = [home, user, login]

for (var module of modules) {
  router.use(module.routes(), module.allowedMethods())
}
export default router
```

As you can see, we imported the `home` module that we have just created in the previous steps. We will create the `user` and `login` modules in the coming sections. After importing these modules, we should register their routes to the router and then export the router. Notice that a prefix, `/public`, is added to these routes. Also, notice that every route is looped and registered to the router with the plain JavaScript `for` loop function.

8. Create the `routes-private.js` file in the `/src/` directory and import all the private routes from the private modules in the `/modules/` directory as follows:

```
// src/routes-private.js
import Router from 'koa-router'

import home from './modules/private/home'
import authenticate from './middlewares/authenticate'

const router = new Router({ prefix: '/private' })
const modules = [home]

for (var module of modules) {
  router.use(authenticate, module.routes(),
module.allowedMethods())
}
export default router
```

In this file, you can see that we will create a private `home` module only in the coming sections. Also, an `authenticate` middleware is imported in this file and added to the private route so that the private module can be protected. After that, we should export the private route with the router and prefix it with `/private`. We will create this `authenticate` middleware in the coming section as well. For now, let's configure our module file paths with Backpack and install the essential Node.js modules that our API essentially depends on.

9. Add the following additional file paths (`./src`, `./src/core`, and `./src/modules`) to the webpack configuration through the Backpack config file:

```
// backpack.config.js
module.exports = {
  webpack: (config, options, webpack) => {
    config.resolve.modules = ['./src', './src/core',
      './src/modules']
    return config
  }
}
```

Creating User Logins and API Authentication

With these additional file paths, we can import our module simply with `import pool from 'core/database/mysql'`, instead of the following:

```
import pool from '../../../../core/database/mysql'
```

> For more information about resolving modules by using the `modules` option in webpack, please visit https://webpack.js.org/configuration/resolve/#resolvemodules.

10. Now we should install Backpack in our project, as well as the other basic and essential Node.js modules that we will need in order to develop this backend app:

    ```
    $ npm i backpack-core
    $ npm i cross-env
    $ npm i koa
    $ npm i koa-bodyparser
    $ npm i koa-favicon
    $ npm i koa-router
    $ npm i koa-static
    ```

    > You should be familiar with these modules as you have learned about them and installed them in Chapter 8, *Adding a Server-Side Framework*, which you can revisit in /chapter-8/nuxt-universal/koa-nuxt/ in our GitHub repository, and also, in Chapter 10, *Adding a Vuex Store*, in /chapter-10/nuxt-universal/nuxtServerInit/, and Chapter 11, *Writing Route Middlewares and Server Middlewares*, in /chapter-11/nuxt-universal/route-middleware/per-route/.

11. Add the following run scripts in `package.json` in the `/backend/` directory:

    ```
    // package.json
    {
      "scripts": {
        "dev": "backpack",
        "build": "backpack build",
        "start": "cross-env NODE_ENV=production node build/main.js"
      }
    }
    ```

    So, the `"dev"` run script is used for developing our API, the `"build"` run script is used for building our API when it is completed, and the `"start"` script is used for serving the API after it is built.

Chapter 12

12. Add the following server configuration to the `index.js` file in the `/config/` directory:

    ```
    // src/config/index.js
    export default {
      server: {
        port: 4000
      },
    }
    ```

    This config file only has a very simple configuration, which is the server, configured to run at port 4000.

13. Import the following modules that you have just installed and register them as middlewares in the `middlewares.js` file in the `/src/` directory as follows:

    ```
    // src/middlewares.js
    import serve from 'koa-static'
    import favicon from 'koa-favicon'
    import bodyParser from 'koa-bodyparser'

    export default (app) => {
      app.use(serve('assets'))
      app.use(favicon('static/favicon.ico'))
      app.use(bodyParser())
    }
    ```

14. Create a middleware that handles the HTTP response with a 200 HTTP status in the `/middlewares/` directory:

    ```
    // src/middlewares/okOutput.js
    export default async (ctx, next) => {
      await next()
      if (ctx.status === 200) {
        ctx.body = {
          status: 200,
          data: ctx.body
        }
      }
    }
    ```

    We will get the following JSON output if the response is OK:

    ```
    {"status":200,"data":{"message":"Hello World!"}}
    ```

[419]

15. Create a middleware that handles an HTTP error status, such as 400, 404, and 500:

    ```
    export default async (ctx, next) => {
      try {
        await next()
      } catch (err) {
        ctx.status = err.status || 500

        ctx.type = 'json'
        ctx.body = {
          status: ctx.status,
          message: err.message
        }

        ctx.app.emit('error', err, ctx)
      }
    }
    ```

    You will get the following JSON response for a 400 error response:

    ```
    {"status":400,"message":"username param is required."}
    ```

16. Create a middleware that handles the HTTP 404 response specifically by throwing a 'Not found' message:

    ```
    // src/middlewares/notFound.js
    export default async (ctx, next) => {
      await next()
      if (ctx.status === 404) {
        ctx.throw(404, 'Not found')
      }
    }
    ```

    We will get the following JSON output for an unknown route:

    ```
    {"status":404,"message":"Not found"}
    ```

17. Import these three middlewares into middlewares.js and register them to the Koa instance just like the other middlewares:

    ```
    // src/middlewares.js
    import errorHandler from './middlewares/errorHandler'
    import notFound from './middlewares/notFound'
    import okOutput from './middlewares/okOutput'

    export default (app) => {
      app.use(errorHandler)
    ```

```
        app.use(notFound)
        app.use(okOutput)
}
```

Notice how we arrange these middlewares in sequence – even though the `errorHandler` middleware is registered first, it is the last middleware that will be re-executed in the upstream cascading in Koa if there is an error in the HTTP response. The upstream cascading will stop at the `okOutput` middleware if the HTTP response status is `200`. Also, note that these middlewares must be registered after the `static`, `favicon`, and `bodyparser` middlewares, which must be called and served publicly first in the downstream cascading.

18. Import the public and private routes from `routes-public.js` and `routes-private.js` and register them after the preceding middlewares as follows:

    ```
    // Import custom local middlewares.
    import routesPublic from './routes-public'
    import routesPrivate from './routes-private'

    export default (app) => {
      app.use(routesPublic.routes(), routesPublic.allowedMethods())
      app.use(routesPrivate.routes(), routesPrivate.allowedMethods())
    }
    ```

19. Import Koa, all middlewares from the `middlewares.js` file, and the server configuration in the `index.js` file in the `/config/` directory, instantiate a Koa instance and pass it to the `middlewares.js` file, and then start the server with this Koa instance:

    ```
    // index.js
    import Koa from 'koa'
    import config from './config'
    import middlewares from './middlewares'

    const app = new Koa()
    const host = process.env.HOST || '127.0.0.1'
    const port = process.env.PORT || config.server.port

    middlewares(app)
    app.listen(port, host)
    ```

Creating User Logins and API Authentication

20. Run this API with `npm run dev` and you should see the app running on your browser at `localhost:4000`. You should get the following output on your browser when you are on `localhost:4000`:

```
{"status":404,"message":"Not found"}
```

This is because there is no route set on / anymore – we have prefixed all our routes with `/public` or `/private`. But if you navigate to `localhost:4000/public`, you will get the following JSON output:

```
{"status":200,"data":{"message":"Hello World!"}}
```

This is the response from the `home` module we have just created in the preceding steps. Also, you should see that your favicon and assets are served correctly at `localhost:4000` – if you have placed any of them inside the `/static/` and `/assets/` directories, for example:

```
localhost:4000/sample-asset.jpg
localhost:4000/favicon.ico
```

You can see your files in these two directories at `localhost:4000`. That is because the `static` and `favicon` middlewares are installed and registered to be executed first in the middleware stacks when the downstream cascading in Koa is taking place.

Well done! Now you have the new working directories ready and a basic API running just like in Chapter 8, *Adding a Server-Side Framework*. Next, you will need to install the other server-side dependencies in the `/backend/` directory and start adding code to the routes in the public `user` and `login` modules and the private `home` module. Let's start with `bcryptjs` in the next section.

> You can find the example app with the preceding structure in `/chapter-12/nuxt-universal/cross-domain/jwt/axios-module/backend/` in our GitHub repository.

Using the bcryptjs module for Node.js

As we mentioned before, `bcryptjs` is used to hash and validate passwords. Please take a look at the simplified steps for further advice on how to use this module in our app:

1. Install the bcryptjs module via npm:

    ```
    $ npm i bcryptjs
    ```

[422]

2. Hash a password by adding `salt` with the password sent from the client in the request body (request), for example, during a new user creation in the `user` module:

   ```
   // src/modules/public/user/_routes/create-user.js
   import bcrypt from 'bcryptjs'

   const saltRounds = 10
   const salt = bcrypt.genSaltSync(saltRounds)
   const hashed = bcrypt.hashSync(request.password, salt)
   ```

   > Note that to speed up our authentication lesson in the chapter, we skip the process of creating a new user. But in a more complete CRUD, you can use this step to hash the password provided by the user.

3. Verify a password by comparing the password sent from the client (request) with the one stored in the database, for example, during the login authentication process in the `login` module as follows:

   ```
   // src/modules/public/login/_routes/local.js
   import bcrypt from 'bcryptjs'

   const isMatched = bcrypt.compareSync(request.password,
     user.password)
   if (isMatched === false) { ... }
   ```

   > Note that you can find out how this step is applied in our backend app in `/chapter-12/nuxt-universal/cross-domain/jwt/axios-module/backend/src/modules/public/login/_routes/local.js` in our GitHub repository.

We will show you how to use `bcryptjs` to verify the incoming password from the client in the coming section. But before hashing and verifying the password from the client, first, we need to connect to our MySQL database in order to establish whether to inject the new user or query the existing ones. For that, we will need the next Node.js module in our app: mysql - a MySQL client. So let's move on to the next section to see how you can install and use it.

> If you want to find more information about this module and some asynchronous examples, please visit https://github.com/dcodeIO/bcrypt.js.

[423]

Using the mysql module for Node.js

We have the MySQL server that we installed in the previous section. Now we will need a MySQL client that we can connect to the MySQL server and perform SQL queries from our server-side program. mysql is the standard MySQL Node.js module that implements the MySQL protocol, thus we can use this module for handling MySQL connection and SQL queries, whether you are on MySQL server or MariaDB server. So, let's get it started in the following steps:

1. Install the `mysql` module via npm:

    ```
    $ npm i mysql
    ```

2. Create the MySQL connection instance in a `mysql.js` file with your MySQL connection details in the subdirectories in the `/src/` directory as follows:

    ```
    // src/core/database/mysql.js
    import util from 'util'
    import mysql from 'mysql'

    const pool = mysql.createPool({
      connectionLimit: 10,
      host : 'localhost',
      user : '<username>',
      password : '<password>',
      database : '<database>'
    })

    pool.getConnection((err, connection) => {
      if (error) {
        // Handle errors ...
      }
      // Release the connection to the pool if no error.
      if (connection) {
        connection.release()
      }
      return
    })
    pool.query = util.promisify(pool.query)
    export default pool
    ```

Let's go through the code we just created in the following notes:

- mysql does not support `async/await`, so we wrapped MySQL's `pool.query` with the `promisify` utility from Node.js. `pool.query` is the function from mysql that handles our SQL query and it returns the result in a callback, for example:

    ```
    connection.query('SELECT ...', function (error, results, fields) {
      if (error) {
        throw error
      }
      // Do something ...
    })
    ```

    With the promisify utility, we have eliminated the callback and now we can use `async/await` as follows:

    ```
    let result = null
    try {
      result = await pool.query('SELECT ...')
    } catch (error) {
      // Handle errors ...
    }
    ```

- `pool.query` is a shortcut function for these three functions, `pool.getConnection`, `connection.query`, and `connection.release`, that we should use together to perform a SQL query in the connection pooling in the mysql module. By using `pool.query`, the connection is automatically released back to the pool when you are done with it. This is the basic underlying structure of the `pool.query` function:

    ```
    import mysql from 'mysql'
    const pool = mysql.createPool(...)

    pool.getConnection(function(error, connection) {
      if (error) { throw error }

      connection.query('SELECT ...', function (error, results,
        fields) {
        connection.release()
        if (error) { throw error }
      })
    })
    ```

Creating User Logins and API Authentication

- In this mysql module, instead of creating and managing the MySQL connections one by one by using `mysql.createConnection`, which can be an expensive operation, we can use `mysql.createPool` for connection pooling, which is a cache of reusable database connections to reduce the cost of establishing fresh connections whenever we want to connect to the database. For more information about connection pooling, please visit https://github.com/mysqljs/mysqlpooling-connections.

3. So, we have abstracted the MySQL connection into the preceding file in the /core/ directory. Now we can use it to fetch the list of users in the user module as follows:

   ```
   // backend/src/modules/public/user/_routes/index.js
   import Router from 'koa-router'
   import pool from 'core/database/mysql'
   const router = new Router()

   router.get('/', async (ctx, next) => {
     try {
       var users = await pool.query(
         'SELECT `id`, `name`, `created_on`
         FROM `users`'
       )
     } catch (err) { ... }

     ctx.type = 'json'
     ctx.body = users
   })

   export default router
   ```

   You can see that we use the same code structure that we have laid out in the previous section to send our request to the MySQL server via the MySQL connection pool. In the query that we send, we tell the MySQL server to return only the fields of `id`, `name`, and `created_on` from the `users` table in the result for us.

4. If you visit the user route at `localhost:4000/public/users`, you should get the following output on your screen:

   ```
   {"status":200,"data":[{"id":1,"name":"Alexandre","created_on":"2019-06-16T22:00:00.000Z"}]}
   ```

Now we have the mysql module for connecting to the MySQL server and databases, and the bcryptjs module for hashing and verifying passwords from the client, so we can refactor and improve the login code that we created roughly in the previous chapter. Let's find out how in the next section.

> If you want to find out more information about the mysql module, please visit https://github.com/mysqljs/mysql.

Refactoring login code on the server side

We have gathered all the essential ingredients in the previous sections, and as soon as we have the MySQL connection pool created, we can refactor and improve our login code from Chapter 10, *Adding a Vuex Store*, and Chapter 11, *Writing Route Middlewares and Server Middlewares*, in the following steps:

1. Import all the dependencies, such as koa-router, jsonwebtoken, bcryptjs, and the MySQL connection pool for the login route as follows:

    ```
    // src/modules/public/login/_routes/local.js
    import Router from 'koa-router'
    import jwt from 'jsonwebtoken'
    import bcrypt from 'bcrypt'
    import pool from 'core/database/mysql'
    import config from 'config'

    const router = new Router()

    router.post('/login', async (ctx, next) => {
      let request = ctx.request.body || {}
      //...
    })

    export default router
    ```

    We imported the config file here for the configuration options of our API, which contains the MySQL database connection details, the options for the server and the static directory, and the secret code for the JWT that we will need later for signing a token.

Creating User Logins and API Authentication

2. Validate the user inputs inside the `post` method for the login route to ensure they are defined and not empty:

   ```
   if (request.username === undefined) {
     ctx.throw(400, 'username param is required.')
   }
   if (request.password === undefined) {
     ctx.throw(400, 'password param is required.')
   }
   if (request.username === '') {
     ctx.throw(400, 'username is required.')
   }
   if (request.password === '') {
     ctx.throw(400, 'password is required.')
   }
   ```

3. Assign the username and password to variables for querying the database when they pass the validation:

   ```
   let username = request.username
   let password = request.password

   let users = []
   try {
     users = await pool.query('SELECT  FROM users WHERE
       username = ?', [username])
   } catch(err) {
     ctx.throw(400, err.sqlMessage)
   }

   if (users.length === 0) {
     ctx.throw(404, 'no user found')
   }
   ```

4. Compare the stored password and the password from the user with bcryptjs if there are results from the MySQL query:

   ```
   let user = users[0]
   let match = false

   try {
     match = await bcrypt.compare(password, user.password)
   } catch(err) {
     ctx.throw(401, err)
   }
   if (match === false) {
     ctx.throw(401, 'invalid password')
   }
   ```

5. Sign a JWT and send it to the client if the user passes all the previous steps and validations:

```
let payload = { name: user.name, email: user.email }
let token = jwt.sign(payload, config.JWT_SECRET, { expiresIn:
  1 * 60 })

ctx.body = {
  user: payload,
  message: 'logged in ok',
  token: token
}
```

6. Run the API with `npm run dev` and test the previous route manually with `curl` on your terminal as follows:

```
$ curl -X POST -d "username=demo&password=123123" -H "Content-Type:
application/x-www-form-urlencoded"
http://localhost:4000/public/login/local
```

You should get the following result if you have logged in successfully:

```
{"status":200,"data":{"user":{"name":"Alexandre","email":"thiamkok.
lau@gmail.com"},"message":"logged in
ok","token":"eyJhbGciOiJIUzI1NiIsInR5cCI6IkpXVCJ9.eyJuYW1lIjoiQWxle
GFuZHJlIiwiZW1haWwiOiJ0aGlhbWtvay5sYXVAZ21haWwuY29tIiwiaWF0IjoxNTgw
MDExNzAwLCJleHAiOjE1ODAwMTE3NjB9.Lhd78jokSGALup6DUYAqWAjl7C-8dLhXjE
ba-KAxy4k"}}
```

Of course, you will get a different token in the preceding response whenever it is signed successfully. Now you have managed to refactor and improve the login code. Next, we will look at how we can verify the preceding token, which will be sent back in the request header from the client side, in the next section. So, keep reading!

Verifying the incoming token on the server side

We have successfully signed a token and returned it to the client when the credentials match what we have stored in the database. But that is only half of the story. We should verify this token each time the client makes a request with it, to access all protected routes guarded by the server-side middleware.

Creating User Logins and API Authentication

So, let's create the middleware and the protected route in the following steps:

1. Create a middleware file in the `/middlewares/` directory inside the `/src/` directory with the following code:

    ```
    // src/middlewares/authenticate.js
    import jwt from 'jsonwebtoken'
    import config from 'config'

    export default async (ctx, next) => {
      if (!ctx.headers.authorization) {
        ctx.throw(401, 'Protected resource, use Authorization header
        to get access')
      }
      const token = ctx.headers.authorization.split(' ')[1]

      try {
        ctx.state.jwtPayload = jwt.verify(token, config.JWT_SECRET)
      } catch (err) {
        // handle error.
      }
      await next()
    }
    ```

    The `if` condition, `!ctx.headers.authorization`, is used to ensure that the client has included the token in the request headers. Since `authorization` comes in with the value in the format `Bearer: [token]`, which has a single space in it, we split the value by that space and only take `[token]` for verification in the `try` and `catch` blocks. If the token is valid, then we let the request through to the next route with `await next()`.

2. Import and inject this middleware to the group of routes that we want to secure with JWT:

    ```
    // src/routes-private.js
    import Router from 'koa-router'
    import home from './modules/private/home'
    import authenticate from './middlewares/authenticate'

    const router = new Router({ prefix: '/private' })
    const modules = [home]

    for (var module of modules) {
      router.use(authenticate, module.routes(),
    module.allowedMethods())
    }
    ```

In this API, we want to secure all routes that fall under the `/private` route. So we will import any routes that we want to secure in this file, for example, the preceding `/home` route. Therefore, when you request this route with `/private/home`, you must include the token in the request to headers to access this route.

That's it. You have managed to create and verify the JWT on the server side. Next, we should look at how we can complete the JWT authentication with Nuxt on the client side in the next section. Let's get going!

Creating frontend authentication

You will find this section easy and familiar because you have built a few authentication Nuxt apps with the dummy backend authentication in the previous two chapters. The difference in this chapter is that we are making cross-domain apps instead of single-domain apps like in the previous two chapters. You can revisit these single-domain Nuxt apps in `/chapter-10/nuxt-universal/nuxtServerInit/` and in `/chapter-11/nuxt-universal/route-middleware/per-route/`.

Furthermore, we will once again use the Nuxt modules that we already covered in *Chapter 6, Writing Plugins and Modules*: `@nuxtjs/axios` and `@nuxtjs/proxy`. You can revisit the Nuxt app that adopts these two modules in `/chapter-6/nuxt-universal/module-snippets/top-level/`. But for now, let's get them installed and configured for this Nuxt app, which we will refactor from the previous chapters, to create the client-side authentication in the following steps:

1. Install `@nuxtjs/axios` and `@nuxtjs/proxy` via npm:

    ```
    $ npm i @nuxtjs/axios
    $ npm i @nuxtjs/proxy
    ```

2. Configure these two modules in the Nuxt config file as follows:

    ```
    // nuxt.config.js
    module.exports = {
      modules: [
        '@nuxtjs/axios',
      ],

      axios: {
        proxy: true
      },

      proxy: {
    ```

Creating User Logins and API Authentication

```
        '/api/': { target: 'http://localhost:4000/', pathRewrite:
        {'^/api/': ''} },
    }
}
```

Since we know the remote API server that we created in the previous sections is running at `localhost:4000`, in this configuration, we assign this API address to the `/api/` key in the `proxy` option.

3. Remove any `import` statement that we used to import the axios Node.js module previously; for example, on the secured page:

   ```
   // pages/secured.vue
   import axios from '~/plugins/axios'
   ```

   This is because we are now using `@nuxtjs/axios` (the Nuxt Axios module) and we will not need to import the vanilla axios Node.js module directly in our code anymore.

4. Call the Nuxt Axios module by using `$axios` and replace `axios` (from the vanilla axios Node.js module), which we used previously in our code for HTTP requests; for example, on the secured page:

   ```
   // pages/secured.vue
   async asyncData ({ $axios, redirect }) {
     const { data } = await $axios.$get('/api/private')
   }
   ```

The Nuxt Axios module is loaded to our Nuxt app via the Nuxt config file in *step 2*, so we can access it from the Nuxt context or `this` by using `$axios`.

We also should refactor the rest of the code in the store and middleware in this app with these two Nuxt modules – `@nuxtjs/axios` and `@nuxtjs/proxy`, and the cookies, Node.js modules (client- and server-side). So let's get to it in the following sections.

Using cookies on the (Nuxt) client side

In this app, we no longer use sessions to "remember" the authenticated data. Instead, we will use the `js-cookie` Node.js module to create cookies to store the data from the remote server.

It is very easy to use this Node.js module to create a cookie that presents across the entire site; for example:

1. Use the following format to set a cookie:

    ```
    Cookies.set(<name>, <value>)
    ```

    Here's the code for if you want to create a cookie that expires 30 days from now:

    ```
    Cookies.set(<name>, <value>, { expires: 30 })
    ```

2. Use the following format to read the cookie:

    ```
    Cookies.get(<name>)
    ```

You can see how easy it is using this Node.js module – all you need is the `set` and `get` methods to set and retrieve your cookies on the client side. So, let's refactor the code in our store in the following steps:

1. Use the `if` ternary condition to import the js-cookie Node.js module when our Nuxt app is processed on the client side only:

    ```
    // store/actions.js
    const cookies = process.client ? require('js-cookie') : undefined
    ```

2. Use the `set` function from js-cookie to store the data from the server as `auth` in the `login` action as follows:

    ```
    // store/actions.js
    export default {
      async login(context, { username, password }) {
        const { data } = await
          this.$axios.$post('/api/public/login/local',
          { username, password })
        cookies.set('auth', data)
        context.commit('setAuth', data)
      }
    }
    ```

3. Use the `remove` function from js-cookie to delete the `auth` cookie in the `logout` action as follows:

    ```
    // store/actions.js
    export default {
      logout({ commit }) {
        cookies.remove('auth')
        commit('setAuth', null)
    ```

[433]

```
      }
   }
```

It is very simple, isn't it? But, you may ask: what do we use this `auth` cookie for, and how? Let's find out in the next section on using cookies on the Nuxt server side.

> For more information and code examples of the Node.js module, please visit https://github.com/js-cookie/js-cookie.

Using cookies on the (Nuxt) server side

Since our authenticated data with JWT has been hashed and stored in a cookie by `js-cookie` as `auth`, we will need to read and parse this cookie whenever we need it. This is where the Node.js module, `cookie`, comes in. Again, we have used this Node.js module in past chapters but we haven't talked about it.

The cookie Node.js module is an HTTP cookie parser and serializer for HTTP servers. It is used to parse the cookie header on the server side. Let's take a look at how we can use it on the `auth` cookie in the following steps:

1. Use the `if` ternary condition to import the cookie Node.js module when our Nuxt app is processed on the server side only:

   ```
   // store/index.js
   const cookie = process.server ? require('cookie') : undefined
   ```

2. Use the `parse` function from the cookie Node.js module to parse the `auth` cookie in the HTTP request headers in the `nuxtServerInit` action as follows:

   ```
   // store/index.js
   export const actions = {
     nuxtServerInit({ commit }, { req }) {
       if (req.headers.cookie && req.headers.cookie.indexOf('auth') > -1) {
         let auth = cookie.parse(req.headers.cookie)['auth']
         commit('setAuth', JSON.parse(auth))
       }
     }
   }
   ```

3. Use the `setHeader` function from the Nuxt Axios module via `$axios` to include the token (JWT) in the HTTP header in the token middleware for accessing the private API routes on the remote server as follows:

```
// middleware/token.js
export default async ({ store, error, $axios }) => {
  if (!store.state.auth.token) {
    // handle error
  }
  $axios.setHeader('Authorization', Bearer:
${store.state.auth.token})
}
```

4. Run the Nuxt app with `npm run dev`. You should get the app running on your browser at `localhost:3000`. You can log in with credentials on the login page and then access the restricted secured page, which is protected by the JWT.

Well done! You have completed the token-based local authentication. You have refactored the code in the store and middleware to get the `js-cookie` and `cookie` Node.js modules to work together and complement each other perfectly on the client and server sides in the Nuxt app for frontend authentication. Also, you have managed to decouple the Nuxt app from the API with the cross-domain approach.

As you can see, using the `js-cookie` and `cookie` Node.js modules for frontend authentication is easy and great. But it also can be achieved with Google OAuth, which we will look into in the next section. Adding Google OAuth to the frontend authentication can give the user an extra option to log in to your app. So, let's get to it.

> You can find the source code of this Nuxt app in `/chapter-12/nuxt-universal/cross-domain/jwt/axios-module/frontend/` in our GitHub repository.
>
> For more information and code examples of the `cookie` Node.js module, please visit https://github.com/jshttp/cookie.
>
> For more information about helpers, such as the `setHeader` helper from the Nuxt Axios module, please visit https://axios.nuxtjs.org/helpers.

Signing in with Google OAuth

OAuth is an open delegated authorization protocol that grants access between websites or apps without exposing user passwords to the parties that have been granted access. It is a very common access delegation used by many companies and websites to identify users with parties such as Google and Facebook that provide OAuth authorization. Let's let our users log in to our app with Google OAuth. This option requires a client ID and a client secret from the Google Developer Console. They can be obtained with the following steps:

1. Create a new project in the Google Developer Console at `https://console.developers.google.com/`.

2. Select **External** on the OAuth **consent screen** tab.

3. Select **OAuth client ID** from the **Create Credentials** drop-down options on the **Credentials** tab, and then select **Web application** for the **Application type**.

4. Provide the name of your OAuth client ID in the **Name** field and the redirect URIs in the **Authorized redirect URIs** field for Google to redirect the user after authenticating on the Google consent page.

5. Enable the Google People API, which provides access to information about profiles and contacts in the API Library from the Library tab.

Once you have a developer account set up and get the **client ID** and **client secret** created by following the previous steps, you are ready to add Google OAuth to the backend authentication in the next section. Let's get to it.

Adding Google OAuth to the backend authentication

For us to sign someone into Google, we need to send them to the Google Login page. From there, they will sign into their account and will be redirected to our app with their Google sign-in details, from which we will extract the Google code and send it back to Google to obtain the user data that we can use in our app. This process requires the `googleapis` Node.js module, which is a client library for using Google APIs.

Let's get it installed and adopted in our code with the following steps:

1. Install the `googleapis` Node.js module via npm:

   ```
   $ npm i googleapis
   ```

2. Create a file with your credentials so Google knows who is making the requests:

   ```
   // backend/src/config/google.js
   export default {
     clientId: '<client ID>',
     clientSecret: '<client secret>',
     redirect: 'http://localhost:3000/login'
   }
   ```

   Note you must replace the preceding `<client ID>` and `<client secret>` values with the ID and secret that you obtain from the Google Developer Console. Also, note that the URL in the `redirect` option must match the redirect URIs in **Authorized redirect URIs** in your Google app API settings.

3. Generate a Google authentication URL with Google OAuth for sending the user to the Google consent page to get permissions from the user to retrieve an access token as follows:

   ```
   // backend/src/modules/public/login/_routes/google/url.js
   import Router from 'koa-router'
   import { google } from 'googleapis'
   import googleConfig from 'config/google'

   const router = new Router()

   router.get('/google/url', async (ctx, next) => {
     const oauth = new google.auth.OAuth2(
       googleConfig.clientId,
       googleConfig.clientSecret,
       googleConfig.redirect
     )

     const scopes = [
       'https://www.googleapis.com/auth/userinfo.email',
       'https://www.googleapis.com/auth/userinfo.profile',
     ]

     const url = oauth.generateAuthUrl({
       access_type: 'offline',
       prompt: 'consent',
   ```

[437]

```
    scope: scopes
  })

  ctx.body = url
})
```

Scopes determine what information and permissions we want from the user when they sign in and then generate the URL. In our case, we want permission to retrieve the information of the user email and profile: `userinfo.email` and `userinfo.profile`. After the user has authenticated on the Google consent page, Google will redirect the user back to our app with a bunch of authenticated data and an authorization code for accessing the user data.

4. Extract the value in the `code` parameter from the authenticated data appended by Google in the returned URL in the previous step. We will come back to the Node.js module, which can help us to extract the `code` parameter from the URL query later, in the next section. Now, let's assume we have extracted the `code` value and sent it to the server side to request tokens with the Google OAuth2 instance in the following basic code structure:

```
// backend/src/modules/public/login/_routes/google/me.js
import Router from 'koa-router'
import { google } from 'googleapis'
import jwt from 'jsonwebtoken'
import pool from 'core/database/mysql'
import config from 'config'
import googleConfig from 'config/google'

const router = new Router()

router.get('/google/me', async (ctx, next) => {

  // Get the code from url query.
  const code = ctx.query.code

  // Create a new google oauth2 client instance.
  const oauth2 = new google.auth.OAuth2(
    googleConfig.clientId,
    googleConfig.clientSecret,
    googleConfig.redirect
  )
  //...
})
```

5. Obtain tokens from Google with the code we just extracted and pass them to Google People, `google.people`, to get the user data with the `get` method and specify what fields relating to the person need to be returned in the `personFields` query parameter:

```
// backend/src/modules/public/login/_routes/google/me.js
...
const {tokens} = await oauth2.getToken(code)
oauth.setCredentials(tokens)

const people = google.people({
  version: 'v1',
  auth: oauth2,
})

const me = await people.people.get({
  resourceName: 'people/me',
  personFields: 'names,emailAddresses'
})
```

You can see that we want only two fields relating to the person from Google in our preceding code, which are `names` and `emailAddresses`. You can find out what other fields relating to the person you want from Google at https://developers.google.com/people/api/rest/v1/people/get. We should get the user data in the JSON format from Google if access is successful, and then we can extract the email from that data to ensure it will match a user in our database in the next step.

6. Retrieve the first email only from the Google person data and query our database to see whether there is any user with that email already:

```
// backend/src/modules/public/login/_routes/google/me.js
...
let email = me.data.emailAddresses[0].value
let users = []

try {
  users = await pool.query('SELECT  FROM users WHERE email = ?',
    [email])
} catch(err) {
  ctx.throw(400, err.sqlMessage)
}
```

7. Send a `'signup required'` message to the client side with the user data from Google if there is no user with that email and ask the user to sign up for an account in our app:

```
// backend/src/modules/public/login/_routes/google/me.js
...
if (users.length === 0) {
  ctx.body = {
    user: me.data,
    message: 'signup required'
  }
  return
}
let user = users[0]
```

8. Sign a JWT with a payload and the JWT secret if there is a match, and then send the token (JWT) to the client side:

```
// backend/src/modules/public/login/_routes/google/me.js
...
let payload = { name: user.name, email: user.email }
let token = jwt.sign(payload, config.JWT_SECRET, { expiresIn: 1 * 60 })

ctx.body = {
  user: payload,
  message: 'logged in ok',
  token: token
}
```

That's it. You have managed to add Google OAuth on the server side in the preceding few steps. Next, we should look at how we can complete the authentication with Nuxt on the client side for Google OAuth in the next section. Let's get going.

> For more information about the googleapis Node.js module, please visit https://github.com/googleapis/google-api-nodejs-client.

Creating frontend authentication for Google OAuth

When Google redirects the user back to our app, we will get a bunch of data on the redirect URL, for example:

```
http://localhost:3000/login?code=4%2F1QGpS37E21TcgQhhIvJZlK1cG4M1jpPJ0I_XPQ
grFjvKUFUJQ3aYuO1zYsqPmKgNb4Wfd8ito88yDjUTD6CKD3E&scope=email%20profile%20h
ttps%3A%2F%2Fwww.googleapis.com%2Fauth%2Fuserinfo.email%20https%3A%2F%2Fwww
.googleapis.com%2Fauth%2Fuserinfo.profile%20openid&authuser=1&prompt=consen
t
```

It is quite difficult to read and decipher when you first look at it, but it is just a query string with parameters appended to our redirect URL:

```
<redirect URL>?
code=4/1QFvWYDSrW...
&scope=email profile...
&authuser=1
&prompt=consent
```

We can use a Node.js module, `query-string`, to parse the query string in the URL, for example:

```
const queryString = require('query-string')
const parsed = queryString.parse(location.search)
console.log(parsed)
```

Then you will get the following JavaScript object in your browser's console:

```
{authuser: "1", code:
"4/1QFvWYDSrWLklhIgRfVR0LJy6Pk0gn5TkjTKWKlRr9pdZveGAHV_pMrxBhicy7Zd6d9nfz0I
QrcLl-VGS-Gu9Xk", prompt: "consent", scope: "email profile
https://www.googleapis.com/auth/user...//www.googleapis.com/auth/userinfo.pro
file openid"}
```

The `code` parameter is what we are interested in the most in the preceding redirect URL as we will need to send it to the server side as you learned in the previous section, in order to obtain the Google user data through the googleapis Node.js module. So, let's get `query-string` installed and create the frontend authentication in our Nuxt app in the following steps:

1. Install the `query-string` Node.js module via npm:

    ```
    $ npm i query-string
    ```

Creating User Logins and API Authentication

2. Create a button on the login page and bind a method called `loginWithGoogle` to dispatch the `getGoogleUrl` method in the store as follows:

```
// frontend/pages/login.vue
<button v-on:click="loginWithGoogle">Google Login</button>

export default {
  methods: {
    async loginWithGoogle() {
      try {
        await this.$store.dispatch('getGoogleUrl')
      } catch (error) {
        let errorData = error.response.data
        this.formError = errorData.message
      }
    }
  }
}
```

3. Call the `/api/public/login/google/url` route in the API in the `getGoogleUrl` method as follows:

```
// frontend/store/actions.js
export default {
  async getGoogleUrl(context) {
    const { data } = await this.$axios.$get('/api/public/login/
      google/url')
    window.location.replace(data)
  }
}
```

The `/api/public/login/google/url` route will send back a Google URL and then we can use it to redirect the user to the Google Login page. From there, the user will decide which Google account to log in to if they have more than one.

4. Extract the query part from the returned URL and send it to the `loginWithGoogle` method in the store when Google redirects the user back to the login page as follows:

```
// frontend/pages/login.vue
export default {
  async mounted () {
    let query = window.location.search

    if (query) {
      try {
        await this.$store.dispatch('loginWithGoogle', query)
```

[442]

```
        } catch (error) {
          // handle error
        }
      }
    }
  }
}
```

5. Extract the code from the `code` parameter in the preceding query part with `query-string` and send it to our API, `/api/public/login/google/me`, using `$axios` as follows:

   ```
   // frontend/store/actions.js
   import queryString from 'query-string'

   export default {
     async loginWithGoogle (context, query) {
       const parsed = queryString.parse(query)
       const { data } = await this.$axios.$get('/api/public/login/
         google/me', {
         params: {
           code: parsed.code
         }
       })

       if (data.message === 'signup required') {
         localStorage.setItem('user', JSON.stringify(data.user))
         this.$router.push({ name: 'signup'})
       } else {
         cookies.set('auth', data)
         context.commit('setAuth', data)
       }
     }
   }
   ```

   We will redirect the user to a sign-up page when we get the `'signup required'` message from the server. But if we get the message with JWT, then we can set a cookie and the authenticated data to the store state. We will leave the sign-up page to your imagination and own effort because it is a form to collect data from the user to be stored in the database.

6. Finally, run the Nuxt app with `npm run dev`. You should get the app running on your browser at `localhost:3000`. You can log in with Google and then access the restricted page, which is protected by the JWT – just like the local authentication.

Creating User Logins and API Authentication

So, there you go – these are the basic steps you take to sign the user in with the Google OAuth API. It is not hard at all, is it? We can also use the Nuxt Auth module to achieve almost the same as we have accomplished here. With this module, you can sign the user in with Auth0, Facebook, GitHub, Laravel Passport, and Google. If you are looking for quick, simple, and zero-boilerplate authentication support for Nuxt, it could be a good option for your project. For more information about this Nuxt module, please visit `https://auth.nuxtjs.org/`. Now let's summarize what you have learned in this chapter in the next section.

> You can find the preceding login option with Google OAuth in `/chapter-12/nuxt-universal/cross-domain/jwt/axios-module/` in our GitHub repository.
>
> For more information about the usage of the `query-string` Node.js module, visit `https://www.npmjs.com/package/query-string`.

Summary

Well done! You have made it this far. After all, it is not difficult to work on web authentication. In this chapter, you have learned what session-based authentication and token-based authentication are, particularly about the JSON Web Token (JWT). You should now know the differences between them and the constituents of a JWT, and how to generate a JWT with the `jsonwebtoken` Node.js module. We have also covered the MySQL Node.js module and used it as part of our authentication system. You have also integrated Google OAuth for signing the user in and then creating the frontend authentication using Nuxt.

In the next chapter, you will learn how to write end-to-end tests in your Nuxt apps. You will learn about the tools you can install and use for writing your end-to-end tests, notably AVA and Nightwatch. Besides this, you will also learn how to use a Node.js module, which is `jsdom`, to make your end-to-end testing possible on the server side. This is because Nuxt technically is a server-side technology and renders our HTML pages on the server side, but there is no DOM on the server side, so we can leverage `jsdom` for that. But rest assured, we will walk you through the steps to get all these tools set up and write your tests. So, stay tuned!

Section 5: Testing and Deployment

In this section, we will write tests and deploy the Nuxt app to a hosting server. We will also learn how to keep our code clean with some JavaScript tools while complying with the coding standard.

This section comprises the following chapters:

- Chapter 13, *Writing End-to-End Tests*
- Chapter 14, *Using Linters, Formatters, and Deployment Commands*

13 Writing End-to-End Tests

Writing tests is part of web development. The more complex and the bigger your app gets, the more you need to test the app, otherwise, it will break at some point and you will spend lots of time fixing bugs and patching things up. In this chapter, you will write end-to-end tests with AVA and jsdom for Nuxt apps, and also get hands-on experience of browser automated testing with Nightwatch. You will learn how to install these tools and set up the testing environment – so let's get started.

The topics we will cover in this chapter are as follows:

- End-to-end testing versus unit testing
- End-to-end testing tools
- Writing tests with `jsdomn` and AVA for Nuxt apps
- Introducing Nightwatch
- Writing tests with Nightwatch for Nuxt apps

End-to-end testing versus unit testing

There are two types of tests commonly practiced for web applications: unit testing and end-to-end testing. You might have heard a lot about unit testing and have done some (or loads) in the past. Unit testing is used to test the small and individual parts of your app, while in contrast, end-to-end testing is to test the overall functions of your app. End-to-end testing involves ensuring the integrated components of an app function as expected. In other words, the entire app is tested in a real-world scenario similar to how a real user would interact with your app. For example, the simplified end-to-end testing of your user login page might involve the following:

1. Load the login page.
2. Provide valid details to the inputs in the login form.
3. Click on the **Submit** button.

4. Log in to the page successfully and see a greeting message.
5. Log out of the system.

What about unit testing? Unit testing runs fast and allows us to precisely identify exact problems and bugs. The main downside of unit testing is that it is time-consuming to write tests for every aspect of your app. And despite the fact that your app has passed the unit tests, the app as a whole may still break.

End-to-end testing can implicitly test many things at once and assure you that you have a working system. End-to-end testing runs slowly compared to unit testing and it can't explicitly point you to the root of the failure of your app. A small change in seemingly insignificant parts of your app can break your entire testing suite.

Combining unit and end-to-end tests for an app can be ideal and compelling because that gives you a more thorough test of your app, but again it can be time-consuming and costly. In this book, we focus on **end-to-end testing** because by default, Nuxt is configured seamlessly with the end-to-end testing tools that you will discover in the next section.

End-to-end testing tools

Nuxt makes end-to-end testing very easy and fun by using the AVA and jsdom Node.js modules together. But before implementing and combining them for the tests in a Nuxt app, let's dive into each of these Node.js modules to see how they work separately so you have a solid basic understanding of these tools. Let's start with jsdom in the next section.

jsdom

In a nutshell, `jsdom` is a JavaScript-based implementation of the W3C Document Object Model (DOM) for Node.js. But, what does it mean? What do we need it for? Imagine you need to manipulate DOM from a raw HTML on the server side in a Node.js app, such as Express and Koa apps, but there is no DOM on the server side and hence there isn't much you can do. This is when jsdom comes to our rescue. It turns the raw HTML into a DOM fragment that works like the DOM on the client side, but inside Node.js. And then, you can use a client-side JavaScript library such as jQuery to manipulate the DOM on Node.js like a charm. The following is an example of basic usage of this for server-side apps:

1. Import jsdom on a server-side app:

```
import jsdom from 'jsdom'
const { JSDOM } = jsdom
```

2. Pass in a string of any raw HTML to the JSDOM constructor and you will get back a DOM object:

```
const dom = new JSDOM(<!DOCTYPE html><p>Hello World</p>)
console.log(dom.window.document.querySelector('p').textContent)
```

The DOM object you get from the preceding code snippet has many useful properties, notably the `window` object, and then you can start manipulating the HTML string you pass in just like on the client side. Now let's apply this tool on the **Koa API**, which you learned about in the previous chapter and which can be found in /chapter-12/nuxt-universal/cross-domain/jwt/axios-module/backend/ in our GitHub repository, to print the Hello world message. Follow these steps:

1. Install jsdom and jQuery via npm:

```
$ npm i jsdom --save-dev
$ npm i jquery --save-dev
```

2. Import jsdom and pass an HTML string, just like we did in the preceding basic usage example:

```
// src/modules/public/home/_routes/index.js
import Router from 'koa-router'
import jsdom from 'jsdom'

const { JSDOM } = jsdom
const router = new Router()

const html = '<!DOCTYPE html><p>Hello World</p>'
const dom = new JSDOM(html)
const window = dom.window
const text = window.document.querySelector('p').textContent
```

3. Output the text to the endpoint:

```
router.get('/', async (ctx, next) => {
  ctx.type = 'json'
  ctx.body = {
    message: text
  }
})
```

Writing End-to-End Tests

You should see the "Hello world" message in JSON format (shown in the following snippet) at `localhost:4000/public` when you run `npm run dev` on your terminal:

```
{"status":200,"data":{"message":"Hello world"}}
```

4. Create a `movie` module in our API and use Axios to fetch an HTML page from the IMDb website, pass the HTML to the JSDOM constructor, import jQuery, and then apply it to the DOM window object created by jsdom as follows:

```
// src/modules/public/movie/_routes/index.js
const url = 'https://www.imdb.com/movies-in-theaters/'
const { data } = await axios.get(url)

const dom = new JSDOM(data)
const $ = (require('jquery'))(dom.window)
```

> Note that Axios must be installed in your project directory via npm, which you do with `npm i axios`.

5. Apply the jQuery object to all movies with the `list_item` class and extract the data (the name and showtime of each movie) as follows:

```
var items = $('.list_item')
var list = []
$.each(items, function( key, item ) {
  var movieName = $('h4 a', item).text()
  var movieShowTime = $('h4 span', item).text()
  var movie = {
    name: movieName,
    showTime: movieShowTime
  }
  list.push(movie)
})
```

6. Output the `list` to the endpoint:

```
ctx.type = 'json'
ctx.body = {
  list: list
}
```

You should see a similar list of movies in the following JSON format at `localhost:4000/public/movies`:

```
{
  "status": 200,
  "data": {
    "list": [{
      "name": " Onward (2020)",
      "showTime": ""
    }, {
      "name": " Finding the Way Back (2020)",
      "showTime": ""
    },
    ...
    ...
    ]
  }
}
```

> You can find these examples in /chapter-13/jsdom/ in our GitHub repository. For more information about this npm package, visit https://github.com/jsdom/jsdom.

You can see how useful this tool is on the server side. It gives us the ability to manipulate the raw HTML as if we were on the client side. Now let's move on to AVA and learn some basic usage of it in the next section before using it together with **jsdom** in our Nuxt app.

Writing End-to-End Tests

AVA

In short, AVA (not Ava or ava, pronounced /ˈeɪvə/) is a JavaScript test runner for Node.js. There are a lot of test runners out there: Mocha, Jasmine, and tape, among others. AVA is another alternative to the existing list. First of all, AVA is simple. It is really easy to set up. Besides, it runs the test in parallel by default, which means your tests will run fast. It works for both frontend and backend Javascript apps. All in all, it's certainly worth a try. Let's get started by creating a simple and basic Node.js app in the following steps:

1. Install AVA via npm and save it to the devDependencies option in the package.json file:

    ```
    $ npm i ava --save-dev
    ```

2. Install Babel core and other Babel packages for us to write ES6 code in our tests for the app:

    ```
    $ npm i @babel/polyfill
    $ npm i @babel/core --save-dev
    $ npm i @babel/preset-env --save-dev
    $ npm i @babel/register --save-dev
    ```

3. Configure the test script in the package.json file as follows:

    ```
    // package.json
    {
      "scripts": {
        "test": "ava --verbose",
        "test:watch": "ava --watch"
      },
      "ava": {
        "require": [
          "./setup.js",
          "@babel/polyfill"
        ],
        "files": [
          "test/**/*"
        ]
      }
    }
    ```

4. Create a `setup.js` file in the root directory with the following code:

   ```
   // setup.js
   require('@babel/register')({
     babelrc: false,
     presets: ['@babel/preset-env']
   })
   ```

5. Create the following class and function that we want to test later in these two separate files in our app:

   ```
   // src/hello.js
   export default class Greeter {
     static greet () {
       return 'hello world'
     }
   }

   // src/add.js
   export default function (num1, num2) {
     return num1 + num2
   }
   ```

5. Create a `hello.js` test in the `/test/` directory for testing `/src/hello.js`:

   ```
   // test/hello.js
   import test from 'ava'
   import hello from '../src/hello'

   test('should say hello world', t => {
     t.is('hello world', hello.greet())
   })
   ```

6. Create another test in a separate file in the `/test/` directory again for testing `/src/add.js`:

   ```
   // test/add.js
   import test from 'ava'
   import add from '../src/add'

   test('amount should be 50', t => {
     t.is(add(10, 50), 60)
   })
   ```

7. Run all the tests on your terminal:

   ```
   $ npm run test
   ```

Writing End-to-End Tests

You also can run the test with the `--watch` flag to enable AVA's watch mode:

```
$ npm run test:watch
```

You should get the following result if the tests pass:

```
✓ add › amount should be 50
✓ hello › should say hello world

2 tests passed
```

> You can find the preceding examples in `/chapter-13/ava/` in our GitHub repository. For more information about this npm package, visit `https://github.com/avajs/ava`.

That is easy and fun, isn't it? It is always rewarding to see our code pass its tests. Now you have a basic understanding of this tool, so it is time to implement it with jsdom in the Nuxt app. Let's get to it in the next section.

Writing tests with jsdomn and AVA for Nuxt apps

You have learned about jsdom and AVA independently and have done some simple tests. Now, we can bring these two packages together into our Nuxt apps. Let's install them in our Nuxt app, which you created in the previous chapter, in `/chapter-12/nuxt-universal/cross-domain/jwt/axios-module/frontend/` using the following steps:

1. Install these two tools via npm and save them to the `devDependencies` option in the `package.json` file:

    ```
    $ npm i ava --save-dev
    $ npm i jsdom --save-dev
    ```

2. Install Babel core and other Babel packages for us to write ES6 code in our tests in the app:

    ```
    $ npm i @babel/polyfill
    $ npm i @babel/core --save-dev
    $ npm i @babel/preset-env --save-dev
    $ npm i @babel/register --save-dev
    ```

[454]

3. Add the AVA configuration to the `package.json` file as follows:

```
// package.json
{
  "scripts": {
    "test": "ava --verbose",
    "test:watch": "ava --watch"
  },
  "ava": {
    "require": [
      "./setup.js",
      "@babel/polyfill"
    ],
    "files": [
      "test/**/*"
    ]
  }
}
```

4. Create a `setup.js` file in the root directory, just like you did in the previous section, but using the following code:

```
// setup.js
require('@babel/register')({
  babelrc: false,
  presets: ['@babel/preset-env']
})
```

5. Prepare the following test template for writing tests in the `/test/` directory:

```
// test/tests.js
import test from 'ava'
import { Nuxt, Builder } from 'nuxt'
import { resolve } from 'path'

let nuxt = null

test.before('Init Nuxt.js', async t => {
  const rootDir = resolve(__dirname, '..')
  let config = {}
  try { config = require(resolve(rootDir, 'nuxt.config.js')) }
    catch (e) {}
  config.rootDir = rootDir
  config.dev = false
  config.mode = 'universal'
  nuxt = new Nuxt(config)
  await new Builder(nuxt).build()
  nuxt.listen(5000, 'localhost')
```

Writing End-to-End Tests

```
})

// write your tests here...

test.after('Closing server', t => {
  nuxt.close()
})
```

The tests will run on `localhost:5000` (or any port you like). You should test on the production build, so turn development mode off in the `config.dev` key and use `universal` in the `config.mode` key if your app was developed for both server and client sides. Then, make sure to close the Nuxt server after the test process is finished.

6. Write the first test to test our home page to ensure that we have correct HTML rendered on this page:

```
// test/tests.js
test('Route / exits and renders correct HTML', async (t) => {
  let context = {}
  const { html } = await nuxt.renderRoute('/', context)
  t.true(html.includes('<p class="blue">My marvelous Nuxt.js
    project</p>'))
})
```

7. Write the second test for the `/about` route to ensure that we have correct HTML rendered on this page:

```
// test/tests.js
test('Route /about exits and renders correct HTML', async (t) => {
  let context = {}
  const { html } = await nuxt.renderRoute('/about', context)
  t.true(html.includes('<h1>About page</h1>'))
  t.true(html.includes('<p class="blue">Something awesome!</p>'))
})
```

8. Write the third test for the `/about` page to ensure the text content, class name, and style are as expected via DOM manipulation on the server side with `jsdom`:

```
// test/tests.js
test('Route /about exists and renders correct HTML and style',
async (t) => {

  function hexify (number) {
    const hexChars =
      ['0','1','2','3','4','5','6','7','8','9','a','b',
      'c','d','e','f']
```

```
      if (isNaN(number)) {
        return '00'
      }
      return hexChars[(number - number % 16) / 16] +
        hexChars[number % 16]
    }

    const window = await nuxt.renderAndGetWindow(
      'http://localhost:5000/about')
    const element = window.document.querySelector('.blue')
    const rgb = window.getComputedStyle(element).color.match(/\d+/g)
    const hex = '' + hexify(rgb[0]) + hexify(rgb[1]) + hexify(rgb[2])

    t.not(element, null)
    t.is(element.textContent, 'Something awesome!')
    t.is(element.className, 'blue')
    t.is(hex, '0000ff')
})
```

You should get the following result if the tests pass with `npm run test`:

```
✓ Route / exits and renders correct HTML (369ms)
✓ Route /about exits and renders correct HTML (369ms)
✓ Route /about exists and renders correct HTML and style (543ms)

3 tests passed
```

You can see that in our third test, we created a `hexify` function to convert a decimal code (R, G, B), computed by the `Window.getComputedStyle` method, to a hex code. For example, you will get `rgb(255, 255, 255)` for the colour you set as `color: white` in your CSS style. So, you will get `rgb(0, 0, 255)` for `0000ff` and the app must convert that to pass the test.

> You can find these tests in /chapter-13/nuxt-universal/ava/ in our GitHub repository.

Well done. You have managed to write simple tests for Nuxt apps. We hope you find it easy and fun to write tests in Nuxt. The complexity of your test depends on what you want to test. Hence, it is very important to first understand what you want to test. Then, you can start writing a test that is sensible, meaningful, and relevant.

Writing End-to-End Tests

However, using jsdom with AVA to test the Nuxt app has some limitations because it does not involve a browser. Remember that jsdom is meant for turning the raw HTML into the DOM on the server side, hence we use the async/await statement to request a page asynchronously for our tests in the preceding exercise. If you want to use a browser to test your Nuxt app, Nightwatch can be a good solution, so we will take a look at it in the next section. Let's move on.

Introducing Nightwatch

Nightwatch is an automated testing framework that provides an end-to-end testing solution for web-based apps. It uses the W3C WebDriver API (it was called Selenium WebDriver formerly) behind the scenes to open the **web browser** to perform operations and assertions on DOM elements. It is a great tool if you want to use a browser to test your Nuxt apps. But before using it in a Nuxt app, let's use it on its own in the following steps to write some simple tests so that you have a basic idea of how it works:

1. Install Nightwatch via npm and save it to the `devDependencies` option in the `package.json` file:

    ```
    $ npm i nightwatch --save-dev
    ```

2. Install GeckoDriver via npm and also save it to the `devDependencies` option in the `package.json` file:

    ```
    $ npm install geckodriver --save-dev
    ```

    Nightwatch relies on WebDriver, so we need to install a specific WebDriver server depending on your **target browser** – for example, if you want to write tests against Firefox only, then you will need to install GeckoDriver.

    In this book, we focus on writing tests against a single browser. But if you want to target multiple browsers such as Chrome, Edge, Safari, and Firefox in parallel, then you will need to install the **Selenium Standalone Server** (also known as Selenium Grid), as follows:

    ```
    $ npm i selenium-server --save-dev
    ```

    > Note that we will be testing on Firefox and Chrome in this book, so this `selenium-server` package will not be used.

[458]

3. Add nightwatch to the test script in the package.json file:

```
// package.json
{
  "scripts": {
    "test": "nightwatch"
  }
}
```

4. Create a nightwatch.json file to configure Nightwatch as follows:

```
// nightwatch.json
{
  "src_folders" : ["tests"],

  "webdriver" : {
    "start_process": true,
    "server_path": "node_modules/.bin/geckodriver",
    "port": 4444
  },

  "test_settings" : {
    "default" : {
      "desiredCapabilities": {
        "browserName": "firefox"
      }
    }
  },

  "launch_url": "https://github.com/lautiamkok"
}
```

In this simple exercise, we want to test the repository search function of github.com on a specific contributor called **Lau Tiam Kok**, so we set https://github.com/lautiamkok in the launch_url option in this configuration.

We will write tests in the /tests/ directory, so we indicate the directory location in the src_folders option. We will test against Firefox only at 4444 (the server port) so we set this information in the webdriver and test_settings options.

> You can find the options for the rest of test settings such as output_folder at https://nightwatchjs.org/gettingstarted/configuration/. If you want to find out the test settings for the Selenium Server, please visit https://nightwatchjs.org/gettingstarted/configuration/selenium-server-settings.

Writing End-to-End Tests

5. Create a `nightwatch.conf.js` file in the project root for setting the driver path **dynamically** to the server path:

```js
// nightwatch.conf.js
const geckodriver = require("geckodriver")
module.exports = (function (settings) {
  settings.test_workers = false
  settings.webdriver.server_path = geckodriver.path
  return settings
})(require("./nightwatch.json"))
```

6. Prepare the following Nightwatch test template in a `.js` file (for example, `demo.js`) in the `/tests/` directory, as follows:

```js
// tests/demo.js
module.exports = {
  'Demo test' : function (browser) {
    browser
      .url(browser.launchUrl)
      // write your tests here...
      .end()
  }
}
```

7. Create a `github.js` file in the `/tests/` directory with the following code:

```js
// tests/github.js
module.exports = {
  'Demo test GitHub' : function (browser) {
    browser
      .url(browser.launchUrl)
      .waitForElementVisible('body', 1000)
      .assert.title('lautiamkok (LAU TIAM KOK) · GitHub')
      .assert.visible('input[type=text][placeholder=Search]')
      .setValue('input[type=text][placeholder=Search]', 'nuxt')
      .waitForElementVisible('li[id=jump-to-suggestion-
        search-scoped]', 1000)
      .click('li[id=jump-to-suggestion-search-scoped]')
      .pause(1000)
      .assert.visible('ul[class=repo-list]')
      .assert.containsText('em:first-child', 'nuxt')
      .end()
  }
}
```

In this test, we want to assert that the repository search function is working as expected so we need to make sure that certain elements and text contents exist and are visible, such as the `<body>` and `<input>` elements, and the text for `nuxt` and `lautiamkok (LAU TIAM KOK) · GitHub`. You should get the following result (assuming the test passes) when you run it with `npm run test`:

```
[Github] Test Suite
===================
Running: Demo test GitHub

  ✓ Element <body> was visible after 34 milliseconds.
  ✓ Testing if the page title equals "lautiamkok (LAU TIAM KOK) ·
    GitHub" - 4 ms.
  ✓ Testing if element <input[type=text][placeholder=Search]> is
    visible - 18 ms.
  ✓ Element <li[id=jump-to-suggestion-search-scoped]> was visible
    after 533 milliseconds.
  ✓ Testing if element <ul[class=repo-list]> is visible - 25 ms.
  ✓ Testing if element <em:first-child> contains text: "nuxt"
    - 28 ms.

OK. 6 assertions passed. (5.809s)
```

> You can find the preceding test in /chapter-13/nightwatch/ in our GitHub repository. For more information on Nightwatch, please visit https://nightwatchjs.org/.

Compared to AVA, Nightwatch is not as minimal as it requires some configuration that can be lengthy and complex, but if you follow the simplest `nightwatch.json` file, it should get you started with Nightwatch quite quickly. So, let's apply what you just have learned in this section to the Nuxt app in the next section.

Writing End-to-End Tests

Writing tests with Nightwatch for Nuxt apps

In this exercise, we want to test the user login authentication that we created in the previous chapter, Chapter 12, *Creating User Logins and API Authentication*, against the **Chrome browser**. We want to make sure the user can log in with their credentials and obtain their user data as expected. We will write the tests in the /frontend/ directory where we kept the Nuxt app, so we will need to modify the package.json file accordingly and write the tests in the following steps:

1. Install ChromeDriver via npm and save it to the devDependencies option in the package.json file:

   ```
   $ npm install chromedriver --save-dev
   ```

2. Change the launch URL to localhost:3000 and other settings as shown in the following code block in the nightwatch.json file for testing against Chrome in the Nightwatch configuration file:

   ```
   // nightwatch.json
   {
     "src_folders" : ["tests"],

     "webdriver" : {
       "start_process": true,
       "server_path": "node_modules/.bin/chromedriver",
       "port": 9515
     },

     "test_settings" : {
       "default" : {
         "desiredCapabilities": {
           "browserName": "chrome"
         }
       }
     },

     "launch_url": "http://localhost:3000"
   }
   ```

3. Create a nightwatch.conf.js file in the project root for setting the driver path **dynamically** to the server path:

   ```
   // nightwatch.conf.js
   const chromedriver = require("chromedriver")
   module.exports = (function (settings) {
     settings.test_workers = false
   ```

```
        settings.webdriver.server_path = chromedriver.path
        return settings
})(require("./nightwatch.json"))
```

4. Create a `login.js` file in the `/tests/` directory with the following code:

```
// tests/login.js
module.exports = {
    'Local login test' : function (browser) {
      browser
        .url(browser.launchUrl + '/login')
        .waitForElementVisible('body', 1000)
        .assert.title('nuxt-e2e-tests')
        .assert.containsText('h1', 'Please login to see the
          secret content')
        .assert.visible('input[type=text][name=username]')
        .assert.visible('input[type=password][name=password]')
        .setValue('input[type=text][name=username]', 'demo')
        .setValue('input[type=password][name=password]',
          '123123')
        .click('button[type=submit]')
        .pause(1000)
        .assert.containsText('h2', 'Hello Alexandre!')
        .end()
    }
}
```

The logic of this test is the same as the test in the previous section. We want to make sure that certain elements and texts are present on the login page before and after logging in.

4. Before running the test, run the Nuxt and API apps at `localhost:3000` and `localhost:4000` on your terminal and then open another terminal with `npm run test` in the `/frontend/` directory. You should get the following result if the test passes:

```
[Login] Test Suite
==================
Running: Local login test

✓ Element <body> was visible after 28 milliseconds.
✓ Testing if the page title equals "nuxt-e2e-tests" - 4 ms.
✓ Testing if element <h1> contains text: "Please login to see the
  secret content" - 27 ms.
✓ Testing if element <input[type=text][name=username]> is
  visible - 25 ms.
✓ Testing if element <input[type=password][name=password]> is
```

Writing End-to-End Tests

```
          visible - 25 ms.
   ✓ Testing if element <h2> contains text: "Hello Alexandre!"
     - 75 ms.

   OK. 6 assertions passed. (1.613s)
```

> Note that you must run the Nuxt app and the API concurrently before running the tests.
>
> You can find the preceding test in `/chapter-13/nuxt-universal/nightwatch/` in our GitHub repository.

Well done. You have finished this short chapter on writing tests for Nuxt apps. The steps and exercises in this chapter have provided you with the basic foundation to expand your tests as your app gets larger and complicated. Let's summarize what you have learned in this chapter in the final section.

Summary

In this chapter, you have learned to use jsdom for server-side DOM manipulation and for writing simple tests with AVA and Nightwatch separately, and then tried using these tools together to run end-to-end tests on our Nuxt app. You also have learned the difference between end-to-end testing and unit testing and their respective pros and cons. Last but not least, you have learned from the exercises in this chapter that Nuxt is configured perfectly by default for you to write end-to-end tests with jsdom and AVA with much less effort.

In the coming chapter, we will cover how to keep our code clean with linters such as ESLint, Prettier, and StandardJS, integrating and mixing them for Vue and Nuxt apps. Finally, you will learn the Nuxt deployment commands and use them to deploy your app to a live server. So, stay tuned.

14
Using Linters, Formatters, and Deployment Commands

Besides writing tests (whether they are end-to-end tests or unit tests), code linting and formatting also are parts of web development. All developers, whether you are a Java, Python, PHP, or JavaScript developer, should know the coding standards in their fields and comply with them to keep your code clean, readable, and formatted for better maintenance in the future. The tools that we commonly use for JavaScript, Vue, and Nuxt apps are ESLint, Prettier, and StandardJS. In this chapter, you will learn to install, configure, and use them with our apps. Finally, after building, testing, and linting your app, you will learn the Nuxt deployment commands to deploy your app to a host.

The topics we will cover in this chapter are the following:

- Introducing Linters – Prettier, ESLint, and StandardJS
- Integrating ESLint and Prettier
- Using ESLint and Prettier for Vue and Nuxt apps
- Deploying Nuxt apps

Introducing linters – Prettier, ESLint, and StandardJS

In a nutshell, a linter is a tool that analyzes source code and flags errors and bugs in the code and styles. The term originated in 1978 from a Unix utility called `lint` that evaluated source code written in C, and was developed by computer scientist Stephen C. Johnson at Bell Labs while debugging the Yacc grammar he was writing. Today, the tools we focus on in this book are Prettier, ESLint, and StandardJS. Let's look into each of them.

Prettier

Prettier is a code formatter that supports many languages such as JavaScript, Vue, JSX, CSS, HTML, JSON, GraphQL, and more. It improves the readability of your code and ensures your code conforms to the rules that it has set for you. It sets a length limit for your lines of code; for example, take a look at the single following line of code:

```
hello(reallyLongArg(), omgSoManyParameters(), IShouldRefactorThis(), isThereSeriouslyAnotherOne())
```

The preceding code is considered lengthy on a single line and is difficult to read, so Prettier will reprint it into multiple lines for you as follows:

```
hello(
  reallyLongArg(),
  omgSoManyParameters(),
  IShouldRefactorThis(),
  isThereSeriouslyAnotherOne()
);
```

Also, any custom or messy styling is also parsed and reprinted, as in the following example:

```
fruits({ type: 'citrus' },
  'orange', 'kiwi')

fruits(
  { type: 'citrus' },
  'orange',
  'kiwi'
)
```

Prettier will print and reformat this into the following, much neater format:

```
fruits({ type: 'citrus' }, 'orange', 'kiwi');

fruits({ type: 'citrus' }, 'orange', 'kiwi');
```

However, if Prettier finds no semicolons in your code, it will insert them for you, just as in the preceding example code. You can turn this feature off if you prefer no semicolons in your code, as is the case with all the code used in this book. Let's turn off this rule with the following steps:

1. Install Prettier via npm to your project:

   ```
   $ npm i prettier --save-dev --save-exact
   ```

2. Parse a specific JavaScript file:

   ```
   $ npx prettier --write src/index.js
   ```

   Or, parse all files in the recursive folders:

   ```
   $ npx prettier --write "src/**/*"
   ```

   Or even try parsing the files in parallel folders:

   ```
   $ npx prettier --write "{scripts,config,bin}/**/*"
   ```

Before committing any change **in-place** (beware!) with the `--write` option, you can use other output options such as the following:

- Use `-c` or `--check` to check whether the given files are formatted and print a human-friendly summary message afterward with the paths to the unformatted files.
- Use `-l` or `--list-different` to print the names of files that are different from Prettier's formatting.

> For more information about this tool, visit `https://prettier.io/`.

Now let's take a look at how we can configure this tool in the next section.

Configuring Prettier

Prettier is built with many options for customization. You can configure Prettier via the following options:

- A `prettier.config.js` or `.prettierrc.js` script in a JavaScript object
- A `package.json` file using a `prettier` key
- A `.prettierrc` file in YAML or JSON with optional extensions: `.json`, `.yaml`, or `.yml`
- A `.prettierrc.toml` file in TOML

It is a good idea to customize Prettier even though you can choose not to. For example, Prettier enforces double quotes and prints semicolons at the ends of statements by default. If we don't want these defaults, we can create a `prettier.config.js` file in our project root directory. Let's use Prettier in the API we have created (we made a copy at `/chapter-14/apps-to-fix/koa-api/` in our GitHub repository) with this configuration in the following steps:

1. Create a `prettier.config.js` file in our project root directory with the following code:

   ```
   // prettier.config.js
   module.exports = {
     semi: false,
     singleQuote: true
   }
   ```

2. Parse all the JavaScript code in the `/src/` directory with the following command:

   ```
   $ npx prettier --write "src/**/*"
   ```

   As you can see, all our files are listed on the terminal when you run `npx prettier --write "src/**/*"`:

   ```
   src/config/google.js 40ms
   src/config/index.js 11ms
   src/core/database/mysql.js 18ms
   src/index.js 8ms
   ...
   ```

   Prettier will highlight the files that have been reprinted and formatted.

> For more format options, check out `https://prettier.io/docs/en/options.html`. You can find this example in `/chapter-14/prettier/` in our GitHub repository.

It is pretty sweet when you see your code "prettified" so effortlessly, isn't it? Let's move on to the next linter, ESLint, to see how it helps to tidy up our code in the next section.

ESLint

ESLint is a pluggable linter for JavaScript. It is designed so that all of its rules are completely pluggable and allows developers to customize the linting rules. ESLint is shipped with some built-in rules to make it useful from the start, but you can dynamically load rules at any point in time. For example, ESLint disallows duplicate keys in object literals (`no-dupe-keys`), and you will get an error for the following code:

```
var message = {
  text: "Hello World",
  text: "qux"
}
```

The correct code under this rule will look like the following:

```
var message = {
  text: "Hello World",
  words: "Hello World"
}
```

ESLint will flag the preceding error and we will have to fix it manually. However, can use the `--fix` option on the command line to automatically fix problems that are more easily fixed without human intervention. Let's see how to do so in the following steps:

1. Install ESLint via npm in your project:

    ```
    $ npm i eslint --save-dev
    ```

2. Set up a configuration file:

    ```
    $ ./node_modules/.bin/eslint --init
    ```

    You will be asked a list of questions similar to the following:

    ```
    ? How would you like to use ESLint? To check syntax, find problems, and enforce code style
    ? What type of modules does your project use? JavaScript modules
    ```

Using Linters, Formatters, and Deployment Commands

```
  (import/export)
? Which framework does your project use? None of these
? Where does your code run? (Press <space> to select, <a> to
  toggle all, <i> to invert selection)Browser
? How would you like to define a style for your project? Use
  a popular style guide
? Which style guide do you want to follow? Standard
(https://github.com/standard/standard)
? What format do you want your config file to be in? JavaScript
...

Successfully created .eslintrc.js file in /path/to/your/project
```

These questions might vary depending on the options/answers you choose for each question.

3. Add the `lint` and `lint-fix` scripts to the `package.json` file:

   ```
   "scripts": {
     "lint": "eslint --ignore-path .gitignore .",
     "lint-fix": "eslint --fix --ignore-path .gitignore ."
   }
   ```

4. Create a `.gitignore` file with the paths and files that we want ESLint to ignore:

   ```
   // .gitignore
   node_modules
   build
   backpack.config.js
   ```

5. Launch ESLint to scan for errors:

   ```
   $ npm run lint
   ```

6. Use `lint-fix` to fix those errors:

   ```
   $ npm run lint-fix
   ```

You can check out the list of ESLint rules at https://eslint.org/docs/rules/. Rules in ESLint are grouped by category: **Possible Errors**, **Best Practices**, **Variables**, **Stylistic Issues**, **ECMAScript 6**, and so on. No rules are enabled by default. You can use the `"extends"`: `"eslint:recommended"` property in a configuration file to enable rules that report common problems, which have a checkmark (✓) in the list.

> For more information about this tool, visit `https://eslint.org/`.

Now let's take a look at how we can configure this tool in the next section.

Configuring ESLint

As we mentioned before, ESLint is a pluggable linter. That means it is completely configurable and that you can switch off every rule, or some of them, or mix custom rules to make ESLint specifically suited for your project. Let's use ESLint in the API we have created with one of the following configurations. There are two methods to configure ESLint:

- Use the JavaScript comments directly with the ESLint configuration information in a file, as in the following example:

    ```
    // eslint-disable-next-line no-unused-vars
    import authenticate from 'middlewares/authenticate'
    ```

- Use a JavaScript, JSON, or YAML file to specify configuration information for an entire directory and all of its subdirectories.

Using the first method can be time-consuming because you may need to provide the ESLint configuration information in every `.js` file, while in the second method, you just need to configure it **once** in a `.json` file. So let's use the second method for our API in the following steps:

1. Create a `.eslintrc.js` file or generate it with `--init` in the root directory with the following rules:

    ```
    // .eslintrc.js
    module.exports = {
      'rules': {
        'no-undef': ['off'],
        'no-console': ['error'],
        'quotes': ['error', 'double']
      }
    }
    ```

[471]

In these rules, we want to make sure to do the following:

- Allow undeclared variables (no-undef) by setting the no-undef option to off
- Disallow the use of the console (no-console) by setting the no-console option to error
- Enforce the consistent use of either backticks, double quotes, or single quotes (quotes) by setting the quotes option to error and double

2. Add the lint and lint-fix scripts to the package.json file:

   ```
   // package.json
   "scripts": {
     "lint": "eslint --ignore-path .gitignore .",
     "lint-fix": "eslint --fix --ignore-path .gitignore ."
   }
   ```

3. Launch ESLint to scan for errors:

   $ npm run lint

   You will get a report like the following if there are any errors:

   ```
   /src/modules/public/login/_routes/google/me.js
       36:11  error  A space is required after '{'  object-
              curly-spacing
       36:18  error  A space is required before '}'  object-
              curly-spacing
   ```

   Even though ESLint can fix your code automatically with the --fix option, you still need to fix some manually, as in the following example:

   ```
   /src/modules/public/user/_routes/fetch-user.js
      9:9  error  'id' is assigned a value but never used
             no-unused-vars
   ```

   > For more information about the configuration, check out https://eslint.org/docs/user-guide/configuring. You can find this example in /chapter-14/eslint/ in our GitHub repository.

It is user-friendly, isn't it? It is indeed another awesome tool just like Prettier. Let's move on to the last linter, StandardJS, to see how it tidies up our code.

[472]

StandardJS

StandardJS or JavaScript Standard Style is a JavaScript style guide, linter, and formatter. It is completely opinionated, meaning that it is completely uncustomizable – no configuration is needed, hence there are no .eslintrc, .jshintrc, or .jscsrc files to manage. It is uncustomizable and unconfigurable. The easiest way to use StandardJS is to install it globally as a Node command-line program. Let's find out how you can use this tool in the following steps:

1. Install StandardJS via npm globally:

    ```
    $ npm i standard --global
    ```

    You can also install it locally for a single project:

    ```
    $ npm i standard --save-dev
    ```

2. Navigate to the directory that you want to inspect and type the following command in the terminal:

    ```
    $ standard
    ```

3. If you install StandardJS locally, then run it with npx instead:

    ```
    $ npx standard
    ```

    You also can add it to the package.json file as follows:

    ```
    // package.json
    {
      scripts": {
        "jss": "standard",
        "jss-fix": "standard --fix"
      },
      "devDependencies": {
        "standard": "^12.0.1"
      },
      "standard": {
        "ignore": [
          "/node_modules/",
          "/build/",
          "backpack.config.js"
        ]
      }
    }
    ```

4. Then the code of your JavaScript project is checked automatically when you run it with npm:

   ```
   $ npm run jss
   ```

   To fix any messy or inconsistent code, try the following command:

   ```
   $ npm run jss-fix
   ```

Even though StandardJS is uncustomizable, it relies on ESLint. The ESLint packages used by StandardJS are as follows:

- `eslint`
- `standard-engine`
- `eslint-config-standard`
- `eslint-config-standard-jsx`
- `eslint-plugin-standard`

While Prettier is a formatter, StandardJS is mostly a linter just like ESLint. If you use `--fix` on your code with StandardJS or ESLint and then run it again with Prettier, you will see that any long lines (which are ignored by StandardJS and ESLint) will be formatted by Prettier.

> For more information about this tool, visit https://standardjs.com/. You should also check out the summary of the standard JavaScript rules at https://standardjs.com/rules.html. You can find an example that uses StandardJS in /chapter-14/standard/ in our GitHub repository.

However, if you are looking for a more flexible and customizable solution that sits in between these tools, you can combine Prettier and ESLint for your project. Let's take a look at how you can achieve that in the next section.

Integrating ESLint and Prettier

Prettier and ESLint complement each other. We can integrate Prettier into the workflow with ESLint. This allows you to use Prettier for formatting your code while letting ESLint focus on linting your code. So, to integrate them, first, we will need the `eslint-plugin-prettier` plugin from ESLint to use Prettier "under" ESLint. Then we can use Prettier to add rules for formatting the code as usual.

However, ESLint contains rules that are formatting-related that can conflict with Prettier, such as `arrow-parens` and `space-before-function-paren`, and that can cause some issues when using them together. To resolve these conflicting issues, we will need the `eslint-config-prettier` config for turning off the ESLint rules that conflict with Prettier. Let's take a look at how you can achieve that in the following steps:

1. Install `eslint-plugin-prettier` and `eslint-config-prettier` via npm:

   ```
   $ npm i eslint-plugin-prettier --save-dev
   $ npm i eslint-config-prettier --save-dev
   ```

2. Enable the plugin and rules of `eslint-plugin-prettier` in the `.eslintrc.json` file:

   ```
   {
     "plugins": ["prettier"],
     "rules": {
       "prettier/prettier": "error"
     }
   }
   ```

3. Override ESLint's rules by extending Prettier's with `eslint-config-prettier` in the `.eslintrc.json` file:

   ```
   {
     "extends": ["prettier"]
   }
   ```

   Note that the value `"prettier"` should be put last in the `extends` array so that Prettier's configurations can override those of ESLint. Also, we can use an `.eslintrc.js` file instead of the JSON file for the preceding configurations because we can add comments in the JavaScript files that can be helpful. So, the following is our configuration for using Prettier under ESLint:

   ```
   // .eslintrc.js
   module.exports = {
     //...
     'extends': ['prettier'],
     'plugins': ['prettier'],
     'rules': {
       'prettier/prettier': 'error'
     }
   }
   ```

4. Configure Prettier in the `package.json` file (or in a `prettier.config.js` file) so that Prettier does not print semicolons in our code and always uses single quotes:

```
{
  "scripts": {
    "lint": "eslint --ignore-path .gitignore .",
    "lint-fix": "eslint --fix --ignore-path .gitignore ."
  },
  "prettier": {
    "semi": false,
    "singleQuote": true
  }
}
```

5. Run `npm run lint-fix` on the terminal to fix and format our code in one shot. After that, you can check the code again with Prettier alone using the `npx prettier` command as follows:

```
$ npx prettier --c "src/**/*"
```

Then you should get the following result on your terminal:

```
Checking formatting...
All matched files use Prettier code style!
```

That means our code has no formatting issues and complies successfully in Prettier code style. It is pretty cool to bring these two tools together to suit our needs and preferences, isn't it? But you are still only half-way through – let's apply these configurations for Vue and Nuxt apps in the next section.

> You can find this integration example in /chapter-14/eslint+prettier/ in our GitHub repository.

Using ESLint and Prettier for Vue and Nuxt apps

The eslint-plugin-vue plugin is an official ESLint plugin for Vue and Nuxt apps. It allows us to inspect the code in the `<template>` and `<script>` blocks in the `.vue` files with ESLint to find any syntax errors, the wrong use of Vue directives, and the Vue style violation against the Vue style guide. Also, we are using Prettier to enforce the code format, so install `eslint-plugin-prettier` and `eslint-config-prettier` just like we did in the previous section for the basic specific configurations that we prefer. Let's get all these sorted in the following steps:

1. Install this `eslint-plugin-vue` plugin using npm:

   ```
   $ npm i eslint-plugin-vue --save-dev
   ```

   You may get some warning:

   ```
   npm WARN eslint-plugin-vue@5.2.3 requires a peer of eslint@^5.0.0
     but none is installed. You must install peer dependencies
       yourself.
   npm WARN vue-eslint-parser@5.0.0 requires a peer of eslint@^5.0.0
     but none is installed. You must install peer dependencies
       yourself.
   ```

   Ignore them because the minimum requirements for `eslint-plugin-vue` are ESLint v5.0.0 or later and Node.js v6.5.0 or later, and you should already have the latest versions.

   > You can check out the minimum requirements at https://eslint.vuejs.org/user-guide/installation. Besides the Vue style guide, you should also check out the Vue rules at https://eslint.vuejs.org/rules/.

2. Add the `eslint-plugin-vue` plugin with its generic rulesets in the ESLint config file:

   ```
   // .eslintrc.js
   module.exports = {
     extends: [
       'plugin:vue/recommended'
     ]
   }
   ```

Using Linters, Formatters, and Deployment Commands

3. Install `eslint-plugin-prettier` and `eslint-config-prettier` and add them to the ESLint config file as well:

```
// .eslintrc.js
module.exports = {
  'extends': [
    'plugin:vue/recommended',
    'plugin:prettier/recommended'
  ],
  'plugins': [
    'prettier'
  ]
}
```

But these are still not enough. You may want to configure some Vue rules to suit your preference. Let's find out some default Vue key rules that we might want to configure in the next section.

> For more information about this `eslint-plugin-vue` plugin, visit https://eslint.vuejs.org/. For Vue directives, please visit https://vuejs.org/v2/api/Directives, and for the Vue style guide, please visit https://vuejs.org/v2/style-guide/.

Configuring Vue rules

There are only four default Vue rules we want to override in this book. You only need to add the preferred rules in the `'rules'` option in the `.eslintrc.js` file just like we did for the `eslint-plugin-prettier` plugin in the previous section. Let's get to it in the following steps:

1. Configure the `vue/v-on-style` rule to "longform" as follows:

```
// .eslintrc.js
'rules': {
  'vue/v-on-style': ['error', 'longform']
}
```

The `vue/v-on-style` rule enforces `shorthand` or `longform` on the `v-on` directive style. The default is set to `shorthand`, for example:

```
<template>
  <!-- ✓ GOOD -->
  <div @click="foo"/>
```

[478]

```
  <!-- ✗ BAD -->
  <div v-on:click="foo"/>
</template>
```

But in this book, `longform` is preferred, as in the following example:

```
<template>
  <!-- ✓ GOOD -->
  <div v-on:click="foo"/>

  <!-- ✗ BAD -->
  <div @click="foo"/>
</template>
```

> For more information about this rule, visit https://eslint.vuejs.org/rules/v-on-style.htmlvue-v-on-style.

2. Configure the `vue/html-self-closing` rule to allow self-closing signs on the void elements as follows:

```
// .eslintrc.js
'rules': {
  'vue/html-self-closing': ['error', {
    'html': {
      'void': 'always'
    }
  }]
}
```

A void element is an HTML element that is not allowed to have contents in any circumstances, such as `<br>`, `<hr>`, `<img>`, `<input>`, `<link>`, and `<meta>`. In writing XHTML, it is mandatory to self-close these elements, such as `<br/>` and `<img src="..." />`. In this book, we want to allow that even though the / character is considered optional in HTML5.

Under the `vue/html-self-closing` rule, you will get errors as a result of self-closing these void elements, even though it aims to enforce the self-closing sign in HTML elements. That's rather confusing, right? In a Vue.js template, we can use either of the following two styles for elements that do not have content:

- `<YourComponent></YourComponent>`
- `<YourComponent/>` (self-closing)

Using Linters, Formatters, and Deployment Commands

Under this rule, the first option is rejected, as in the following example:

```
<template>
  <!-- ✓ GOOD -->
  <MyComponent/>

  <!-- ✗ BAD -->
  <MyComponent></MyComponent>
</template>
```

However, it also rejects the self-closing void elements:

```
<template>
  <!-- ✓ GOOD -->
  <img src="...">

  <!-- ✗ BAD -->
  <img src="..." />
</template>
```

In other words, void elements are not allowed to have self-closing signs in the Vue rules. So the value for the `html.void` option is set to `'never'` by default. So if you want to allow self-closing signs on these void elements, as in this book, then set the value to `'always'`.

> For more information about this rule, visit https://eslint.vuejs.org/rules/html-self-closing.htmlvue-html-self-closing.

3. Configure the `vue/max-attributes-per-line` rule to turn off this rule as follows:

```
// .eslintrc.js
'rules': {
  'vue/max-attributes-per-line': 'off'
}
```

The `vue/max-attributes-per-line` rule aims to enforce one attribute per line. By default, an attribute is considered to be in a new line when there is a line break between two attributes. The following is an example of how this looks under this rule:

```
<template>
  <!-- ✓ GOOD -->
  <MyComponent lorem="1"/>
  <MyComponent
```

[480]

```
      lorem="1"
      ipsum="2"
  />
  <MyComponent
      lorem="1"
      ipsum="2"
      dolor="3"
  />

  <!-- ✗ BAD -->
  <MyComponent lorem="1" ipsum="2"/>
  <MyComponent
      lorem="1" ipsum="2"
  />
  <MyComponent
      lorem="1" ipsum="2"
      dolor="3"
  />
</template>
```

However, this rule conflicts with Prettier. We should let Prettier handle cases like this, which is why we will turn this rule off.

> For more information about this rule, visit https://eslint.vuejs.org/rules/max-attributes-per-line.htmlvue-max-attributes-per-line.

4. Configure the `eslint/space-before-function-paren` rule:

   ```
   // .eslintrc.js
   'rules': {
     'space-before-function-paren': ['error', 'always']
   }
   ```

   The `eslint/space-before-function-paren` rule aims to enforce a space before a function declaration's parentheses. It is ESLint's default behavior to add the space and it is also a defined rule in StandardJS. See the following examples:

   ```
   function message (text) { ... } // ✓ ok
   function message(text) { ... }  // ✗ avoid

   message(function (text) { ... }) // ✓ ok
   message(function(text) { ... })  // ✗ avoid
   ```

Using Linters, Formatters, and Deployment Commands

However, under the preceding rule, you will get errors like the following when you use Prettier:

```
/middleware/auth.js
  1:24 error Delete · prettier/prettier
```

We will ignore the errors from Prettier because we want to follow the rule in Vue. But currently, there is no option from Prettier to disable that yet from https://prettier.io/docs/en/options.html. If you happen to remove that space because of Prettier, you can add it back by setting the value to `'always'` under this Vue rule.

> For more information about this rule, visit https://eslint.org/docs/rules/space-before-function-paren and https://standardjs.com/rules.html.

5. Because ESLint targets only `.js` files by default, include the `.vue` extension with the `--ext` option (or a glob pattern) in the ESLint command to run ESLint with the preceding configurations on the terminal:

```
$ eslint --ext .js,.vue src
$ eslint "src/**/*.{js,vue}"
```

You also can run it with the custom commands in the `scripts` option with `.gitignore` in the `package.json` file as follows:

```
// package.json
"scripts": {
  "lint": "eslint --ext .js,.vue --ignore-path .gitignore .",
  "lint-fix": "eslint --fix --ext .js,.vue --ignore-path
    .gitignore ."
}

// .gitignore
node_modules
build
nuxt.config.js
prettier.config.js
```

[482]

ESLint will ignore files defined in the preceding .gitignore snippet while linting all of the JavaScript and Vue files. It is a good idea to lint files on hot reloading via webpack. Just add the following snippet to the Nuxt config file to run ESLint whenever you save your code:

```
// nuxt.config.js
...
build: {
 extend(config, ctx) {
    if (ctx.isDev && ctx.isClient) {
      config.module.rules.push({
        enforce: "pre",
        test: /\.(js|vue)$/,
        loader: "eslint-loader",
        exclude: /(node_modules)/
      })
    }
  }
}
```

> You can find an example that uses this plugin with ESLint in /chapter-14/eslint-plugin-vue/integrate/ in our GitHub repository.

As you can see in this and the previous sections, mixing ESLint and Prettier in a single config file can be problematic. The hassle you get may not be worth the effort in making them work together "as a team." Why not try to run them separately without coupling them? Let's find out how you can do this for Nuxt apps in the next section.

Running ESLint and Prettier separately in Nuxt apps

Another possible solution to the conflict between ESLint and Prettier, especially on `space-before-function-paren`, is not to integrate them at all, but run them to format and lint our code separately. So let's get this working in the following steps:

1. Create the scripts separately for Prettier and ESLint in the `package.json` file as follows:

    ```
    // package.json
    "scripts": {
    "prettier": "prettier --check \"
     {components,layouts,pages,store,middleware,plugins}/**/*.{vue,js}
       \"", "prettier-fix": "prettier --write
       {components,layouts,pages,store,middleware,plugins}
       /**/*.{vue,js}\"", "lint": "eslint --ext .js,.vue
       --ignore-path .gitignore .",
       "lint-fix": "eslint --fix --ext .js,.vue --ignore-path
         .gitignore ."
    }
    ```

    So now we can completely forget about `eslint-plugin-prettier` and the `eslint-config-prettier` config in our workflow. We still keep `eslint-plugin-vue` and the rules that we have already configured in this chapter, but remove Prettier completely from the `.eslintrc.js` file:

    ```
    // .eslintrc.js
    module.exports = {
      //...
      'extends': [
        'standard',
        'plugin:vue/recommended',
        // 'prettier' // <- removed this.
      ]
    }
    ```

2. Run Prettier first, then ESLint, when we want to analyze our code:

    ```
    $ npm run prettier
    $ npm run lint
    ```

3. Again, run Prettier first, then ESLint, when we want to fix the format and to lint our code:

```
$ npm run prettier-fix
$ npm run lint-fix
```

You can see that this solution keeps our workflow clearer and cleaner in this way. No more conflict – it's a breeze. Sweet.

> You can find an example that runs ESLint and Prettier separately in /chapter-14/eslint-plugin-vue/separate/ in our GitHub repository.

Well done. You have made it through the first major part of this chapter. We hope you will start, or have already started, writing beautiful and readable code for your Vue and Nuxt apps, and making use of these amazing formatters and linters. As your Nuxt learning in the book nears its end, we will walk you through how you can deploy the Nuxt app in the next section. So keep reading.

Deploying Nuxt apps

Besides the code linting and formatting, app deployment, too, is a part of the web development workflow. We need to deploy our apps to a server or a host somewhere remotely so that the public can access the app publicly. Nuxt comes with the built-in commands that we can use to deploy our app. They are as follows:

- nuxt
- nuxt build
- nuxt start
- nuxt generate

The nuxt command is one that you are now familiar with using on your terminal:

```
$ npm run dev
```

Using Linters, Formatters, and Deployment Commands

If you open the `package.json` file that is generated by Nuxt when installing the project with the `create-nuxt-app` scaffolding tool, you can see these commands are pre-configured in the `"scripts"` snippet, as follows:

```
// package.json
"scripts": {
  "dev": "nuxt",
  "build": "nuxt build",
  "start": "nuxt start",
  "generate": "nuxt generate"
}
```

You can launch the command on your terminal with the following Node.js command line:

```
$ npm run <command>
```

The `nuxt` command is used for development with hot-reloading on the development server on `localhost:3000`, while the others are for production deployment. Let's take a look at how you can use them to deploy your Nuxt app in the next section.

> You can also use common arguments such as `--help` with any of these commands. If you want to find out more, please visit https://nuxtjs.org/guide/commandslist-of-commands.

Deploying a Nuxt universal server-side rendered app

We hope that from working through all the previous chapters, you know that you have been developing Nuxt universal **server-side rendered** (SSR) apps. An SSR app is an app that renders your app content on the server side. This kind of app requires a specific server to run your apps, such as a Node.js and Apache server, while a universal SSR app like that you've been creating with Nuxt runs on both the server and client sides. This kind of apps requires a specific server too. A Nuxt universal SSR app can be deployed with just two commands on the terminal. Let's take a look at how you can do it in the following steps:

1. Launch the `nuxt build` command via npm to build the app with webpack and minify the JavaScript and CSS:

   ```
   $ npm run build
   ```

You should get the following build result:

```
> [your-app-name]@[your-app-name] start /var/path/to/your/app
> nuxt build
i Production build
i Bundling for server and client side
i Target: server
✓ Builder initialized
✓ Nuxt files generated
...
...
```

2. Launch the `nuxt start` command via npm to start the server in production mode:

    $ npm run start

    You should get the following start status:

    ```
    > [your-app-name]@[your-app-name] start /var/path/to/your/app
    > nuxt start

    Nuxt.js @ v2.14.0

    > Environment: production
    > Rendering: server-side
    > Target: server

    Memory usage: 28.8 MB (RSS: 88.6 MB)
    ```

That's all it takes to deploy a Nuxt universal SSR app – just two command lines. It's a piece of cake, isn't it? However, if you don't have a Node.js server to host your app, or for any reason you just want to deploy your app as a static site, you can generate it from a Nuxt universal SSR app. Let's find out how you can achieve that in the next section.

Deploying a Nuxt static-generated (pre-rendered) app

To generate a Nuxt static generated app from the Nuxt universal SSR app, we will use the sample website we created in the previous chapters for this exercise. You can find this sample in /chapter-14/deployment/sample-website/ in our GitHub repository. So let's get cracking with the following steps:

1. Make sure you have the following "generate" run script in the package.json file as follows:

    ```
    "scripts": {
      "generate": "nuxt generate"
    }
    ```

2. Change the target project in the Nuxt config file to static:

    ```
    // nuxt.config.js
    export default {
      target: 'static'
    }
    ```

3. Generate the 404 page by configuring the generate option in the Nuxt config file:

    ```
    // nuxt.config.js
    export default {
      generate: {
        fallback: true
      }
    }
    ```

    Nuxt does not generate your custom 404 page, nor its default one. If you want to include this page in your static app, you can set fallback: true in the generate option in the config file.

4. Launch the nuxt generate command via npm to build the app and generate an HTML file for each route:

    ```
    $ npm run generate
    ```

Nuxt has a crawler that scans the links and generates dynamic routes and their async contents (the data rendered with the `asyncData` and `fetch` methods) automatically for you. So you should get every route of your app as follows:

```
i Generating output directory: dist/
i Generating pages with full static mode
✓ Generated route "/contact"
✓ Generated route "/work-nested"
✓ Generated route "/about"
✓ Generated route "/work"
✓ Generated route "/"
✓ Generated route "/work-nested/work-sample-4"
✓ Generated route "/work-nested/work-sample-1"
✓ Generated route "/work-nested/work-sample-3"
✓ Generated route "/work-nested/work-sample-2"
✓ Generated route "/work/work-sample-1"
✓ Generated route "/work/work-sample-4"
✓ Generated route "/work/work-sample-2"
✓ Generated route "/work/work-sample-3"
✓ Client-side fallback created: 404.html
i Ready to run nuxt serve or deploy dist/ directory
```

> Note that you will still need to use `generate.routes` for generating routes that the crawler cannot detect.

5. If you look inside your project root directory, you should find a `/dist/` folder generated by Nuxt with everything ready inside that you need to deploy the app to the static hosting server. But before that, you can test your production static app from the `/dist/` directory with the `nuxt serve` command on your terminal:

```
$ npm run start
```

You should get the following output on your terminal:

```
Nuxt.js @ v2.14.0

> Environment: production
> Rendering: server-side
> Target: static
Listening: http://localhost:3000/

i Serving static application from dist/
```

6. Now you can point your browser to `localhost:3000` and see that the app is running just like SSR, but in fact, it is a static-generated app.

We will come back to this configuration in the next chapter for deploying Nuxt **single-page application** (**SPA**) apps. You can see that it involves just a bit of work to go for this type of deployment and it is totally worth it because there are benefits in deploying your app "statically," such as you can get your static files hosted on static hosting servers, which are relatively cheaper than a Node.js server. We will show you how to serve your static site on this kind of server just like **GitHub Pages** in the next chapter. Even though there are benefits in deploying the Nuxt universal SSR app "statically," there are the following caveats that you must take into account:

- The Nuxt context given to the `asyncData` and `fetch` methods will lose the HTTP `req` and `res` objects from Node.js.
- The `nuxtServerInit` action will not be available in the store.

So if you have a Nuxt app that relies heavily on these items in the preceding list, then it is probably not a good idea to generate your Nuxt universal SSR app into static files because they are server-side features. However, we can imitate the `nuxtServerInit` action on the client side with the client-side cookies, which we will also show you in the next chapter. But for now, let's move on to the next section to find out what kind of hosting servers you can choose from to host your Nuxt apps.

> If you want to find out more about the `generate` property/option and other options, such as the `fallback` and `routes` options, that you can configure with this property, please visit https://nuxtjs.org/api/configuration-generate.

Hosting the Nuxt universal SSR app on virtual private servers

When it comes to hosting Node.js apps, a **virtual private server** (**VPS**) and dedicated servers are better options because you will have the complete freedom to set up the Node.js environment for your apps. And whenever Node.js releases new versions, you should update your environment as well. Only with a VPS server can you upgrade and tweak your environment anytime you need to.

A VPS provider such as Linode or Vultr offers affordable VPS hosting pricing if you are looking for a Linux server and will install the infrastructure that you need from scratch. What these VPS providers give you is an empty virtual machine with your preferred Linux distribution, for example, Ubuntu. The process of building the infrastructure of your needs is the same as how you install Node.js, MongoDB, MySQL, and so on, when you just have a Linux distribution freshly installed on your local machine. For more about these VPS providers, please visit the following links:

- `https://welcome.linode.com/` for Linode
- `https://www.vultr.com/` for Vultr

After you have the Node.js environment and the infrastructure set up to meet your requirements, you can upload your Nuxt app to this kind of host, then build and start the app very easily on your terminal through the **Secure Shell** (**SSH**) function provided by these hosting providers:

```
$ npm run build
$ npm run start
```

What about a shared hosting server? Let's take a look at what you have to choose from in the next section.

Hosting the Nuxt universal SSR app on shared hosting servers

Bear in mind that not all hosts are Node.js-friendly and shared hosting servers for Node.js are relatively rare compared to the shared hosting servers for PHP. But all shared hosting servers are the same – what you can do is usually severely restricted and you must follow the strict rules set by the provider. You can check out the following shared hosting servers providers:

- **Reclaim Hosting**, at `https://reclaimhosting.com/shared-hosting/`
- **A2 Hosting**, at `https://www.a2hosting.com/nodejs-hosting`

In a shared hosting server, for example, at Reclaim Hosting, most likely you cannot run the Nuxt commands to start your app. Instead, you will need to provide an application start file to the server and this file must be called `app.js` and placed in your project root directory.

If you would like to go for Reclaim Hosting, you can use their test environment at `https://stateu.org/` to see how it works for you. But keep in mind that advanced setups are not possible. The good news is that Nuxt provides a Node.js module, `nuxt-start`, to start Nuxt apps in production mode in a shared hosting server like this. So let's find out how in the following steps:

1. Install `nuxt-start` via npm locally:

    ```
    $ npm i nuxt-start
    ```

2. Create an `app.js` file in your project root directory with the following code to start the Nuxt app:

    ```js
    // app.js
    const { Nuxt } = require('nuxt-start')
    const config = require('./nuxt.config.js')

    const nuxt = new Nuxt(config)
    const { host, port } = nuxt.options.server

    nuxt.listen(port, host)
    ```

    Alternatively, you can use Express or Koa to start your Nuxt app. The following example assumes you are using Express:

    ```js
    // app.js
    const express = require('express')
    const { Nuxt } = require('nuxt')
    const app = express()

    let config = require('./nuxt.config.js')
    const nuxt = new Nuxt(config)
    const { host, port } = nuxt.options.server

    app.use(nuxt.render)
    app.listen(port, host)
    ```

    In this code, we import the `express` and `nuxt` modules and the `nuxt.config.js` file, and then use the Nuxt app as the middleware. It is the same if you are using Koa – you only need to use Nuxt as the middleware.

3. Upload the Nuxt app to the server with this `app.js` file in it and follow the instructions from the host to install the app dependencies via npm and then run `app.js` to start your app.

That's all you need to do. There are limitations in these shared hosting servers. You have less control with the Node.js environment in these servers. But you can get your universal SSR Nuxt apps up and running if you follow the strict rules that are set by server providers.

> You can find the preceding sample code and others in `/chapter-14/deployment/shared-hosting/reclaimhosting.com/` in our GitHub repository for hosting the Nuxt universal SSR app at Reclaim Hosting.
>
> For more information about `nuxt-start`, please visit https://www.npmjs.com/package/nuxt-start.

You can see that it is not perfect and has its limitations, but it is reasonable if you are looking for shared hosting. If this is not ideal for you, then the last option is to go for the static site hosting servers, as we'll see in the next section.

Hosting the Nuxt static generated app on static site hosting servers

With this option, you will have to lose the server side of Nuxt. But the good news is that there are many popular hosts for hosting a static-generated Nuxt app and you can serve it on almost any host online, quickly. Let's find out how in the following steps:

1. Change `server` to `static` as the target in the Nuxt config file, as follows:

   ```
   // nuxt.config.js
   export default {
     target: 'static'
   }
   ```

2. Launch the `nuxt generate` commands locally via npm to generate the static files for your Nuxt app:

   ```
   $ npm run generate
   ```

3. Upload all the content in the `/dist/` folder generated by Nuxt to the host.

The following list details the hosts you can choose from. The deployment processes for all of them are well documented on the Nuxt site. You should check out the Nuxt FAQ at https://nuxtjs.org/faq to check deployment examples and see how to deploy the static generated Nuxt app to any of these specific hosts:

- AWS w/ S3 (Amazon Web Services) at https://nuxtjs.org/faq/deployment-aws-s3-cloudfront
- GitHub Pages at https://nuxtjs.org/faq/github-pages
- Netlify at https://nuxtjs.org/faq/netlify-deployment
- Surge at https://nuxtjs.org/faq/surge-deployment

We will guide you through the deployment of Nuxt SPA apps on GitHub Pages in the next chapter. But for now, this is the end of this chapter on formatting, linting, and deploying the Nuxt universal SSR app. Let's summarize what you have learned in this chapter.

Summary

Well done. You have made it this far. It is been quite a journey. In this chapter, we covered JavaScript linters and formatters, notably ESLint, Prettier, and StandardJS for Nuxt apps and also for JavaScript apps in general. You have learned how to install and configure them for your needs and preferences. We also covered the Nuxt commands to deploy Nuxt apps and the options available for hosting the Nuxt app, whether it is a universal SSR app or a static generated site.

In the coming chapter, we will learn how to create an SPA with Nuxt and deploy it to GitHub Pages. You will see the slight difference between traditional SPAs and the SPA in Nuxt (let's called it **Nuxt SPA**). We will guide you through the process of setting up the SPA development environment in Nuxt, refactoring the universal SSR Nuxt authentication app that you have created in the previous chapters, and turning it into a Nuxt SPA and a static-generated Nuxt SPA. Lastly, you will learn to deploy the static-generated SPA to GitHub Pages. So keep reading.

Section 6: The Further Fields

In this section, we will learn about what else we can do with Nuxt. We will learn how to develop a single-page app (SPA) in Nuxt, using PHP rather than JavaScript to create a cross-domain and external API data platforms to feed our Nuxt app, developing a real-time application with Nuxt, and using (headless) CMS and GraphQL with Nuxt.

This section comprises the following chapters:

- Chapter 15, *Creating an SPA with Nuxt*
- Chapter 16, *Creating a Framework-Agnostic PHP API for Nuxt*
- Chapter 17, *Creating a Real-Time App with Nuxt*
- Chapter 18, *Creating a Nuxt App with CMS and GraphQL*

15
Creating an SPA with Nuxt

In the previous chapters, we created a variety of Nuxt apps in `universal` mode. These were universal server-side rendered (SSR) apps. This means they are apps that run on both the server and client sides. Nuxt gives us another option for developing **single-page apps** (**SPA**), just like we can do with Vue and other SPA frameworks, such as Angular and React. In this chapter, we're going to guide you through how to develop, build, and deploy an SPA in Nuxt and see what makes it differ from the traditional SPAs that are available.

In this chapter, we will cover the following topics:

- Understanding classic SPAs and Nuxt SPAs
- Installing a Nuxt SPA
- Developing a Nuxt SPA
- Deploying a Nuxt SPA

Let's get started!

Understanding classic SPAs and Nuxt SPAs

An SPA, also referred to as a classic SPA, is an app that loads once on a browser and does not require us to reload and re-render the page throughout the life of the app. This differs from multiple-page applications (MPAs) in which every change and every data exchange with the server requires that we rerender the entire page anew, from the server to the browser.

In a classic/traditional SPA, the HTML that's served to the client is relatively empty. JavaScript will dynamically render the HTML and content once it gets to the client. React, Angular, and Vue are popular choices for creating classic SPAs. However, don't get confused with the Nuxt app in spa mode (let's called it **Nuxt SPA**), even though Nuxt offers you the option to develop an "SPA" with just one line of configuration, as follows:

```
// nuxt.config.js
export default {
  mode: 'spa'
}
```

Nuxt's SPA mode simply means that you lose the server-side features of Nuxt and Node.js, as we learned in Chapter 14, *Using Linters, Formatters, and Deployment Commands*, on turning a universal SSR Nuxt app into a static-generated (pre-rendered) Nuxt app. The same goes for the spa-mode Nuxt app – when you use the preceding configuration, your spa-mode Nuxt app will become a purely **client-side app**.

But the spa-mode Nuxt app is quite different from the classic SPA that you create from the Vue CLI, React, or Angular. This is because, after building the app, the pages and routes of your (classic) SPA will be dynamically rendered by JavaScript at runtime. On the other hand, the pages in a spa-mode Nuxt app will be pre-rendered during build time, and the HTML in each page is as "empty" as the classic SPA. This is where things start to get confusing. Let's take a look at the following examples. Let's say you have the following pages and routes in your Vue app:

```
src
├── favicon.ico
├── index.html
├── components
│   ├── about.vue
│   ├── secured.vue
│   └── ...
└── routes
    ├── about.js
    ├── secured.js
    └── ...
```

Your app will be built into the following distribution:

```
dist
├── favicon.ico
├── index.html
├── css
│   └── ...
└── js
    └── ...
```

Here, you can see that only the `index.html`, `/css/`, and `/js/` folders are built into the `/dust/` folder. This means that the pages and routes of your app will be dynamically rendered by JavaScript at runtime. However, let's say you have the following pages in your spa-mode Nuxt app:

```
pages
├── about.vue
├── secured.vue
├── ...
└── users
    ├── about.js
    ├── index.vu
    └── _id.vue
```

Your app will be built into the following distribution:

```
dist
├── index.html
├── favicon.ico
├── about
│   └── index.html
├── secured
│   └── index.html
├── users
│   └── index.html
└── ...
```

As you can see, every page and route of your app is built with an `index.html` file and placed in the `/dust/` folder – just like the static site that you generate for a universal SSR Nuxt app. So, here, we can say that the spa-mode Nuxt app you will build and deploy is a "static" SPA, as opposed to the classic SPA, which is "dynamic". Of course, you can still deploy your spa-mode Nuxt app as if it were a universal SSR Nuxt app using the following deployment commands. This will make it "dynamic" at runtime:

```
$ npm run build
$ npm run start
```

But deploying a Nuxt SPA app on a Node.js host can be overkill because there must be some good reasons for you to go for a spa-mode Nuxt app and don't want to use a Node.js host for your SPAs. Hence, **pre-rendering** the Nuxt SPA into a static-generated app (let's call it a **static-generated Nuxt SPA**) is probably more sensible. You can pre-render your Nuxt SPA with the `nuxt export` command easily, just like the universal SSR Nuxt app.

This is what this chapter is all about: developing a Nuxt app in spa mode and generating the required static HTML files before deploying them to a static hosting server such as GitHub Pages. So, let's get started by installing and setting up the environment.

Installing a Nuxt SPA

Installing a Nuxt SPA is the same as installing Nuxt universal SSR using the `create-nuxt-app` scaffolding tool. Let's get started:

1. Install a Nuxt project via your terminal using the Nuxt scaffolding tool:

    ```
    $ npx create-nuxt-app <project-name>
    ```

2. Answer the questions that appear and pick the **Single Page App** option when asked for the **Rendering mode**:

    ```
    ? Project name
    ? Project description
    //...
    ? Rendering mode:
      Universal (SSR / SSG)
    > Single Page App
    ```

    After the installation is completed, if you inspect the Nuxt config file in your project's root directory, you should see that the `mode` option was configured as an SPA for you during the installation process:

    ```
    // nuxt.config.js
    export default {
      mode: 'spa'
    }
    ```

3. Start Nuxt development mode in your terminal:

    $ npm run dev

    You should see that **only** the code on the client-side is compiled on your terminal:

    ```
    ✓ Client
      Compiled successfully in 1.76s
    ```

You will no longer see any code compiled on the server-side that you would normally see for the Nuxt app in `universal` mode:

```
✓ Client
  Compiled successfully in 2.75s

✓ Server
  Compiled successfully in 2.56s
```

As you can see, it is rather easy to get the spa-mode environment started in Nuxt. You can also set up this spa-mode **manually** just by adding the `spa` value to the `mode` option in the Nuxt config file. Now, let's develop a Nuxt SPA.

Developing a Nuxt SPA

One major important thing to bear in mind when developing a Nuxt SPA is the Nuxt context that's given to the `asyncData` and `fetch` methods, will lose their `req` and `res` objects because these objects are Node.js HTTP objects. In this section, we'll create a simple user login authentication, which you should already be familiar with. However, this time, we will make it in the Nuxt SPA. We will also create a page for listing users using dynamic routes, as we learned about in `Chapter 4`, *Adding Views, Routes, and Transitions*. Let's get started:

1. Prepare the following `.vue` files or just make a copy from the previous chapter, as follows:

   ```
   -| pages/
   ---| index.vue
   ---| about.vue
   ---| login.vue
   ---| secret.vue
   ---| users/
   -----| index.vue
   -----| _id.vue
   ```

2. Prepare the Vuex store with the store state, mutations, actions, and the index file for handling user login authentication, as follows:

   ```
   -| store/
   ---| index.js
   ---| state.js
   ---| mutations.js
   ---| actions.js
   ```

As we mentioned in the previous chapter, we will lose the nuxtServerInit action in the store when we generate the Nuxt Universal SSR app **statically**, so it is the same in the Nuxt SPA – we will not have this server action on the client-side. Thus, we will need a client-side nuxtServerInit action to imitate the server-side nuxtServerInit action. We'll learn how to do this next.

Creating the client-side nuxtServerInit action

The methods and properties in these files are the same as those we had in past exercises, except for the nuxtServerInit action:

```
// store/index.js
const cookie = process.server ? require('cookie') : undefined

export const actions = {
  nuxtServerInit ({ commit }, { req }) {
    if (
      req
      && req.headers
      && req.headers.cookie
      && req.headers.cookie.indexOf('auth') > -1
    ) {
      let auth = cookie.parse(req.headers.cookie)['auth']
      commit('setAuth', JSON.parse(auth))
    }
  }
}
```

There is no server involved in the Nuxt SPA since nuxtServerInit is called by Nuxt from the server-side only. So, we will need a solution for that. We can use the Node.js js-cookie module to store the authenticated data on the client-side when the user logs in, which makes it the best candidate to replace the server-side cookie. Let's learn how to achieve this:

1. Install the Node.js js-cookie module via npm:

    ```
    $ npm i js-cookie
    ```

2. Create a custom method called `nuxtClientInit` (you can choose any name you like if you wish) in the store actions to retrieve the user data in the cookie. Then, set it back to the desired state for the specified situation when the user refreshes the browser:

```
// store/index.js
import cookies from 'js-cookie'

export const actions = {
  nuxtClientInit ({ commit }, ctx) {
    let auth = cookies.get('auth')
    if (auth) {
      commit('setAuth', JSON.parse(auth))
    }
  }
}
```

As you may recall, the store `nuxtServerInit` action is always called on the server-side when refreshing the page. The same happens with this `nuxtClientInit` method; it should be called every time on the client-side when refreshing the page. However, it won't be called **automatically**, so we can use a plugin to call it each time **before** the Vue root is initiated.

3. Create a plugin called `nuxt-client-init.js` in the `/plugins/` directory that will call the `nuxtClientInit` method through the `dispatch` method in the store:

```
// plugins/nuxt-client-init.js
export default async (ctx) => {
  await ctx.store.dispatch('nuxtClientInit', ctx)
}
```

Remember that we can access the Nuxt context in plugins before the Vue root is initiated. The store is added to the Nuxt context, so, we can access the store actions and the `nuxtClientInit` method is what we are interested in here.

4. Now, add this plugin to the Nuxt config file in order to install the plugin:

```
// nuxt.config.js
export default {
  plugins: [
    { src: '~/plugins/nuxt-client-init.js', mode: 'client' }
  ]
}
```

Now, every time you refresh the browser, the `nuxtClientInit` method will be called and the state will be repopulated by this method before the Vue root is initiated. As you can see, it isn't straightforward to imitate the `nuxtClientInit` action when we lose the full power of Nuxt as a universal JavaScript app. But if you must go for a Nuxt SPA, then this issue can be resolved with the `nuxtClientInit` method we just created.

Next, we will create some custom Axios instances using Nuxt plugins. This should be something that you are quite familiar with already. However, being able to create custom Axios instances is useful because you can always fall back to the **vanilla** version of Axios when you need to, even though we have the **Nuxt Axios module** as well. So, let's move on!

Creating multiple custom Axios instances with plugins

In this spa-mode exercise, we will need two Axios instances to make API calls to the following addresses:

- `localhost:4000` for user authentication
- `jsonplaceholder.typicode.com` for fetching users

We will use the vanilla Axios (`https://github.com/axios/axios`) as it gives us the flexibility to create multiple instances of Axios with some custom configurations. Let's get started:

1. Install the vanilla `axios` via npm:

    ```
    $ npm i axios
    ```

2. Create an `axios` instance on the page you need it:

    ```
    // pages/users/index.vue
    const instance = axios.create({
      baseURL: '<api-address>',
      timeout: <value>,
      headers: { '<x-custom-header>': '<value>' }
    })
    ```

But creating the `axios` instance directly on a page is not ideal. Ideally, we should be able to extract this instance and reuse it anywhere. Through the Nuxt plugin, we can create the Axios extracted instance. There are two methods we can follow to create them. We'll look at the first method in the next section.

Installing the custom Axios plugin in the Nuxt config file

In previous chapters, you learned that we can create a plugin with the `inject` method and install the plugin through the Nuxt `config` file. Besides using the `inject` method, it is worth knowing that we can also inject a plugin **directly** into the Nuxt context. Let's take a look at how to do this:

1. Create an `axios-typicode.js` file in the `/plugins/` directory, import the vanilla `axios`, and create the instance, as follows:

    ```
    // plugins/axios-typicode.js
    import axios from 'axios'

    const instance = axios.create({
      baseURL: 'https://jsonplaceholder.typicode.com'
    })

    export default (ctx, inject) => {
      ctx.$axiosTypicode = instance
      inject('axiosTypicode', instance)
    }
    ```

    As you can see, after creating the `axios` instance, we inject the plugin through the Nuxt context (`ctx`), use the `inject` method, and then export it.

2. Install this plugin in the Nuxt config file:

    ```
    // nuxt.config.js
    export default {
      plugins: [
        { src: '~/plugins/axios-typicode.js', mode: 'client' }
      ]
    }
    ```

    You must set the `mode` option to `client` because we **only** need it on the client-side.

3. You can access this plugin from anywhere you like. In this example, we want to use this plugin on the user index page to fetch the list of users:

    ```
    // pages/users/index.vue
    export default {
      async asyncData({ $axiosTypicode }) {
        let { data } = await $axiosTypicode.get('/users')
        return { users: data }
    ```

```
    }
}
```

In this plugin, we injected the custom `axios` instance into the Nuxt context (`ctx`) directly as `$axiosTypicode` so that we can call it directly by using the JavaScript destructuring assignment syntax to unpack it as `$axiosTypicode`. We also injected the plugin using the `inject` method, so we also call this plugin by using `ctx.app`, as follows:

```
// pages/users/index.vue
export default {
  async asyncData({ app }) {
    let { data } = await app.$axiosTypicode.get('/users')
    return { users: data }
  }
}
```

It isn't too hard to create a custom Axios plugin, is it? If you install the plugin through the Nuxt config file, this means it is a global JavaScript function and that you can access it from anywhere. But if you don't want to install it as a global plugin, you can skip installing it in the Nuxt config file. This brings us to the second method of creating a Nuxt plugin.

Importing the custom Axios plugin manually

Another method of creating the custom Axios instance does not involve the Nuxt config at all. We can just export the custom instance as a regular JavaScript function and then import it directly into the page where we need it. Let's take a look at how to do this:

1. Create an `axios-api.js` file in the `/plugins/` directory, import the vanilla `axios`, and create the instance, as follows:

   ```
   // plugins/axios-api.js
   import axios from 'axios'

   export default axios.create({
     baseURL: 'http://localhost:4000',
     withCredentials: true
   })
   ```

   As you can see, we're no longer using the `inject` method; instead, we export the instance directly.

2. Now, we can import it manually when we need it. In this example, we need it in the `login` action method, as follows:

```
// store/actions.js
import axios from '~/plugins/axios-api'

async login({ commit }, { username, password }) {
  const { data } = await axios.post('/public/users/login', {
  username, password })
  //...
}
```

As you can see, we must import this plugin **manually** because it is not plugged into the Nuxt lifecycle.

3. Import it and set the `Authorization` header on this `axios` instance in the `token` middleware, as follows:

```
// middleware/token.js
import axios from '~/plugins/axios-api'

export default async ({ store, error }) => {
  //...
  axios.defaults.headers.common['Authorization'] = Bearer:
  ${store.state.auth.token}
}
```

Even though we have to import the plugin manually when following this method, at least we have extracted the following setting into a plugin that we can reuse wherever it is needed:

```
{
  baseURL: 'http://localhost:4000',
  withCredentials: true
}
```

> You can find the code for the Nuxt SPA, along with these two methods, in `/chapter-15/frontend/` in this book's GitHub repository.

Once you have created, tested, and linted all the code and files, you are ready to deploy the Nuxt SPA. So, let's get to it!

Deploying a Nuxt SPA

We can deploy a Nuxt SPA just like we can deploy universal SSR Nuxt apps if we have a Node.js runtime server. If we don't, then we can only deploy the SPA as a static site to a static hosting server such as **GitHub Pages**. You can deploy a static-generated Nuxt SPA as follows:

1. Make sure that you have set the value to `spa` in the `mode` option in the Nuxt config file:

   ```
   // nuxt.config.js
   export default {
     mode: 'spa'
   }
   ```

2. Make sure you have the following run scripts in the `package.json` file as well:

   ```
   {
     "scripts": {
       "generate": "nuxt generate"
     }
   }
   ```

3. Run `npm run generate`, just like you would for the universal SSR Nuxt app. You should see the following output in the terminal:

   ```
   i Generating output directory: dist/
   i Generating pages
   ✓ Generated /about
   ✓ Generated /login
   ✓ Generated /secret
   ✓ Generated /users
   ✓ Generated /
   ```

   In the preceding output, if you navigate to the `/dist/` folder inside the project, you will find an `index.html` file at the root, as well as `index.html` files in each subfolder, along with the route name. However, you will not find any of these pages in the dynamic routes that were generated, such as `/users/1`. This is because dynamic routes are not generated in spa-mode, as opposed to universal mode.

Also, if you open the index.html file in the /dist/ folder, you will find all the index.html files are exactly the same – just some "empty" HTML elements, similar to the classic SPA. Furthermore, each index.html file does not contain its individual meta information, only the common ones from nuxt.config.js. The meta information of these pages will be hydrated (filled and updated) at runtime. Due to this, it may seem counter-intuitive and "half-baked" for a "static" SPA. On top of that, no static payload is generated. This means that if you navigate to localhost:3000/users on your browser, you will notice that this page is still requesting its data from https://jsonplaceholder.typicode.com/users instead of fetching the data from the payload like the universal SSR Nuxt app does. This is because Nuxt does not generate the static content in spa mode, even though you have set static for the target property in the Nuxt config file. To overcome these issues, we can generate the static content we need from the universal mode.

4. Change spa to universal for the mode option in the Nuxt config file:

```
// nuxt.config.js
export default {
  mode: 'universal'
}
```

5. Run npm run generate so that Nuxt will make the REST API calls to the API to retrieve the users and export their contents to local static payloads. You will see the following output:

```
i Generating output directory: dist/
i Generating pages with full static mode
✓ Generated /about
✓ Generated /secret
✓ Generated /login
✓ Generated /users
✓ Generated /users/1
✓ Generated /users/2
...
...
✓ Generated /users/10
✓ Generated /
```

Notice that there is no dynamic routes are generated in the preceding output. If you navigate to the /dist/ folder again, you should see that the /users/ folder now contains multiple folders, each with the owns user ID. Each of these folders contains an index.html file that contains the contents for that specific user. Now, each index.html file contains its own individual meta information and payload generated in /dist/_nuxt/static/.

Creating an SPA with Nuxt

6. Change `universal` back to `spa` for the `mode` option in the Nuxt config file:

   ```
   // nuxt.config.js
   export default {
     mode: 'spa'
   }
   ```

7. Now, run `npm run build` on your terminal. You should see the following output:

   ```
   Hash: c36ee9714ee9427ac1ff
   Version: webpack 4.43.0
   Time: 5540ms
   Built at: 11/07/2020 07:58:09
                           Asset       Size  Chunks
   Chunk Names
   ../server/client.manifest.json   9.31 KiB          [emitted]
                        LICENSES   617 bytes          [emitted]
                 app.922dbd1.js     57 KiB         0  [emitted]
                   [immutable] app
         commons/app.7236c86.js    182 KiB         1  [emitted]
                   [immutable] commons/app
         pages/about.75fcd06.js    667 bytes        2  [emitted]
                   [immutable] pages/about
         pages/index.76b5c20.js    784 bytes        3  [emitted]
                   [immutable] pages/index
         pages/login.09e509e.js     3.14 KiB        4  [emitted]
                   [immutable] pages/login
       pages/secured.f086299.js     1.36 KiB        5  [emitted]
                   [immutable] pages/secured
     pages/users/_id.e1c568c.js     1.69 KiB        6  [emitted]
                   [immutable] pages/users/_id
    pages/users/index.b3e7aa8.js    1.5 KiB        7  [emitted]
                   [immutable] pages/users/index
                 runtime.266b4bf.js  2.47 KiB       8  [emitted]
                   [immutable] runtime
   + 1 hidden asset
   Entrypoint app = runtime.266b4bf.js commons/app.7236c86.js
   app.922dbd1.js
   i Ready to run nuxt generate
   ```

8. Ignore the `Ready to run nuxt generate` message. Instead, test your production static SPA from the `/dist/` directory first with the `nuxt start` command on your terminal:

   ```
   $ npm run start
   ```

You should get the following output:

```
Nuxt.js @ v2.14.0

> Environment: production
> Rendering: client-side
> Target: static
Listening: http://localhost:3000/

i Serving static application from dist/
```

Now, routes such as `localhost:3000/users` will no longer request their data from `https://jsonplaceholder.typicode.com`. Instead, they will fetch the data from the payload in the `/static/` folder, which can be found inside the `/dist/` folder.

9. Finally, just deploy this `/dist/` directory only to your static hosting server.

If you are looking for a free static hosting server, consider using GitHub Pages. Using this, you can have a domain name for your site in the following format:

```
<username>.github.io/<app-name>
```

GitHub also allows you to serve your site with a custom domain name rather than using theirs. For more information, follow the guide from the GitHub Help site: `https://help.github.com/en/github/working-with-github-pages/configuring-a-custom-domain-for-your-github-pages-site`. However, in this book, we will show you how to serve your site on the GitHub's `github.io` domain name. We'll learn how to do this in the next section.

> You can find the code for this section in `/chapter-15/frontend/` in this book's GitHub repository.

Deploying to GitHub Pages

GitHub Pages is a static site hosting service from GitHub that hosts and publishes the static files (HTML, CSS, and JavaScript only) in your GitHub repository. You can get your static site hosted in GitHub Pages as long as you have a user account on GitHub and a GitHub repository created for your site.

> Please visit https://guides.github.com/features/pages/ to find out how to get started with GitHub Pages.

You just need to go to the **Settings** section on your GitHub repository and scroll down to the **GitHub Pages** section. Then, you need to click the **Choose a theme** button to start the process of creating your static site.

Deploying the static version of your Nuxt SPA to GitHub Pages is fairly easy – you just need to make some minor configuration changes to the Nuxt config file and then use the `git push` command to upload it to your GitHub repository. When you create a GitHub repository and if you are creating GitHub Pages, the URL of the static pages, by default, will be served in the following format:

```
<username>.github.io/<repository-name>
```

So, you will need to add this `<repository-name>` to the `router` base option in the Nuxt config file, as follows:

```js
export default {
  router: {
    base: '/<repository-name>/'
  }
}
```

But changing the base name will interfere with `localhost:3000` when developing the Nuxt app. Let's learn how to resolve this:

1. Create an `if` condition for the development and production GitHub Pages in the Nuxt config file, as follows:

   ```js
   // nuxt.config.js
   const routerBase = process.env.DEPLOY_ENV === 'GH_PAGES' ? {
     router: {
       base: '/<repository-name>/'
     }
   } : {}
   ```

   This condition simply adds `/<repository-name>/` to the `base` key of the `router` option if the `DEPLOY_ENV` option has `GH_PAGES` in the process environment.

2. Add this `routerBase` constant to your Nuxt configuration in the config file using the `spread` operator:

   ```
   // nuxt.config.js
   export default {
     ...routerBase
   }
   ```

3. Set the `DEPLOY_ENV='GH_PAGES'` scripts in the `package.json` file:

   ```
   // package.json
   "scripts": {
     "build:gh-pages": "DEPLOY_ENV=GH_PAGES nuxt build",
     "generate:gh-pages": "DEPLOY_ENV=GH_PAGES nuxt generate"
   }
   ```

   Using one of these two npm scripts, the value of `/<repository-name>/` won't be injected into your Nuxt configuration and interfere with the dev process when running `npm run dev` for development.

4. Change `spa` to `universal` for the `mode` option in the Nuxt config file, just as in *step 4* in the previous section, to generate the static payloads and pages with the `nuxt generate` command:

   ```
   $ npm run generate:gh-pages
   ```

5. Change `universal` back to `spa` for the `mode` option in the Nuxt config file, just as in *step 6* in the previous section, to build the SPA with the `nuxt build` command:

   ```
   $ npm run build:gh-pages
   ```

6. Push the files in the `/dist/` folder that were generated by Nuxt to GitHub Pages through your GitHub repository.

That's it for deploying a Nuxt SPA to GitHub Pages. However, make sure you have an empty `.nojekyll` file included in the `/dist/` folder when pushing your static site to GitHub Pages.

Jekyll is a simple, blog-aware, static site generator. It transforms plain text into static websites and blogs. GitHub Pages is powered by Jekyll behind the scenes and, by default, it does not build any files or directories that start with a dot ".", or an underscore "_", or end with a tilde "~". This will be a problem when serving the static site in GitHub Pages because a subfolder called _nuxt is also generated inside the /dist/ folder when building the Nuxt SPA; this /_nuxt/ folder will be ignored by Jekyll. To fix this, we need to include an empty .nojekyll file in the /dist/ folder to turn off Jekyll. This file is generated when we build the static pages for the Nuxt SPA, so make sure to push it to your GitHub repository as well.

Well done – you have made it through another short chapter of this book! Nuxt SPAs are a great option if you want to build an SPA in Nuxt instead of using Vue or other frameworks such as Angular and React. However, if you are offering web services such as social media sites that require immediate or real-time publications, a static-generated Nuxt SPA probably isn't a good choice. It all depends on the nature of your business and whether you want to go for the full power of Nuxt, the universal SSR, or the client-side only version of Nuxt - Nuxt SPA. Next, we'll summarize what we have learned in this chapter.

Summary

In this chapter, we have learned how to develop, build, and deploy an SPA in Nuxt and see what makes it different from a classic SPA. We also learned that Nuxt SPAs can be a good option for developing apps, but developing a Nuxt SPA means that we will lose the nuxtServerInit action and the req and res HTTP objects. However, we can use the client-side js-cookies (or localStorage) and the Nuxt plugin to imitate the nuxtServerInit action. Last but not least, we learned how to publish and serve the static-generated Nuxt SPA on GitHub Pages.

So far in this book, we have only been using JavaScript for all our Nuxt apps and APIs. However, in the coming chapters, we will explore how we can take Nuxt further so that we can work with another language, **PHP**. We will walk you through the HTTP messages and PHP standards, writing CRUD operations with PHP database frameworks, and serving a PHP API for the Nuxt app. Read on!

16
Creating a Framework-Agnostic PHP API for Nuxt

In previous chapters, such as Chapter 8, *Adding a Server-Side Framework*, and Chapter 9, *Adding a Server-Side Database*, you learned how to create APIs using Nuxt's default server with Node.js JavaScript frameworks such as Koa and Express. In Chapter 12, *Creating User Logins and API Authentication*, you learned how to create APIs using an external server with the same Node.js JavaScript framework – Koa.

In this chapter, we will guide you through how to create APIs using an external server with **PHP: Hypertext Preprocessor** (or simply PHP) instead. In Chapter 9, *Adding a Server-Side Database*, you also learned how to use MongoDB to manage the database. However, in this chapter, we will use MySQL instead, which you used with Koa in Chapter 12, *Creating User Logins and API Authentication*.

Most importantly, in this chapter, you will learn all about PHP standards and the **PHP Standards Recommendations (PSRs)**. In particular, you will learn about PSR-4 for autoloading, PSR-7 for HTTP messages, and PSR-15 for composing middleware components and handling HTTP server requests. We will put together the packages that are based on these PSR standards from different vendors such as Zend Framework and The PHP League to make a **framework-agnostic** PHP RESTful API for our Nuxt app.

In this chapter, we will cover the following topics:

- Introducing PHP
- Understanding HTTP messages and PHP standards
- Writing CRUD operations with PHP database frameworks
- Integrating with Nuxt

Let's get started!

Introducing PHP

PHP has come a long way. It existed long before Node.js and was created by Rasmus Lerdorf in 1994. It stood for **Personal Home Page** originally. The PHP reference implementation is now produced by The PHP Group (https://www.php.net/). PHP was originally developed as a templating language that allowed us to mix HTML with PHP code itself, just like Twig (https://twig.symfony.com/) and Pug (https://pugjs.org/) do these days.

Now, PHP is more than just a templating language. Over the years, it has evolved into a general-purpose scripting language and object-oriented language, especially suited for server-side web development. You can still use it for templating, but we should make use of its full power in modern PHP development. If you want to check out what else PHP can do, visit https://www.php.net/manual/en/intro-whatcando.php.

At the time of writing this book, the current stable version of PHP is 7.4.x. If you are getting started with PHP, start with PHP 7.4. If you are using PHP 7.2 or 7.3, you should consider upgrading it to PHP 7.4 as it contains several bug fixes. For more about the changes in this release, visit https://www.php.net/ChangeLog-7.php.

In this book, we will guide you through how to install or upgrade to PHP 7.4 on Ubuntu with Apache2 support. Let's get started!

Installing or upgrading PHP

If you are on macOS, please use this guide: https://phptherightway.com/mac_setup. If you are on Windows, then please use this guide: https://phptherightway.com/windows_setup.

We're using an Apache2 HTTP server but you can use an Nginx HTTP server if you have it installed on your machine already. Now, follow these simple steps to install PHP:

1. Run the following commands to update the local packages on your Ubuntu server and install Apache2:

   ```
   $ sudo apt update
   $ sudo apt install apache2
   ```

2. After installing Apache2, verify it with the -v option:

   ```
   $ apache2 -v
   Server version: Apache/2.4.41 (Ubuntu)
   Server built: 2019-08-14T14:36:32
   ```

You can use the following commands to stop, start, and enable the Apache2 service so that it always starts up when the server boots up:

```
$ sudo systemctl stop apache2
$ sudo systemctl start apache2
$ sudo systemctl enable apache2
```

You can use the following command to check the status of Apache2:

```
$ sudo systemctl status apache2
```

You should always get `active (running)` as the output in your terminal:

```
apache2.service - The Apache HTTP Server
 Loaded: loaded (/lib/systemd/system/apache2.service; enabled;
vendor preset: enabled)
 Active: active (running) since Thu 2020-08-06 13:17:25 CEST; 52min
ago
 //...
```

3. Run the following commands to install PHP 7.4:

   ```
   $ sudo apt update
   $ sudo apt install php
   ```

4. You should also install PHP 7.4-related modules and extensions that may be needed when developing PHP apps:

   ```
   $ sudo apt install -y php7.4-
   {bcmath,bz2,curl,gd,intl,json,mbstring,xml,zip,mysql}
   ```

5. Disable PHP 7.3 (if you are on PHP 7.3) and then enable PHP 7.4:

   ```
   $ sudo a2dismod php7.3
   $ sudo a2enmod php7.4
   ```

If you are installing PHP for the first time, then you don't have to disable the older version. If you want to uninstall PHP and all its related modules, you can use the following command:

```
$ sudo apt-get purge 'php*'
```

6. Restart the Apache2 and PHP services:

    ```
    $ sudo service apache2 restart
    ```

7. Now, you can verify the PHP you just installed with the following command:

    ```
    $ php -v
    ```

You should get the following version information:

```
PHP 7.4.8 (cli) (built: Jul 13 2020 16:46:22) ( NTS )
Copyright (c) The PHP Group
Zend Engine v3.4.0, Copyright (c) Zend Technologies
  with Zend OPcache v7.4.8, Copyright (c), by Zend Technologies
```

Now that you have Apache2 and PHP 7.4 installed, the next thing you should do is configure PHP. We'll do this in the next section.

Configuring PHP 7.4

Now that Apache2 and PHP are installed, you may want to configure PHP so that you can use it according to what suits your PHP apps. The default PHP configuration file is located at `/etc/php/7.4/apache2/php.ini`, so follow these steps to configure your version of PHP 7.4:

1. Run the following command to edit or configure PHP 7.4:

    ```
    $ sudo nano /etc/php/7.4/apache2/php.ini
    ```

    You may need to change the default allowance of `upload_max_filesize` for uploaded files:

    ```
    upload_max_filesize = 2M
    ```

    You can find more information about this configuration at http://php.net/upload-max-filesize.

    2 MB maximum for uploaded files can be considered small for PHP apps. So, go ahead and change it to suit your needs, as follows:

    ```
    upload_max_filesize = 32M
    ```

The following are some other important lines/PHP directives to consider:

```
post_max_size = 48M
memory_limit = 256M
max_execution_time = 600
```

You can find more information about the preceding PHP directives and other directives for configuring your PHP at https://www.php.net/manual/en/ini.core.php.

2. Restart Apache for the aforementioned modified PHP settings to take effect:

```
$ sudo service apache2 restart
```

PHP 7.4 is powerful. You can just have it installed and serving your site for development without relying on the Apache server if you don't want to install Apache on your local development machine. In the next section, you'll learn how to use PHP 7.4 without the Apache server.

Running PHP apps with a built-in PHP web server

Since PHP 5.4, you can run PHP scripts and apps with the built-in PHP web server, without needing a common web server such as Apache or Nginx. As long as you have PHP 7.4 installed, you can skip the preceding Apache installation. To start the PHP server, just open a terminal from your project's root directory and run the following command:

```
$ php -S 0.0.0.0:8181
```

If you want to start the app from a specific document root directory, such as from the `public` directory, in the project directory called `www`, do the following:

```
$ cd ~/www
$ php -S localhost:8181 -t public
```

Let's create a classic "Hello World" example that will be served up by this built-in PHP web server to see whether everything is set up correctly:

1. Create a simple "Hello World" message page in a PHP file, as follows:

```
// public/index.php
<?php
echo 'Hello world!';
```

2. Navigate to your project directory and start it with the built-in PHP web server by using the preceding command. The terminal should show the following information:

   ```
   [Sun Mar 22 09:12:37 2020] PHP 7.4.4 Development Server (http://localhost:8181) started
   ```

3. Now, load `localhost:8181` on your browser. You should see **Hello world!** on your screen, without any errors.

> If you want to learn about this built-in web server, visit https://www.php.net/features.commandline.webserver.

Next, you'll learn how to arm yourself with some PHP standards. You'll also understand what HTTP messages are and why we need PSR for modern PHP apps.

Understanding HTTP messages and PSRs

Hypertext Transfer Protocol (HTTP) is a communication protocol between client computers and web servers. A web browser such as Chrome, Safari, or Firefox can be the web client or the user-agent, while a web application on a computer that's listening on some port can be the web server. Web clients are not only browsers but any application that can speak to the web server, such as cURL or Telnet.

A client opens a connection via the internet to make a request to the server and waits until they receive a response from the server. The request contains request information, while the response contains status information and the requested content. These two types of exchanged data are called HTTP messages. They are just bodies of text encoded in ASCII and they span multiple lines in the following structure:

```
Start-line
HTTP Headers

Body
```

This looks very simple and straightforward, doesn't it? Although this may be the case, let's elaborate on this structure:

- `Start-line` describes the implemented request method (such as `GET`, `PUT`, or `POST`), the request target (usually a URI), and the HTTP version or the status (such as 200, 404, or 500) of the response and the HTTP version. `Start-line` is always a single line.
- The `HTTP Headers` line describes the specific details (meta-information) of the request or the response, such as `Host`, `User-Agent`, `Server`, `Content-type`, and so on.
- The blank line indicates that all the meta-information for the request has been sent.
- `Body` (or, message body) contains the exchanged data of the request (such as the content of an HTML form) or the response (such as the content of an HTML document). The message body is optional (sometimes, it is not needed in the request for requesting data from the server).

Now, let's use cURL to see how the data of the HTTP request and response is exchanged:

1. Serve the PHP "Hello World" app that you learned about in the previous section on `localhost:8181` using the built-in PHP web server:

    ```
    $ php -S localhost:8181 -t public
    ```

2. Open a new tab on your terminal and run the following cURL script:

    ```
    $ curl http://0.0.0.0:8181 \
      --trace-ascii \
      /dev/stdout
    ```

    You should see that the request message is displayed in the first part, as follows:

    ```
    == Info: Trying 0.0.0.0:8181...
    == Info: TCP_NODELAY set
    == Info: Connected to 0.0.0.0 (127.0.0.1) port 8181 (0)
    => Send header, 76 bytes (0x4c)
    0000: GET / HTTP/1.1
    0010: Host: 0.0.0.0:8181
    0024: User-Agent: curl/7.65.3
    003d: Accept: /
    004a:
    ```

Here, you can see that the blank line is represented at `004a:` and that there is no message body in the request at all. The response message is displayed in the second part, as follows:

```
== Info: Mark bundle as not supporting multiuse
<= Recv header, 17 bytes (0x11)
0000: HTTP/1.1 200 OK
<= Recv header, 20 bytes (0x14)
0000: Host: 0.0.0.0:8181
<= Recv header, 37 bytes (0x25)
0000: Date: Sat, 21 Mar 2020 20:33:09 GMT
<= Recv header, 19 bytes (0x13)
0000: Connection: close
<= Recv header, 25 bytes (0x19)
0000: X-Powered-By: PHP/7.4.4
<= Recv header, 40 bytes (0x28)
0000: Content-type: text/html; charset=UTF-8
<= Recv header, 2 bytes (0x2)
0000:
<= Recv data, 12 bytes (0xc)
0000: Hello world!
== Info: Closing connection 0
```

Here, you can see the status is `200 OK` in the start line in the response. But in the preceding example, we did not send any data, so there is no message body in the request message. Let's create another very basic PHP script, as follows:

1. Create a PHP page with the PHP `print` function so that it displays POST data, as follows:

   ```
   // public/index.php
   <?php
   print_r($_POST);
   ```

2. Serve the page on `localhost:8181` using the built-in PHP web server:

   ```
   $ php -S localhost:8181 -t public
   ```

3. Send some data over cURL on your terminal:

   ```
   $ curl http://0.0.0.0:8181 \
     -d "param1=value1&param2=value2" \
     --trace-ascii \
     /dev/stdout
   ```

This time, the request message will be displayed in the first part, along with the message body:

```
== Info: Trying 0.0.0.0:8181...
== Info: TCP_NODELAY set
== Info: Connected to 0.0.0.0 (127.0.0.1) port 8181 (0)
=> Send header, 146 bytes (0x92)
0000: POST / HTTP/1.1
0011: Host: 0.0.0.0:8181
0025: User-Agent: curl/7.65.3
003e: Accept: /
004b: Content-Length: 27
005f: Content-Type: application/x-www-form-urlencoded
0090:
=> Send data, 27 bytes (0x1b)
0000: param1=value1&param2=value2
== Info: upload completely sent off: 27 out of 27 bytes
```

The response message is displayed in the second part, as follows:

```
== Info: Mark bundle as not supporting multiuse
<= Recv header, 17 bytes (0x11)
0000: HTTP/1.1 200 OK
<= Recv header, 20 bytes (0x14)
0000: Host: 0.0.0.0:8181
<= Recv header, 37 bytes (0x25)
0000: Date: Sat, 21 Mar 2020 20:43:06 GMT
<= Recv header, 19 bytes (0x13)
0000: Connection: close
<= Recv header, 25 bytes (0x19)
0000: X-Powered-By: PHP/7.4.4
<= Recv header, 40 bytes (0x28)
0000: Content-type: text/html; charset=UTF-8
<= Recv header, 2 bytes (0x2)
0000:
<= Recv data, 56 bytes (0x38)
0000: Array.(. [param1] => value1. [param2] => value2.).
Array
(
    [param1] => value1
    [param2] => value2
)
== Info: Closing connection 0
```

4. Here, you can also see the request message and the request message for the `PUT` method over cURL on your terminal:

```
$ curl -X PUT http://0.0.0.0:8181 \
  -d "param1=value1&param2=value2" \
  --trace-ascii \
  /dev/stdout
```

5. The same applies for the `DELETE` method over cURL, as follows:

```
$ curl -X DELETE http://0.0.0.0:8181 \
  -d "param1=value1&param2=value2" \
  --trace-ascii \
  /dev/stdout
```

6. Last but not least, we also can use the Developer Tools in Google Chrome to help us inspect the exchanged data. Let's create another simple PHP script that will receive data from the URI:

```
// public/index.php
<?php
print_r($_GET);
```

7. Send some data on your browser by using `0.0.0.0:8181/?param1=value1&param2=value2`. By doing this, the data is sent as `param1=value1&param2=value2`, as shown in the following screenshot:

> If you want to know more about HTTP and HTTP messages, please visit https://developer.mozilla.org/en-US/docs/Web/HTTP for HTTP in general and https://developer.mozilla.org/en-US/docs/Web/HTTP/Messages for HTTP messages specifically.

When it comes to server-side development, HTTP messages are better encapsulated in objects so that they are easier to work with. For example, Node.js has a built-in HTTP module (https://nodejs.dev/the-nodejs-http-module) for HTTP communication, in which you can get the HTTP messages objects from the callback in the http.createServer() method when using it to create an HTTP server:

```
const http = require('http')

http.createServer((request, response) => {
  response.writeHead(200, {'Content-Type': 'text/plain'})
  response.end('Hello World')
}).listen(8080)
```

If you are using a Node.js framework such as Koa, you can find the HTTP messages objects in ctx, as follows:

```
const Koa = require('koa')
const app = new Koa()

app.use(async ctx => {
  ctx
  ctx.request
  ctx.response
})
```

In the preceding code, ctx is the Koa context, while ctx.request is the HTTP request message and ctx.response is the HTTP response message. We can do the same in Express; you can find the HTTP messages as follows:

```
const express = require('express')
const app = express()

app.get('/', (req, res) => res.send('Hello World!'))
```

Unlike Node.js, PHP has never had built-in HTTP message objects like these. There are a bunch of ways to get and set the web data, both manually and directly, just like we saw in the previous PHP examples, by using superglobals ($_GET, $_POST) and the built-in functions (echo, print_r). If you want to catch the incoming request, you can use $_GET, $_POST, $_FILE, $_COOKIE, $_SESSION, or any other superglobals (https://www.php.net/manual/en/language.variables.superglobals.php), depending on the situation.

The same goes for returning a response: you use global functions such as `echo`, `print`, and `header` to set response headers manually. In the past, PHP developers and frameworks had their own ways of implementing HTTP messages. This led to a time where different frameworks had different abstractions to **represent** HTTP messages, and any app based on a specific implementation of HTTP messages could hardly be interoperable in the project for using other frameworks. This lack of industry standards made the components of a framework tightly coupled. If you didn't start with a framework, you would end up building one yourself.

But today, the PHP community has learned and enforced PHP standards and recommendations. You don't have to fully comply with these standards and recommendations; you can ignore them if you have philosophical reasons that urge you to. But they are a measure with a good intention to end the PHP war – at least commercially and collaboratively. And once for all, PHP developers can focus on PHP standards rather than frameworks in a framework-agnostic way. When we talk about PHP standards, we tend to refer to the PSR, a PHP specification defined and published by the PHP Framework Interop Group (PHP-FIG). PSR-7: HTTP message interfaces is one of the specifications suggested by the PHP-FIG members and was voted for according to the established protocol that they agreed upon.

PSR-7 was officially accepted in May 2015. It is basically used to standardize HTTP message interfaces. Before jumping into PSR-7, we should know about some other PSR numbers as well, notably PSR-12 (replacement of PSR-2), PSR-4, and PSR-15. We will guide you through them in this book so that you can write reusable, framework-agnostic apps and components that can be used on their own or can be interoperable with other frameworks, whether they are a full-stack or micro frameworks. Let's get started!

Why PSRs?

Internally, PHP never tells developers how they should write their PHP code. For example, Python uses indentation to indicate a block of code, while for other programming languages such as PHP and JavaScript, indentation in code is done for readability. The following is an example of what Python will accept:

```
age = 20
if age == 20:
    print("age is 20")
```

Python will return an error if there's no indentation:

```
if age == 20:
print("age is 20")
```

The number of spaces is up to the coder's preference, but you must use at least one and have the same number of spaces for other lines in the same block; otherwise, Python will return an error:

```
if age == 20:
 print("age is 20")
   print("age is 20")
```

On the other hand, in PHP, you can write the following:

```
if (age == 20) {
print("age is 20");
}
```

The following is valid in PHP too:

```
if (age == 20) {
 print("age is 20");
   print("age is 20");
}
```

Python internally enforces readability and tidiness for code. PHP does not. You can imagine that without some basic enforcement, and depending on the experience of the coder, PHP code can end up very messy, ugly, and unreadable. Perhaps the low barrier to entry in PHP web development plays a part in that. So, your PHP code must adhere to a common code style to make it easy for collaboration and maintenance.

> There are a few PHP coding standards around for specific frameworks, but they are more or less based on (or similar to) PSR standards:
>
> - **Zend Coding Standard** at `https://framework.zend.com/manual/2.4/en/ref/coding.standard.html`
> - **Symfony Coding Standards** at `https://symfony.com/doc/master/contributing/code/standards.html`
> - **CakePHP Coding Standards** at `https://book.cakephp.org/3.0/en/contributing/cakephp-coding-conventions.html`
> - **FuelPHP Coding Standards** at `https://fuelphp.com/docs/general/coding_standards.html`
> - **WordPress Coding Standards** at `https://codex.wordpress.org/WordPress_Coding_Standards`

Pragmatically, your code should adhere to the framework that you are tied to, and that specific framework only. But if you are only using some components or libraries from the framework, then you can comply with any combination of PSRs, or the coding standards made by PEAR. The PEAR Coding Standards can be found at https://pear.php.net/manual/en/standards.php.

This book focuses on a variety of PSRs because this chapter aims to create framework-agnostic PHP apps. You don't have to agree with PSR, but if you are looking for a standard to start a project with and do not have any standard of your own within your organization, it might be a good place to start. You can find out more about the PSR at https://www.php-fig.org/psr/.

On top of what we have mentioned here, you should also check out **PHP: The Right Way** at https://phptherightway.com/. It outlines things that a modern PHP coder can use as references, from setting up PHP, dependency management with **Composer** (which we will cover later in this chapter), coding style guides (in which PSRs are recommended), dependency injection, databases, templating, to testing frameworks and more. It is a good start for new PHP coders who want to avoid the mistakes of the past and find links to authoritative PHP tutorials on the web. It is also a good place for experienced PHP coders who need a quick reference and updates from the PHP community at large, or anything they might have missed in the past few years.

Now, let's dive into PSRs, starting with **PSR-12**.

PSR-12 – Extended Coding Style guide

PSR-12 is a revised coding style guide of PSR-2 that takes PHP 7 into account. The PSR-12 specification was approved on 9 August 2019. Since PSR-2 was accepted in 2012, many changes have been made to PHP that have had some impact on coding style guidelines, the most notable of which is **return type declarations**, which are introduced in PHP 7 and not described in PSR-2. Hence, a standard should be defined for using them so that they can be adopted by the wider PHP community before individual PHP coders implement their standards, which might conflict with each other eventually.

For example, the **return type declarations** that have been added in PHP 7 simply specifies the type of value that a function should return. Let's take a look at the following function, which adopts the **return type declarations**:

```
declare(strict_types = 1);

function returnInt(int $value): int
{
```

```
        return $value;
}

print(returnInt(2));
```

You will get the correct result of 2 as an integer. However, let's see what happens if you change the code inside the `returnInt` function, as follows:

```
function returnInt(int $value): int
{
    return $value + 1.0;
}
```

PHP will give up with the following error:

```
PHP Fatal error: Uncaught TypeError: Return value of returnInt() must be of
the type int, float returned in ...
```

So, to cater for the need of this new feature of PHP 7, PSR-12 requires you to use a single space after the colon, followed by the type declaration for the methods with the return type declaration. Also, the colon and declaration must be on the same line as the argument list's closing parenthesis with no spaces between the two characters. Let's take a look at a simple example that has a `return` type declaration:

```
class Fruit
{
    public function setName(int $arg1, $arg2): string
    {
        return 'kiwi';
    }
}
```

Some rules are kept the same in PSR-2 and PSR-12. For example, in both PSRs, you must not use tabs for indentation but four single spaces instead. But the rule in PSR-2 regarding the list of blocks has been revised. Now, in PSR-12, the blocks that use statements for importing classes, functions, and constants must be separated by a single blank line, even though there is just one import of them. Let's take a quick look at some code that complies with this rule:

```
<?php

/**
 * The block of comments...
 */

declare(strict_types=1);
```

```
namespace VendorName\PackageName;

use VendorName\PackageName\{ClassX as X, ClassY, ClassZ as Z};
use VendorName\PackageName\SomeNamespace\ClassW as W;

use function VendorName\PackageName\{functionX, functionY, functionZ};

use const VendorName\PackageName\{ConstantX, ConstantY, ConstantZ};

/**
 * The block of comments...
 */
class Fruit
{
    //...
}
```

Now, you should notice that, in PSR-12, you must use a single blank line right after the opening `<?php` tag. However, in PSR-2, this isn't necessary. For example, you can write the following:

```
<?php
namespace VendorName\PackageName;

use FruitClass;
use VegetableClass as Veg;
```

It is worth knowing that PSR-2 was extended from PSR-1, which was a basic coding standard, but since PSR-12 was accepted, PSR-2 is now officially deprecated.

> To implement these PSRs for your code, please visit the following sites:
>
> - `https://www.php-fig.org/psr/psr-1/` for the PSR-1: Basic Coding Standard
> - `https://www.php-fig.org/psr/psr-2/` for the PSR-2: Coding Style Guide (deprecated)
> - `https://www.php-fig.org/psr/psr-12/` for the PSR-12: Extended Coding Style
>
> If you want to find out the new features in PHP 7, such as scalar type declarations and return type declarations, please visit `https://www.php.net/manual/en/migration70.new-features.php`.

PSR-12 helps PHP coders write more readable and structured code, so it is worth adopting it in your code when writing in PHP. Now, let's move on to **PSR-4**, which allows us to use autoloading in PHP.

PSR-4 – Autoloader

In the old days of PHP, if you wanted to bring a third-party library into your PHP project, or bring in your functions and classes from separate PHP files, you would use `include` or `require` statements. With the arrival of PHP autoloading, you would use the `__autoload` magic method (which is now deprecated since PHP 7.2) or `spl_autoload` to automatically call your code. Then came **true namespace** support in PHP 5.3, where developers and frameworks can devise their approaches to prevent naming collisions. But still, it was quite far from ideal because of the battle between different approaches. You can imagine a situation where you have two frameworks – framework A and framework B – and individual developers disagreeing with each other and implementing their own ways to achieve the same result. This was madness.

Today, we comply with PSR-4 (which is the successor of PSR-0) to standardize the autoloading approach and bind developers and frameworks together. It specifies the standard for autoloading classes from **file paths**. It also describes the location of the file. So, a **fully qualified class name** should adhere to the following form:

```
\<NamespaceName>(\<SubNamespaceNames>)\<ClassName>
```

In this rule, we have the following:

- The namespace for a fully qualified class must have a top-level vendor namespace, which is the `<NamespaceName>` part in the preceding code.
- You can use one or more sub-namespaces, as shown by the `<SubNamespaceNames>` part of the preceding code.
- Then, you must end the namespace with your class name, as shown by the `<ClassName>` part of the preceding code.

So, if you are writing an autoloader, it is recommended to use this standard. However, you don't have to (and probably shouldn't) go through the hassle of writing your own autoloader while complying with PSR-4. This is because you can use **Composer** to help you do this. Composer is a package manager for PHP. It is akin to npm in Node.js. It was initially released in 2012. Since then, it has been used by all modern PHP frameworks and PHP coders alike. This means you can focus more on your code development and worry less about the interoperability of different packages and libraries that you are going to bring into your project environment.

Creating a Framework-Agnostic PHP API for Nuxt

> Before we start, make sure you have Composer installed on your system. Depending on your system, you can follow the following guides to install Composer:
>
> - https://getcomposer.org/doc/00-intro.md and https://getcomposer.org/download/ from the official Composer site
> - https://phptherightway.com/dependency_management from **PHP: The Right Way**

The current version is 1.10.9. Follow these steps to install Composer and make use of the autoloader that it offers:

1. Install Composer in your current directory by running the following script in your terminal:

   ```
   $ php -r "copy('https://getcomposer.org/installer', 'composer-setup.php');"
   $ php -r "if (hash_file('sha384', 'composer-setup.php') === 'e5325b19b381bfd88ce90a5ddb7823406b2a38cff6bb704b0acc289a09c8128d4a8ce2bbafcd1fcbdc38666422fe2806') { echo 'Installer verified'; } else { echo 'Installer corrupt'; unlink('composer-setup.php'); } echo PHP_EOL;"
   ```

2. Run the Composer setup file, as follows:

   ```
   $ sudo php composer-setup.php
   ```

   You should get the following output in your terminal:

   ```
   All settings correct for using Composer
   Downloading...

   Composer (version 1.10.9) successfully installed to: /home/lau/composer.phar
   Use it: php composer.phar
   ```

3. Remove the Composer setup file, as follows:

   ```
   $ php -r "unlink('composer-setup.php');"
   ```

4. Verify the installation by running `php composer.phar` on your terminal. If you want to use Composer **globally**, then move Composer to `/usr/local/bin` (if you are using Linux/Unix):

   ```
   $ sudo mv composer.phar /usr/local/bin/composer
   ```

5. Now, you can run Composer globally. To verify it, just run the following command:

   ```
   $ composer
   ```

   You should see the logo for Composer, as well as its available commands and options:

   ```
      _____
     / ____/___  ____ ___  ____  ____  _____  _____
    / /   / __ \/ __ `__ \/ __ \/ __ \/ ___/ _ \/ ___/
   / /___/ /_/ / / / / / / /_/ / /_/ (__  )  __/ /
   \____/\____/_/ /_/ /_/ .___/\____/____/\___/_/
                       /_/
   Composer version 1.10.9 2020-07-16 12:57:00
   ...
   ...
   ```

   Alternatively, you can use the `-V` option to check the version you've installed directly:

   ```
   $ composer -V
   Composer version 1.10.9 2020-07-16 12:57:00
   ```

6. Now that you have Composer installed on your system, simply navigate to your project's root through your terminal and use `composer require`, followed by `<package-name>`, to install any third-party packages (also known as dependencies) that you need in your project, as follows:

   ```
   $ composer require monolog/monolog
   ```

7. After installing the required packages, you can go to your project root. You should see that a `composer.json` file has been created that contains the dependency of your project in a `require` key:

   ```
   {
       "require": {
           "monolog/monolog": "^2.0"
       }
   }
   ```

8. If you want to install all the dependencies again next time, you can just run the `install` command, as follows:

```
$ composer install
```

9. When you have installed your project dependencies, whether that be with the `require` or `install` command, you will always get a `/vendor/` folder generated by Composer that contains all your dependencies. An `autoload.php` file will always be generated and located inside the `/vendor/` folder. You then can include this file and start using the classes that those packages provide straight away, as follows:

```
require __DIR__ . '/vendor/autoload.php';

$log = new Monolog\Logger('name');
$log->pushHandler(new
Monolog\Handler\StreamHandler('path/to/your.log',
Monolog\Logger::WARNING));
$log->addWarning('Foo');
$log->error('Bar');
```

10. Most importantly, you can even add your classes to the autoloader by adding the `autoload` key, along with your custom namespace, to the `composer.json` file. For example, you can have your classes stored in an `/src/` folder in the project root, on the same level where the `/vendor/` directory is:

```
{
    "autoload": {
        "psr-4": {"Spectre\\": "src/"}
    }
}
```

If you have the source files in multiple locations, you can use an array, `[ ]`, to associate it with your custom namespace, as follows:

```
{
    "autoload": {
        "psr-4": {
            "Spectre\\": [
                "module1/",
                "module2/"
            ]
        }
    }
}
```

Composer will register a PSR-4 autoloader for the Spectre namespace. After that, you can start writing your classes. For example, you can create a /src/Foo.php file that contains a Spectre\Foo class. After that, just run dump-autoload on your terminal to regenerate the autoload.php file inside the /vendor/ directory. You also can add multiple custom namespaces to the autoload field, as follows:

```
{
    "autoload": {
        "psr-4": {
            "Spectre\\": [
                //...
            ],
            "AnotherNamespace\\": [
                //...
            ]
        }
    }
}
```

Besides PSR-4, Composer also supports PSR-0. You can add a PSR-0 key to the composer.json file.

> For more information and examples of how to use PSR-0 with Composer, please visit https://getcomposer.org/doc/04-schema.mdautoload. However, please note that PSR-0 is now deprecated. If you want to read more about these two PSRs, please visit https://www.php-fig.org/psr/psr-0/ for PSR 0 (deprecated) and https://www.php-fig.org/psr/psr-4/ for PSR-4.
>
> If you want to know about Monolog, which we used in the preceding example for logging in PHP, please visit https://github.com/Seldaek/monolog. If you want to read more about Autoloading Classes in PHP, please visit https://www.php.net/manual/en/language.oop5.autoload.php.

As soon as you have armed yourself with knowledge about PSR-12 and PSR-4, it will be easier for you to build PHP apps that comply with other PSRs. The other two PSRs that this book focuses on are PSR-7 and PSR-15. Let's move on and look at **PSR-7** first.

PSR-7 – HTTP Message Interfaces

Earlier, we mentioned that PHP does not have HTTP request and response message objects, which is why PHP frameworks and coders came out with different abstractions to represent (or "imitate") HTTP messages in the past. Luckily, in 2015, PSR-7 came to the rescue to end these "disagreements" and differences.

PSR-7 is a set of common interfaces (abstractions) that specify public methods for HTTP messages and URIs when communicating over HTTP. In object-oriented programming (OOP), an interface is, in fact, an abstraction of the actions (public methods) that an object (a class) must implement, without defining the complexities and details of how these actions are implemented. For example, the following table shows the methods that your HTTP message classes must implement when composing them so that they comply with the PSR-7 specification.

The specified methods for accessing and modifying the request and response objects are as follows:

To access	To modify
`getProtocolVersion()`	`withProtocolVersion($version)`
`getHeaders()`	`withHeader($name, $value)`
`hasHeader($name)`	`withAddedHeader($name, $value)`
`getHeader($name)` `getHeaderLine($name)`	`withoutHeader($name)`
`getBody()`	`withBody(StreamInterface $body)`

The specified methods for accessing and modifying just **request** objects are as follows:

To access	To modify
• getRequestTarget() • getMethod() • getUri() • getServerParams() • getCookieParams() • getQueryParams() • getUploadedFiles() • getParsedBody() • getAttributes() • getAttribute($name, $default = null)	• withMethod($method) • withRequestTarget($requestTarget) • withUri(UriInterface $uri, $preserveHost = false) • withCookieParams(array $cookies) • withQueryParams(array $query) • withUploadedFiles(array $uploadedFiles) • withParsedBody($data) • withAttribute($name, $value) • withoutAttribute($name)

The specified methods for accessing and modifying just **response** objects are as follows:

To access	To modify
• getStatusCode() • getReasonPhrase()	• withStatus($code, $reasonPhrase = '')

Since PSR-7 was accepted on 18 May 2015, many packages have been made based on it. You can develop your own version as long as you implement the interfaces and methods specified in PSR-7. However, you might be "reinventing the wheel" since there are PSR-7 HTTP messages packages out there already – unless you have some strong reasons to do so. So, for the sake of getting it started quickly, let's use zend-diactoros from Zend Framework. We will "reuse" the PSR knowledge (PSR-12 and PSR-4) you gained in the previous sections to create a simple "Hello World" server-side app with HTTP messages. Let's get started:

1. Create a /public/ directory in the app root with an index.php file in it. Add the following lines to it to bootstrap the app environment:

   ```
   // public/index.php
   chdir(dirname(__DIR__));
   require_once 'vendor/autoload.php';
   ```

   In these two lines of code, we have changed the current directory from /path/to/public to /path/to so that we can import the autoload.php file by writing vendor/autoload.php instead of ../vendor/autoload.php.

Creating a Framework-Agnostic PHP API for Nuxt

The `__DIR__` (magic) constant is used to get the directory path of the current file, which is `index.php`, in the `/path/to/public/` directory. The `dirname` function is then used to get the parent directory's path, which is `/path/to`. The `chdir` function is then used to change the current directory.

Note that in the upcoming sections on PSRs, we will use this pattern to bootstrap the app environment and import the autoload file. Please visit the following links to find out more about the constants and functions mentioned previously:

- The `__DIR__` (magic) constant: https://www.php.net/manual/en/language.constants.predefined.php
- The `dirname` function: https://www.php.net/manual/en/function.dirname.php
- The `chdir` function: https://www.php.net/manual/en/function.chdir.php

Also, note that you must run all the incoming PHP apps on a terminal by using the built-in PHP web server, as follows:

```
$ php -S localhost:8181 -t public
```

2. Install `zend-diactoros` into the app's root directory via Composer:

```
$ composer require zendframework/zend-diactoros
```

3. To marshal an incoming request, you should create a request object in the `index.php` file in the `/public/` directory, as follows:

```
$request = Zend\Diactoros\ServerRequestFactory::fromGlobals(
    $_SERVER,
    $_GET,
    $_POST,
    $_COOKIE,
    $_FILES
);
```

[538]

4. Now, we can create a response object and manipulate the response, as follows:

   ```
   $response = new Zend\Diactoros\Response();
   $response->getBody()->write("Hello ");
   ```

5. Note that the `write` method is specified in the stream interface (`StreamInterface`) and that we can also append more data by making multiple calls with this method:

   ```
   $response->getBody()->write("World!");
   ```

6. We can then manipulate the headers if needed:

   ```
   $response = $response
       ->withHeader('Content-Type', 'text/plain');
   ```

7. Note that the headers should be added after data is written to the body. Then, that's it – you have managed to transform the simple PHP "Hello World" app that you learned about at the beginning of this chapter into a modern PHP app with PSR-7! However, if you run this PSR-7 "Hello World" app on your browser with `php -S localhost:8181 -t public` from your terminal, you will see nothing on the screen. This is because we did not **emit** the response to the browser with **PSR-15 HTTP Server Request Handlers** and **PSR-7 HTTP Response Emitter**, which we will cover in the next section. If you want to see the output, for now, you can access the data by using the `getBody` method and then using `echo`:

   ```
   echo $response->getBody();
   ```

8. If you inspect the `Content-type` of your page through the Developer Tools on Chrome, you'll get `text/html` instead of `text/plain`, which is what we modified with the `withHeader` method. We will get the correct content type with the emitter in the next chapter.

> For more information about `zend-diactoros` and their advanced usage, please visit https://docs.zendframework.com/zend-diactoros/. Besides `zend-diactoros` from Zend Framework, you also can use the HTTP messages package from other frameworks and libraries:
>
> - Guzzle and PSR-7 from Guzzle at http://docs.guzzlephp.org/en/latest/psr7.html
> - HTTPlug from PHP-HTTP at http://docs.php-http.org/en/latest/
> - The PSR-7 Bridge from Symfony at https://symfony.com/doc/master/components/http_foundation.html
> - Slim at http://www.slimframework.com
>
> You should check out the PSR-7 documentation at https://www.php-fig.org/psr/psr-7/ for more information about this PSR. If you are new to PHP interfaces, please visit https://www.php.net/manual/en/language.oop5.interfaces.php for further reading.

From the PSR-7 documentation, you can find out the rest of the public methods that are not mentioned in this book. They should be expected in any PSR-7 HTTP messages package, such as `zend-diactoros`. It is useful to know about these methods so you know what you can do with them. You also can use the built-in PHP `get_class_methods` method at runtime to list all the methods that you can use in the request and response objects. For example, for the `request` object, you can do the following:

```
$request = Zend\Diactoros\ServerRequestFactory::fromGlobals(
    //...
);
print_r(get_class_methods($request));
```

You will get a list of request methods in an array that you can call. The same goes for the `response` object; you will get a list of response methods in an array by doing this:

```
$response = new Zend\Diactoros\Response();
print_r(get_class_methods($response));
```

Now, let's move on and look at **PSR-15**, where we'll find out how to emit the response to the client (browser).

PSR-15 – HTTP Server Request Handlers (request handlers)

PSR-7 was a great step in the PHP community, but it is only halfway to the goal that **could** free PHP coders from monolithic MVC frameworks and allow them to compose agnostic PHP apps out of a range of reusable middlewares. It only defines HTTP messages (the request and the response); it never defines how to deal with them afterward. So, we need a request handler to process the request in order to produce a response.

Like PSR-7, PSR-15 is a set of common interfaces, but they take things a step further and specify the standard for request handlers (HTTP server request handlers) and middleware (HTTP server request middleware). It was accepted on 22 January 2018. We will cover the HTTP server request middleware in the next section. Now, let's understand the HTTP server request handlers in the PSR-15 interface, `RequestHandlerInterface`:

```
// Psr\Http\Server\RequestHandlerInterface

namespace Psr\Http\Server;

use Psr\Http\Message\ResponseInterface;
use Psr\Http\Message\ServerRequestInterface;

interface RequestHandlerInterface
{
    public function handle(ServerRequestInterface $request) :
      ResponseInterface;
}
```

As you can see, this is a very simple interface. It only has one specified public method, `handle`, which only accepts a PSR-7 HTTP request message and **must** return a PSR-7 HTTP response message. We will use the `zend-httphandlerrunner` component from Zend Framework, which implements this interface, to provide utilities that we can use to emit PSR-7 responses. Let's get it hooked up to the app:

1. Install `zend-httphandlerrunner` via Composer:

   ```
   $ composer require zendframework/zend-httphandlerrunner
   ```

2. As soon as we have it installed in our project environment, we can send the response that we created previously to the browser, as follows:

   ```
   //...
   $response = $response
   ```

```
        ->withHeader('Content-Type', 'text/plain');

(new Zend\HttpHandlerRunner\Emitter\SapiEmitter)->emit($response);
```

If you inspect `Content-Type` of your page again through the Developer Tools on Chrome, you'll get the correct content type, which is `text/plain`.

> For more information about `zend-httphandlerrunner`, visit https://docs.zendframework.com/zend-httphandlerrunner/. For more information about PSR-15, visit https://www.php-fig.org/psr/psr-15/.

Besides `zend-httphandlerrunner`, you can also use Http Response Emitter from Narrowspark at https://github.com/narrowspark/http-emitter to handle the request and emit the response. Now, let's move on and look at the **second interface** of PSR-15: `MiddlewareInterface`.

PSR-15 – HTTP Server Request Handlers (middleware)

The middleware interface in PSR-15 has the following abstraction:

```
// Psr\Http\Server\MiddlewareInterface

namespace Psr\Http\Server;

use Psr\Http\Message\ResponseInterface;
use Psr\Http\Message\ServerRequestInterface;
use Psr\Http\Server\RequestHandlerInterface;

interface MiddlewareInterface
{
    public function process(
        ServerRequestInterface $request,
        RequestHandlerInterface $handler
    ) : ResponseInterface;
}
```

Again, you can see it is a very simple interface. It only has one specified public method process for middleware implementation. The component (middleware) that implements this interface will only accept a PSR-7 HTTP request message and a PSR-15 HTTP server request handler and then **must** return a PSR-7 HTTP response message.

We will use the `zend-stratigility` components from Zend Framework, which implement this interface, to allow us to create PSR-15 middleware in our app. Let's learn how to get it hooked up to the app:

1. Install `zend-stratigility` via Composer:

    ```
    $ composer require zendframework/zend-stratigility
    ```

2. As soon as we have it installed in our project environment, we will import the `middleware` function and `MiddlewarePipe` class, as follows:

    ```
    use function Zend\Stratigility\middleware;

    $app = new Zend\Stratigility\MiddlewarePipe();

    // Create a request
    $request = Zend\Diactoros\ServerRequestFactory::fromGlobals(
        //...
    );
    ```

3. Then, we can use this `middleware` function to create **three** middlewares and attach them to the pipeline, as follows:

    ```
    $app->pipe(middleware(function ($request, $handler) {
        $response = $handler->handle($request);
        return $response
            ->withHeader('Content-Type', 'text/plain');
    }));

    $app->pipe(middleware(function ($request, $handler) {
        $response = $handler->handle($request);
        $response->getBody()->write("User Agent: " .
         $request->getHeader('user-agent')[0]);
        return $response;
    }));

    $app->pipe(middleware(function ($request, $handler) {
        $response = new Zend\Diactoros\Response();
        $response->getBody()->write("Hello world!\n");
        $response->getBody()->write("Request method: " .
         $request->getMethod() . "\n");
        return $response;
    }));
    ```

4. As you can see, the "Hello World" code block we created previously now is a piece of middleware that's stacked with other middleware. Finally, we can generate a **final** response from these pieces of middleware and emit it to the browser, as follows:

```
$response = $app->handle($request);
(new Zend\HttpHandlerRunner\Emitter\SapiEmitter)->
  emit($response);
```

You should get a result similar to the following on your browser at `0.0.0.0:8181`:

```
Hello world!
Request method: GET
User Agent: Mozilla/5.0 (X11; Linux x86_64) AppleWebKit/537.36
  (KHTML, like Gecko) Chrome/77.0.3865.90 Safari/537.36
```

For more information about `zend-stratigility`, visit https://docs.zendframework.com/zend-stratigility/.

> Besides `zend-stratigility`, you can also use the following packages to create your middleware:
> - Northwoods Broker at https://github.com/northwoods/broker
> - Relay at https://relayphp.com/

So, there you go. With the help of several interoperable components, we have bootstrapped a modern PHP app that complies with PSR-12, PSR-7, and PSR-15, which means you can freely pick (agnostically) from a broad range of vendor implementations of those standards for your HTTP messages, request handler, and middleware. But we haven't finished yet. As you may have noticed, the app we have created is just a one-page app that runs on a single "route" at `0.0.0.0:8181`. It doesn't have any other routes, such as `/about`, `/contact`, and so on. Therefore, we need a router that implements PSR-15. We'll cover this in the next section.

PSR-7/PSR-15 router

We will use Route from The League of Extraordinary Packages (a PHP developer group) so that we have a PSR-7 routing system and dispatch our PSR-15 middleware on it. In short, Route is a fast PSR-7 routing/dispatcher package.

It is a PSR-15 server request handler and can handle the invocation of a stack of middleware. It is built on top of FastRoute (https://github.com/nikic/FastRoute) by Nikita Popov.

Let's learn how to get it hooked up to the app:

1. Install league/route via Composer:

    ```
    $ composer require league/route
    ```

2. Once you have it installed, we can refactor our "Hello World" component with a route, as follows:

    ```
    use Psr\Http\Message\ResponseInterface;
    use Psr\Http\Message\ServerRequestInterface;

    $request = Zend\Diactoros\ServerRequestFactory::fromGlobals(
        //...
    );

    $router = new League\Route\Router;

    $router->map('GET', '/', function (ServerRequestInterface $request) : ResponseInterface {
        $response = new Zend\Diactoros\Response;
        $response->getBody()->write('<h1>Hello, World!</h1>');
        return $response;
    });
    ```

3. Then, we just have to create a PSR-7 HTTP response by using a dispatch method from Route and emitting it to the browser:

    ```
    $response = $router->dispatch($request);
    (new Zend\HttpHandlerRunner\Emitter\SapiEmitter)->emit($response);
    ```

    Check out the list of HTTP request methods (get, post, put, delete, and so on) that you can use at https://route.thephpleague.com/4.x/route. What's more, we can attach middleware to our app.

4. If you want to lock down the entire app, you can add the middleware to the router, as follows:

    ```
    use function Zend\Stratigility\middleware;

    $router = new League\Route\Router;
    $router->middleware(<middleware>);
    ```

5. If you want to lock down a group of routes, you can add the middleware to the group, as follows:

   ```
   $router
       ->group('/private', function ($router) {
           // ... add routes
       })
       ->middleware(<middleware>)
   ;
   ```

6. If you want to lock down a specific route, you can add the middleware to that route, as follows:

   ```
   $router
       ->map('GET', '/secret', <SomeController>)
       ->middleware(<middleware>)
   ;
   ```

7. For example, you can use Route with `zend-stratigility`:

   ```
   use function Zend\Stratigility\middleware;

   $router = new League\Route\Router;
   $router->middleware(middleware(function ($request, $handler) {
       //...
   }));
   ```

8. If you don't want to use the `middleware` function or prefer not to use `zend-stratigility` at all, you can create anonymous middleware, as follows:

   ```
   use Psr\Http\Message\ResponseInterface;
   use Psr\Http\Message\ServerRequestInterface;
   use Psr\Http\Server\MiddlewareInterface;
   use Psr\Http\Server\RequestHandlerInterface;

   $router = new League\Route\Router;

   $router->middleware(new class implements MiddlewareInterface {
       public function process(ServerRequestInterface $request,
       RequestHandlerInterface $handler) : ResponseInterface
       {
           $response = $handler->handle($request);
           return $response->withHeader('X-Clacks-Overhead',
           'GNU Terry Pratchett');
       }
   });
   ```

As long as you comply with PSR7 and PSR-15 by implementing the `process` method in your middleware, there's no need for `zend-stratigility` at all. If you want to create class-based middleware in a separate PHP file, please check out the example provided at https://route.thephpleague.com/4.x/middleware/.

> For more information about Route from The League of Extraordinary Packages, visit https://route.thephpleague.com/. You can also check out other packages that have been created by this group of developers at https://thephpleague.com/. Besides Route from The League of Extraordinary, you can also use the following packages for HTTP routers based on PSR-7 and PSR-15:
>
> - `delolmo/symfony-router` at https://github.com/delolmo/symfony-router
> - `middlewares/aura-router` at https://github.com/middlewares/aura-router
> - `middlewares/fast-route` at https://github.com/middlewares/fast-route
> - `timtegeler/routerunner` at https://github.com/timtegeler/routerunner
> - `sunrise-php/http-router` at https://github.com/sunrise-php/http-router

You may need a dispatcher to use with some of these packages. The advantage of using Route from The League of Extraordinary Packages is that it provides a router and a dispatcher in one package.

With that, we have composed an agnostic PHP app by using PSR-12, PSR-4, PSR-7, and PSR-15. But our PHP API isn't done yet. There's one more task to do – we need to add a database framework for CRUD operations. We will guide you through this task in the next section.

Writing CRUD operations with PHP database frameworks

As you may recall from Chapter 9, *Adding a Server-Side Database*, **CRUD** stands for **c**reate, **r**ead, **u**pdate, and **d**elete. In that chapter, we used MongoDB to create CRUD operations. In this section, we will use MySQL to create backend authentication. We will use MySQL with PHP in the PHP app we have just created with PSRs. So, let's start by creating the table that we will need in the MySQL database.

Creating MySQL tables

Make sure you have installed MySQL Server on your local machine and created a database called `nuxt-php`. Once you've done that, follow these steps to finish up the first part of our API:

1. Insert the following SQL query to create the table in the database:

    ```
    CREATE TABLE user (
      uuid varchar(255) NOT NULL,
      name varchar(255) NOT NULL,
      slug varchar(255) NOT NULL,
      created_on int(10) unsigned NOT NULL,
      updated_on int(10) unsigned NOT NULL,
      UNIQUE KEY slug (slug)
    ) ENGINE=MyISAM DEFAULT CHARSET=utf8;
    ```

    The first thing you will have noticed is that we are using `uuid` instead of `id` like we did in Chapter 12, *Creating User Logins and API Authentication*. UUID stands for **Universally Unique Identifier**. There may be reasons why and benefits that will make you want to choose UUIDs over auto increment keys for indexing records in database tables. For example, you can create a UUID without connecting to the database. It is practically unique across apps, so you can easily combine data from different databases and never get a clash. To generate UUIDs in a PHP app, we can use `ramsey/uuid` by Ben Ramsey to help us generate RFC 4122 (https://tools.ietf.org/html/rfc4122) version 1, 3, 4, and 5 UUIDs.

2. So, let's install `ramsey/uuid` via Composer:

    ```
    $ composer require ramsey/uuid
    ```

3. Now, you can use this package to generate version 1 of UUID, as follows:

```
use Ramsey\Uuid\Uuid;

$uuid1 = Uuid::uuid1();
echo $uuid1->toString();
```

> If you want to find out more information about this package, visit https://github.com/ramsey/uuid.

Now, let's learn how to use PHP to work with MySQL databases and find out why we need a database framework to speed up our development in PHP.

Using Medoo as a database framework

In the old days of PHP, developers used MySQL functions (https://www.php.net/manual/en/ref.mysql.php) to manage MySQL databases. Then, the MySQLi extension (https://www.php.net/manual/en/book.mysqli.php) came to replace MySQL functions, which are now deprecated. However, now, developers are encouraged to use **PHP Data Objects (PDO)** (https://www.php.net/manual/en/book.pdo.php). PDO is a built-in PHP interface abstraction, just like PSR-7 and PSR-15 are. It is a data-access abstraction layer that provides a consistent interface (a unified API) for accessing and managing databases (for example, MySQL and PostgreSQL), which means regardless of which database you are using, you use the same functions to query and fetch data. It supports the following databases:

• CUBRID • MS SQL Server • Firebird • IBM	• Informix • MySQL • Oracle • ODBC and DB2	• PostgreSQL • SQLite • 4D

Note that PDO is a data-access abstraction layer, not a database abstraction layer. Hence, depending on which database you use, a PDO driver for that database must be installed for using PDO. We are using a MySQL database, so we must make sure that the `PDO_MYSQL` driver is installed. In Ubuntu, you can use the following command to check whether you have the PDO extension is enabled and that `PDO_MYSQL` driver is installed in your environment:

```
$ php -m
```

Creating a Framework-Agnostic PHP API for Nuxt

You should get a list of PHP modules. Look for `PDO` and `pdo_mysql`:

```
[PHP Modules]
...
PDO
pdo_mysql
...
```

Another more specific option you can use to check for PDO and its drivers is as follows:

```
$ php -m|grep -i pdo
PDO
pdo_mysql
```

If you just want to search for PDO drivers, do the following:

```
$ php -m|grep -i pdo_
pdo_mysql
```

You can also create a PHP page with `phpinfo()` to look for them. Alternatively, you can use the `getAvailableDrivers` method, as follows:

```
print_r(PDO::getAvailableDrivers());
```

You should get a list of PDO drivers, as follows:

```
Array
(
    [0] => mysql
)
```

Alternatively, there are some built-in PHP functions that can help you:

```
extension_loaded ('PDO'); // returns boolean
extension_loaded('pdo_mysql'); // returns boolean
get_loaded_extensions(); // returns array
```

If you don't see any PDO drivers, then you must install the driver for MySQL support. Follow these steps to do so:

1. Search for the package name (Ubuntu):

   ```
   $ apt-cache search php7.4|grep mysql
   php7.4-mysql - MySQL module for PHP
   ```

2. Install `php7.4-mysql` and restart your Apache server:

   ```
   $ sudo apt-get install php7.4-mysql
   $ sudo service apache2 restart
   ```

Once you have the `PDO_MYSQL` driver in place, you can start writing CRUD operations immediately. For example, let's write an `insert` operation, as follows:

1. Create the MySQL database connection:

   ```
   $servername = "localhost";
   $username = "<username>";
   $password = "<password>";
   $dbname = "<dbname>";
   $connection = new PDO(
       "mysql:host=$servername;dbname=$dbname",
       $username,
       $password
   )
   ```

   > Note that `<username>`, `<password>`, and `<dbname>` are placeholders for the actual connection details. You must change them according to your own database settings.

2. Prepare the SQL query and `bind` parameters:

   ```
   $stmt = $connection->prepare("
       INSERT INTO user (
           uuid,
           name,
           slug,
           created_on,
           updated_on
       ) VALUES (
           :uuid,
           :name,
           :slug,
           :created_on,
           :updated_on
       )
   ");
   $stmt->bindParam(':uuid', $uuid);
   $stmt->bindParam(':name', $name);
   $stmt->bindParam(':slug', $slug);
   $stmt->bindParam(':created_on', $createdOn);
   $stmt->bindParam(':updated_on', $updatedOn);
   ```

3. Insert a fresh row:

   ```
   $uuid = "25769c6c-d34d-4bfe-ba98-e0ee856f3e7a";
   $name = "John Doe";
   ```

```
$slug = "john-doe";
$createdOn = (new DateTime())->getTimestamp();
$updatedOn = $createdOn;
$stmt->execute();
```

This is not ideal because you have to `prepare` the statement every time and bind parameters where they needed, and this takes quite a lot of lines to operate. For this reason, we should pick a PHP database framework to accelerate development. **Medoo** (https://medoo.in/) is one of the choices out there. It is lightweight and very easy to integrate and use.

Let's get it installed and hooked up to our app:

1. Install Medoo via Composer:

   ```
   $ composer require catfan/medoo
   ```

2. If everything is set and in place, you can import Medoo and pass in an array of configuration to start the database connection, just as we did previously in the vanilla approach:

   ```
   use Medoo\Medoo;

   $database = new Medoo([
       'database_type' => 'mysql',
       'database_name' => '<dbname>',
       'server' => 'localhost',
       'username' => '<username>',
       'password' => '<password>'
   ]);
   ```

That's it for establishing a connection to the MySQL database through this database framework. You can find the actual usage of this snippet in `/chapter-16/nuxt-php/proxy/backend/core/mysql.php` in this book's GitHub repository. We will show you how to implement it in the upcoming section, but for now, let's explore how to write some basic CRUD operations with Medoo.

Inserting records

You can use the `insert` method when you want to insert new records into a table, as follows:

```
$database->insert('user', [
    'uuid' => '41263659-3c1f-305a-bfac-6a7c9eab0507',
    'name' => 'Jane',
```

```
    'slug' => 'jane',
    'created_on' => '1568072289'
]);
```

> If you want to find out more details about this method, visit https://medoo.in/api/insert.

Querying records

You can use the `select` method when you want to list records from a table, as follows:

```
$database->select('user', [
    'uuid',
    'name',
    'slug',
    'created_on',
    'updated_on',
]);
```

The `select` method gives you a list of records. If you just want to select a specific row, you can use the `get` method, as follows:

```
$database->get('user', [
    'uuid',
    'name',
    'slug',
    'created_on',
    'updated_on',
], [
    'slug' => 'jane'
]);
```

> If you want to find out more details, visit https://medoo.in/api/select for the `select` method and https://medoo.in/api/get for the `get` method.

Updating records

You can use the `update` method when you want to modify the data of a record in a table, as follows:

```
$database->update('user', [
    'name' => 'Janey',
    'slug' => 'jane',
    'updated_on' => '1568091701'
], [
    'uuid' => '41263659-3c1f-305a-bfac-6a7c9eab0507'
]);
```

> If you want to find out more details about this method, visit https://medoo.in/api/update.

Deleting records

You can use the `delete` method when you want to remove a record from a table, as follows:

```
$database->delete('user', [
    'uuid' => '41263659-3c1f-305a-bfac-6a7c9eab0507'
]);
```

If you want to find out more details about this method, visit https://medoo.in/api/delete.

That's it regarding how to write basic CRUD operations with Medoo and PDO.

> Please check out Medoo's documentation at https://medoo.in/doc for the rest of the methods that you can use. There are other alternatives to Medoo, such as Doctrine DBAL at https://github.com/doctrine/dbal and Eloquent at https://github.com/illuminate/database.

In this section, you studied a handful of PSRs and CRUD operations. Next, we will cover how to put all these together and integrate them with Nuxt. Since PHP and JavaScript are two different languages, the only way for them to talk to each other is through JSON in the API.

But before we write a script that will enable that, we should look into the cross-domain application structure for these two programs. We have been using cross-domain application structures for our Nuxt apps since Chapter 12, *Creating User Logins and API Authentication*, so this should be familiar to you. Let's get started!

Structuring cross-domain app directories

Again, just like when structuring cross-domain app directories, the following is our holistic view for Nuxt and our PHP API:

```
// Nuxt app
front-end
├── package.json
├── nuxt.config.js
└── pages
    ├── index.vue
    └── ...

// PHP API
backend
├── composer.json
├── vendor
│   └── ...
├── ...
└── ...
```

Individually, the directory structure for Nuxt remains the same. We only have to make a slight change to the API directory's structure, as follows:

```
// PHP API
backend
├── composer.json
├── middlewares.php
├── routes.php
├── vendor
│   └── ...
├── public
│   └── index.php
├── static
│   └── ...
├── config
│   └── ...
├── core
│   └── ...
├── middleware
│   └── ...
```

Creating a Framework-Agnostic PHP API for Nuxt

```
└── module
    └── ...
```

The directory structure for the PHP API is a suggestion. You can always design a structure that you prefer and that suits you the most. So, at a glance, we have the following:

- The `/vendor/` directory is where all the third-party packages or dependencies are kept.
- The `/public/` directory only contains an `index.php` file that initiates our API.
- The `/static/` directory for static files, such as a favicon.
- The `/config/` directory stores the configuration files, such as MySQL files.
- The `/core/` directory stores the common objects and functions that we can use across the app.
- The `/middleware/` directory stores our PSR-15 middleware.
- The `/module/` directory stores the custom modules we will create later, just as we did in Chapter 12, *Creating User Logins and API Authentication*, with Koa.
- The `composer.json` file is always located at the root level.
- The `middlewares.php` file is the core location for importing middleware from the `/middleware/` directory.
- The `routes.php` file is the core location for importing routes from the `/module/` directory.

Once you have the structure ready, you can start writing the top-level code that will glue the other code from the different locations and directory into a single app in the `index.php` file in the `/public/` directory. So, let's get started:

1. Put the `foreach` loop in the `routes.php` file to iterate each module that you will create later:

   ```
   // backend/routes.php
   $modules = require './config/routes.php';

   foreach ($modules as $module) {
       require './module/' . $module . 'index.php';
   }
   ```

2. Create a `routes.php` file in the `/config/` directory that will list the filename of your module, as follows:

   ```
   // backend/config/routes.php
   return [
       'Home/',
   ```

```
        'User/'.
        //...
];
```

3. In this PHP API, the `middlewares.php` file will import a piece of middleware that is used to decorate the CRUD operation's output:

    ```
    // backend/middlewares.php
    require './middleware/outputDecorator.php';
    ```

    This decorator will print the CRUD operation's output in JSON in the following format:

    ```
    {"status":<status code>,"data":<data>}
    ```

4. Create a file called `outputDecorator.php` in the `/middleware/` directory that contains the following code. This will wrap the operation's output in the preceding format:

    ```
    // backend/middleware/outputDecorator.php
    use function Zend\Stratigility\middleware;

    $router->middleware(middleware(function ($request, $handler) {
        $response = $handler->handle($request);
        $existingContent = (string) $response->getBody();
        $contentDecoded = json_decode($existingContent, true);
        $status = $response->getStatusCode();
        $data = [
            "status" => $status,
            "data" => $contentDecoded
        ];
        $payload = json_encode($data);

        $response->getBody()->rewind();
        $response->getBody()->write($payload);

        return $response
            ->withHeader('Content-Type', 'application/json')
            ->withStatus($status);
    }));
    ```

    Here, we use the `middleware` method from the `zend-stratigility` component to create the decorator middleware. Then, we lock down the entire application with this middleware by using the router from `league/route` by The League of Extraordinary.

5. Create a `mysql.php` file in the `/core/` directory that returns the Medoo instance for the MySQL connection:

```php
// backend/core/mysql.php
$dbconfig = require './config/mysql.php';
$mysql = new Medoo\Medoo([
    'database_type' => $dbconfig['type'],
    'database_name' => $dbconfig['name'],
    'server' => $dbconfig['host'],
    'username' => $dbconfig['username'],
    'password' => $dbconfig['password']
]);
return $mysql;
```

6. As we mentioned earlier, the `/public/` directory only contains an `index.php` file. This is used to initiate our program, so it contains the script that you learned about previously regarding PSRs:

```php
// backend/public/index.php
chdir(dirname(__DIR__));
require_once 'vendor/autoload.php';

$request = Zend\Diactoros\ServerRequestFactory::fromGlobals(
    //...
);

$router = new League\Route\Router;
try {
    require 'middlewares.php';
    require 'routes.php';
    $response = $router->dispatch($request);
} catch(Exception $exception) {
    // handle errors
}

(new Zend\HttpHandlerRunner\Emitter\SapiEmitter)->emit($response);
```

Here, you can see that the `middlewares.php` and `routes.php` files are imported into this file to produce a PSR-7 response. They are wrapped in the `try` and `catch` blocks to catch any HTTP errors, such as 404 and 506 errors. Due to this, any output from the module and any errors will be emitted to the browser through the last line. Hopefully, this has given you a bird's-eye view on this simple API. Now, let's move on and dive into the `/module/` directory in more detail to learn how to create modules and routes.

Creating the API's public routes and their modules

Creating the API's public routes and their modules is very similar to the API you learned to build in the previous chapters of this book; the main difference is the language. We used JavaScript and the Node.js framework – Koa, previously, while for the API in this chapter, we are using PHP and PSRs to create a framework-agnostic API. So, let's get started:

1. Create two directories in the /module/ directory: one called Home and another called User. These two sub-directories are the modules in this API. In each module, create a /_routes/ directory and an index.php file that will import the routes from the /_routes/ directory, as follows:

   ```
   └── module
       ├── Home
       │   ├── index.php
       │   └── _routes
       │       └── hello_world.php
       └── User
           ├── index.php
           └── _routes
               └── ...
   ```

2. In the Home module, output a "Hello world!" message and map it to the / route, as follows:

   ```
   // module/Home/_routes/hello_world.php
   use Psr\Http\Message\ResponseInterface;
   use Psr\Http\Message\ServerRequestInterface;

   $router->get('/', function (ServerRequestInterface $request) :
     ResponseInterface {
       return new Zend\Diactoros\Response\JsonResponse(
         'Hello world!');
   });
   ```

3. In the User module, write the CRUD operations so that we can create, read, update, and delete our users. So, in the /_routes/ directory, create five files called fetch_user.php, fetch_users.php, insert_user.php, and update_user.php, and delete_user.php. In each of these files, we will map the route for each of the CRUD operations in the /Controller/ directory:

   ```
   └── User
       ├── index.php
   ```

[559]

```
├── _routes
│   ├── delete_user.php
│   ├── fetch_user.php
│   │   ...
└── Controller
    └── ...
```

4. For example, in the `fetch_users.php` file, we will define a `/users` route for listing all the users, as follows:

   ```
   // module/User/_routes/fetch_users.php
   use Psr\Http\Message\ResponseInterface;
   use Psr\Http\Message\ServerRequestInterface;

   $router->get('/users', function (ServerRequestInterface $request) :
   ResponseInterface {
       $database = require './core/mysql.php';
       $users = (new Spectre\User\Controller\
        Fetch\Users($database))->fetch();
       return new Zend\Diactoros\Response\JsonResponse($users);
   });
   ```

   Here, you can see that we import the Medoo instance as `$database` and pass it the controller that will perform the **Read** operation and then call the `fetch` method to get all the available users.

5. So, the next thing we will do is create some CRUD directories: `Insert`, `Fetch`, `Update`, and `Delete`. In each of these CRUD directories, we will store the PSR-4 classes inside the `/Controller/` directory, as follows:

   ```
   └── Controller
       ├── Controller.php
       ├── Insert
       │   └── User.php
       ├── Fetch
       │   ├── User.php
       │   └── Users.php
       ├── Update
       │   └── User.php
       └── Delete
           └── User.php
   ```

6. First of all, create an `abstract` class that can be extended by the classes in the CRUD directories. This class will only accept the `Medoo\Medoo` database in its constructor, as follows:

```php
// module/User/Controller/Controller.php
namespace Spectre\User\Controller;

use Medoo\Medoo;

abstract class Controller
{
    protected $database;

    public function __construct(Medoo $database)
    {
        $this->database = $database;
    }
}
```

7. Import the preceding `abstract` class and extend it to any other classes that need to connect to the MySQL database, as follows:

```php
// module/User/Controller/Fetch/Users.php
namespace Spectre\User\Controller\Fetch;

use Spectre\User\Controller\Controller;

class Users extends Controller
{
    public function fetch()
    {
        $columns = [
            'uuid',
            'name',
            'slug',
            'created_on',
            'updated_on',
        ];
        return $this->database->select('user', $columns);
    }
}
```

In this class, we use the `select` method to fetch all the users from the `user` table in the MySQL database. Medoo will return an `Array` containing the list of users or an empty `Array` if there are no users. This result will then be converted into JSON using the `JsonResponse` method from `zend-diactoros` in the `fetch_users.php` file.

Finally, it will be decorated by the middleware in the `/middleware/` directory. This will result in the following output:

```
{"status":200,"data":[{"uuid":"...","name":"Jane","slug":"jane",...},{...},
{...}]}
```

That's it regarding the PHP API. It's pretty easy, isn't it? In this exercise, we will skip the task of dealing with CORS on the API side as we will be using the Nuxt Axios and Proxy modules to handle CORS seamlessly and effortlessly for us in the Nuxt app that we are going to create. So, let's get started!

> You can find this PHP API in `/chapter-16/nuxt-php/proxy/backend/` and the rest of the CRUD classes of this API in `/chapter-16/nuxt-php/proxy/backend/module/User/Controller/` in this book's GitHub repository.

Integrating with Nuxt

The `@nuxtjs/axios` module is well integrated with the `@nuxtjs/proxy` module and is very useful in many cases. Preventing the CORS problem is one of the benefits of using these two modules together. You learned how to install and use them in *Chapter 6, Writing Plugins and Modules*. Let's recap:

1. Install the `@nuxtjs/axios` and `@nuxtjs/proxy` modules via npm:

    ```
    $ npm install @nuxtjs/axios
    $ npm install @nuxtjs/proxy
    ```

2. Register `@nuxtjs/axios` in the `modules` option in the Nuxt config file, as follows:

    ```
    // nuxt.config.js
    module.exports = {
      modules: [
        '@nuxtjs/axios'
      ],

      axios: {
        proxy: true
      },

      proxy: {
        '/api/': { target: 'http://0.0.0.0:8181',
    ```

[562]

```
            pathRewrite: {'^/api/': ''} }
    }
}
```

Note that it is not required to register the @nuxtjs/proxy module when you are using it with @nuxtjs/axios, as long as it is installed and in the dependencies field in package.json.

In the preceding configuration, we use /api/ as the proxy for http://0.0.0.0:8181, which is where our PHP API is running. So, whenever we use /api/ in any of our API endpoint requests, it is calling 0.0.0.0:8181. For example, let's say you are making an API call, as follows:

```
$axios.get('/api/users')
```

The @nuxtjs/axios and @nuxtjs/proxy modules will convert that /api/users endpoint into the following:

```
http://0.0.0.0:8181/api/users
```

But since we don't use /api/ in our PHP API's routes, we use pathRewrite in the configuration to remove it during the call. Then, the actual URL that's sent by the @nuxtjs/axios and @nuxtjs/proxy modules to the API is as follows:

```
http://0.0.0.0:8181/users
```

> Once more, visit the following links for more information about these two modules:
> - https://axios.nuxtjs.org/ for @nuxtjs/axios
> - https://github.com/nuxt-community/proxy-module for @nuxtjs/proxy

After the installation and configuration are in place, we can start creating the **frontend UI** for communicating with the PHP API. We'll look at this in the next section.

Creating CRUD pages

Again, this is not a completely new task to you as this is almost the same as creating the CRUD pages you learned to create in Chapter 9, *Adding a Server-Side Database*. Let's recap:

1. Create the following pages in the /pages/users/ directory for sending and fetching data:

    ```
    users
    ├── index.vue
    ├── _slug.vue
    ├── add
    │   └── index.vue
    ├── update
    │   └── _slug.vue
    └── delete
        └── _slug.vue
    ```

2. For example, use the following script to fetch all the available users:

    ```
    // pages/users/index.vue
    export default {
      async asyncData ({ error, $axios }) {
        try {
          let { data } = await $axios.get('/api/users')
          return {
            users: data.data
          }
        } catch (err) {
          // handle errors.
        }
      }
    }
    ```

The scripts, templates, and directory structure in this Nuxt app are the same as the app you learned to create in Chapter 9, *Adding a Server-Side Database*. The difference is that an _id was used in that chapter but in this chapter, we're using _slug. By now, you should be able to complete the rest of the CRUD pages on your own. However, you can always revisit the following sections in Chapter 9, *Adding a Server-Side Database*, for more information:

- *Creating an Add page*
- *Creating an Update page*
- *Creating a Delete page*

Once you have created these pages, you can run the Nuxt app with `npm run dev`. You should see the app running on your browser at `localhost:3000`.

> You can find the complete source code for this app in `/chapter-16/nuxt-php/proxy/frontend/nuxt-universal/` in this book's GitHub repository.
>
> If you don't want to use the `@nuxtjs/axios` and `@nuxtjs/proxy` modules in this Nuxt app, you can find the complete source regarding how to enable CORS in the PHP API for the Nuxt app in `/chapter-16/nuxt-php/cors/` in this book's GitHub repository.
>
> You can also find a copy of the database saved as `user.sql` in `/chapter-16/nuxt-php/` in this book's GitHub repository.

Now, let's summarize what you've learned in this long chapter. We hope you have enjoyed this chapter and found it inspiring.

Summary

In this chapter, you have not only managed to decouple a Nuxt app from an API, similar to what you did in Chapter 12, *Creating User Logins and API Authentication*, but you also managed to write an API in a different language, PHP, one of the most popular server-side scripting languages in web development. You learned how to install PHP and Apache in order to run PHP apps or use the built-in PHP web server for development, all while complying with PSR-12, PSR4, PSR7, and PSR-15 in order to build a modern framework-agnostic app. You also learned to use the PHP database framework known as Medoo for writing CRUD operations, reusing the Nuxt app from Chapter 9, *Adding a Server-Side Database*, but with a few modifications, and gluing the frontend UI and the backend API together perfectly. Now, you also understand HTTP messages in more detail and know how to use PDO for modern PHP database management. Well done.

In the next chapter, you will discover what else you can do with Nuxt in terms of real-time apps. Here, you will learn about **Socket.io** and **RethinkDB**. We will walk you through the installation process for these two technologies. Then, you will learn how to perform real-time CRUD operations in a RethinkDB database, write real-time code in JavaScript with Socket.io, and integrate them with the Nuxt app. This will be another interesting and exciting chapter that we will guide you through. So, stay tuned!

17
Creating a Real-Time App with Nuxt

In this chapter, we are going to venture a bit further with Nuxt to see how we can use it to work with other frameworks for making real-time apps. We will continue using Koa as the backend API but "enhance" it with RethinkDB and Socket.IO. In other words, we will turn our backend API into a **real-time API** with these two awesome frameworks and tools. At the same time, we will turn our frontend Nuxt app into a **real-time Nuxt app** with help from them as well. You can develop these two real-time apps on the single-domain approach if you prefer. However, this book favors the cross-domain approach so that we don't mix up the frontend and the backend dependencies and get confused over time. So, this will be another interesting and exciting chapter for you to learn from!

In this chapter, we will cover the following topics:

- Introducing RethinkDB
- Integrating RethinkDB with Koa
- Introducing Socket.IO
- Integrating Socket.IO with Nuxt

Let's get started!

Introducing RethinkDB

RethinkDB is an open-source JSON database for real-time apps. It pushes JSON data to your apps in real-time from the database whenever a change occurs in the database tables that you subscribe to their real-time feeds – changefeeds. Despite that the changefeeds lies at the heart of RethinkDB's real-time functionality, you can skip this functionality if you want to. You can use RethinkDB just like MongoDB to store and query your NoSQL database.

Even though you can use the Change Streams in MongoDB to access the real-time data changes but it requires some configuration to get it started, while the real-time feeds are ready for use by default in RethinkDB and you can tap in right away without any configuration. Let's get started by installing the **RethinkDB server** in your system and see how you can use it in the next section.

Installing RethinkDB Server

At the time of writing this book, the current stable version of RethinkDB is **2.4.0 (Night Of The Living Dead)**, released on 19 December 2019. There are a few ways to install a RethinkDB server, depending on the platform (Ubuntu, or OS). You can check out the guide at `https://rethinkdb.com/docs/install/` for your platform. Note Windows is not supported yet in 2.4.0. For more information about this issue for Windows, please visit `https://rethinkdb.com/docs/install/windows`.

In this book, we will install RethinkDB 2.4.0 on **Ubuntu 20.04 LTS** (Focal Fossa). It works the same if you are on Ubuntu 19.10 (Eoan Ermine), Ubuntu 19.04 (Disco Dingo), or the older versions of Ubuntu, such as 18.04 LTS (Bionic Beaver). Let's get started:

1. Add the RethinkDB repository to your list of Ubuntu repositories, as follows:

    ```
    $ source /etc/lsb-release && echo "deb https://download.rethinkdb.com/apt $DISTRIB_CODENAME main" | sudo tee /etc/apt/sources.list.d/rethinkdb.list
    ```

2. Get the public key of RethinkDB using `wget`:

    ```
    $ wget -qO- https://download.rethinkdb.com/apt/pubkey.gpg | sudo apt-key add -
    ```

    You should get an **OK** message on your terminal for the preceding command line.

3. Update your version of Ubuntu and install RethinkDB:

    ```
    $ sudo apt update
    $ sudo apt install rethinkdb
    ```

4. Verify RethinkDB:

    ```
    $ rethinkdb -v
    ```

    You should get the following output on the terminal:

    ```
    rethinkdb 2.4.0~0eoan (CLANG 9.0.0 (tags/RELEASE_900/final))
    ```

RethinkDB comes with an administrative UI for you to manage databases on a browser at `localhost:8080`. This can be very handy and useful during project development. If you ever want to uninstall RethinkDB and remove all its databases, you can do so with the following commands:

```
$ sudo apt purge rethinkdb.
$ sudo rm -r /var/lib/rethinkdb
```

The administrative UI that came with the installation is like the PHP Adminer that you used to manage the MySQL databases for the PHP API in the previous chapter. You can use the RethinkDB administrative UI to add databases and tables by using the graphical buttons on the UI or using the RethinkDB query language (in JavaScript), **ReQL**. We'll explore the administrative UI and ReQL in the following section.

Introducing ReQL

ReQL is the query language of RethinkDB and is used for manipulating the JSON documents in RethinDB databases. The queries are constructed automatically by calling RethinkDB's built-in chainable functions on the server-side. These functions are embedded in the driver in various programming languages JavaScript, Python, Ruby, and Java. You can check out the ReQL commands/functions at the following links:

- JavaScript at `https://rethinkdb.com/api/javascript/`
- Python at `https://rethinkdb.com/api/python/`
- Ruby at `https://rethinkdb.com/api/ruby/`
- Java at `https://rethinkdb.com/api/java/`

We will be using JavaScript in this book. Let's use the Data Explorer on the administrative UI to perform some CRUD operations by using the respective ReQL commands. You can navigate to the page where the Data Explorer is or point your browser to `localhost:8080/#dataexplorer` and start playing with the queries, as shown here. The default top-level namespace on the Data Explorer is `r`, so the ReQL commands must be chained to this namespace.

However, we can change this `r` namespace and call anything we like when using the driver in our app, which we will do in the next section. For now, let's stick to the default namespace, `r`, for this exercise:

1. Create a database:

   ```
   r.dbCreate('nuxtdb')
   ```

   Click the **Run** button. You should get a result similar to the following on the screen showing that one database has been created with the database name you chose and that an ID was generated by RethinkDB:

   ```
   {
     "config_changes": [
       {
         "new_val": {
           "id": "353d11a4-adc8-4958-a4ae-a82c996dcb9f",
           "name": "nuxtdb"
         },
         "old_val": null
       }
     ],
     "dbs_created": 1
   }
   ```

   > If you want to find out more information about the `dbCreate` ReQL command, please visit https://rethinkdb.com/api/javascript/db_create/.

2. Create a table in an existing database; for example, create a `user` table in the `nuxtdb` database:

   ```
   r.db('nuxtdb').tableCreate('user')
   ```

   Click the **Run** button. You should get a result similar to the following on the screen showing that one table has been created with an ID generated by RethinkDB for you and other information about the table that you created:

   ```
   {
     "config_changes": [{
       "new_val": {
         "db": "nuxtdb",
         "durability": "hard",
         "id": "259e0066-1ffe-4064-8b24-d1c82e515a4a",
         "indexes": [],
         "name": "user",
   ```

```
            "primary_key": "id",
            "shards": [{
               "nonvoting_replicas": [],
               "primary_replica": "lau_desktop_opw",
               "replicas": ["lau_desktop_opw"]
            }],
            "write_acks": "majority",
            "write_hook": null
         },
         "old_val": null
      }],
      "tables_created": 1
}
```

> If you want to find out more information about the `tableCreate` ReQL command, please visit https://rethinkdb.com/api/javascript/table_create/.

3. Insert new documents into the `user` table:

```
r.db('nuxtdb').table('user').insert([
  { name: "Jane Doe", slug: "jane" },
  { name: "John Doe", slug: "john" }
])
```

Click the **Run** button. You should get a result similar to the following on the screen, showing that two documents have been inserted with keys generated by RethinkDB for you:

```
{
  "deleted": 0,
  "errors": 0,
  "generated_keys": [
     "7f7d768d-0efd-447d-8605-2d460a381944",
     "a144001c-d47e-4e20-a570-a29968980d0f"
  ],
  "inserted": 2,
  "replaced": 0,
  "skipped": 0,
  "unchanged": 0
}
```

Creating a Real-Time App with Nuxt

> If you want to find out more information about the `table` and `insert` ReQL commands, please visit https://rethinkdb.com/api/javascript/table/ and https://rethinkdb.com/api/javascript/insert/, respectively.

4. Retrieve documents from the `user` table:

    ```
    r.db('nuxtdb').table('user')
    ```

    Click the **Run** button. You should get a result similar to the following on the screen, showing two documents from the `user` table:

    ```
    [{
      "id": "7f7d768d-0efd-447d-8605-2d460a381944",
      "name": "Jane Doe",
      "slug": "jane"
    }, {
      "id": "a144001c-d47e-4e20-a570-a29968980d0f",
      "name": "John Doe",
      "slug": "john"
    }]
    ```

    You can chain the `count` method to the query if you want to count the total documents in a table, as follows:

    ```
    r.db('nuxtdb').table('user').count()
    ```

    You should get 2 in the `user` table after injecting the new documents.

    > If you want to find out more information about the `count` ReQL command, please visit https://rethinkdb.com/api/javascript/count/.

5. Update the documents in the `user` table by filtering the table with the `slug` key:

    ```
    r.db('nuxtdb').table('user')
    .filter(
      r.row("slug").eq("john")
    )
    .update({
      name: "John Wick"
    })
    ```

[572]

Click the **Run** button. You should get the following result on the screen, showing that one document has been replaced:

```
{
  "deleted": 0,
  "errors": 0,
  "inserted": 0,
  "replaced": 1,
  "skipped": 0,
  "unchanged": 0
}
```

> If you want to find out more information about the `filter` and `update` ReQL commands, please visit https://rethinkdb.com/api/javascript/filter/ and https://rethinkdb.com/api/javascript/update/, respectively.
>
> Also, if you want to find out more information about the `row` and `eq` ReQL commands, please visit https://rethinkdb.com/api/javascript/row/ and https://rethinkdb.com/api/javascript/eq/, respectively.

6. Delete a document from the `user` table by filtering the table with the `slug` key:

```
r.db('nuxtdb').table('user')
.filter(
  r.row("slug").eq("john")
)
.delete()
```

Click the **Run** button. You should get the following result on the screen, showing that one document has been deleted:

```
{
  "deleted": 1,
  "errors": 0,
  "inserted": 0,
  "replaced": 0,
  "skipped": 0,
  "unchanged": 0
}
```

If you want to delete all the documents in a table, then simply chain the `delete` method to the table without filtering, as follows:

```
r.db('nuxtdb').table('user').delete()
```

> If you want to find out more information about the `delete` ReQL command, please visit https://rethinkdb.com/api/javascript/delete/.

It is fun and easy in using ReQL commands, isn't it? You don't have to read through all the ReQL commands and study each of them in great detail to be productive. You just have to know what you want to do and find the commands you need from the ReQL command reference/API page based on the programming language that you already know about. Next, you will find out how to add the **RethinkDB client** or driver to your app. Let's get to it!

Integrating RethinkDB with Koa

In this section, we will build a simple API following the PHP APIs that we created in the previous chapter to list, add, update, and delete users. In the previous API, we used PHP and MySQL, while in this chapter, we will use JavaScript and RethinkDB. We will still use Koa as the framework for our API. But this time, we will restructure the API directory so that the structure is consistent (as much as possible) with the directory structure you already familiar with for the Nuxt app and PHP API. So, let's get started!

Restructuring API directories

Remember the default directory structure that you get in your project when using Vue CLI, which you learned about in *Chapter 11, Writing Route Middleware and Server Middleware*? After installing a project with Vue CLI, if you take a look inside the project directory, you will see a barebones project structure in which you can find a `/src/` directory to develop your components, pages, and routes, as follows:

```
├── package.json
├── babel.config.js
├── README.md
├── public
│   ├── index.html
│   └── favicon.ico
└── src
    ├── App.vue
    ├── main.js
    ├── router.js
    ├── components
    │   └── HelloWorld.vue
```

```
└── assets
    └── logo.png
```

We have been using this kind of standard structure for the cross-domain apps since Chapter 12, *Creating User Logins and API Authentication*. For example, the following is the directory structure for Koa APIs, which you made previously:

```
backend
├── package.json
├── backpack.config.js
├── static
│   └── ...
└── src
    ├── index.vue
    ├── ...
    ├── modules
    │   └── ...
    └── core
        └── ...
```

But this time, we will eliminate the /src/ directory from the APIs that we are going to make in this chapter. So, let's move everything in the /src/ directory up to the top level and reconfigure how we bootstrap the app, as follows:

1. Create the following files and folders in the project's root directory:

```
backend
├── package.json
├── backpack.config.js
├── middlewares.js
├── routes.js
├── configs
│   ├── index.js
│   └── rethinkdb.js
├── core
│   └── ...
├── middlewares
│   └── ...
├── modules
│   └── ...
└── public
    └── index.js
```

Again, the directory structure here is merely a suggestion; you can design your directory structure as you wish so that it suits you the most. But let's take a glance at this suggested directory and study what these folders and files are used for:

- The /configs/ directory is used to store the app's basic information and the RethinkDB database connection's details.
- The /public/ directory is used to store the files for initiating the app.
- The /modules/ directory is used to store the modules of the app, such as the 'user' module, which we will create in the upcoming sections.
- The /core/ directory is used to store the common functions or classes that can be used throughout the app.
- The middlewares.js file is the core location for importing middleware from the /middlewares/ and /node_modules/ directories.
- The routes.js file is the core location for importing routes from the /modules directory.
- The backpack.config.js file is used to customize the webpack configuration for our app.
- The package.json file contains the scripts and dependencies of our app and is always located at the root level.

2. Point the entry file to the index.js file in the /public/ directory:

```
// backpack.config.js
module.exports = {
  webpack: (config, options, webpack) => {
    config.entry.main = './public/index.js'
    return config
  }
}
```

Remember that the default entry file in Backpack is an index.js file in the /src/ directory. Since we have moved this index file to the /public/ directory, we must configure this entry point through the Backpack config file.

> If you want to know more about the entry points in webpack, please visit https://webpack.js.org/concepts/entry-points/.

3. Add aliases for the /configs, /core, /modules, and /middlewares paths to the resolve option in the webpack configuration before returning the config object in the Backpack config file:

```
// backpack.config.js
const path = require('path')

config.resolve = {
  alias: {
    Configs: path.resolve(__dirname, 'configs/'),
    Core: path.resolve(__dirname, 'core/'),
    Modules: path.resolve(__dirname, 'modules/'),
    Middlewares: path.resolve(__dirname, 'middlewares/')
  }
}
```

Using aliases to resolve the file path in our app is very useful and handy. Typically, we import files using the relative paths, like this:

```
import notFound from '../../Middlewares/notFound'
```

Instead of doing this, now, we can import files from anywhere with the alias that tucks away the relative path, thus making our code neater:

```
import notFound from 'Middlewares/notFound'
```

> If you want to find out more about the alias and resolve options in webpack, please visit https://webpack.js.org/configuration/resolve/resolvealias.

Once you have the preceding structure ready and the entry file sorted, you can start applying the CRUD operations with RethinkDB to this API. But first, you will need to install the **RethinkDB JavaScript client** into your project. So, let's get started!

Adding and using the RethinkDB JavaScript client

Depending on the programming knowledge you have, there are several official client drivers you can choose from regarding JavaScript, Ruby, Python, and Java. There are many community-supported drivers as well, such as PHP, Perl, and R. You can check them out at https://rethinkdb.com/docs/install-drivers/.

In this book, we will be using the RethinkDB JavaScript client driver. We will guide you through the installation and how to use the CRUD operations using this driver in the following steps:

1. Install the RethinkDB JavaScript client driver via npm:

   ```
   $ npm i rethinkdb
   ```

2. Create a `rethinkdb.js` file that will contain the RethinkDB server connection details in the `/configs/` directory, as follows:

   ```
   // configs/rethinkdb.js
   export default {
     host: 'localhost',
     port: 28015,
     dbname: 'nuxtdb'
   }
   ```

3. Create a `connection.js` file for opening a RethinkDB server connection with the preceding connection details in the `/core/` directory, as follows:

   ```
   // core/database/rethinkdb/connection.js
   import config from 'Configs/rethinkdb'
   import rethink from 'rethinkdb'

   const c = async () => {
     const connection = await rethink.connect({
       host: config.host,
       port: config.port,
       db: config.dbname
     })
     return connection
   }
   export default c
   ```

4. Also, create an open connection middleware with an `open.js` file in the `/middlewares/` directory and bind it to the Koa context as another option to connect to RethinkDB, as follows:

   ```
   // middlewares/database/rdb/connection/open.js
   import config from 'Configs/rethinkdb'
   import rdb from 'rethinkdb'

   export default async (ctx, next) => {
     ctx._rdbConn = await rdb.connect({
       host: config.host,
       port: config.port,
   ```

```
        db: config.dbname
    })
    await next()
}
```

> **TIP**
> It is a good practice, which we learned from PHP's PSR-4, to use the directory path to describe your middleware (or CRUD operations) so that you don't have to use a long name to describe your file. For example, you might want to name this middleware `rdb-connection-open.js` to describe what it is **as clearly as possible** if you are not using a descriptive directory path for it. But if you are using the directory path to describe the middleware, then you can just name the file something as simple as `open.js`.

5. Create a close connection middleware with a `close.js` file in the `/middlewares/` directory and bind it to the Koa context as the last middleware, as follows:

```
// middlewares/database/rdb/connection/close.js
import config from 'Configs/rethinkdb'
import rdb from 'rethinkdb'

export default async (ctx, next) => {
    ctx._rdbConn.close()
    await next()
}
```

6. Import the `open` and `close` connection middleware in the root `middlewares.js` file and register them to the app, as follows:

```
// middlewares.js
import routes from './routes'
import rdbOpenConnection from
'Middlewares/database/rdb/connection/open'
import rdbCloseConnection from
'Middlewares/database/rdb/connection/close'

export default (app) => {
    //...
    app.use(rdbOpenConnection)
    app.use(routes.routes(), routes.allowedMethods())
    app.use(rdbCloseConnection)
}
```

Here, you can see that the `open` connection middleware is registered **before** all the module routes and that the `close` connection middleware is registered **last** so that they are called first and last, respectively.

7. In the upcoming steps, we will use the following template code with a Koa router and the RethinkDB client driver to make the CRUD operation. For example, the following code shows how we apply the template code for fetching all the users from the `user` table in the `user` module:

```js
// modules/user/_routes/index.js
import Router from 'koa-router'
import rdb from 'rethinkdb'

const router = new Router()
router.get('/', async (ctx, next) => {
  try {
    // perform verification on the incoming parameters...
    // perform a CRUD operation:
    let result = await rdb.table('user')
      .run(ctx._rdbConn)

    ctx.type = 'json'
    ctx.body = result
    await next()

  } catch (err) {
    ctx.throw(500, err)
  }
})
export default router
```

Let's go through this code and understand what it does. Here, you can see that we are using a custom top-level namespace, `rdb`, for the RethinkDB client driver, as opposed to the `r` namespace that you have practiced on `localhost:8080`. Also, when using the RethinkDB client driver in our app, we must always call the `run` method at the end of the ReQL commands with the RethinkDB server connection to construct the query and pass it onto the server for execution.

Furthermore, we must call the `next` method at the end of the code so that we can pass the execution of the app to the next piece of middleware, especially the `close` connection middleware, which is used to close the RethinkDB connection. We should perform checks on the incoming parameters and data from the client before performing any CRUD operations. Then, we should wrap our code in `try-catch` blocks to catch and throw any potential errors.

> Note that in the upcoming steps, we will skip writing the parameter verification and the try-catch statement from the code to avoid lengthy and repetitive code lines and blocks, but you should have them included in your actual code.

8. Create a `create-user.js` file in the `/_routes/` folder in the `user` module with the following code for injecting new users into the `user` table in the database:

```
// modules/user/_routes/create-user.js
router.post('/user', async (ctx, next) => {
  let result = await rdb.table('user')
    .insert(document, {returnChanges: true})
    .run(ctx._rdbConn)

  if (result.inserted !== 1) {
    ctx.throw(404, 'insert user failed')
  }
  ctx.type = 'json'
  ctx.body = result
  await next()
})
```

We should throw the error if the insertion fails and pass the error message to the Koa `throw` method with the HTTP error code so that we can catch them with the `try-catch` blocks and display them on the frontend.

9. Create a `fetch-user.js` file in the `/_routes/` folder in the `user` module to fetch a specific user from the `user` table by using the `slug` key, as follows:

```
// modules/user/_routes/fetch-user.js
router.get('/:slug', async (ctx, next) => {
  const slug = ctx.params.slug
  let user = await rdb.table('user')
    .filter(searchQuery)
    .nth(0)
    .default(null)
    .run(ctx._rdbConn)

  if (!user) {
    ctx.throw(404, 'user not found')
  }

  ctx.type = 'json'
  ctx.body = user
  await next()
})
```

We added the `nth` command in the query to display the document by its position. In our case, we just want to get the first document, so we pass a `0` integer to this method. We also added the `default` command to return a `null` exception if no users are found in the `user` table.

10. Create an `update-user.js` file in the `/_routes/` folder in the `user` module for updating the existing user in the `user` table by using the document ID, as follows:

```
// modules/user/_routes/update-user.js
router.put('/user', async (ctx, next) => {
  let body = ctx.request.body || {}
  let objectId = body.id

  let timestamp = Date.now()
  let updateQuery = {
    name: body.name,
    slug: body.slug,
    updatedAt: timestamp
  }

  let result = await rdb.table('user')
    .get(objectId)
    .update(updateQuery, {returnChanges: true})
    .run(ctx._rdbConn)

  if (result.replaced !== 1) {
    ctx.throw(404, 'update user failed')
  }

  ctx.type = 'json'
  ctx.body = result
  await next()
})
```

We added the `get` command in the query to fetch the specific document by its ID first, before running the update.

11. Create a `delete-user.js` file in the `/_routes/` folder in the `user` module for deleting the existing user from the `user` table by using the document ID, as follows:

```
// modules/user/_routes/delete-user.js
router.del('/user', async (ctx, next) => {
  let body = ctx.request.body || {}
  let objectId = body.id
```

```
        let result = await rdb.table('user')
          .get(objectId)
          .delete()
          .run(ctx._rdbConn)

        if (result.deleted !== 1) {
          ctx.throw(404, 'delete user failed')
        }

        ctx.type = 'json'
        ctx.body = result
        await next()
      })
```

12. Lastly, refactor the CRUD operation for listing all the users from the `user` table that you just created in *step 7* by adding an `orderBy` command to the query in the `index.js` file, which is kept in the `/_routes/` folder, as follows:

```
    // modules/user/_routes/index.js
    router.get('/', async (ctx, next) => {
      let cursor = await rdb.table('user')
        .orderBy(rdb.desc('createdAt'))
        .run(ctx._rdbConn)

      let users = await cursor.toArray()
      ctx.type = 'json'
      ctx.body = users
      await next()
    })
```

We added the `orderBy` command to the query so that we can sort the documents by their creation dates descendingly (the latest first). Also, the documents returned by the RethinkDB database are always contained in a **cursor object** as a callback from the CRUD operation, so we must use the `toArray` command to iterate through the cursor and convert the object into an array.

> If you want to find out more about the `orderBy` and `toArray` commands, please visit https://rethinkdb.com/api/javascript/order_by/ and https://rethinkdb.com/api/javascript/to_array/, respectively.

With that, you have implemented the CRUD operations with RethinkDB in your API successfully. Again, this is easy and fun, isn't it? But we still can improve the "quality" of the document we store in the database by enforcing schema in the RethinkDB databases. We'll learn how to do this in the next section.

Enforcing schema in RethinkDB

Just like the BSON databases in MongoDB, the JSON databases in RethinkDB are also **schemaless**. This means no blueprints and no formula or integrity constraints are imposed on the databases. No organized rule of how the database is constructed can pose the issue of integrity in our databases. Certain documents can contain different and unwanted keys in the same table (or "collection" in MongoDB), along with the documents that have the correct keys. You may inject some keys by mistake or forget to inject the required keys and values. So, it can be a good idea to enforce some sort of schema in our JSON or BSON databases if you want to keep the data in your documents organized. There is no internal feature from RethinkDB (or MongoDB) for enforcing the schema, but we can create custom functions to impose some basic schema with the Node.js Lodash module. Let's explore how to do this:

1. Install the Lodash module via npm:

    ```
    $ npm i lodash
    ```

2. Create a `utils.js` file in the `/core/` directory and import `lodash` to create a function called `sanitise`, as follows:

    ```js
    // core/utils.js
    import lodash from 'lodash'

    function sanitise (options, schema) {
      let data = options || {}

      if (schema === undefined) {
        const err = new Error('Schema is required.')
        err.status = 400
        err.expose = true
        throw err
      }

      let keys = lodash.keys(schema)
      let defaults = lodash.defaults(data, schema)
      let picked = lodash.pick(defaults, keys)

      return picked
    }
    export { sanitise }
    ```

    This function simply picks the default keys that you set and ignores any additional keys that are not in the "schema".

> We are using the following methods from Lodash. For more information about each of them, please visit the following links:
> https://lodash.com/docs/4.17.15#keys for the `keys` method
> https://lodash.com/docs/4.17.15#defaults for the `defaults` method
> https://lodash.com/docs/4.17.15#pick for the `pick` method

3. Create a `user` schema in the `user` module with the following keys that only you want to accept:

    ```
    // modules/user/schema.js
    export default {
      slug: null,
      name: null,
      createdAt: null,
      updatedAt: null
    }
    ```

4. Import the `sanitise` method and the preceding schema into the route that you want to enforce the schema; for example, in the `create-user.js` file:

    ```
    // modules/user/_routes/create-user.js
    let timestamp = Date.now()
    let options = {
      name: body.name,
      slug: body.slug,
      createdAt: timestamp,
      username: 'marymoe',
      password: '123123'
    }

    let document = sanitise(options, schema)
    let result = await rdb.table('user')
      .insert(document, {returnChanges: true})
      .run(ctx._rdbConn)
    ```

In the preceding code, the example fields, `username` and `password`, won't be injected into the document in the `user` table when sanitizing the data before insertion.

You can see that this `sanitise` function only performs a simple validation. If you need more complicated and advanced data validation, you can use the Node.js joi module from the hapi web framework.

> If you want to find out more about this module, please visit https://hapi.dev/module/joi/.

Creating a Real-Time App with Nuxt

The next thing you must explore is the **changefeeds** in RethinkDB. This is the main purpose of this chapter – to show you how to make use of the real-time feature of RethinkDB to create real-time apps. So, let's explore and play with the changefeeds in RethinkDB!

Introducing changefeeds in RethinkDB

Before applying the changefeeds in our app with the RethinkDB client driver, let's use the Data Explorer from the Administration UI again at `localhost:8080/#dataexplorer` to see the real-time feeds in real time on the screen:

1. Paste in the following ReQL query and click the **Run** button:

    ```
    r.db('nuxtdb').table('user').changes()
    ```

    You should see the following information on your browser screen:

    ```
    Listening for events...
    Waiting for more results
    ```

2. Open another tab on your browser and point it to `localhost:8080/#dataexplorer`. Now, you have two data explorers. Drag one out from the browser tab so that you can place them side by side. Then, insert the new documents into the `user` table from one of the data explorers:

    ```
    r.db('nuxtdb').table('user').insert([
      { name: "Richard Roe", slug: "richard" },
      { name: "Marry Moe", slug: "marry" }
    ])
    ```

    You should get the following result:

    ```
    {
      "deleted": 0,
      "errors": 0,
      "generated_keys": [
        "f7305c97-2bc9-4694-81ec-c5acaed1e757",
        "5862e1fa-e51c-4878-a16b-cb8c1f1d91de"
      ],
      "inserted": 2,
      "replaced": 0,
      "skipped": 0,
      "unchanged": 0
    }
    ```

At the same time, you should see the other Data Explorer displaying the following feeds instantaneously in real time:

```
{
  "new_val": {
    "id": "f7305c97-2bc9-4694-81ec-c5acaed1e757",
    "name": "Richard Roe",
    "slug": "richard"
  },
  "old_val": null
}

{
  "new_val": {
    "id": "5862e1fa-e51c-4878-a16b-cb8c1f1d91de",
    "name": "Marry Moe",
    "slug": "marry"
  },
  "old_val": null
}
```

Hooray! You have just made real-time feeds effortlessly with RethinkDB! Notice that you will always get these two keys, `new_val` and `old_val`, in each of the real-time feeds. They have the following implications:

- If you get the data in `new_val` but it's `null` in `old_val`, that means the new document is injected into the database.
- If you get the data in both `new_val` and `old_val`, that means the existing document is updated in the database.
- If you get the data in `old_val` but it's `null` in `new_val`, that means the existing document is removed from the database.

You will get to use these keys when we use them in the Nuxt app in the last section of this chapter. So, don't worry too much about them for now. Instead, the next challenge is to implement it in the API and the Nuxt app. To do that, we will need another Node.js module – **Socket.IO**. So, let's explore how this module can help you to achieve that.

Introducing Socket.IO

Just like HTTP, WebSocket is a communication protocol, but it provides full-duplex (bidirectional) communication between the client and the server. Unlike HTTP, the WebSocket connection always remains open for real-time data transfer. So, in WebSocket apps, the server can send data to the client without having the client initiate the request.

Also, unlike the HTTP schema that starts with HTTP or HTTPS for Hypertext Transfer Protocol Secure, the WebSocket protocol schema starts with `ws` or `wss` for WebSocket Secure; for example:

```
ws://example.com:4000
```

Socket.IO is a JavaScript library that uses the WebSocket protocol and polling as the fallback option for creating real-time web apps. It supports any platform, browser, or device and handles all the degradation for the server and client to get the full-duplex communication in real time. Most browsers support the WebSocket protocol these days anyway, including Google Chrome, Microsoft Edge, Firefox, Safari, and Opera. But when using Socket.IO, we must use its client-side and server-side libraries together. The client-side library runs inside the browser, while the server-side library runs on your server-side Node.js app. So, let's get these two libraries working in our apps.

> If you want to find out more about Socket.IO, please visit https://socket.io/.

Adding and using Socket.IO server and client

We will add the Socket.IO server to the API that we have been building in the last few sections, and then add the Socket.IO client to the Nuxt app eventually. But before adding it to the Nuxt app, we will add it to a simple HTML page so that we have a bird's-eye view of how the Socket.IO server and Socket.IO client work together. Let's learn how to do so:

1. Install the Socket.IO server via npm:

    ```
    $ npm i socket.io
    ```

2. Create an `index.js` file in the `/configs/` directory to store the server setting if you haven't done so yet:

    ```
    // configs/index.js
    export default {
      server: {
        port: 4000
      },
    }
    ```

    From this simple setting, we will be serving our API at port 4000.

3. Import `socket.io` and bind it to the Node.js HTTP object with the new instance of Koa to create a new instance of Socket.IO, as follows:

```
// backend/koa/public/index.js
import Koa from 'koa'
import socket from 'socket.io'
import http from 'http'
import config from 'Configs'
import middlewares from '../middlewares'

const app = new Koa()
const host = process.env.HOST || '127.0.0.1'
const port = process.env.PORT || config.server.port
middlewares(app)

const server = http.createServer(app.callback())
const io = socket(server)

io.sockets.on('connection', socket => {
  console.log('a user connected: ' + socket.id)
  socket.on('disconnect', () => {
    console.log('user disconnected: ' + socket.id)
  })
})
server.listen(port, host)
```

After creating the new instance of Socket.IO, we can start listening to the Socket.IO `connection` event for the incoming socket from the `socket` callback. We log the incoming socket to the console with its ID. We also log the incoming socket's `disconnect` event when it is disconnected. Lastly, notice that we start and serve the app on `localhost:4000` by using the native Node.js HTTP, as opposed to using the HTTP inside Koa, which we used to do:

```
app.listen(4000)
```

4. Create a `socket-client.html` page and import the Socket.IO client via CDN. Create a new instance of it by passing `localhost:4000` as the specific URL, as follows:

```
// frontend/html/socket-client.html
<script src="https://cdn.jsdelivr.net/npm/socket.io-
 client@2/dist/socket.io.js"></script>

<script>
  var socket = io('http://localhost:4000/')
</script>
```

Now, if you browse this HTML page on your browser, or when you refresh the page, you should see the console printing the log with the socket ID, as follows:

```
a user connected: abeGnarBnELo33vQAAAB
```

You should also see the console printing the log with the socket ID when you close the HTML page, as follows:

```
user disconnected: abeGnarBnELo33vQAAAB
```

That's all you need to do in order to connect the server and client sides of Socket.IO. This is extremely simple and easy, isn't it? But all we're doing here is connecting and disconnecting the server and client. We need more from them – we want to transmit data simultaneously. To do that, we just need to emit and receive events from and to each other, which we'll do in the upcoming steps.

> If you want to use the local version of the Socket.IO client, you can point the script tag's URL source to `/node_modules/socket.io-client/dist/socket.io.js`.

5. Create an emit event from the server by using the `emit` method from the Socket.IO server, as follows:

```
// backend/koa/public/index.js
io.sockets.on('connection', socket => {
  io.emit('emit.onserver', 'Hi client, what you up to?')
  console.log('Message to client: ' + socket.id)
})
```

Here, you can see that we emit the event with a simple message through the custom event called `emit.onserver` and log the activity to the console. Notice that we can only emit the event when the connection is established. Then, we can listen to this custom event on the client-side and log the message coming from the server, as follows:

```
// frontend/html/socket-client.html
socket.on('emit.onserver', function (message) {
  console.log('Message from server: ' + message)
})
```

6. So, now, if you refresh the page again on your browser, you should see the console printing the log with the socket ID, as follows:

```
Message to client: abeGnarBnELo33vQAAAB // server side
Message from server: Hi client, what you up to? // client side
```

7. Create an emit event from the client by using the `emit` method from the Socket.IO client, as follows:

```
// frontend/html/socket-client.html
<script
  src="https://code.jquery.com/jquery-3.4.1.slim.min.js"
  integrity="sha256-pasqAKBDmFT4eHoN2ndd61N370kFiGUFyTiUHWhU7k8="
  crossorigin="anonymous"></script>

<button class="button-sent">Send</button>

$('.button-sent').click(function(e){
  e.preventDefault()

  var message = 'Hi server, how are you holding up?'
  socket.emit('emit.onclient', message)
  console.log('Message sent to server.')

  return false
})
```

Here, you can see that, first, we install jQuery via CDN and create a `<button>` with the jQuery `click` event. Secondly, we emit the Socket.IO custom event called `emit.onclient` with a simple message when the button is clicked. Lastly, we log the activity to the console.

8. After that, we can listen to the Socket.IO custom event on the server-side and log the message coming from the client, as follows:

```
// backend/koa/public/index.js
socket.on('emit.onclient', (message) => {
  console.log('Message from client, '+ socket.id + ' :' + message);
})
```

9. If you refresh the page again on your browser, you should see the console printing the log, along with the socket ID, as follows:

```
Message sent to server. // client side
Message from client, abeGnarBnELo33vQAAAB: Hi server,
how are you holding up? // server side
```

You now know how to transmit data back and forth in real time with Socket.IO – just by emitting custom events and listening to them. The next thing you should know about is how to integrate Socket.IO with the changefeeds in RethinkDB in order to transmit the real-time data from the database to the client. So, keep reading!

Integrating Socket.IO server and RethinkDB changefeeds

Remember that you fiddled with the RethinkDB changefeeds previously, using the Data Explorer from the Administration UI again at `localhost:8080/#dataexplorer`. To subscribe to a changefeed, you just have to chain the ReQL `changes` command to the query, as follows:

```
r.db('nuxtdb').table('user').changes()
```

The RethinkDB changefeeds contain real-time data that's emitted from the RethinkDB database to our API, which means we need to catch these feeds on the server-side with the Socket.IO server and emit them to the client. So, let's learn how to catch them by refactoring the API we have been developing throughout this chapter:

1. Install the Socket.IO server via npm into your API:

    ```
    $ npm i socket.io
    ```

2. Create an asynchronous anonymous arrow function in a `changefeeds.js` file in the `/core/` directory with the following code:

    ```
    // core/database/rethinkdb/changefeeds.js
    import rdb from 'rethinkdb'
    import rdbConnection from './connection'

    export default async (io, tableName, eventName) => {
      try {
        const connection = await rdbConnection()
        var cursor = await rdb.table(tableName)
          .changes()
          .run(connection)

        cursor.each(function (err, row) {
          if (err) {
            throw err
          }
          io.emit(eventName, row)
        })
      } catch( err ) {
        console.error(err);
      }
    }
    ```

In this function, we import `rethinkdb` as `rdb` and our RethinkDB database connection as `rdbConnection`, and then use the following items as the parameters of this function:

- The instance of the Socket.IO server
- The Socket.IO emit custom event name that you will want to use
- The RethinkDB table name that you want to subscribe to its changefeed

The changefeed will return the documents in a cursor object as a callback, so we iterate through the cursor object and emit each row of the document with the custom event name.

3. Import the `changefeeds` function as `rdbChangeFeeds` in the app root in the `/public/` directory and integrate it with the rest of the existing code in the `index.js` file, as follows:

```
// public/index.js
import Koa from 'koa'
import socket from 'socket.io'
import http from 'http'
import config from 'Configs'
import middlewares from '../middlewares'
import rdbChangeFeeds from 'Core/database/rethinkdb/changefeeds'

const app = new Koa()
const host = process.env.HOST || '127.0.0.1'
const port = process.env.PORT || config.server.port
middlewares(app)

const server = http.createServer(app.callback())
const io = socket(server)
io.sockets.on('connection', socket => {
  //...
})

rdbChangeFeeds(io, 'user', 'user.changefeeds')
server.listen(port, host)
```

In the preceding code, the table name we want to subscribe to is `user` and the emit event name we want to call is `user.changefeeds`. So, we pass them into the `rdbChangeFeeds` function with the `socket.io` instance. That's all you need to do to integrate Socket.IO and RethinkDB once only and globally.

Well done! You have managed to integrate Koa, RethinkDB, and Socket.IO on the server-side and created a real time API. But what about the client side, and how do we listen to the event being emitted from the API? We'll find out in the next section.

Integrating Socket.IO with Nuxt

The Nuxt app we are going to build is very similar to the one we had in the previous chapter, where we had a `/users/` directory that contains the following CRUD pages in the `/pages/` directory for adding, updating, listing, and deleting users:

```
users
├── index.vue
├── _slug.vue
├── add
│   └── index.vue
├── update
│   └── _slug.vue
└── delete
    └── _slug.vue
```

You can copy these files from the previous chapter. The only major change and difference in this app is the `<script>` block, where we will list users in real time by listening to the emit event from the Socket.IO server. To do that, we will need to use the Socket.IO client, which you learned in the *Adding and using Socket.IO server and client* section with the simple HTML page. So, let's find out how to implement what we already know into the Nuxt app:

1. Install the Socket.IO client via npm into your Nuxt project:

    ```
    $ npm i socket.io-client
    ```

2. Create the following variables for the app's protocol, hostname, and the cross-domain ports in the Nuxt config file so that we can reuse them later:

    ```
    // nuxt.config.js
    const protocol = 'http'
    const host = process.env.NODE_ENV === 'production' ? 'a-cool-domain-name.com' : 'localhost'

    const ports = {
    ```

```
    local: '8000',
    remote: '4000'
}

const remoteUrl = protocol + '://' + host + ':' + ports.remote +
'/'
```

These variables are made for the following situations:

- The `host` variable is used to take the value of `a-cool-domain-name.com` when the Nuxt app is in production; that is, when you run the app with `npm run start`. Otherwise, it just takes `localhost` as the default value.
- The `local` key in the `ports` variable is used to set a server port for the Nuxt app and it is set to `8000`. Remember that the default port that Nuxt serves the app is `3000`.
- The `remote` key in the `ports` variable is used to tell the Nuxt app what server port the API is on, which is `4000`.
- The `remoteUrl` variable is used to concatenate the API with the preceding variables.

3. Apply the preceding variables to the `env` and `server` options in the Nuxt config file, as follows:

```
// nuxt.config.js
export default {
  env: {
    remoteUrl
  },
  server: {
    port: ports.local,
    host: host
  }
}
```

So, with this configuration, we can access the `remoteUrl` variable again when serving the app via the following methods:

- `process.env.remoteUrl`
- `context.env.remoteUrl`

Creating a Real-Time App with Nuxt

Also, in this configuration, we have changed the Nuxt app's default server port to `8000` in the `server` option. The default port is `3000`, while the default host is `localhost`. But you may want to use a different port for some reason. That's why we looked at how to change them here.

> If you want to find out more about the `server` configuration and other options such as `timing` and `https`, please visit https://nuxtjs.org/api/configuration-server.
>
> If you want to find out more about the `env` configuration, please visit https://nuxtjs.org/api/configuration-envthe-env-property.

4. Install the Nuxt Axios and Proxy modules and configure them in the Nuxt config file, as follows:

```js
// nuxt.config.js
export default {
  modules: [
    '@nuxtjs/axios'
  ],

  axios: {
    proxy: true
  },

  proxy: {
    '/api/': {
      target: remoteUrl,
      pathRewrite: {'^/api/': ''}
    }
  }
}
```

Notice that we have reused the `remoteUrl` variable in the `proxy` option. So, every API request we make that starts with `/api/` will be converted into `http://localhost:4000/api/`. But since we don't have `/api/` in the routes in the API, we remove this `/api/` section from the request URL with the `pathRewrite` option before sending it off to the API.

5. Create a plugin in the `/plugin/` directory for abstracting the instance of the Socket.IO client so that we can reuse it anywhere:

```js
// plugins/socket.io.js
import io from 'socket.io-client'
```

[596]

```
const remoteUrl = process.env.remoteUrl
const socket = io(remoteUrl)

export default socket
```

Notice that we have reused the `remoteUrl` variable via `process.env.remoteUrl` in the Socket.IO client instance. This means the Socket.IO client will call the Socket.IO server at `localhost:4000`.

6. Import the `socket.io` client plugin into the `<script>` block and fetch the list of users with the `@nuxtjs/axios` module in the `index` file. This index file is kept in the `/users/` directory, under `pages`:

```
// pages/users/index.vue
import socket from '~/plugins/socket.io'

export default {
  async asyncData ({ error, $axios }) {
    try {
      let { data } = await $axios.get('/api/users')
      return { users: data.data }
    } catch (err) {
      // Handle the error.
    }
  }
}
```

7. After fetching and setting the users with the `asyncData` method, use the Socket.IO plugin to listen to the `user.changefeeds` event in the `mounted` method for any new real-time feeds from the server, as follows:

```
// pages/users/index.vue
export default {
  async asyncData ({ error, $axios }) {
    //...
  },
  mounted () {
    socket.on('user.changefeeds', data => {
      if (data.new_val === undefined && data.old_val === undefined)
{
        return
      }
      //...
    })
  }
}
```

Here, you can see that we always check the `data` callback to make sure that `new_val` and `old_val` are defined in the incoming feed. In other words, we want to ensure these two keys are always present in the feed before proceeding to the following lines.

8. After checking this, if we receive data in the `new_val` key but the `old_val` key is empty, this means a new user has been added to the server. If we get a new feed from the server side, we will prepend the new user data to the top of the `user` array by using the JavaScript `unshift` function, as follows:

```
// pages/users/index.vue
mounted () {
  //...
  if(data.old_val === null && data.new_val !== null) {
    this.users.unshift(data.new_val)
  }
}
```

Then, if we receive data in the `old_val` key but the `new_val` key is empty, this means an existing user has been deleted from the server. So, to pop off an existing user from the array by its index (its position/location in the array), we can use the JavaScript `splice` function. But first, we must find the index of the user by its ID using the JavaScript `map` function, as follows:

```
// pages/users/index.vue
mounted () {
  //...
  if(data.new_val === null && data.old_val !== null) {
    var id = data.old_val.id
    var index = this.users.map(el => {
      return el.id
    }).indexOf(id)
    this.users.splice(index, 1)
  }
}
```

Lastly, if we receive data in both the `new_val` and `old_val` keys, this means a current user has been updated. So, if a user has been updated, we must find the user's index in the array first and then replace it with the JavaScript `splice` function., as follows:

```
// pages/users/index.vue
mounted () {
  //...
  if(data.new_val !== null && data.old_val !== null) {
    var id = data.new_val.id
```

[598]

```
        var index = this.users.findIndex(item => item.id === id)
        this.users.splice(index, 1, data.new_val)
      }
    }
```

Note that we use the JavaScript `findIndex` function instead as another alternative to the `map` function.

If you want to find out more information about the JavaScript standard built-in functions we have used here for manipulating the JavaScript arrays, please visit the following links:

- https://developer.mozilla.org/en-US/docs/Web/JavaScript/Reference/Global_Objects/Array/unshift for the `unshift` function
- https://developer.mozilla.org/en-US/docs/Web/JavaScript/Reference/Global_Objects/Array/splice for the `splice` function
- https://developer.mozilla.org/en-US/docs/Web/JavaScript/Reference/Global_Objects/Array/map for the `map` function
- https://developer.mozilla.org/en-US/docs/Web/JavaScript/Reference/Global_Objects/Array/findIndex for the `findIndex` function

9. Add the following template to the `<template>` block to display the users, as follows:

```
// pages/users/index.vue
<div>
  <h1>Users</h1>
  <ul>
    <li v-for="user in users" v-bind:key="user.uuid">
      <nuxt-link :to="'/users/' + user.slug">
        {{ user.name }}
      </nuxt-link>
    </li>
  </ul>
  <nuxt-link to="/users/add">
    Add New
  </nuxt-link>
</div>
```

In this template, you can see that we simply loop the user data we get from the `asyncData` method with `v-for` and bind the user `uuid` to each looped element. After that, any real-time feed that occurs in the `mounted` method will update the user data and the template reactively.

10. Run the Nuxt app with `npm run dev`. You should the following information on your terminal:

    ```
    Listening on: http://localhost:8000/
    ```

11. Open two tabs on your browser side by side, or two different browsers side by side, and point them to `localhost:8000/users`. Add a new user from one of the tabs (or browsers) at `localhost:8000/users/add`. You should see that the newly added user is shown on all the tabs (or browsers) instantly and concurrently, in real time, without you needing to refresh them.

> You can find all the code and apps in this chapter in `/chapter-17/frontend/` and `/chapter-17/backend/` in this book's GitHub repository.

Well done – you have made it! We hope you found this application fun and easy and that it inspires you to venture further with what you've learned so far. Let's summarize what we have learned in this chapter.

Summary

In this chapter, you managed to install and use RethinkDB and Socket.IO to turn the ordinary backend API and frontend Nuxt app into real-time apps. You learned how to manipulate the JSON data by creating, reading, updating, and deleting them on the server side with RethinkDB through the RethinkDB Administration UI, and then used the RethinkDB client driver with Koa. Most importantly, you learned how to manipulate the real time feeds in RethinkDB, known as changefeeds, through the RethinkDB Administration UI as well, and then integrated them with the Socket.IO server and Koa on the server side. Furthermore, you used the Socket.IO server to emit data with custom events and the Socket.IO client to listen to the event and catch the data in real-time on the client side with the Nuxt app. Wasn't it a fun ride?

Chapter 17

In the next chapter, we will take Nuxt further with third-party APIs, **content management systems** (**CMS**), and GraphQL. You will be introduced to WordPress API, Keystone, and GraphQL. You will then learn how to create custom content types and custom routes to extend the WordPress API so that you can integrate it with Nuxt and stream remote images from the WordPress project. You will be developing custom CMS using Keystone, installing and securing PostgreSQL for Keystone app development, as well as securing MongoDB, which you learned how to install in Chapter 9, *Adding a Server-Side Database*. Most importantly and excitingly, you will learn the differences between the REST API and the GraphQL API; build a GraphQL API with GraphQL.js, Express, and Apollo Server; understand the GraphQL schema and its resolvers; use the Keystone GraphQL API; and then integrate them with Nuxt. It will definitely be another fun ride, so buckle up and get ready!

18
Creating a Nuxt App with a CMS and GraphQL

In the previous chapters, you have been creating APIs from scratch so that they work with Nuxt apps. Building a personalized API can be rewarding and fulfilling, but it may not suit every situation. Building an API from the bottom-up is time-consuming. In this chapter, we are going to explore third-party systems that can provide us with the API services we need without having us build them from scratch. Ideally, we want to use a system that can help us manage our content – a **content management system** (**CMS**).

WordPress and Drupal are popular CMSes. They are packed with APIs that are worth looking into. In this book, we will be using **WordPress**. Besides CMSes such WordPress, we will also look into **headless CMSes**. A headless CMS is just like WordPress but is a pure API service without the frontend presentation, which can be done in Nuxt, just as we have been doing throughout this book. **Keystone** will be the headless CMS that we will explore in this book. However, the WordPress API and the Keystone API are two different kinds of API. Specifically, the former is a **REST API**, while the latter is a **GraphQL API**. But what are they? In short, a REST API is an API that uses HTTP requests to `GET`, `PUT`, `POST`, and `DELETE` data. The APIs you created in the previous chapters are REST APIs. GraphQL is an API that implements the GraphQL specification (technical standard).

GraphQL APIs are an alternative to REST APIs. To demonstrate how we can deliver the same result using these two different kinds of API, we will use the sample Nuxt app website we provided in `Chapter 4`, *Adding Views, Routes. and Transitions*. This can be found in `/chapter-4/nuxt-universal/sample-website/` in this book's GitHub repository. We will refactor the existing pages (home, about, projects, content, and the project subpages), which consist of text and images (featured images, fullscreen images, and individual project images). We will also refactor the navigation by getting data from the APIs instead of hardcoding them, just like we did for the other Nuxt apps in the previous chapters. With a CMS, we can get navigation data dynamically through the API, regardless of whether it is a REST or a GraphQL API.

Furthermore, we are going to generate static Nuxt pages (you learned about these in Chapter 14, *Using Linters, Formatters, and Deployment Commands*, and Chapter 15, *Creating an SPA with Nuxt*) with these CMSes. So, by the end of this chapter, you will have a full and final view of what you have learned throughout this book.

In this chapter, we will cover the following topics:

- Creating headless REST APIs in WordPress
- Introducing Keystone
- Introducing GraphQL
- Integrating Keystone, GraphQL, and Nuxt

Let's get started by looking into the WordPress REST API.

Creating headless REST APIs in WordPress

WordPress (WordPress.org) is an open source PHP CMS for general-purpose website development. It is not "headless" by default; it is stacked with a template system. This means the view and the data are intertwined. However, since 2015 (WordPress 4.4), the REST API infrastructure has been integrated into WordPress core for developers, and now all the default endpoints can be accessed if you append `/wp-json/` to your website-based URL. You can also extend the WordPress REST API and add your own custom endpoints. So, we can easily use WordPress as a "headless" REST API by ignoring the view. You will find out how to achieve this in the upcoming sections. To speed up the development process, we will install the following WordPress plugins:

- **Advanced Custom Fields (ACF)** for creating custom meta boxes. For more information about this plugin, please visit `https://www.advancedcustomfields.com/`
- **The ACF Repeater Field** for creating a repeatable set of subfields. It is an ACF premium add-on (`https://www.advancedcustomfields.com/add-ons/`). You can purchase it from `https://www.advancedcustomfields.com/add-ons/repeater-field/`. Alternatively, you can get it by default from ACF PRO at `https://www.advancedcustomfields.com/pro/`
- **Rewrite Rules Inspector** for inspecting and flushing your rewrite rules in WordPress. For more information about this plugin, please visit `https://wordpress.org/plugins/rewrite-rules-inspector/`

You can create your own plugins and meta boxes if you prefer not to use any of these. Please check out how to create custom meta boxes at `https://developer.wordpress.org/plugins/metadata/custom-meta-boxes/`. Also, check out how to develop custom plugins at `https://developer.wordpress.org/plugins/intro/`.

> For more information about the WordPress REST API, please visit `https://developer.wordpress.org/rest-api/`.

To develop and extend the WordPress REST API with these plugins or with yours, first, you will need to download WordPress and install the program on your machine. We'll learn how to do this in the next section.

Installing WordPress and creating our first pages

There are a few ways we can install and serve WordPress:

- By unpacking the downloaded WordPress `.zip` file and installing it from a directory
- By using the WordPress CLI (`https://make.wordpress.org/cli/handbook/` or `https://wp-cli.org/`)
- By setting up a port using Apache (which can be a bit of pain)
- By using the built-in PHP server

We will use the built-in PHP server in this book as it is the simplest way to get WordPress started and will make it easier to move it around in the future if we need to, as long as it is served on the same port; for example, `localhost:4000`. So, let's find out how to do this:

1. Create a directory (make it writable as well) and download and unzip WordPress in there. You can download WordPress from `https://wordpress.org/`. You should see some `.php` files with `/wp-admin/`, `/wp-content/`, and `/wp-includes/` directories in your unzipped WordPress directory.
2. Create a MySQL database (for example, `nuxt-wordpress`) through the PHP Adminer.
3. Navigate to the directory and serve WordPress with built-in PHP, as follows:

    ```
    $ php -S localhost:4000
    ```

4. Point your browser to `localhost:4000` and install WordPress with the required MySQL credentials (database name, username, and password) and your WordPress user account information (username, password, and email address).
5. Log into the WordPress admin UI with your user credentials at `localhost:4000/wp-admin/` and create some main pages (home, about, projects, contact) under the `Pages` label.
6. Navigate to **Menus** from under **Appearance** and create the site navigation by adding `menu-main` to the **Menu Name** input field.
7. Select all the pages (contact, about, projects, home) that appear under **Add menu items** and click **Add to Menu** to add them to `menu-main` as navigation items. You can drag and sort the items so that they are read in this order: home, about, projects, contact. Then, click the **Save Menu** button.
8. (Optional) Change the WordPress permalinks from the **Plain** option to the **Custom Structure** (with a value of `/%postname%/`, for example) in **Permalinks**, under **Settings**.
9. Download the plugins we mentioned previously and unpack them into a `/plugins/` directory. This can be found inside the `/wp-content/` directory. Then, activate them through the admin UI.

If you inspect the `wp_options` table in the `nuxt-wordpress` database, you should see that port `4000` is recorded successfully in the `siteurl` and `home` fields. So, from now on, you can move your WordPress project directory wherever you like, as long as you run it with the built-in PHP server at this port.

Although we have the data of our main pages and navigation in WordPress, we still need the data of the subpages of the `Projects` page. We can add them to the `Page` label and then just attach them to the `Projects` page. But these pages will share an identical content type (which is called post type in WordPress) – the `page` post type. It is better to organize them in a separate post type so that they can be managed more easily. We'll find out how to create custom post types in WordPress in the next section.

> For more details about the WordPress installation process, please visit https://wordpress.org/support/article/how-to-install-wordpress/.

Creating custom post types in WordPress

We can create custom post types in WordPress from the `functions.php` file in any WordPress theme. However, since we are not going to use the WordPress template system to deliver the view for our content, we can just extend a **child theme** from the default theme that is provided by WordPress. Then, we can just activate the child theme in **Themes**, under **Appearance**. We'll use the "Twenty Nineteen" theme to extend our child theme and then create the custom post types from there. Let's get started:

1. Create a directory called `twentynineteen-child` in the `/themes/` directory and create a `style.css` file that contains the following content:

   ```
   // wp-content/themes/twentynineteen-child/style.css
   /*
    Theme Name: Twenty Nineteen Child
    Template: twentynineteen
    Text Domain: twentynineteenchild
   */
   
   @import url("../twentynineteen/style.css");
   ```

   `Theme Name`, `Template`, and `Text Domain` are the minimum required header comments for extending a theme, followed by importing its parent's `style.css` file. These header comments must be put at the top of the file.

   > If you want to include more header comments in this child theme, please visit `https://developer.wordpress.org/themes/advanced-topics/child-themes/`.

2. Create a `functions.php` file in the `/twentynineteen-child/` directory and create the custom post type using this format and WordPress' `register_post_type` function, as follows:

   ```
   // wp-content/themes/twentynineteen-child/functions.php
   function create_something () {
       register_post_type('<name>', <args>);
   }
   add_action('init', 'create_something');
   ```

[607]

So, to add our custom post type, just use `project` as the type name and provide some arguments:

```
// wp-content/themes/twentynineteen-child/functions.php
function create_project_post_type () {
    register_post_type('project', $args);
}
add_action('init', 'create_project_post_type');
```

We can add labels and what content fields we want to support to the custom post type UI, as follows:

```
$args = [
    'labels' => [
        'name' => __('Project (Pages)'),
        'singular_name' => __('Project'),
        'all_items' => 'All Projects'
    ],
    //...
    'supports' => ['title', 'editor', 'thumbnail', 'page-attributes'],
];
```

> For more information about the `register_post_type` function, please visit https://developer.wordpress.org/reference/functions/register_post_type/.
>
> For more information about the custom post type UI, please visit https://wordpress.org/plugins/custom-post-type-ui/.

3. (Optional) We can also add support for `category` and `tag` for this custom post type, as follows:

```
'taxonomies' => [
    'category',
    'post_tag'
],
```

However, these are global category and tag instances, which means they are shared with other post types such as the `Page` and `Post` post types. So, if you want to specify specific categories for the `Project` post type only, use the following code:

```
// wp-content/themes/twentynineteen-child/functions.php
add_action('init', 'create_project_categories');
function create_project_categories() {
```

[608]

```
    $args = [
        'label' => __('Categories'),
        'has_archive' => true,
        'hierarchical' => true,
        'rewrite' => [
            'slug' => 'project',
            'with_front' => false
        ],
    ];
    $postTypes = ['project'];
    $taxonomy = 'project-category';
    register_taxonomy($taxonomy, $postTypes, $args);
}
```

> For more information about registering taxonomies, please visit https://developer.wordpress.org/reference/functions/register_taxonomy/.

4. (Optional) It may be a good idea to disable Gutenberg completely for all post types if you find it difficult to use:

```
// wp-content/themes/twentynineteen-child/functions.php
add_filter('use_block_editor_for_post', '__return_false', 10);
add_filter('use_block_editor_for_post_type', '__return_false', 10);
```

5. Activate the child theme in the WordPress admin UI and start adding `project` type pages to the **Projects** label.

You will notice that the content fields (`title`, `editor`, `thumbnail`, `page-attributes`) that you can use to add content to the project pages are very limited. We need more specific content fields, such as content fields for adding multiple project images and a fullscreen image. This is the same issue we had with the `home` page because we need another content field so that we can add multiple slide images as well. To add more of these content fields, we will need custom meta boxes. You can use the ACF plugin or create your own custom meta boxes and include them in the `functions.php` file or create them as a plugin. Alternatively, you can use another different meta box plugin such as Meta Box (https://metabox.io/). It is entirely up to you.

Once you have created the custom content fields and added the required content to each project page, you can extend the WordPress REST API for project pages, main pages, and navigation. We'll learn how to do this in the next section.

Extending the WordPress REST API

The WordPress REST API can be accessed with `/wp-json/` and is the entry route that's appended to your site-based URLs. For example, you can see all the other available routes by pointing your browser to `localhost:4000/wp-json/`. You will see what endpoints are available in every route, as these can be either GET or POST endpoints. For example, the `/wp-json/wp/v2/pages` route has a GET endpoint for listing pages and a POST endpoint for creating a page. You can find out more about these default routes and endpoints at https://developer.wordpress.org/rest-api/reference/.

However, if you have custom post types and custom content fields, then you will need custom routes and endpoints. We can create custom versions of these by registering them with the `register_rest_route` function in the `functions.php` file, as follows:

```
add_action('rest_api_init', function () { , and then followed by the
available endpoint
    $args = [
        'methods' => 'GET',
        'callback' => '<do_something>',
    ];
    register_rest_route(<namespace>, <route>, $args);
});
```

Let's learn how to extend the WordPress REST API:

1. Create a global namespace and endpoints for fetching the navigation and a single page:

    ```
    // wp-content/themes/twentynineteen-child/functions.php
    $namespace = 'api/v1/';

    add_action('rest_api_init', function () use ($namespace) {
        $route = 'menu';
        $args = [
            'methods' => 'GET',
            'callback' => 'fetch_menu',
        ];
        register_rest_route($namespace, $route, $args);
    });

    add_action('rest_api_init', function () use ($namespace) {
        $route = 'page/(?P<slug>[a-zA-Z0-9-]+)';
        $args = [
            'methods' => 'GET',
            'callback' => 'fetch_page',
        ];
    ```

```
    register_rest_route($namespace, $route, $args);
});
```

Notice that we pass the global namespace to each block of `add_action` by using the PHP `use` keyword in the anonymous functions. For more information about the PHP `use` keyword and anonymous functions, please visit https://www.php.net/manual/en/functions.anonymous.php.

> For more information about the `register_rest_route` function from WordPress, please visit https://developer.wordpress.org/reference/functions/register_rest_route/.

2. Create endpoints for fetching a single project page and listing project pages:

```
// wp-content/themes/twentynineteen-child/functions.php
add_action('rest_api_init', function () use ($namespace) {
    $route = 'project/(?P<slug>[a-zA-Z0-9-]+)';
    $args = [
        'methods' => 'GET',
        'callback' => 'fetch_project',
    ];
    register_rest_route($namespace, $route, $args);
});

add_action('rest_api_init', function () use ($namespace) {
    $route = 'projects/(?P<page_number>\d+)';
    $args = [
        'methods' => 'GET',
        'callback' => 'fetch_projects',
    ];
    register_rest_route($namespace, $route, $args);
});
```

3. Create a `fetch_menu` function for fetching the `menu-main` navigation items:

```
// wp-content/themes/twentynineteen-child/functions.php
function fetch_menu ($data) {
    $menu_items = wp_get_nav_menu_items('menu-main');

    if (empty($menu_items)) {
        return [];
    }

    return $menu_items;
}
```

We use the `wp_get_nav_menu_items` function from WordPress to help us fetch the navigation.

> For more information about the `wp_get_nav_menu_items` function, please visit https://developer.wordpress.org/reference/functions/wp_get_nav_menu_items/.

4. Create a `fetch_page` function for fetching a page by slug (or path):

```
// wp-content/themes/twentynineteen-child/functions.php
function fetch_page ($data) {
    $post = get_page_by_path($data['slug'], OBJECT, 'page');

    if (!count((array)$post)) {
        return [];
    }
    $post->slides = get_field('slide_items', $post->ID);

    return $post;
}
```

Here, we use the `get_page_by_path` function from WordPress to fetch the page. For more information about this function, please visit https://developer.wordpress.org/reference/functions/get_page_by_path/.

We also use the `get_field` function from the ACF plugin to fetch the list of slide images that are attached to the page and then push them to the `$post` object as `slides`. For more information about this function, please visit https://www.advancedcustomfields.com/resources/get_field/.

5. Create a `fetch_project` function in order to fetch a single project page:

```
// wp-content/themes/twentynineteen-child/functions.php
function fetch_project ($data) {
    $post = get_page_by_path($data['slug'], OBJECT, 'project');

    if (!count((array)$post)) {
        return [];
    }
    $post->fullscreen = get_field('full_screen_image', $post->ID);
    $post->images = get_field('image_items', $post->ID);

    return $post;
}
```

Again, we use the WordPress `get_page_by_path` function for fetching a page for us and the ACF `get_field` function for fetching images (the fullscreen image and project images) attached to the project page and then push them to the `$post` object as `fullscreen` and `images`.

6. Create a `fetch_projects` function for fetching a list of project pages, 6 items per page:

```
// wp-content/themes/twentynineteen-child/functions.php
function fetch_projects ($data) {
    $paged = $data['page_number'] ? $data['page_number'] : 1;
    $posts_per_page = 6;
    $post_type = 'project';
    $args = [
        'post_type' => $post_type,
        'post_status' => ['publish'],
        'posts_per_page' => $posts_per_page,
        'paged' => $paged,
        'orderby' => 'date'
    ];
    $posts = get_posts($args);

    if (empty($posts)) {
        return [];
    }

    foreach ($posts as &$post) {
        $post->featured_image = get_the_post_thumbnail_url($post->ID);
    }
    return $posts;
}
```

Here, we used the `get_posts` function from WordPress with the required arguments to fetch the list. For more information about this function, please visit https://developer.wordpress.org/reference/functions/get_posts/.

Then, we loop each project page and push their featured images into the `get_the_post_thumbnail_url` function from WordPress. For more information about this function, please visit https://developer.wordpress.org/reference/functions/get_the_post_thumbnail_url/.

[613]

7. We also need to compute the data (the previous page number and next page number) in order to make pagination for project pages, so instead of just returning $posts, return it as items in the following array with the pagination data:

```
$total = wp_count_posts($post_type);
$total_max_pages = ceil($total->publish / $posts_per_page);

return [
    'items' => $posts,
    'total_pages' => $total_max_pages,
    'current_page' => (int)$paged,
    'next_page' => (int)$paged === (int)$total_max_pages ? null : $paged + 1,
    'prev_page' => (int)$paged === 1 ? null : $paged - 1,
];
```

Here, we used the wp_count_posts function to count the total published project pages. For more information about this function, please visit https://developer.wordpress.org/reference/functions/wp_count_posts/.

8. Log into the WordPress admin UI, go to **Rewrite Rules** under **Tools**, and click the **Flush Rules** button to refresh the WordPress rewrite rules.
9. Go to your browser and test the custom API routes that you have just created:

```
/wp-json/api/v1/menu
/wp-json/api/v1/page/<slug>
/wp-json/api/v1/projects/<number>
/wp-json/api/v1/project/<slug>
```

You should see a bunch of JSON raw data printed on your browser screen. The JSON raw data can be difficult to read, but you can use **JSONLint**, a JSON validator, for pretty-printing your data at https://jsonlint.com/. Alternatively, you can just use **Firefox**, which has the option to pretty-print your data.

> You can find the entire code for this in /chapter-18/cross-domain/backend/wordpress/, in this book's GitHub repository. You can find a sample database (nuxt-wordpress.sql) in it too. The default **username** and **password** in this sample database for logging into the WordPress admin UI is **admin**.

Well done! You have successfully extended the WordPress REST API so that it supports custom post types. We don't need to develop any new theme in WordPress to view our content because this will be handled by Nuxt. We can keep WordPress' existing themes for previewing the content. This means we are only using WordPress to host our site content remotely, including all the media files (images, videos, and so on). Furthermore, we can generate static pages using Nuxt (just like we did in the previous chapters) and stream all the media files from WordPress to our Nuxt project so that we can host them locally. We'll learn how to do this in the next section.

Integrating with Nuxt and streaming images from WordPress

Integrating Nuxt with the WordPress REST API is similar to when you integrated with the cross-domain APIs you learned about and created in the previous chapters. However, in this section, we will improve the plugin that we use to load images by requiring them from the `/assets/` directory. But since our images are uploaded to the WordPress CMS and are kept in the `/uploads/` directory in our WordPress project, we need to refactor our asset loader plugin so that it requires the images from the `/assets/` directory when they are found in there; otherwise, we just load them remotely from WordPress. Let's get started:

1. Set `remote URL` for the Axios instance in the Nuxt config file, as follows:

   ```
   // nuxt.config.js
   const protocol = 'http'
   const host = process.env.NODE_ENV === 'production' ? 'your-domain.com' : 'localhost'
   const ports = {
     local: '3000',
     remote: '4000'
   }
   const remoteUrl = protocol + '://' + host + ':' + ports.remote

   module.exports = {
     env: {
       remoteUrl: remoteUrl,
     }
   }
   ```

2. Create an Axios instance and inject it into the Nuxt context directly as `$axios`. Also, add this Axios instance to the app option into the context using the `inject` function:

```js
// plugins/axios.js
import axios from 'axios'

let baseURL = process.env.remoteUrl
const api = axios.create({ baseURL })

export default (ctx, inject) => {
  ctx.$axios = api
  inject('axios', api)
}
```

3. Refactor the asset loader plugin, as follows:

```js
// plugins/utils.js
import Vue from 'vue'

Vue.prototype.$loadAssetImage = src => {
  var array = src.split('/')
  var last = [...array].pop()
  if (process.server && process.env.streamRemoteResource === true)
  {
    var { streamResource } = require('~/assets/js/stream-resource')
    streamResource(src, last)
    return
  }

  try {
    return require('~/assets/images/' + last)
  } catch (e) {
    return src
  }
}
```

Here, we split the image URL string into an array, get the image's filename (for example, `my-image.jpg`) from the last item in the array, and store it in the `last` variable. We then require the image locally using the filename (`last`). If an error is thrown, that means the image does not exist in the `/assets/` directory, so we just return the image's URL (`src`) as it is.

However, we will stream the image from the remote URL to the /assets/ directory using a streamResource function when our app is running on the server-side and the streamRemoteResource option is true. You will find out how to create this option (just like the remoteURL option) in the upcoming step.

4. Create a stream-resource.js file with the streamResource function in the /assets/ directory, as follows:

```js
// assets/js/stream-resource.js
import axios from 'axios'
import fs from 'fs'

export const streamResource = async (src, last) => {
  const file = fs.createWriteStream('./assets/images/' + last)
  const { data } = await axios({
    url: src,
    method: 'GET',
    responseType: 'stream'
  })
  data.pipe(file)
}
```

In this function, we use plain Axios to request the data of the remote resource by specifying stream as the response type. We then use the createWriteStream function from the Node.js built-in File System (fs) package with the necessary filepath to create the image in the /assets/ directory.

> For more information about the fs package and its createWriteStream function, please visit https://nodejs.org/api/fs.html and https://nodejs.org/api/fs.html#fs_fs_createwritestream_path_options.
>
> For more information about the Node.js stream's pipe event in the response data and the Node.js stream itself, please visit https://nodejs.org/api/stream.html#stream_event_pipe and https://nodejs.org/api/stream.html#stream_stream.

5. Register both plugins in the Nuxt config file:

```js
// nuxt.config.js
plugins: [
  '~/plugins/axios.js',
  '~/plugins/utils.js',
],
```

6. Refactor the home page's `index.vue` in the `/pages/` directory in order to use these two plugins, as follows:

```
// pages/index.vue
async asyncData ({ error, $axios }) {
  let { data } = await $axios.get('/wp-json/api/v1/page/home')
  return {
    post: data
  }
}

<template v-for="slide in post.slides">
  <img :src="$loadAssetImage(slide.image.sizes.medium_large)">
</template>
```

Here, we used `$axios` from our plugin to request the WordPress API. After receiving the data, we populated it in the `<template>` block. The `$loadAssetImage` function is used to run logic on how to load and process the image for us.

The rest of the pages in the `/pages/` directory should be refactored and follow the same pattern we followed for the home page. They are `/about.vue`, `/contact.vue`, `/projects/index.vue`, `/projects/_slug.vue`, and `/projects/pages/_number.vue`. Also, you need to do this for the component in the `/components/` directory; that is, `/projects/project-items.vue`. You can find the repository path to these completed files in the GitHub repositories provided at the end of this section.

7. Create another script command with a custom environment variable, `NUXT_ENV_GEN`, and put `stream` as its value in the `package.json` file in our Nuxt project:

```
// package.json
"scripts": {
  "generate": "nuxt generate",
  "stream": "NUXT_ENV_GEN=stream nuxt generate"
}
```

In Nuxt, if you create an environment variable prefixed with `NUXT_ENV_` in the `package.json` file, it will be injected into the Node.js process environment automatically. After doing this, you can access it throughout the app via the `process.env` object – including other custom properties you might set in the `env` property in the Nuxt config file

> For more information about the env property in Nuxt, please visit https://nuxtjs.org/api/configuration-env/.

8. Define the streamRemoteResource option for the asset loader plugin (which we refactored in *step 3*) in the env property in the Nuxt config file, as follows:

```js
// nuxt.config.js
env: {
  streamRemoteResource: process.env.NUXT_ENV_GEN === 'stream' ?
    true : false
},
```

This streamRemoteResource option will be set to true when we get the stream value from the NUXT_ENV_GEN environment variable; otherwise, it is always set to false. So, when this option is set to true, the asset loader plugin will start streaming the remote resources to the /assets/ directory for us.

9. (Optional) If the Nuxt crawler fails to detect the dynamic routes for some unknown reasons, then generate these routes manually in the generate option in the Nuxt config file, as follows:

```js
// nuxt.config.js
import axios from 'axios'
export default {
  generate: {
    routes: async function () {
      const projects = await axios.get(remoteUrl + '/wp-json/api/v1/projects')
      const routesProjects = projects.data.map((project) => {
        return {
          route: '/projects/' + project.post_name,
          payload: project
        }
      })

      let totalMaxPages = Math.ceil(routesProjects.length / 6)
      let pagesProjects = []
      Array(totalMaxPages).fill().map((item, index) => {
        pagesProjects.push({
          route: '/projects/pages/' + (index + 1),
          payload: null
        })
      })
```

```
            const routes = [ ...routesProjects, ...pagesProjects ]
            return routes
        }
    }
}
```

In this optional step, we used Axios to fetch all the child pages that belong to the `projects` post type, and used the JavaScript `map` method to loop these pages in order to generate their routes. And then, we took the length of the child pages to work out how many maximum pages in number (`totalMaxPages`) by dividing the child pages by six (making six items per page). After that, we converted the `totalMaxPages` number into an array by using the JavaScript `Array` object, and then used the Javascript `fill`, `map`, and `push` methods to loop the array in order to generate the dynamic routes for pagination. Lastly, we concatenated the routes from the child pages and pagination with the JavaScript spread operator, and then return them as a single array for Nuxt to generate the dynamic routes for us.

> For more information about the JavaScript `map`, `fill`, and `push` methods, please visit https://developer.mozilla.org/en-US/docs/Web/JavaScript/Reference/Global_Objects/Array/map, https://developer.mozilla.org/en-US/docs/Web/JavaScript/Reference/Global_Objects/Array/fill, and https://developer.mozilla.org/en-US/docs/Web/JavaScript/Reference/Global_Objects/Array/push, respectively.

10. Run the `stream` command first, followed by the `generate` command on your terminal, as follows:

    ```
    $ npm run stream && npm run generate
    ```

    We use the `stream` command to stream the remote resources to the `/assets/` directory by generating the first batch of static pages, then the `generate` command to regenerate the static pages. At this point, webpack will process the images in the `/assets/` directory and export them to the `/dist/` folder with the static pages. So, after running these two commands, you should see that the remote resources are streamed and processed in `/assets/` and `/dist/`. You can navigate to these two directories and inspect the downloaded resources.

    > You can find the Nuxt app of this section in `/chapter-18/cross-domain/frontend/nuxt-universal/nuxt-wordpress/axios-vanilla/` in this book's GitHub repository.

Well done! You have successfully integrated Nuxt with the WordPress REST API and streamed remote resources for static pages. WordPress may not be everyone's choice since it does not comply with **PHP Standards Recommendations (PSRs)** (https://www.php-fig.org/) and has its own way of getting things done. But it was released in 2003 before PSR and many modern PHP frameworks. It has been able to support countless businesses and individuals ever since. Of course, it has evolved and offers one of the most user-friendly admin UIs for editors and developers alike.

If this hasn't convinced you to use WordPress as an API, there are other options. In the next section, we are going to look at an alternative to REST APIs – GraphQL APIs – and an alternative to WordPress in Node.js – Keystone. Keystone uses GraphQL to deliver its API. Before diving into GraphQL, we'll take a look at Keystone and learn how to develop customized CMS.

Introducing Keystone

Keystone is a scalable headless CMS for building GraphQL APIs in Node.js. It is open source and equipped with a very decent admin UI where you can manage your content. Just like WordPress, you can create custom content types in Keystone called **lists** and then query your contents through the GraphQL API. You create lists from source, just like you create REST APIs. You add what you need for your API so that it is highly scalable and extensible.

To use Keystone, first, you need to prepare a database for storing your content. Keystone supports MongoDB and PostgreSQL. You need to install and configure one of them and then find out the connection string for Keystone. You learned about MongoDB in Chapter 9, *Adding a Server-Side Database*, so using it again as the database for Keystone should not be an issue for you. But what about PostgreSQL? Let's find out.

> For more information about Keystone, please visit https://www.keystonejs.com/.

Installing and securing PostgreSQL (Ubuntu)

PostgreSQL, also known as Postgres, is an object-relational database system, often compared with MySQL, which is a (purely) relational database management system (RDBMS). Both are open source and use tables but have their differences.

Creating a Nuxt App with a CMS and GraphQL

For example, Postgres is largely SQL compliant while MySQL is partially compliant, and MySQL performs faster in terms of read speed while PostgreSQL is faster at injecting complex queries. For more information about Postgres, please visit https://www.postgresql.org/.

You can install Postgres on many different operating systems, including Linux, macOS, and Windows. Depending on your operating system, you can follow the official guide at https://www.postgresql.org/download/ to install it on your machine. We will show you how to install and secure it on Linux, specifically Ubuntu, in the following steps:

1. Update your local package index and install Postgres from Ubuntu's default repositories using Ubuntu's apt packaging system:

   ```
   $ sudo apt update
   $ sudo apt install postgresql postgresql-contrib
   ```

2. Verify Postgres by checking its version:

   ```
   $ psql -v
   ```

   If you get the following output, this means you have installed it successfully:

   ```
   /usr/lib/postgresql/12/bin/psql: option requires an argument -- 'v'
   Try "psql --help" for more information.
   ```

   The number **12** in the path indicates you have Postgres version 12 on your machine.

3. Enter the Postgres shell from your terminal:

   ```
   $ sudo -u postgres psql
   ```

   You should get an output similar to the following on your terminal:

   ```
   postgres@lau-desktop:~$ psql
   psql (12.2 (Ubuntu 12.2-2.pgdg19.10+1))
   Type "help" for help.

   postgres=
   ```

4. List the default users using the Postgres \du command:

   ```
   postgres= \du
   ```

[622]

You should get two default users, as follows:

```
Role name
----------
postgres
root
```

We will add a new administrative user (or role) to the list using an interactive prompt on our terminal. However, we need to exit the Postgres shell first:

```
postgres= \q
```

5. Type in the following command with the `--interactive` flag:

    $ sudo -u postgres createuser --interactive

    You should see the following two questions regarding the name of the new role and whether the role should have superuser permissions:

    ```
    Enter name of role to add: user1
    Shall the new role be a superuser? (y/n) y
    ```

    Here, we called the new user `user1`. It has superuser permissions, just like the default users do.

6. Log into the Postgres shell with `sudo -u postgres psql` to verify the new user with the `\du` command. You should see that it has been added to the list.

7. Add a password to the new user with the following SQL query:

    ```
    ALTER USER user1 PASSWORD 'password';
    ```

    If you get the following output, then you have successfully added a password for this user:

    ```
    ALTER ROLE
    ```

8. Exit the Postgres shell. Now, you can use PHP's Adminer (https://www.adminer.org/) to log into Postgres with this user and, from there, add a new database that will be required when you install Keystone later. Then, you can use the following format for the Postgres connection string for the database you have just created:

    ```
    postgres://<username>:<password>@localhost/<dbname>
    ```

Note that a password is always required for any user to log into the database from Adminer for security reasons. So, it is a good practice to add security to your database, especially for production, regardless of whether it is a MySQL, Postgres, or MongoDB database. What about MongoDB? You learned to install and use it in previous chapters, but it hasn't been secured yet. We'll find out how to do this in the next section.

Installing and securing MongoDB (Ubuntu)

By now, you should know how to install MongoDB. So, in this section, we will focus on securing databases in MongoDB. To secure MongoDB, we will start by adding an administrative user to MongoDB, as follows:

1. Connect to the Mongo shell from your terminal:

    ```
    $ mongo
    ```

2. Select the `admin` database and add a new user with a username and password (for example, root and password) to this database, as follows:

    ```
    > use admin
    > db.createUser(
      {
        user: "root",
        pwd: "password",
        roles: [ { role: "userAdminAnyDatabase", db: "admin" },
          "readWriteAnyDatabase" ]
      }
    )
    ```

3. Exit the shell and open the MongoDB configuration file from your terminal:

    ```
    $ sudo nano /etc/mongod.conf
    ```

4. Look for the `security` section, remove the hash, and add the `authorization` setting, as shown here:

    ```
    // mongodb.conf
    security:
      authorization: "enabled"
    ```

5. Save and exit the file and restart MongoDB:

    ```
    $ sudo systemctl restart mongod
    ```

6. Verify the configuration by checking the status of MongoDB:

   ```
   $ sudo systemctl status mongod
   ```

   If you see an `"active"` status, that means you have configured it correctly.

7. Log in as `"root"` with the password and the `--authenticationDatabase` option. Also, supply the name of the database where the user is stored, which is `"admin"` in this case:

   ```
   $ mongo --port 27017 -u "root" -p "password" --authenticationDatabase "admin"
   ```

8. Create a new database (for example, `test`) and attach a new user to it:

   ```
   > use test
   db.createUser(
     {
       user: "user1",
       pwd: "password",
       roles: [ { role: "readWrite", db: "test" } ]
     }
   )
   ```

9. Exit and test the database by logging in as `user1`:

   ```
   $ mongo --port 27017 -u "user1" -p "password" --authenticationDatabase "test"
   ```

10. Test whether you can access this `test` database but not other databases:

    ```
    > show dbs
    ```

    If you receive no output, that means you are only authorized to access this database after authentication. You can use the following format to supply the MongoDB connection string for Keystone or any other apps (for example, Express, Koa, and so on):

    ```
    mogodb://<username>:<password>@localhost:27017/<dbname>
    ```

Again, it is good practice to add security to the database, especially for production, but it is easier and faster to develop apps with MongoDB without authentication enabled. You can always disable it for local development and just enable it in the production server.

Now, both database systems (Postgres and MongoDB) are ready and you can choose either of them to build your Keystone app. So, let's get to it!

Installing and creating Keystone apps

There are two ways to start a Keystone project – from scratch or by using the Keystone scaffolding tool known as `keystone-app`. If you are going to do it from scratch, you need to install any Keystone-related packages manually. These include the minimum required Keystone's packages and the additional Keystone packages that you need to build your app. Let's take a look at this manual installation:

1. Create a project directory and install the minimum required packages – the Keystone package itself, the Keystone GraphQL package (which is considered as an app in Keystone), and a database adapter:

    ```
    $ npm i @keystonejs/keystone
    $ npm i @keystonejs/app-graphql
    $ npm i @keystonejs/adapter-mongoose
    ```

2. Install the additional Keystone packages that you need, such as the Keystone Admin UI package (which is considered an app in Keystone) and the Keystone field package for registering lists:

    ```
    $ npm i @keystonejs/app-admin-ui
    $ npm i @keystonejs/fields
    ```

3. Create an empty `index.js` file in your root directory and import the packages you have just installed:

    ```
    // index.js
    const { Keystone } = require('@keystonejs/keystone')
    const { GraphQLApp } = require('@keystonejs/app-graphql')
    const { AdminUIApp } = require('@keystonejs/app-admin-ui')
    const { MongooseAdapter } = require('@keystonejs/adapter-mongoose')
    const { Text } = require('@keystonejs/fields')
    ```

4. Create a new instance of Keystone and pass the new instance of the database adapter to it, as follows:

    ```
    const keystone = new Keystone({
      name: 'My Keystone Project',
      adapter: new MongooseAdapter({ mongoUri:
    'mongodb://localhost/your-
        db-name' }),
    })
    ```

Chapter 18

> Check out the following guide to learn how to configure the Mongoose adapter: `https://www.keystonejs.com/keystonejs/adapter-mongoose/`. We will cover this again when we install Keystone with the scaffolding tool.

5. Create a simple list – a `Page` list, for example – and define the fields that you will need in order to store the data for every single item in this list:

    ```
    keystone.createList('Page', {
      fields: {
        name: { type: Text },
      },
    })
    ```

    It is a convention to capitalize the name of the list for GraphQL. We will cover this soon.

6. Export the `keystone` instance and the apps so that they can be executed:

    ```
    module.exports = {
      keystone,
      apps: [new GraphQLApp(), new AdminUIApp()]
    }
    ```

7. Create a `package.json` file (if you haven't done so already) and add the following `keystone` command to the scripts, as follows:

    ```
    "scripts": {
      "dev": "keystone"
    }
    ```

8. Start the app by running the `dev` script on your terminal:

    ```
    $ npm run dev
    ```

    You should see the following output on your terminal. This means you have started the app successfully:

    ```
     Command: keystone dev
    ✓ Validated project entry file ./index.js
    ✓ Keystone server listening on port 3000
    ✓ Initialised Keystone instance
    ✓ Connected to database
    ✓ Keystone instance is ready at http://localhost:3000
    ∞ Keystone Admin UI: http://localhost:3000/admin
    ∞ GraphQL Playground: http://localhost:3000/admin/graphiql
    ∞ GraphQL API: http://localhost:3000/admin/api
    ```

[627]

Well done! You have your first and simplest Keystone app up and running. In this app, you have a GraphQL API at `localhost:3000/admin/api`, a GraphQL Playground at `localhost:3000/admin/graphiql`, and a Keystone Admin UI at `localhost:3000/admin`. But how do we use the GraphQL API and GraphQL Playground? Rest assured, we will get to that in the upcoming section.

It is not difficult at all to start a new Keystone app, is it? You just need to install what Keystone requires and what you need. However, the easiest way to kick off a Keystone app is by using the scaffolding tool. The benefit of using the scaffolding tool is that it comes with some optional samples of Keystone apps during the installation process and they can be very useful as guides and templates. These optional samples are as follows:

- **Starter**: This example demonstrates basic user authentication using Keystone.
- **Todo**: This example demonstrates a simple app for adding items to a `Todo` list, along with some frontend integration (HTML, CSS, and JavaScript).
- **Blank**: This example provides a basic starting point, along with the Keystone Admin UI, GraphQL API, and GraphQL Playground. These are just like the ones in the manual installation but without the Keystone `field` package.
- **Nuxt**: This example demonstrates a simple integration with Nuxt.js.

We will go for the **blank** option because it provides us with the basic packages we need so that we can build our lists on top of them. Let's take a look:

1. Create a fresh Keystone app with any name on your terminal:

   ```
   $ npm init keystone-app <app-name>
   ```

2. Answer the questions that Keystone asks about, as follows:

   ```
   ✓ What is your project name?
   ✓ Select a starter project: Starter / Blank / Todo / Nuxt
   ✓ Select a database type: MongoDB / Postgre
   ```

3. After the installation is complete, move into your project directory:

   ```
   $ cd <app-name>
   ```

4. If you are using secured Postgres, then just provide the connection string, along with the username, password, and database for Keystone:

   ```
   // index.js
   const adapterConfig = { knexOptions: { connection: 'postgres://
     <username>:<password>@localhost/<dbname>' } }
   ```

Note that you just have to remove `<username>:<password>@` from the string if you don't have authentication enabled. Then, run the following command to install the database tables:

```
$ npm run create-tables
```

> For more information about the Knex database adapter, please visit `https://www.keystonejs.com/quick-start/adapters` or visit knex.js at `http://knexjs.org/`. It is a query builder for PostgreSQL, MySQL, and SQLite3.

5. If you are using secured MongoDB, then just provide the connection string, along with the username, password, and database for Keystone:

   ```
   // index.js
   const adapterConfig = { mongoUri:
   'mogodb://<username>:<password>@localhost:27017/<dbname>' }
   ```

   Note that you just have to remove `<username>:<password>@` from the string if you don't have authentication enabled.

   > For more information about the Mongoose database adapter, please visit `https://www.keystonejs.com/keystonejs/adapter-mongoose/` or visit Mongoose at `https://mongoosejs.com/`. MongoDB is a **schemaless** database system by nature, so this adapter is used as a schema solution to model the data in our app.

6. Change the server default port from `3000` to `4000` to serve the Keystone app. You can do this by simply adding `PORT=4000` to the `dev` script, as follows:

   ```
   // package.json
   "scripts": {
     "dev": "cross-env NODE_ENV=development PORT=4000 ...",
   }
   ```

   The reason we changed the port for Keystone to `4000` is because we are reserving port `3000` for Nuxt apps.

7. Install `nodemon` in our project. This will allow us to monitor changes in our Keystone app so that it can reload the server for us:

   ```
   $ npm i nodemon --save-dev
   ```

8. After installing this package, add the `nodemon --exec` command to the `dev` script, as follows:

```
// package.json
"scripts": {
  "dev": "... nodemon --exec keystone dev",
}
```

> For more information about nodemon, please visit https://nodemon.io/.

9. Start the development server for our Keystone app with the following command:

```
$ npm run dev
```

You should see the following output on your terminal. This means you have installed the Keystone app successfully:

```
✓ Keystone instance is ready at http://localhost:4000
∞ Keystone Admin UI: http://localhost:4000/admin
∞ GraphQL Playground: http://localhost:4000/admin/graphiql
∞ GraphQL API: http://localhost:4000/admin/api
```

This is the same as performing the manual installation but on a different port. In this app, you have a GraphQL API at `localhost:4000/admin/api`, a GraphQL Playground at `localhost:4000/admin/graphiql`, and a Keystone Admin UI at `localhost:4000/admin`. Before we can do anything with the GraphQL API and GraphQL Playground, we must add lists to our Keystone app and start injecting data from the Keystone Admin UI. We'll start adding lists and fields to the app in the next section.

> You can find the apps we created from both of these installation techniques in `/chapter-18/keystone/` in this book's GitHub repository.

Creating lists and fields

In Keystone, lists are schemas. A schema is a data model that has types that describe our data. It is the same in Keystone: a list schema is composed of fields that have types to describe the data they accept, just like we had in the manual installation, in which we have a `Page` list composed of a single `name` field with a `Text` type.

There are many different field types in Keystone, such as `File`, `Float`, `Checkbox`, `Content`, `DateTime`, `Slug`, and `Relationships`. You can find out about the rest of the Keystone field types that you need in their documentation at https://www.keystonejs.com/.

To add fields and their types to the list, you just have to install the Keystone packages that hold those field types in your project directory. For example, the `@keystonejs/fields` package holds the `Checkbox`, `Text`, `Float`, and `DateTime` field types, among others. You can find out about the rest of the field types at https://www.keystonejs.com/keystonejs/fields/fields. After you have the required field type packages installed, you can just import them and unpack the field types you need by using the JavaScript destructuring assignment for list creation.

However, lists can grow over time, which means they can become messy and difficult to keep up with. So, it is a good idea to create lists in **separate** files in a /list/ directory for better maintainability, as follows:

```
// lists/Page.js
const { Text } = require('@keystonejs/fields')

module.exports = {
  fields: {...},
}
```

Then, you just have to import it into the `index.js` file. So, let's find out what schema/lists and other Keystone packages we need to build our Keystone app. The lists that we are going to create are as follows:

- A `Page` schema/list for storing main pages such as `home`, `about`, `contact`, and `projects`
- A `Project` schema/list for storing project pages
- An `Image` schema/list for storing images for main and project pages
- A `Slide Image` schema/list for storing images for main pages only
- A `Nav Link` schema/list for storing the site links

The Keystone packages that we are going to use to create these lists are as follows:

- **Static file app**: This package is used to serve static files such as images, CSS, and JavaScript so that they can be accessed publicly by the client. For more information, please visit https://www.keystonejs.com/keystonejs/app-static/.

- **File adapters**: This package is used to support the `File` field type, which is used to upload files to a local or remote cloud-based location. For more information, please visit https://www.keystonejs.com/keystonejs/file-adapters/.
- **WYSIWYG**: This package is used to render a WYSIWYG editor in the Keystone Admin UI using TinyMCE. For more information about this package, please visit https://www.keystonejs.com/keystonejs/fields-wysiwyg-tinymce/. For the information about TinyMCE, please visit https://www.tiny.cloud/.

Now, let's install and use them to create our lists:

1. Install the Keystone packages that we mentioned previously via npm:

   ```
   $ npm i @keystonejs/app-static
   $ npm i @keystonejs/file-adapters
   $ npm i @keystonejs/fields-wysiwyg-tinymce
   ```

2. Import `@keystonejs/app-static` into `index.js` and define the path and the folder name where you want to keep the static files:

   ```
   // index.js
   const { StaticApp } = require('@keystonejs/app-static');

   module.exports = {
     apps: [
       new StaticApp({
         path: '/public',
         src: 'public'
       }),
     ],
   }
   ```

3. Create a `File.js` file in the `/lists/` directory. Then, define the fields for the `Image` list using the `File`, `Text`, and `Slug` field types from `@keystonejs/fields` and `LocalFileAdapter` from `@keystonejs/file-adapters`. This will allow you to upload files to the local location; that is, `/public/files/`:

   ```
   // lists/File.js
   const { File, Text, Slug } = require('@keystonejs/fields')
   const { LocalFileAdapter } = require('@keystonejs/file-adapters')

   const fileAdapter = new LocalFileAdapter({
     src: './public/files',
     path: '/public/files',
   })
   ```

```
module.exports = {
  fields: {
    title: { type: Text, isRequired: true },
    alt: { type: Text },
    caption: { type: Text, isMultiline: true },
    name: { type: Slug },
    file: { type: File, adapter: fileAdapter, isRequired: true },
  }
}
```

In the preceding code, we defined a list of fields (`title`, `alt`, `caption`, `name`, and `file`) so that we can store the meta-information about every uploaded file. It is good practice to have the `name` field in every list schema so that we can store a unique name in this field that we can use as the label in Keystone Admin UI. We can use it to identify each injected list item easily. To generate a unique name for this field, we can use the `Slug` type, which, by default, generates the unique name from the `title` field.

> For more information about the field types that we used in the preceding code, please visit the following links:
> - https://www.keystonejs.com/keystonejs/fields/src/types/file/ for the `File` type
> - https://www.keystonejs.com/keystonejs/fields/src/types/text/ for the `Text` type
> - https://www.keystonejs.com/keystonejs/fields/src/types/slug/ for the `Slug` type

For more information about `LocalFileAdapter`, please visit https://www.keystonejs.com/keystonejs/file-adapters/localfileadapter.

Our app files can be uploaded to Cloudinary using `CloudinaryFileAdapter`.

> For more information about how to set up an account so that you can host files on Cloudinary, please visit https://cloudinary.com/.

4. Create a `SlideImage.js` file in the `/lists/` directory and define the fields that are identical to the ones in the `File.js` file with an additional field type, `Relationship`, so that you can link the slide image to the project page:

```
// lists/SlideImage.js
const { Relationship } = require('@keystonejs/fields')

module.exports = {
  fields: {
    // ...
    link: { type: Relationship, ref: 'Project' },
  },
}
```

> For more information about the `Relationship` field, please visit https://www.keystonejs.com/keystonejs/fields/src/types/relationship/.

5. Create a `Page.js` file in the `/lists/` directory and define the fields for the `Page` list using the `Text, Relationship, Slug,` and `Wysiwyg` field types from `@keystonejs/fields` and `@keystonejs/fields-wysiwyg-tinymce`, as follows:

```
// lists/Page.js
const { Text, Relationship, Slug } = require('@keystonejs/fields')
const { Wysiwyg } = require('@keystonejs/fields-wysiwyg-tinymce')

module.exports = {
  fields: {
    title: { type: Text, isRequired: true },
    excerpt: { type: Text, isMultiline: true },
    content: { type: Wysiwyg },
    name: { type: Slug },
    featuredImage: { type: Relationship, ref: 'Image' },
    slideImages: { type: Relationship, ref: 'SlideImage', many:
      true },
  },
}
```

In the preceding code, we defined a list of fields (`title`, `excerpt`, `content`, `name`, `featuredImage`, and `slideImages`) so that we can store the data of every main page that we will inject into this content type. Note that we link `featuredImage` to the `Image` list and link `slideImages` to the `SlideImage` list. We want to allow multiple images to be placed in the `slideImages` field, so we set the `many` option to `true`.

> For more information about these one-to-many and many-to-many relationships, please visit https://www.keystonejs.com/guides/new-schema-cheatsheet.

6. Create a `Project.js` file in the `/lists/` directory and define the fields that are identical to the ones in the `File.js` file for the `Project` list with two additional fields (`fullscreenImage` and `projectImages`):

```
// lists/Project.js
const { Text, Relationship, Slug } = require('@keystonejs/fields')
const { Wysiwyg } = require('@keystonejs/fields-wysiwyg-tinymce')

module.exports = {
  fields: {
    //...
    fullscreenImage: { type: Relationship, ref: 'Image' },
    projectImages: { type: Relationship, ref: 'Image', many:
      true },
  },
}
```

7. Create a `NavLink.js` file in the `/lists/` directory and define the fields (`title`, `order`, `name`, `link`, `subLinks`) for the `NavLink` list using the `Text`, `Relationship`, `Slug`, and `Integer` field types from `@keystonejs/fields`, as follows:

```
// lists/NavLink.js
const { Text, Relationship, Slug, Integer } =
require('@keystonejs/fields')

module.exports = {
  fields: {
    title: { type: Text, isRequired: true },
    order: { type: Integer, isRequired: true },
    name: { type: Slug },
    link: { type: Relationship, ref: 'Page' },
    subLinks: { type: Relationship, ref: 'Project', many: true },
```

```
    },
}
```

Here, we use the `order` field to sort the link items by their numeric positions in the GraphQL query. You will learn about this soon. The `subLinks` field is an example that demonstrates how you can make simple sublinks in Keystone. So, we can add multiple sublinks to the main links by attaching the project pages to this field, which is linked to the `Project` list using the `Relationship` field type.

> For more information about the `Integer` field type, please visit https://www.keystonejs.com/keystonejs/fields/src/types/integer/.

8. Import the files from the `/lists/` directory and start creating the list schema from them, as follows:

```
// index.js
const PageSchema = require('./lists/Page.js')
const ProjectSchema = require('./lists/Project.js')
const FileSchema = require('./lists/File.js')
const SlideImageSchema = require('./lists/SlideImage.js')
const NavLinkSchema = require('./lists/NavLink.js')

const keystone = new Keystone({ ... })

keystone.createList('Page', PageSchema)
keystone.createList('Project', ProjectSchema)
keystone.createList('Image', FileSchema)
keystone.createList('SlideImage', SlideImageSchema)
keystone.createList('NavLink', NavLinkSchema)
```

9. Start the app by running the `dev` script on your terminal:

```
$ npm run dev
```

You should see a list of URLs on your terminal identical to the ones shown in the previous section. This means you have started the app successfully on `localhost:4000`. So, now, you can point your browser to `localhost:4000/admin` and start injecting content and uploading files from the Keystone Admin UI. Once you have the content and data ready, you can query them using the GraphQL API and GraphQL Playground. But before you can do that, you should learn what a GraphQL is and how to create and use it independently from Keystone. So, let's find out!

> You can find the source code for this app in `/chapter-18/cross-domain/backend/keystone/` in this book's GitHub repository.

Introducing GraphQL

GraphQL is an open source query language, server-side runtime (execution engine), and specification (technical standard). But what does it mean? What is it? GraphQL is a query language, which is what the "QL" part of GraphQL stands for. To be specific, it is a client query language. But again, what does it mean? The following example will address any doubts you have about GraphQL queries:

```
{
  planet(name: "earth") {
    id
    age
    population
  }
}
```

GraphQL queries like the previous one are used in HTTP clients such as Nuxt or Vue to send the query to the server in exchange for a JSON response, as follows:

```
{
  "data": {
    "planet": {
      "id": 3,
      "age": "4543000000",
      "population": "7594000000"
    }
  }
}
```

As you can see, you get the specific data for the fields (`age` and `population`) that you requested and nothing more. This is what makes GraphQL distinctive and gives the client the power to request exactly what they want. It's cool and exciting, isn't it? But what is it in the server that returns the GraphQL response? A GraphQL API server (server-side runtime).

GraphQL queries are sent by the client to a GraphQL API server over an HTTP endpoint via the `POST` method to the server as a string. The server extracts and processes the query string. Then, just like any typical API server, the GraphQL API will fetch the data from a database or other services/APIs and return it to the client in a JSON response.

So, can we use a server such as Express as a GraphQL API server? Yes and no. All qualified GraphQL servers must implement two core components, as specified in the GraphQL specification, that validate and process and then return the data: a schema and resolvers.

A GraphQL schema is a collection of type definitions that consist of objects that the client can request and the fields that the objects have. On the other hand, GraphQL resolvers are functions that are attached to the fields that return values when the client makes a query or mutation. For example, the following is the type definition for finding a planet:

```
type Planet {
  id: Int
  name: String
  age: String
  population: String
}

type Query {
  planet(name: String): Planet
}
```

Here, you can see that GraphQL uses a strongly typed schema – each field must be defined with a type that can be a scalar type (which is a single value that can be an integer, Boolean, or string) or an object type. The `Planet` and `Query` types are object types, while `String` and `Int` are scalar types. Each of the fields in the object types must be resolved with a function, as follows:

```
Planet: {
  id: (root, args, context, info) => root.id,
  name: (root, args, context, info) => root.name,
  age: (root, args, context, info) => root.age,
  population: (root, args, context, info) => root.population,
}

Query: {
  planet: (root, args, context, info) => {
    return planets.find(planet => planet.name === args.name)
  },
}
```

The preceding example was written in JavaScript, but a GraphQL server can be written in any programming language as long as you follow and implement what is outlined in the GraphQL specification at https://spec.graphql.org/. The following are some examples of GraphQL implementations in different languages:

- GraphQL.js (JavaScript) at https://github.com/graphql/graphql-js
- graphql-php (PHP) at https://github.com/webonyx/graphql-php
- Graphene (Python) at https://github.com/graphql-python/graphene
- GraphQL Ruby (Ruby) at https://github.com/rmosolgo/graphql-ruby

You are free to create a new implementation as long as you comply with the GraphQL specification, but we're only going to use GraphQL.js in this book. Now, you probably have some deeper questions – what exactly is the query type? We know that it is an `object` type, but why do we need it? Do we need to have it in the schema? The short answer is yes.

We'll look at this in more detail in the next section and find out why it is required regardless. We will also find out how to use Express as a GraphQL API server. So, keep reading.

Understanding the GraphQL schema and resolvers

The example schema and resolvers for finding a planet that we discussed in the previous section presume that we use the GraphQL schema language, which helps us create the GraphQL schema required by the GraphQL server. We can easily create a GraphQL.js `GraphQLSchema` instance from the GraphQL schema language using the `makeExecutableSchema` function from a Node.js package called GraphQL Tools.

> You can find out more information about this package at https://www.graphql-tools.com/ or https://github.com/ardatan/graphql-tools.

The GraphQL schema language is a "shortcut" – a shorthand notation for constructing your GraphQL schema and its type system. Before making use of this shorthand notation, we should take a look at how a GraphQL schema is built from the low-level objects and functions such as GraphQLObjectType, GraphQLString, GraphQLList, and so on from GraphQL.js, which implements the GraphQL specification. Let's install these packages and create a simple GraphQL API server with Express:

1. Install Express, GraphQL.js, and GraphQL HTTP Server Middleware via npm:

```
$ npm i express
$ npm i express-graphql
$ npm i graphql
```

GraphQL HTTP Server Middleware is a piece of middleware that allows us to create a GraphQL HTTP server with any HTTP web framework that implements the way Connect supports a middleware, such as Express, Restify, and Connect itself.

> For more information about these packages, please visit the following links:
> - https://github.com/graphql/express-graphql for GraphQL HTTP Server Middleware
> - https://github.com/senchalabs/connect for Connect
> - https://expressjs.com/ for Express
> - http://restify.com/ for Restify

2. Create an index.js file in the project's root and import express, express-graphql and graphql, using the require method:

```
// index.js
const express = require('express')
const graphqlHTTP = require('express-graphql')
const graphql = require('graphql')

const app = express()
const port = process.env.PORT || 4000
```

3. Create a dummy data with a list of planets:

```
// index.js
const planets = [
  { id: 3, name: "earth", age: 4543000000, population:
    7594000000 },
  { id: 4, name: "mars", age: 4603000000, population: 0 },
]
```

4. Define the Planet object type and the fields that the client can query:

```
// index.js
const planetType = new graphql.GraphQLObjectType({
  name: 'Planet',
  fields: {
  id: { ... },
  name: { ... },
  age: { ... },
  population: { ... },
})
```

Note that it is a convention to capitalize the object type in the name field for the GraphQL schema's creation.

5. Define various types and how you want to resolve the value for each field:

```
// index.js
id: {
  type: graphql.GraphQLInt,
  resolve: (root, orgs, context, info) => root.id,
},
name: {
  type: graphql.GraphQLString,
  resolve: (root, orgs, context, info) => root.name,
},
age: {
  type: graphql.GraphQLString,
  resolve: (root, orgs, context, info) => root.age,
},
population: {
  type: graphql.GraphQLString,
  resolve: (root, orgs, context, info) => root.population,
},
```

Notice that every resolver function accepts the following four arguments:

- `root`: The object or value that's resolved from the parent object type (the Query in *step 6*).
- `args`: Arguments that the field can receive if they are set. See *step 8*.
- `context`: A mutable JavaScript object that holds the top-level data that is shared across all the resolvers. It is the Node.js HTTP request object (`IncomingMessage`) by default in our case when using Express. We can modify this context object and add general data that we want to be shared, such as authentication and database connections. See *step 10*.
- `info`: A JavaScript object that holds information about the current field such as its field name, return type, parent type (`Planet`, in this case), and the general schema details.

We can omit them if they aren't needed for resolving the value for the current field.

6. Define the `Query` object type and the fields that the client can query:

```
// index.js
const queryType = new graphql.GraphQLObjectType({
  name: 'Query',
  fields: {
    hello: { ... },
    planet: { ... },
  },
})
```

7. Define the type and resolve how you want to return the value for the `hello` field:

```
// index.js
hello: {
  type: graphql.GraphQLString,
  resolve: (root, args, context, info) => 'world',
}
```

8. Define the type and resolve how you want to return the value for the `planet` field:

   ```
   // index.js
   planet: {
     type: planetType,
     args: {
       name: { type: graphql.GraphQLString }
     },
     resolve: (root, args, context, info) => {
       return planets.find(planet => planet.name === args.name)
     },
   }
   ```

   Notice that we passed the `Planet` object type that we created and stored in the `planetType` variable to the `planet` field in the `Query` object type so that a relationship between them can be established.

9. Construct a GraphQL schema instance with the required `query` field and the `Query` object type that you have just defined with the fields, types, arguments, and resolvers in it, as follows:

   ```
   // index.js
   const schema = new graphql.GraphQLSchema({ query: queryType })
   ```

   Note that the `query` key must be provided as the GraphQL query root type so that our query can be chained down to the fields in the `Planet` object type. We can say that the `Planet` object type is a subtype or a child of the `Query` object type (the root type) and that their relationship must be established in the parent object (`Query`) using the `type` field in the `planet` field.

10. Use the GraphQL HTTP Server Middleware as a piece of middleware with the GraphQL schema instance to establish the GraphQL server on an endpoint permitted by Express called `/graphiql`, as follows:

    ```
    // index.js
    app.use(
      '/graphiql',
      graphqlHTTP({ schema, graphiql: true }),
    )
    ```

    It is recommended to set the `graphiql` option to `true` so that we can use the GraphQL IDE when the GraphQL endpoint is loaded on the browser.

At this top level, you can also modify the context of your GraphQL API by using the `context` option inside the `graphqlHTTP` middleware, as follows:

```
context: {
  something: 'something to be shared',
}
```

By doing this, you can access this top-level data from any resolver. This can be very useful. Cool, isn't it?

11. Finally, after all the data has been loaded, start the server with the `node index.js` command on your terminal with the following line in the `index.js` file:

    ```
    // index.js
    app.listen(port)
    ```

12. Point your browser to `localhost:4000/graphiql`. You should see the GraphQL IDE, a UI where you can test your GraphQL API. So, type the following query into the input area on the left-hand side:

    ```
    // localhost:4000/graphiql
    {
      hello
      planet (name: "earth") {
        id
        age
        population
      }
    }
    ```

    You should see that the preceding GraphQL query has been exchanged with a JSON object on the right-hand side when you hit the play button:

    ```
    // localhost:4000/graphiql
    {
      "data": {
        "hello": "world",
        "planet": {
          "id": 3,
          "age": "4543000000",
          "population": "7594000000"
        }
      }
    }
    ```

Well done – you have managed to create a basic GraphQL API server with Express using the low-level approach! We hope this has given you a full picture of how a GraphQL API server can be created with the GraphQL schema and resolvers. We also hope that you can see the relationship between these two core components in GraphQL and that we have answered yours questions; that is, what exactly is the `Query` type? Why do we need it? Do we need to have it in the schema? The answer is yes, the query (object) type is a root object type (usually called a root `Query` type) that must be provided when creating the GraphQL schema.

But you may still have some questions and complaints, particularly regarding the resolvers – surely you find it tedious and dumb to define the resolvers in *step 5* for the fields in the `Planet` object type because they do nothing except return the values that are resolved from the query object. Is there any way to avoid this painful repetition? The answer is yes: you don't specify them for every field in your schema, and this lies in the **default resolver**. But how do we do this? We'll find out in the next section.

> You can find this and other examples in `/chapter-18/graphql-api/graphql-express/` in this book's GitHub repository.

Understanding GraphQL default resolvers

When no resolver has been specified for a field, by default, this field will take on the value of the property in the object that's been resolved by the parent – that is, if that object has a property name that matches the field name. So, the fields in the `Planet` object type can be refactored as follows:

```
fields: {
  id: { type: graphql.GraphQLInt },
  name: { type: graphql.GraphQLString },
  age: { type: graphql.GraphQLString },
  population: { type: graphql.GraphQLString },
}
```

The values of these fields will fall back to the properties in the object that's been resolved by the parent (the query type) under the hood, as follows:

```
root.id
root.name
root.age
root.population
```

So, put the other way around, when a resolver is specified explicitly for a field, this resolver will always be used, even if the parent's resolver returns any value for that field. For example, let's specify a value explicitly for the `id` field in the `Planet` object type, as follows:

```
fields: {
  id: {
    type: graphql.GraphQLInt,
    resolve: (root, orgs, context, info) => 2,
  },
}
```

We already know that the default ID values for Earth and Mars are 3 and 4 and that they are resolved by the `Query` object type (the parent), as shown in *step 8* in the previous section. But these resolved values will never be used because they are overridden by the value in the ID's resolver. So, let's query Earth or Mars, as follows:

```
{
  planet (name: "mars") {
    id
  }
}
```

In this case, you will always get 2 in the JSON response:

```
{
  "data": {
    "planet": {
      "id": 2
    }
  }
}
```

This is very clever, isn't it? It saves us from painful repetition – that is, if you have tons of fields in an object type. However, so far, we have been following the most painful way to construct our schema by working with GraphQL.js. This is because we wanted to see and understand how a GraphQL schema is created from the low-level types. We probably wouldn't want to take this long and winding road in real life, especially in a large project. Instead, we should prefer using the GraphQL schema language to build the schema and resolvers for us. In the next section, we will show you how to create a GraphQL API server easily with the GraphQL schema language and **Apollo Server** as an alternative to GraphQL HTTP Server Middleware. So, read on!

Creating a GraphQL API with Apollo Server

Apollo Server is an open source and GraphQL spec-compliant server developed by the Apollo platform for building GraphQL APIs. We can use it standalone or with other Node.js web frameworks such as Express, Koa, Hapi, and so on. We will use Apollo Server as it is in this book, but if you want to use it with other frameworks, please visit https://github.com/apollographql/apollo-serverinstallation-integrations.

In this GraphQL API, we will create a server that queries a collection of books by title and author. Let's get started:

1. Install Apollo Server and GraphQL.js via npm as the project dependencies:

   ```
   $ npm i apollo-server
   $ npm i graphql
   ```

2. Create an index.js file in the project root directory and import the ApolloServer and gql functions from the apollo-server package:

   ```
   // index.js
   const { ApolloServer, gql } = require('apollo-server')
   ```

   The gql function is used to parse GraphQL operations and the schema language by wrapping them with template literal tags (or tagged template literals). For more information about template literals and tagged templates, please visit https://developer.mozilla.org/en-US/docs/Web/JavaScript/Reference/Template_literals.

3. Create the following static data, which holds the lists of authors and posts:

   ```
   // index.js
   const authors = [
     { id: 1, name: 'author A' },
     { id: 2, name: 'author B' },
   ]

   const posts = [
     { id: 1, title: 'Post 1', authorId: 1 },
     { id: 2, title: 'Post 2', authorId: 1 },
     { id: 3, title: 'Post 3', authorId: 2 },
   ]
   ```

4. Define the `Author`, `Post`, and `Query` object types, along with the fields that the client can query:

```
// index.js
const typeDefs = gql`
  type Author {
    id: Int
    name: String
  }

  type Post {
    id: Int
    title: String
    author: Author
  }

  type Query {
    posts: [Post]
  }
`
```

Note that we can shorthand the `Author`, `Post`, and `Query` object types as the `Author` type, the `Post` type, and the `Query` type. It is just clearer than using "object type" to describe them because that is what they are. Remember that apart from being an object type by nature, the `Query` type is also the root type in GraphQL schema creation.

Notice how we establish the relationship of `Author` with `Post` and `Post` with `Query` – the type for the `author` field is the `Author` type. The `Author` type has simple scalar types for its fields (`id`, `name`), while the `Post` type has simple scalar types (`id`, `title`) and the `Author` type (`author`) for its field. The `Query` type has the `Post` type for its only field, which is `posts`, but it is a list of posts, so we must use the type modifier to wrap the `Post` type with open and closed square brackets to indicate that this `posts` field will resolve with an array of `Post` objects.

> For more information about the type modifier, please visit https://graphql.org/learn/schema/lists-and-non-null.

5. Define resolvers to specify how you want to resolve the value for the `posts` field in the `Query` type and the `author` field in the `Post` type:

```
// index.js
const resolvers = {
  Query: {
    posts: (root, args, context, info) => posts
  },
  Post: {
    author: root => authors.find(author => author.id ===
      root.authorId)
  },
}
```

Notice how the GraphQL schema language has helped us **decouple** the resolvers from the object types and that they are simply defined in a single JavaScript object. The resolvers in the JavaScript object are "magically" connected with the object types, as long as the property names for our resolvers map the field names in the type definitions. Hence, this JavaScript object is called a resolver map. Before defining resolvers, we must also define the **top-level** property names (`Query`, `Post`) in the resolver map so that they match the object types (`Author`, `Post`, `Query`) in the type definitions. But we don't need to define any specific resolvers for the `Author` type in this resolver map because the values for the fields (`id`, `name`) in `Author` are resolved by the default resolvers automatically.

Another point to note is that the values for the fields (`id`, `title`) in the `Post` type are also resolved by the default ones. If you don't like using property names to define resolvers, you can use resolver functions instead, as long as the function names correspond with the field names in the type definitions. For example, the resolvers for the `author` field can be rewritten as follows:

```
Post: {
  author (root) {
    return authors.find(author => author.id === root.authorId)
  },
}
```

6. Construct a GraphQL schema instance from `ApolloServer` with the type definitions and resolvers. Then, start the server, as follows:

```
// index.js
const server = new ApolloServer({ typeDefs, resolvers })

server.listen().then(({ url }) => {
```

Creating a Nuxt App with a CMS and GraphQL

```
        console.log(`Server ready at ${url}`)
})
```

7. Launch your GraphQL API with the `node` command on your terminal:

    ```
    $ node index.js
    ```

8. Point your browser to `localhost:4000`. You should see the GraphQL Playground loaded on your screen. From there, you can test your GraphQL API. So, type the following query into the input area on the left-hand side:

    ```
    {
      posts {
        title
        author {
          name
        }
      }
    }
    ```

You should see that the preceding GraphQL query has been exchanged with a JSON object on the right-hand side when you hit the play button:

```
{
  "data": {
    "posts": [
      {
        "title": "Post 1",
        "author": {
          "name": "author A"
        }
      },
      ...
    ]
  }
}
```

This is beautiful and wonderful, isn't it? That's how easily we can build a GraphQL API with the GraphQL schema language and Apollo Server. It is worth knowing the long and painful way of how a GraphQL schema and resolvers are created before adopting the shorthand method. Once you have this basic concrete knowledge, you should be able to query the data you have stored with Keystone with ease. We have only covered a few of GraphQL's types in this book, including the scalar type, the object type, the query type, and the type modifier. There are a few other types you should check out, such as the mutation type, the enumeration type, the union and input types, and interface. Please check them out at https://graphql.org/learn/schema/.

> If you want to learn more about GraphQL, please visit `https://graphql.org/learn/`. For more information about Apollo Server, visit `https://www.apollographql.com/docs/apollo-server/`.
>
> You can find the code that was used in this section, along with other example GraphQL type definitions, in `/chapter-18/graphql-api/graphql-apollo/` in this book's GitHub repository.

Now, let's learn how to use the Keystone GraphQL API.

Using the Keystone GraphQL API

The GraphQL Playground for the Keystone GraphQL API is located at `localhost:4000/admin/graphiql`. Here, we can test the list we created through the Keystone admin UI at `localhost:4000/admin`. Keystone will generate four top-level GraphQL queries automatically for **every** list that's created. For example, we will get the following queries for the `page` list we created in the previous section:

- `allPages`

    This query can be used to fetch all the items from the `Page` list. We can also search, limit, and filter the result, as follows:

    ```
    {
      allPages (orderBy: "name_DESC", skip: 0, first: 6) {
        title
        content
      }
    }
    ```

- `_allPagesMeta`

    This query can be used to fetch all meta-information about items in the `Page` list, such as the total count of all matched items, which can be useful for pagination. We can also search, limit, and filter the result, as follows:

    ```
    {
      _allPagesMeta (search: "a") {
        count
      }
    }
    ```

- Page

    This query can be used to fetch a single item from the Page list. We can **only** use a where parameter with an id key to fetch the page, as follows:

    ```
    {
      Page (where: { id: $id }) {
        title
        content
      }
    }
    ```

- _PagesMeta

    This query can be used to fetch the meta-information about the Page list itself, such as its name, access, schema, and fields, as follows:

    ```
    {
      _PagesMeta {
        name
        access {
          read
        }
        schema {
          queries
          fields {
            name
          }
        }
      }
    }
    ```

As you can see, these four queries, along with the filter, limit, and sorting parameters, provide us with enough power to fetch the specific data that we need and nothing more. What's more is that, in GraphQL, we can fetch **multiple** resources with a **single** request, as follows:

```
{
  _allPagesMeta {
    count
  },
  allPages (orderBy: "name_DESC", skip: 0, first: 6) {
    title
    content
  }
}
```

This is amazing and fun, isn't it? In a REST API, you may have to send multiple requests to multiple API endpoints for multiple resources. GraphQL offers us an alternative to solve this infamous issue of REST APIs that has bothered both frontend and backend developers. Note that these four top-level queries also apply to other lists we have created, including `Project`, `Image`, and `NavLink`.

> For more information about these four top-level queries and the filter, limit, and sorting parameters, as well as the GraphQL mutations and execution steps, which are not covered in this book, please visit `https://www.keystonejs.com/guides/intro-to-graphql/`.
>
> If you want to learn about how to query a GraphQL server in general, please visit `https://graphql.org/learn/queries/`.

Now that you have basic knowledge of GraphQL and are aware of Keystone's top-levels GraphQL queries, it's time to learn how to use them in the Nuxt app.

Integrating Keystone, GraphQL, and Nuxt

Keystone's GraphQL API endpoint is located at `localhost:4000/admin/api`. As opposed to a REST API, which usually has multiple endpoints, GraphQL API usually has **one single endpoint** for all queries. So, we will use this endpoint to send our GraphQL queries from the Nuxt app. It is good practice to always test our queries on the GraphQL Playground first to confirm that we get the result we need and then use those tested queries in our frontend apps. Besides, we should always use the `query` keyword in our queries in the frontend app to fetch data from the GraphQL API.

In this exercise, we will refactor the Nuxt app that we built for the WordPress API. We will be looking at the `/pages/index.vue`, `/pages/projects/index.vue`, `/pages/projects/_slug.vue`, and `/store/index.js` files. We will still be using Axios to help us send the GraphQL query. Let's take a look at how to get the GraphQL query and Axios working together:

1. Create a variable that will store the GraphQL query in order to fetch the title of the home page and the slide images that we attached to it:

    ```
    // pages/index.vue
    const GET_PAGE = `
      query {
        allPages (search: "home") {
          title
          slideImages {
    ```

[653]

```
          alt
          link {
            name
          }
          file {
            publicUrl
          }
        }
      }
    }
  }
```

We only need the slug from the project page that the image will link to, so the name field is the only field we will query. And we only need the relative public URL of the image, so the `publicUrl` field is the only field we want from the image file object. Also, we use the `allPages` query instead of `Page` because it is easier to get the page by its slug, which is *home* in this case.

2. Send the query to the GraphQL API endpoint using the `post` method from Axios:

```
// pages/index.vue
export default {
  async asyncData ({ $axios }) {
    let { data } = await $axios.post('/admin/api', {
      query: GET_PAGE
    })
    return {
      post: data.data.allPages[0]
    }
  },
}
```

Notice that we only need the first item from the array in the data that's returned from the GraphQL API, so we use 0 to locate this first item.

Note that we should also refactor `/pages/about.vue`, `/pages/contact.vue`, `/pages/projects/index.vue`, and `/pages/projects/pages/_number.vue` following the same pattern of how we refactored this home page. You can find the path to this book's GitHub repository, which contains the complete code, at the end of this section.

3. Create a variable that will store the query and allow you to fetch multiple resources from the endpoint, as follows:

   ```
   // components/projects/project-items.vue
   const GET_PROJECTS = `
     query {
       _allProjectsMeta {
         count
       }
       allProjects (orderBy: "name_DESC", skip: ${ skip }, first: ${
        postsPerPage }) {
         name
         title
         excerpt
         featuredImage {
           alt
           file {
             publicUrl
           }
         }
       }
     }
   `
   ```

   As you can see, we are fetching the total count of project pages through `_allProjectsMeta` and the list of project pages through `allProjects` with the `orderBy`, `skip`, and `first` filters. The data for the `skip` and `first` filters will be passed in as variables; that is, `skip` and `postsPerPage`, respectively.

4. Compute the data for the `skip` variable from the route parameters, set 6 to the `postsPerPage` variable, and then send the query to the GraphQL API endpoint using the `post` method from Axios:

   ```
   // components/projects/project-items.vue
   data () {
     return {
       posts: [],
       totalPages: null,
       currentPage: null,
       nextPage: null,
       prevPage: null,
     }
   },

   async fetch () {
     const postsPerPage = 6
     const number = this.$route.params.number
   ```

```
    const pageNumber = number === undefined ? 1 : Math.abs(
      parseInt(number))
    const skip = number === undefined ? 0 : (pageNumber - 1)
     * postsPerPage

    const GET_PROJECTS = `...`

    let { data } = await $axios.post('/admin/api', {
      query: GET_PROJECTS
    })

    //... continued in step 5.
  }
```

As you can see, we compute the `pageNumber` data from the route parameters, which we can only access via `this.$route.params` in the `fetch` method. The `skip` data is computed from `pageNumber` and `postsPerPage` before we pass it to the GraphQL query and fetch our data. Here, we will get 1 for `pageNumber` and 0 for `skip` on the `/projects` or `/projects/pages/1` route, 2 for `pageNumber` and 6 for `skip` on the `/projects/pages/2` route, and so on. Also, we must make sure that any intentional negative data in the route (for example, `/projects/pages/-100`) will be made positive by using the JavaScript `Math.abs` function.

> For more information about the JavaScript `Math.abs` function, please visit https://developer.mozilla.org/en-US/docs/Web/JavaScript/Reference/Global_Objects/Math/abs.

5. Create the pagination (the next page and the previous page) from the `count` field that's returned from the server, and then return the data as usual for the `<template>` block, as follows:

```
// components/projects/project-items.vue
let totalPosts = data.data._allProjectsMeta.count
let totalMaxPages = Math.ceil(totalPosts / postsPerPage)

this.posts = data.data.allProjects
this.totalPages = totalMaxPages
this.currentPage = pageNumber
this.nextPage = pageNumber === totalMaxPages ? null : pageNumber + 1
this.prevPage = pageNumber === 1 ? null : pageNumber - 1
```

6. Create a variable that will store the query for fetching a single project page by the slug from the endpoint, as follows:

```
// pages/projects/_slug.vue
const GET_PAGE = `
  query {
    allProjects (search: "${ params.slug }") {
      title
      content
      excerpt
      fullscreenImage { ... }
      projectImages { ... }
    }
  }
`
```

Here, we are fetching the project page through `allProjects` with the `search` filter. The data for the `search` filter will be passed in from the `params.slug` parameter. The fields we will query in `fullscreenImage` and `fullscreenImage` are the same as the ones in `featuredImage`; you can find them in *step 3*.

7. Send the query to the GraphQL API endpoint using the `post` method from Axios:

```
// pages/projects/_slug.vue
async asyncData ({ params, $axios }) {
  const GET_PAGE = `...`

  let { data: { data: result } } = await $axios.post('/admin/api',
  {
    query: GET_PAGE
  })

  return {
    post: result.allProjects[0],
  }
}
```

Notice that you can also destructure nested objects or arrays and assign a variable to the value. In the preceding code, we have assigned `result` as the variable in order to store the value of the `data` property that's returned by GraphQL.

[657]

8. Create a variable that will store the query for fetching the list of `NavLinks` from the endpoint with the `orderBy` filter, as follows:

   ```
   // store/index.js
   const GET_LINKS = `
     query {
       allNavLinks (orderBy: "order_ASC") {
         title
         link {
           name
         }
       }
     }
   `
   ```

9. Send the query to the GraphQL API endpoint using the `post` method from Axios and then commit the data to the store state:

   ```
   // store/index.js
   async nuxtServerInit({ commit }, { $axios }) {
     const GET_LINKS = `...`
     let { data } = await $axios.post('/admin/api', {
       query: GET_LINKS
     })
     commit('setMenu', data.data.allNavLinks)
   }
   ```

10. (Optional) Just like the *step 9* in the *Integrating with Nuxt and streaming images from WordPress* section, if the Nuxt crawler fails to detect the dynamic routes for some unknown reasons, then generate these routes manually in the generate option in the Nuxt config file, as follows:

```
// nuxt.config.js
import axios from 'axios'

export default {
  generate: {
    routes: async function () {
      const GET_PROJECTS = `
        query {
          allProjects { name }
        }
      `
      const { data } = await axios.post(remoteUrl + '/admin/api', {
        query: GET_PROJECTS
      })
      const routesProjects = data.data.allProjects.map(project => {
```

```
      return {
        route: '/projects/' + project.name,
        payload: project
      }
    })

    let totalMaxPages = Math.ceil(routesProjects.length / 6)
    let pagesProjects = []
    Array(totalMaxPages).fill().map((item, index) => {
      pagesProjects.push({
        route: '/projects/pages/' + (index + 1),
        payload: null
      })
    })

    const routes = [ ...routesProjects, ...pagesProjects ]
    return routes
  }
},
}
```

In this optional step, you can see that we use the same JavaScript built-in object and methods – `Array`, `map`, `fill` and `push`, just as in the *Integrating with Nuxt and streaming images from WordPress* section, to work out the dynamic routes for the child pages and pagination for us, and then return them as a single array for Nuxt to generate their dynamic routes.

11. Run the following script commands for either development or production:

    ```
    $ npm run dev
    $ npm run build && npm run start
    $ npm run stream && npm run generate
    ```

Remember that if you want to generate static pages and host the images in the same location, we have the ability to stream the remote images to the `/assets/` directory so that webpack can process these images for us. So, if you want to do that, then just as we've done previously, run `npm run stream` first to stream the remote images to your local disc and then run `npm run generate` to regenerate the static pages with the images before hosting them somewhere.

> You can find the code for this exercise in `/chapter-18/cross-domain/frontend/nuxt-universal/nuxt-keystone` in this book's GitHub repository.
>
> Apart from using Axios, you can also use Nuxt Apollo module to send GraphQL queries to the server. For more information about this module and its usage, please visit `https://github.com/nuxt-community/apollo-module`.

Well done! You have successfully integrated Nuxt with the Keystone GraphQL API and streamed remote resources for static pages – just like did with the WordPress REST API. We hope that Keystone and GraphQL, in particular, have shown you another exciting API option. You can even take the GraphQL knowledge you have learned in this chapter further and develop your GraphQL API for Nuxt apps. You can also take Nuxt to the next level with many other technologies, just like some of those we have walked you through in this book. This book has been quite a journey. We hope it has benefitted you regarding web development and that you can take what you have learned from this book as far as you can. Now, let's summarize what you have learned in this chapter.

Summary

In this chapter, you managed to create custom post types and routes to extend the WordPress REST API, integrated with Nuxt, and streamed the remote resources from WordPress to generate static pages. You also managed to customize a CMS from Keystone by creating lists and fields. You then learned how to create a GraphQL API at a low level with GraphQL.js and at a high level with the GraphQL schema language and Apollo Server. Now that you've grasped the foundations of GraphQL, you can query the Keystone GraphQL API from the Nuxt app using GraphQL queries and Axios. And last, not least, you can stream remote resources from the Keystone project to the Nuxt project to generate static pages. Well done!

This has been a very long journey. You've gone from learning about the directory structure of Nuxt to adding pages, routes, transitions, components, Vuex stores, plugins, and modules, and then to creating user logins and API authentication, writing end-to-end tests, and creating Nuxt SPAs (static pages). You've also integrated Nuxt with other technologies, tools, and frameworks, including MongoDB, RethinkDB, MySQL, PostgreSQL, and GraphQL; Koa, Express, Keystone, and Socket.IO; PHP and PSRs; Zurb Foundation and Less CSS; and Prettier, ESLint, and StandardJS.

Chapter 18

We hope that this has been an inspiring journey and that you will adopt Nuxt in your projects wherever it fits and take it further to benefit yourself as well as the community. Keep coding, be inspiring, and stay inspired. We wish you all the best.

Note that a final app example of this book can be found on the author's website. It's a solely static-generated web app made entirely with Nuxt's `static` target and GraphQL! Please have a look and explore it at `https://lauthiamkok.net/`.

Other Books You May Enjoy

If you enjoyed this book, you may be interested in these other books by Packt:

Clean Code in JavaScript
James Padolsey

ISBN: 978-1-78995-764-8

- Understand the true purpose of code and the problems it solves for your end-users and colleagues
- Discover the tenets and enemies of clean code considering the effects of cultural and syntactic conventions
- Use modern JavaScript syntax and design patterns to craft intuitive abstractions
- Maintain code quality within your team via wise adoption of tooling and advocating best practices
- Learn the modern ecosystem of JavaScript and its challenges like DOM reconciliation and state management
- Express the behavior of your code both within tests and via various forms of documentation

Building Forms with Vue.js
Marina Mosti

ISBN: 978-1-83921-333-5

- Learn all about the basics of creating reusable form components with the Vue framework
- Understand v-model and how it plays a role in form creation
- Create forms that are completely powered and generated by a schema, either locally or from an API endpoint
- Understand how Vuelidate allows for easy declarative validation of all your form's inputs with Vue's reactivity system
- Connect your application with a Vuex-powered global state management
- Use the v-mask library to enhance your inputs and improve user experience (UX)

Leave a review - let other readers know what you think

Please share your thoughts on this book with others by leaving a review on the site that you bought it from. If you purchased the book from Amazon, please leave us an honest review on this book's Amazon page. This is vital so that other potential readers can see and use your unbiased opinion to make purchasing decisions, we can understand what our customers think about our products, and our authors can see your feedback on the title that they have worked with Packt to create. It will only take a few minutes of your time, but is valuable to other potential customers, our authors, and Packt. Thank you!

Index

A

A2 Hosting
   reference link 491
Abide plugin, in Foundation
   reference link 67
actions, Vuex
   about 332
   mapActions helper 334
Adminer
   reference link 410
Advanced Custom Fields (AFC)
   reference link 604
AFC premium add-on
   reference link 604
AFC Repeater Field 604
aliases 40
Angular Universal
   URL 26
Anime.js
   reference link 141
anonymous functions
   reference link 611
AOS
   adding 78, 79, 80, 81
API public/private modules
   creating 413, 415, 416, 417, 418, 419, 420, 422
API public/private routes
   creating 413, 414, 416, 417, 418, 419, 420, 422
API
   modules, creating 559, 560, 561
   public routes, creating 559, 560, 561
Apollo Server
   reference link 650
   used, for creating GraphQL API 647, 648, 650

app template
   customizing 108
applications
   types 20
asset management
   reference link 57
asset serving 55, 56, 57
assets directory 36
async Nuxt modules, writing
   about 213
   async/await, using 213
   Promise, returning 214, 215
async/await
   using 275
asyncData method 118
asyncData
   about 274
   context, accessing 276
   data, fetching 281, 282
   dynamic route data, accessing 277
   errors, handling 278, 279, 280
   fetching, with Axios 280
   listening, to query changes 278
   req/res objects, accessing 277
Autoloader 531
AVA
   about 452, 453
   reference link 454
   tests, writing for Nuxt apps 454, 455, 457
Axios
   async data, fetching 280
   data, fetching 281, 282
   installing 280
   query change 283
axios
   reference link 38
   URL 207

B

Babel Loader
  URL 12
Babel
  URL 12
backend authentication
  API public/private modules, creating 413, 415, 416, 417, 418, 419, 420, 422
  API public/private routes, creating 413, 414, 416, 417, 418, 419, 420, 422
  bcryptjs module, using for Node.js 422, 423
  creating 409
  cross-domain app directories, structuring 411, 412, 413
  Google OAuth, adding 436, 438, 439, 440
  incoming token, verifying on server side 429, 430
  login code, refactoring on server side 427, 428, 429
  mysql module, using for Node.js 424, 425, 426
  MySQL, using as server database 410, 411
Backpack
  about 259
  configuring 260, 261
  Express app, creating 261
  installing 260, 261
  reference link 259
basic mixins
  creating 182
basic routes
  creating 93
bcryptjs module
  about 411
  reference link 423
  using, for Node.js 422, 423
beforeRouteEnter guard 369
beforeRouteLeave guard 369
beforeRouteUpdate guard 370
Binary JSON (BSON) 287
Bootstrap
  URL 60
BootstrapVue
  reference link 218
build-only modules, Nuxt
  reference link 213

built-in HTTP module, Node.js
  reference link 525
built-in PHP web server
  reference link 520
built-in transition, Motion UI
  reference link 70

C

CakePHP Coding Standards
  reference link 527
changefeeds
  about 586, 587
  Socket.IO server, integrating with 592, 593, 594
checkbox element
  v-model, using in 233, 235
checkbox elements
  Boolean, replacing 244
child component events
  listening to 151, 152
  values, emitting 152
child components
  data, passing to 148, 149
child theme 607
classic SPAs 497, 498, 499
client-only plugins
  injecting 204, 206
CoffeeScript
  reference link 74
component data 185
component files 187
component names
  defining 184
components directory 37
components
  about 147, 148
  multi-word component names 185
  naming conventions 184
Composer
  about 531
  installing 532, 533, 534, 535
  reference link 531
Connect framework 397
connection pooling
  reference link 426
content delivery networks (CDNs) 60

[668]

context
  accessing, in asyncData 276
cookie Node.js module, code example
  reference link 435
cookies
  about 405
  using, on (Nuxt) client side 433, 434
  using, on (Nuxt) server side 434, 435
create-nuxt-app
  creating 33
  using 32, 34
createWriteStream function
  reference link 617
cross-domain app directories
  structuring 411, 412, 413, 555, 556, 557, 558
CRUD operations, with PHP database frameworks
  Medoo, using as database framework 549, 550, 552
  MySQL tables, creating 548
  records, deleting 554
  records, inserting 552
  records, querying 553
  records, updating 554
  writing 548
CRUD pages
  creating 564
CSS animations
  creating, with Motion UI 68, 69, 70
  transitions, making with 135, 136, 137
CSS transitions
  creating, with Motion UI 68, 69, 70
custom Axios plugin manually
  importing 506, 507
custom Axios plugin
  installing, in Nuxt config file 505
custom error pages
  creating 116, 117
custom HTML head
  creating 109
custom input components
  creating, with v-model 153, 154
  models, customizing 154, 156
custom layouts
  creating 114, 115
custom meta tags
  creating, for Nuxt pages 113
custom pages
  creating 117, 118
custom plugin
  writing, in Vue 193, 194
custom post types
  creating, in WordPress 607, 608, 609
custom routes
  creating 90
custom server middleware
  creating 400
custom transitions
  creating 127
custom validation
  applying, to Nuxt application 251, 252
custom views
  creating 107

D

data, injecting with MongoDB CRUD
  about 294
  documents, deleting 300, 301
  documents, inserting 294
  documents, querying 295, 296, 297
  documents, updating 298, 299
data
  merging 275, 276
database management system (DBMS) 287
default layout
  modifying 114
default meta tags
  customizing, in Nuxt apps 113
dependencies
  installing, for Koa apps 265, 267
destructuring assignment
  reference link 119
directory structure
  about 35
  aliases 40
  assets directory 36
  components directory 37
  layouts directory 37
  middleware directory 39
  nuxt.config.js file 40
  package.json file 39

pages directory 37
plugins directory 38
static directory 36
store directory 38
dynamic nested routes
  creating 101, 102, 103
dynamic routes
  creating 94, 95
dynamic value bindings
  creating 243

E

ECMAScript 2015, features
  reference link 14
end-to-end testing, tools
  about 448
  AVA 452, 453, 454
  jsdom 448, 449, 450, 451
end-to-end testing
  versus unit testing 447, 448
env property
  reference link 618
ESLint rules
  reference link 470
ESLint
  about 469
  configuring 471, 472
  installing 469
  integrating, with Prettier 474
  reference link 471
  using, for Vue and Nuxt apps 477
Express app
  creating, with Backpack 261
  using, as Nuxt's server middleware 393, 394, 395
Express
  using, as Nuxt's server middleware 396
Extended Coding Style guide 528, 529, 530
external Vue plugins
  importing, without SSR support 197, 198

F

fetch method
  about 120
  reference link 121

fields
  creating 630
file adapters
  reference link 632
file-loader
  reference link 57
Font Awesome
  reference link 223
forms, validating with data bindings
  about 236, 237
  checkbox elements, validating 239
  radio elements, validating 240
  select elements, validating 241, 242, 243
  text elements, validating 237, 238
  textarea elements, validating 238
forms
  handling, in Vuex store 345
  validating, with VeeValidate 248, 249
Foundation Icon Fonts 3
  icons, adding 71
Foundation MediaQuery
  reference link 65
Foundation utilities
  reference link 65
Foundation
  adding, as UI framework 60, 61
  grid layouts, creating 62
  JavaScript plugins, using from 64, 65, 66
  JavaScript utilities, using from 64, 65, 66, 67
  reference link 251
  website navigations, creating 62
frontend authentication
  cookies, using on (Nuxt) client side 432, 433, 434
  cookies, using on (Nuxt) server side 434, 435
  creating 431, 432
  creating, for Google OAuth 441, 442
FuelPHP Coding Standards
  reference link 527
functions
  injecting, into Nuxt context 200, 201, 202
  injecting, into Vue instance 199, 201, 202

G

generate option 54
  about 54
  reference link 54
getters, Vuex
  about 327
  mapGetters helper 329, 330
GitHub Pages
  about 511
  Nuxt SPA, deploying to 512, 513
  reference link 512
global components
  registering 174
  registering, in Nuxt 178
  registering, in Vue 174
global functions
  writing, in Nuxt 198, 199
global guards
  creating 366, 367
global middlewares
  writing 385, 386, 387
global mixins
  creating 183, 184
Google OAuth authentication 409
Google OAuth
  about 435
  adding, to backend authentication 436, 438, 439, 440
  frontend authentication, creating for 441, 442
  signing in with 436
GraphQL API
  creating, with Apollo Server 647, 648, 650
GraphQL server
  queries, reference link 653
GraphQL
  about 637, 638
  default resolvers 645, 646
  reference link 650
  resolvers 638, 639, 640, 642, 644
  schema 638, 639, 640, 644
grid layouts
  creating, with Foundation 62

H

Handlebars
  URL 26
head method 121
headless REST APIs
  creating, in WordPress 604, 605
hooks, Nuxt's life cycle events
  reference link 229
HTTP message interfaces 536, 537, 539
HTTP messages 520, 521, 525, 526
HTTP Server Request Handlers (middleware) 542, 543, 544
HTTP Server Request Handlers (request handlers) 541
Hypertext Transfer Protocol (HTTP) 404, 520

I

icons
  adding, with Foundation Icon Fonts 3 71
in-component guards
  creating 369, 370, 371, 372
incoming token
  verifying, on server side 429, 430
Integer field type
  reference link 636

J

JavaScript addEventListener
  reference link 65
JavaScript EventTarget
  reference link 65
JavaScript hooks
  transitions, creating with 137, 139
JavaScript Math.abs function
  reference link 656
JavaScript plugins
  using, from Foundation 64, 65, 66
JavaScript utilities
  using, from Foundation 64, 65, 66
jQuery animate function
  reference link 78
jQuery UI
  adding 75, 78
jsdom

about 448, 449, 450
reference link 451
tests, writing for Nuxt apps 454, 455, 457
JSON Web Tokens (JWTs)
about 406, 407
Node.js modules, using for 408
JSONLint
reference link 614
JSONPlaceholder
reference link 214
JWT standard fields
reference link 407

K

key attributes
in v-for loops 156, 157, 160, 161
reusable elements, controlling with 161
Keystone apps
creating 626, 627, 628, 630
installing 626, 627, 628, 630
Keystone GraphQL API
reference link 653
using 651, 653
Keystone
about 621
reference link 621
Knex database adapter
reference link 629
Koa API 449
Koa apps
dependencies, installing for 265, 267
Koa community
reference link 413
koa-router
about 265
reference link 266
Koa.js
reference link 265
Koa
about 262
cascading, working 264, 265
configuring 263
ctx 263
installing 262
integrating, with Nuxt 268, 269

middleware, adding 271, 273
MongoDB, integrating with 301
reference link 262
RethinkDB, integrating with 574
routes, adding 270
using, as Nuxt server middlewares 397, 398, 400

L

Laravel Pug
reference link 21
Lau Tiam Kok 459
layout property 121
layouts directory 37
layoutTransition option 53
layoutTransition property
transitions, making with 133, 134, 135
Leaner Style Sheets (Less)
adding 72, 73, 74
linters
about 466
ESLint 469
Prettier 466
StandardJS 473
Linux distribution
reference link 410
Linux Ubuntu 19.10
reference link 410
lists
creating 630, 632, 634, 635, 636
loading property 121, 123, 124
local authentication 409
local components
registering 174
registering, in Vue/Nuxt 175, 176, 177
login code
refactoring, on server side 427, 428, 429

M

MariaDB server
reference link 410
MediaQuery utility 64
Medoo
URL 552
Meta Box

[672]

reference link 609
middleware directory 39
middleware property 127
middleware
　about 364
　writing, with Vue Router 364
mixins
　creating 181
　using 180
models
　customizing, in custom input components 154, 156
module dependencies 55
modules option
　reference link 418
modules, Vuex
　about 335
　local state 336
　namespacing 337, 338
　root state 336
MongoDB Community Edition, installing on Ubuntu
　reference link 288
MongoDB Community Edition
　reference link 288
MongoDB CRUD operations
　reference link 293
　writing 293
MongoDB driver
　configuring 304
　installing 301
　simple app, creating with 302, 303
MongoDB Enterprise
　reference link 288
MongoDB queries
　collection, creating 292
　database, creating 291
　writing 291
MongoDB, $currentDate
　reference link 298
MongoDB, $or selector
　reference link 297
MongoDB, $set operator
　reference link 298
MongoDB, with Koa
　document, deleting 312

document, fetching 309, 310
document, injecting 306, 307, 308
document, updating 310
MongoDB driver, configuring 304
ObjectId 305, 306
ObjectId method 305, 306
simple app, creating with MongoDB driver 302, 303
MongoDB
　about 287, 288
　connecting, to server 289, 290
　installing 288
　installing, on Ubuntu 624, 625
　installing, on Ubuntu 20.04 288, 289
　integrating, with Koa 301
　securing 624, 625
Mongoose adapter
　configuration link 627
Mongoose
　reference link 629
Monolog
　reference link 535
Motion UI
　CSS animations and transitions, creating 68, 69, 70
　reference link 70
multi-page applications (MPAs) 13
multiple custom Axios instances
　creating, with plugins 504
mutations, Vuex
　about 330, 331
　mapMutations helper 331
mysql 423
MySQL client 423
mysql module
　reference link 427
　using, for Node.js 424, 425, 426
MySQL
　using, as server database 410, 411
MySQLi extension
　reference link 549

N

navigation guard arguments
　from 373

[673]

next 373
to 373
navigation guards
  global guards 366, 367, 368
  in-component guards 369
  per-route guards 368, 369
  using 366
nested routes
  creating 96, 97, 98, 99
Next
  URL 26
Nightwatch
  about 458, 459, 460, 461
  used, for writing tests for Nuxt apps 462, 463
Node.js module, code example
  reference link 434
Node.js modules
  using, for JWT 408
Node.js stream
  reference link 617
Node.js
  bcryptjs module, using 422, 423
  mysql module, using 424, 425, 426
nodemon
  reference link 630
non-global mixins
  creating 181, 182
non-string 245
Nuxt application
  build option 46
  buildModules option 45
  components option 44
  configuring 41
  css option 43
  custom validation, applying to 251, 252
  default meta tags, customizing 113
  deploying 485, 486
  dev option 46
  dir option 51
  env option 49
  ESLint and Prettier, running separately 484, 485
  generate option 54
  head option 42
  installing 34
  layoutTransition option 53

loading option 53
mode option 42
modules option 45
pageTransition option 53
plugins option 44
rootDir option 47
router option 50
server option 49
srcDir option 48
target option 42
Nuxt config file
  about 41
  custom Axios plugin, installing in 505
Nuxt context
  functions, injecting into 200, 201
  reference link 14, 276
Nuxt default webpack config
  reference link 225
Nuxt FAQ
  reference link 494
Nuxt HTTP module
  URL 27, 284
Nuxt module snippets, writing
  about 215
  addPlugin helper, using 217, 218
  CSS library, adding 221, 223
  custom webpack loaders, registering 223, 224, 225
  custom webpack plugins, registering 226, 227
  Lodash templates 220
  tasks, creating on specific hooks 227, 228, 229
  top-level options, using 215, 216, 217
Nuxt module snippets
  Lodash templates, using 219
Nuxt modules
  basic module, writing 208, 209, 210, 211, 213
  writing 207, 208
Nuxt Pages
  add page, creating for adding new users 313
  custom meta tags, creating for 113
  delete page, creating for deleting existing users 315
  integrating with 313
  update page, creating for updating existing users 314
Nuxt server middlewares

[674]

Express, using as 393, 394, 395, 396
Koa, using as 397, 398, 399
writing 392, 393
Nuxt SPA
　about 498, 499
　deploying 508, 509, 510, 511
　deploying, to GitHub Pages 512, 513
　developing 501, 502
　installing 500, 501
Nuxt static generated app
　deploying 488, 490
　hosting, on static site hosting servers 493
Nuxt universal SSR app
　deploying 486, 487
　hosting, on shared hosting servers 491
　hosting, on virtual private servers 490
Nuxt view 107
nuxt.config.js file 40
Nuxt.js
　reference link 16
Nuxt
　about 11
　code, bundling with webpack 18, 20
　code, splitting with webpack 18, 20
　CSS, writing with preprocessor 15, 16
　ES2015+ JavaScript (ES6), writing 14, 15
　extending, with modules and plugins 16
　global components, registering 178
　global functions, writing 198, 199
　head element, managing 18
　installing 32
　integrating with 562, 563
　integrating, with Keystone GraphQL API 653, 655, 657, 659
　Koa, integrating with 268, 269
　local components, registering 175, 176, 177
　need for 13
　route middlewares, writing 384
　single-file components, writing 13
　Socket.IO, integrating with 594, 595, 596, 597, 598, 599, 600
　transitions. adding between routes 17
　using, as single-page app 28, 29
　using, as static site generator 28
　using, as universal SSR app 26, 27

Vue plugins, importing into 196
nuxtServerInit action
　creating 502, 503

O

options, Nuxt app
　reference link 46

P

package.json file 39
packages, MongoDB driver
　references 301
pages directory 37
pages
　about 118
　asyncData method 118
　fetch method 120
　head method 121
　layout property 121
　loading property 121, 123, 124
　middleware property 127
　scrollToTop property 126
　transition property 126
　validate method 126
pageTransition option 53
pageTransition property
　transitions, making with 130, 131, 132, 133
Panini
　reference link 70
PEAR Coding Standards
　reference link 528
per-route guards
　creating 368, 369
per-route middlewares
　writing 388, 389, 390, 391
Personal Home Page 516
PHP 7.4
　configuring 518, 519
PHP Adminer
　reference link 623
PHP apps
　running, with built-in PHP web server 519, 520
PHP Group
　reference link 516
PHP script

[675]

creating 522, 523, 524
PHP setup, on macOS
  reference link 516
PHP setup, on Windows
  reference link 516
PHP Standards Recommendations (PSR)
  reference link 621
PHP Standards
  need for 526, 527
PHP
  about 516
  installing 516, 517, 518
  reference link 516
  upgrading 516, 517, 518
phpMyAdmin
  reference link 410
plugins directory 38
plugins
  multiple custom Axios instances, creating 504
PostgreSQL
  download link 622
  installing, on Ubuntu 621, 623, 624
  securing 622, 623, 624
Prettier
  about 466
  configuring 468
  ESLint, integrating with 475
  installing 467
  URL 467
  using, for Vue and Nuxt apps 477
production-ready modules, Nuxt Community
  reference link 207
promise object
  returning 274
Promise support, Vuex
  reference link 322
prop definitions 186, 187
props
  data, passing to child components 148, 149
ProvidePlugin function
  reference link 46
PSR-0
  reference link 535
PSR-12 528, 529, 530
PSR-15 541, 542, 543, 544

reference link 542
PSR-4 531
PSR-7 536, 537, 539, 540
PSR-7/PSR-15 router 544, 545, 546, 547
Pug
  reference link 74, 516
  URL 21, 26

Q

query and projection operators, MongoDB
  reference link 297
query selectors, MongoDB
  reference link 296, 311

R

radio element
  strings, replacing with dynamic properties 245
  v-model, using in 233, 235
real-time app, Nuxt
  API directories, restructuring 574, 576, 577
  RethinkDB JavaScript client, adding 577, 578, 580, 581, 582, 583
  Socket.IO client, adding 588, 590, 591
  Socket.IO server, adding 588, 590, 591
Reclaim Hosting
  reference link 491
relational database management systems (RDBMSes) 287
Relationship field
  reference link 634
release changes, PHP
  reference link 516
ReQL 569, 570, 572, 573
ReQL commands/functions
  reference link 569
RethinkDB JavaScript client
  installation link 577
  using 577, 578, 580, 581, 582, 583
RethinkDB server
  about 568
  installing 568, 569
RethinkDB
  about 567, 568
  changefeeds 586, 587
  integrating, with Koa 574

schema, enforcing 584, 585
return type declarations 528
reusable elements
  controlling, with key attributes 161
Rewrite Rules Inspector
  reference link 604
route middlewares
  writing, in Nuxt 384
route params
  validating 104, 105
router middleware
  reference link 266
routes
  basic routes, creating 93
  creating, with Vue Router 91, 92, 93
  dynamic nested routes 102
  dynamic nested routes, creating 101, 103
  dynamic routes, creating 94, 95
  nested routes, creating 96, 97, 98, 99
  unknown routes, handling with _.vue files 105, 106

S

Sass (Syntactically Awesome Style Sheets)
  reference link 74
schema cheatsheet
  reference link 635
scoped slot data properties, Validation Observer
  reference link 255
scrollToTop property 126
Scss (Sassy Cascaded Style Sheets)
  reference link 74
select elements
  v-model, using in 235, 236
select options elements
  strings, replacing with objects 245
Selenium Standalone Server 458
self-closing components 188, 189
server side
  incoming token, verifying 429, 430
  login code, refactoring 427, 428, 429
server-only plugins
  injecting 204, 206
server-side rendering (SSR) 11
session authentication flow 405

session-based authentication
  about 404
sessions 404
setHeader helper
  reference link 435
shared hosting servers
  Nuxt universal SSR app, hosting on 491
single-file component filename casing 188
single-file components
  compiling, with webpack 166
  data, passing 166, 169
  listening, to events 166, 169
single-file Vue components
  compiling, with webpack 164, 165
  creating 162
single-page application (SPA) 11
Socket.IO client
  using 588, 590, 591
Socket.IO server
  integrating, with changefeeds 592, 593, 594
  using 588, 590, 591
Socket.IO
  about 587
  integrating, with Nuxt 594, 595, 596, 597, 598, 599, 600
  URL 588
StandardJS
  about 473, 474
  installing 473
  reference link 474
state management pattern, Vuex 320, 321
state, Vuex
  about 324
  accessing 324
  mapState helper 325
static assets
  versus webpack assets 57, 58
static directory 36
static file app
  reference link 631
static pages 25
static site hosting servers
  Nuxt static generated app, hosting on 493
static-generated app
  about 25, 26

advantages 25
disadvantages 26
store directory 38
stream's pipe event
   reference link 617
style guide, Vue
   reference link 189
Style Sherpa
   reference link 70
svg-transform-loader
   reference link 225
Swiper
   about 84
   adding 81
   reference link 84
Symfony Coding Standards
   reference link 527

T

taxonomy registration
   reference link 609
template literals
   reference link 647
text element
   v-model, using in 232, 233
textarea element
   v-model, using in 232, 233
token authentication flow 407, 408
token-based authentication
   about 406
traditional server-side rendered app
   about 20
   advantages 21
   disadvantages 21
traditional single-page app (SPA)
   about 22
   advantages 22
   disadvantages 23
transition modes 142
transition property 126
transitions
   creating, with JavaScript hooks 137, 139
   making, with CSS animations 135, 136, 137
   making, with layoutTransition property 133, 134, 135

making, with pageTransition property 130, 131, 132, 133
Twig
   reference link 516
   URL 26
two-way computed property
   using 347
type modifier
   reference link 648

U

Ubuntu 20.04
   MongoDB, installing on 288, 289
Ubuntu
   MongoDB, installing 624, 625
   PostgreSQL, installing 621, 623, 624
unit testing
   versus end-to-end testing 447, 448
universal (SSR) 11
universal server-side rendered app (SSR)
   about 23
   advantages 24
   disadvantages 24
Universally Unique Identifier (UUID) 548
update operators, MongoDB
   reference link 311
url-loader
   reference link 57
user middleware 384

V

v-bind directive
   using 346, 347
v-for loops
   key attribute 156, 157, 160, 161
v-model
   about 231, 232
   custom input components, creating 153, 154
   using, in checkbox element 233, 235
   using, in radio element 233, 235
   using, in select elements 235, 236
   using, in text element 232, 233
   using, in textarea element 232, 233
v-on directive
   using 346, 347

validate method 126
VeeValidate
  reference link 250
  used, for validating forms 248, 249
virtual private servers
  Nuxt universal SSR app, hosting on 490
Vue app
  creating, with simple HTML page 374, 375
Vue apps
  metadata, creating with Vue Meta 111
Vue CLI
  about 376
  installing 376, 377
  middlewares, writing 379, 380, 382, 384
  project structure 377, 378
Vue components, Nuxt
  adding 169
  copyright component, refactoring 172, 173, 174
  navigation and social links, refactoring 170, 171
Vue components
  about 146, 147
  reference link 162
Vue instance
  functions, injecting into 199
Vue instances 147
Vue Loader
  URL 12
Vue Meta
  about 109
  installing 110, 111
  reference link 110
  URL 12
Vue plugins
  importing, into Nuxt 196
  writing 192
Vue Router Multiguard
  reference link 379
Vue Router
  about 90
  installing 91, 365
  middleware, writing 364
  reference link 90, 366
  routes, creating 91, 92, 93
  URL 12
Vue rules

configuring 478, 479, 482
Vue Server Renderer
  URL 12
Vue slots
  reference link 250
Vue transitions 128, 129
Vue, modifiers
  .lazy 247
  .number 247
  .trim 247
  using 246
vue-loader
  reference link 57
vue-template-compiler
  reference link 57
Vue.js
  reference link 16
Vue
  custom plugin, writing 193, 194
  global components, registering 174
  local components, registering 175, 176, 177
  URL 12
Vuex store 379, 381
Vuex store modules
  structuring 341
Vuex store, in Nuxt
  fetch method, using 354
  module files, using 352
  module mode, using 348, 351
  nuxtServerInit action, using 356, 357, 358
  using 348
Vuex store
  forms, handling 345
Vuex, core concepts
  about 323
  actions 332
  getters 327
  modules 335
  mutations 330, 331
  state 324
Vuex
  about 320, 322
  advanced store module structure, creating 343, 344
  architecture 319

[679]

  installing 322
  reference link 348
  simple store, creating 323
  state management pattern 320, 321
  store module structure, creating 341
  URL 12
vuexpress
  reference link 21

W

webpack assets
  versus static assets 57, 58
webpack features
  reference link 19
webpack
  reference link 46, 57
  single-file components 165, 166
  single-file components, compiling 164
  URL 12
website navigations
  creating, with Foundation 62
WordPress CLI
  reference link 605
WordPress Coding Standards
  reference link 527
WordPress REST API
  extending 610, 611, 612, 613, 614, 615
WordPress
  custom post types, creating 607, 608, 609
  headless REST APIs, creating 604, 605
  images, streaming 615, 616, 618, 621
  installation link 606
  installing 605, 606
  Nuxt, integrating with 615, 616, 618, 621
  pages, creating 605, 606
WYSIWYG
  reference link 632

X

XY Grid and Navigation, in Foundation
  reference link 63

Z

Zend Coding Standard
  reference link 527
zend-httphandlerrunner
  reference link 542

Printed in Great Britain
by Amazon